Contents

D0183795

Geography
for the IB Diploma

Global
Interactions
Paul Guinness

Cambridge University Press's mission is to advance learning, knowledge and research worldwide.

Our IB Diploma resources aim to:
- encourage learners to explore concepts, ideas and topics that have local and global significance
- help students develop a positive attitude to learning in preparation for higher education
- assist students in approaching complex questions, applying critical-thinking skills and forming reasoned answers.

CAMBRIDGE
UNIVERSITY PRESS

CAMBRIDGE
UNIVERSITY PRESS

University Printing House, Cambridge CB2 8BS, United Kingdom

Cambridge University Press is part of the University of Cambridge.

It furthers the University's mission by disseminating knowledge in the pursuit of education, learning and research at the highest international levels of excellence.

www.cambridge.org
Information on this title: www.cambridge.org/9780521147323

© Cambridge University Press 2011

First published 2011
5th printing 2014

Printed in India by Replika Press Pvt. Ltd

A catalogue record for this publication is available from the British Library

ISBN 978-0-521-14732-3 Paperback

Cover image: Ron Brown/SuperStock

Header images: Hiroyuki Otsu/amanaimages/Corbis (globe); imagebroker/Alamy (forest); Ron Gilling/Lineair/Still Pictures (man and donkey)

Background images: iStock (compass); Shutterstock/Mark Breck (Joshua Tree, National Park); all other background images courtesy of Andrew Oliver

Illustrations by Kathy Baxendale
Reviewer: Ian Lycett, Head of IB Geography at Impington Village College, UK

Introduction

Global Interactions covers the Specification for the Higher Level extension of the Diploma Programme geography course. Knowledge of the core theme (Patterns and Change) is assumed, so students also need to study this (and three optional themes) in order to pass the course at the Higher Level. The Higher Level extension is assessed in Paper 3 of the examination, accounting for 20% of the total assessment.

The syllabus sees the study of global interactions as having a broader perspective than a conventional study of globalisation, suggesting a two-way and complex process whereby cultural traits and commodities may be adopted, adapted or resisted by different societies. It is emphasised that the process is neither universal nor inevitable. The focus is on the interactions, flows and exchanges that arise from the disparities existing between places.

This book follows the order of the Specification, which is organised into seven sections. Each sub-section in the specification is the subject of a chapter, with the exception of 'Defining glocalisation' and 'Adoption of globalisation' which are combined into one chapter in Section 7. The overall objective of this book is to provide comprehensive coverage of all topics included in the Higher Level extension. Key concepts are carefully explained and exemplified in case studies from a range of locations.

The first two sections, 'Measuring global interactions' and 'Changing space – the shrinking world', provide the foundation for the rest of the book by examining the patterns and processes of globalisation and the technological advances that have been so important to the rapid progress of this phenomenon. Although not explicitly specified in the syllabus, Section 1 examines the definition, evolution and dimensions of globalisation to provide you with a firm understanding of the essentials of the subject prior to consideration of globalisation indices and the identification of the global core and periphery.

Section 3 discusses economic interactions and flows between the developed core areas and the peripheries. The role of major international institutions is an important part of this process. Flows of labour and information are also considered in this section. Environmental change is the subject of Section 4, where there is a clear link with Section 3 of the core theme. A number of major global issues are examined in this section, which closes with a discussion of the global homogenisation of landscapes. 'Sociocultural exchanges' is the title of Section 5, which begins by examining the range of ways in which cultural traits can be examined. The development and spread of consumer culture is a key element of this section, which ends with consideration of the concept of cultural imperialism.

Section 6 analyses the political outcomes of global interactions, concentrating on concerns about loss of sovereignty and various responses to such concerns. Section 7 concentrates on the impact of globalisation at the local level. Here students are encouraged to examine the impact of global interaction in the region in which they live. The concept of glocalisation has gained widespread acceptance and the role of civil societies.

The dynamic nature of the process of globalisation is stressed in each section. The controversial nature of many aspects of globalisation is examined with reference to a range of case studies.

The content of each chapter is posed at the start as a series of key questions closely reflecting the wording of the 'Development' section of the Specification. Each chapter includes a 'Theory of Knowledge' link highlighting issues of particular relevance to the study of the theory of knowledge. While these links are kept deliberately brief, they are designed to point you in the right direction to enable you to explore such issues in more detail.

Each main section of text within a chapter finishes with an 'Activities' section, allowing both students and teachers to check on the knowledge and understanding gained in terms of both concepts and content. A key 'Geographical skill' is highlighted in each chapter. Geographical skills reflect the subject's distinctive methodology and approach. While you are not expected to cover all the geographical skills in your study of the Higher Level extension, you should acquire or cement a significant number of the skills set out in the Specification. 'Discussion points' and 'Research ideas' are a regular feature of the book. The first suggest ideas for group debate, while the research ideas can be used as extension exercises on both an individual and a group basis. Each chapter concludes with definitions of key terms (highlighted in bold in each chapter) and examination-style questions, modelled on essay questions for Paper 3 (the HL paper).

Case studies are an important part of this book, with countries highlighted at different levels of economic development. Some countries are featured in several chapters, allowing you to develop a good overall understanding of such nations, but there are, too, more fleeting references to other nations across the world. Key countries featured in this coursebook are also featured in the Core theme coursebook, *Patterns and Change*. This will allow you to further develop your knowledge of a range of interesting countries. The aim throughout is to debate issues of national, regional and global importance, highlighting both the positive and negative aspects of change.

The Standard Level and Higher Level Diploma Programme geography course sets four Assessment Objectives. Having followed the course at either level you should be able to:

- demonstrate knowledge and understanding of specified content (35%)

- demonstrate application and analysis of knowledge and understanding (35%)

- demonstrate synthesis and evaluation (20%)

- select, use and apply a variety of appropriate skills and techniques (10%).

(The figures in brackets show the weighting of the Assessment Objectives for Paper 3.)

Full details of the Assessment Objectives for the Diploma Programme geography course can be found in the IBO Geography Guide. Higher Level students are required to study the core theme, the Higher Level extension and three optional themes. Standard Level students study the core theme and two optional themes. Internal assessment accounts for 20% of the total assessment at Higher Level and 20% at Standard Level.

Paul Guinness

01 Global participation

KEY QUESTIONS

- What is globalisation?
- What are the merits and limitations of the main globalisation indices?
- How can these indices be represented spatially?

McDonald's in Beijing – McDonald's is perhaps the most well-known symbol of globalisation.

Globalisation

What is globalisation?

The word **globalisation** was not in common usage until about 1960. In 1961 Webster became the first major dictionary to give a definition of globalisation. However, the word was not recognised as academically significant until the early to mid 1980s. Since then its use has increased dramatically. Some see the concept of globalisation as the key idea by which we understand the transition of human society into the third millennium. Figure 1 shows how the number of articles mentioning 'globalisation' in *The Economist* changed between 1979 and 2009. There was a dramatic rise in the mid 1990s compared with the earlier period.

The International Baccalaureate (IB) syllabus uses the International Monetary Fund (IMF) definition of globalisation, which is: 'The growing interdependence of countries worldwide through the increasing volume and variety of cross-border transactions in goods and services and of international capital flows, and through the more rapid and widespread diffusion of technology.' The IB is an example of educational globalisation, with schools from a large number of countries following its courses. Almost 3000 schools in over 130 countries now offer IB programmes. The photo below shows a leading IB school in Basle, Switzerland, which has hosted international conferences about the IB.

A leading IB school in Basle, Switzerland.

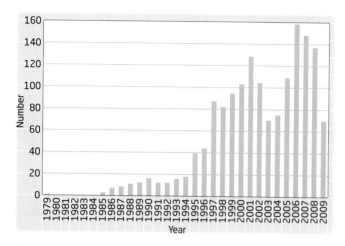

Figure 1 *Articles in* The Economist *that mention 'globalisation'.*

Globalisation is a very controversial process. Some see it as a generally positive process, but there are others who are very concerned about the ways in which globalisation is operating (Figure 2). Critics see it as justifying the spread of Western culture and **capitalism**. To counter this a formidable **anti-capitalism** movement has developed in recent decades.

Research idea

Look at a variety of magazines covering a range of subjects in your school library. How many articles are there covering some aspect of globalisation? Make a list and discuss it in class.

Theory of Knowledge

There is a wide variety of definitions of globalisation as this is a concept that spans so many subjects and affects virtually every country in the world to some degree. Definitions can be considerably influenced by the perspective of the writer. On what basis can we choose between competing definitions and why might it be important to do so?

'Globalisation has the potential to bring major improvements in productivity, innovation and creativity. But it's being overshadowed by a corporate-led plan for economic integration which threatens to undermine the whole project. Instead of helping build a better world for all, the current free-market model is eroding both democracy and equity.'

W. Ellwood, *The No-Nonsense Guide to Globalisation*

'Globalisation is a myth due to economic illiteracy. It comes down to mass ignorance.'

Alan Rugman, Oxford University management scholar

'The world's corporate and political leadership is undertaking a restructuring of global politics and economics that may prove as historically significant as any event since the Industrial Revolution. This restructuring is happening at tremendous speed, with little public disclosure of its profound consequences affecting democracy, human welfare, local economics, and the natural world.'

The International Forum on Globalisation

'Although there are undoubtedly globalising forces at work we do not have a fully globalised world economy.'

Peter Dicken, *Global Shift*

'Globalisation does not necessarily imply homogenisation or integration. It merely implies greater connectedness and de-territorialisation.'

Malcolm Waters, *Globalisation*

Figure 2 *Some views on globalisation.*

The global economy

Figure 3 shows Peter Dicken's view of the global economy. **Transnational corporations (TNCs)** and nation-states are the two major shapers of the global economy. They are embedded within a triangular nexus of interactions consisting of firm–firm, state–state and firm–state relationships. The impact of such relationships is evident at all scales: local, national and global. Advances in technology have been vital in establishing and strengthening such relationships.

Nation-states individually and collectively set the rules for the global economy but the bulk of investment is through TNCs, which are the main drivers of **global shift**. It is this process that has resulted in the emergence of an increasing

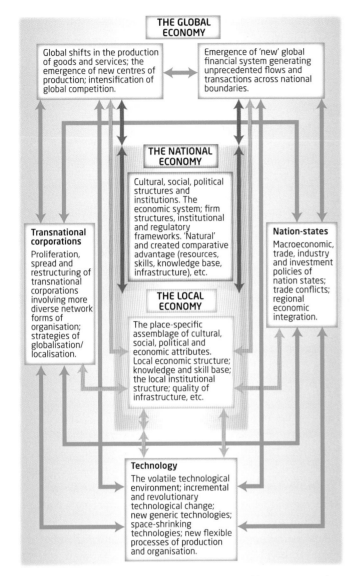

Figure 3 *The globalising process as a system of interconnected elements and scales.*

Level	Countries	GNP per capita 2005 ($)
1	Japan: a developed country	38 984
2	First generation NICs, e.g. Taiwan	16 764
3	Second generation NICs, e.g. Malaysia	4 963
4	Third generation NICs, e.g. China	1 735
5	Fourth generation NICs, e.g. Vietnam	623
6	Poorest countries, e.g. Mongolia	380

Table 1 *Countries at different levels of economic development.*

Beijing street market: China is a third generation NIC.

number of **newly industrialised countries (NICs)** since the 1960s. Under this process, manufacturing industries at first and more recently services have relocated in significant numbers from developed countries to selected developing countries.

In Asia four generations of NIC can be recognised in terms of the timing of industrial development and their current economic characteristics. Within this region, only Japan is at a higher economic level than the NICs (Table 1) because it is a long-standing developed country, but there are a number of countries at much lower levels of economic development. The latter form the poorest nations in the region.

Nowhere else in the world is the filter-down concept of industrial location better illustrated than in Asia. When Japanese companies first decided to locate abroad in the quest for cheap labour, they looked to the most developed of their neighbouring countries, particularly South Korea and Taiwan.

What were the reasons for the phenomenal rates of economic growth recorded in South Korea, Taiwan, Hong Kong and Singapore from the 1960s? What was it that set this group of 'Asian tigers' apart from so many others? From the vast literature that has appeared on the subject the following factors are usually given prominence:

● A good initial level of hard and soft infrastructure provided the preconditions for structural economic change.

● As in Japan previously, the land-poor NICs stressed people as their greatest resource, particularly through the expansion of primary and secondary education but also through specialised programmes to develop scientific, engineering and technical skills.

- Cultural traditions in these countries revere education and achievement.

- The Asian NICs became globally integrated at a 'moment of opportunity' in the structure of the world system, distinguished by the geostrategic and economic interests of core capitalist countries (especially the USA and Japan) in extending their influence in East and South-east Asia.

- All four countries had distinct advantages in terms of geographical location. Singapore is strategically situated to funnel trade flows between the Indian and Pacific Oceans and its central location in the region has facilitated its development as a major financial, commercial and administrative/managerial centre. Hong Kong has benefited from its position astride the trade routes between North-east and South-east Asia, as well as acting as the main link to the outside world for south-east China. South Korea and Taiwan were ideally located to expand trade and other ties with Japan.

- The ready availability of bank loans, often extended at government behest and at attractive interest rates, allowed South Korea's chaebol in particular to pursue market share and to expand into new fields.

Most other countries in the region lacked the physical infrastructure and skill levels required by Japanese companies. Companies from elsewhere in the developed world, especially the USA, also recognised the advantages of locating branch plants in such countries. As the economies of the first generation NICs developed, the level of wages increased, resulting in:

- Japanese and Western TNCs seeking locations in second generation NICs where improvements in physical and human infrastructures now satisfied their demands but where wages were still low

- indigenous companies from the first generation NICs also moving routine tasks to their cheaper labour neighbours such as Malaysia and Thailand.

With time, the process also included the third generation NICs, a significant factor in the recent very high growth rates in China and India. The least developed countries in the region, nearly all hindered by conflict of one sort or another at some time in recent decades, are now beginning to be drawn into the system. The recent high level of investment into Vietnam makes it reasonable to think of the country as an example of a fourth generation Asian NIC.

As their industrialisation processes have matured, the NICs have occupied a more intermediate position in the regional division of labour between Japan and other less developed Asian countries.

Taking water home from a well – rural Mongolia, one of the poorest countries in Asia.

The dimensions of globalisation

The ties that bind the world together are, first, the economic ones (Figure 4) of trade, investment and migration. The movement of goods, money and people around the globe brings far-off places closer together. The World Trade Organisation – the successor of the General Agreement on Tariffs and Trade (GATT) – has played a vital (and controversial) role in the increase in world trade. Relationships are also political. The increasing role played by the United Nations (UN) around the world epitomises the developing cooperation between nations even if the outcome of peacekeeping operations sometimes fails to match the original objective. The period after the Second World War has also witnessed the rapid development of trade blocs. Most countries are now in some sort of trade agreement with their regional neighbours. The European Union is the most advanced model of this important phenomenon.

Geographical skill

Look at Figure 4. If you are in a classroom with others, divide into groups, with each group discussing one dimension of globalisation. From the existing knowledge of each group, try to elaborate on the information given in the chart. Report back on your conclusions.

Dimension	Characteristics
Economic	Under the auspices of first the GATT and latterly the WTO, world trade has expanded rapidly. Transnational corporations have been the major force in the process of increasing economic interdependence, and the emergence of different generations of NICs has been the main evidence of success in the global economy. However, the frequency of anti-capitalist demonstrations in recent years shows that many people have grave concerns about the direction the global economy is taking. Many less developed countries and a significant number of regions within the developed countries feel excluded from the benefits of globalisation.
Urban	A hierarchy of global cities has emerged to act as the command centres of the global economy. New York, London and Tokyo are at the highest level of this hierarchy. Competition within and between the different levels of the global urban hierarchy is intensifying.
Social/cultural	Western culture has diffused to all parts of the world to a considerable degree through TV, cinema, the Internet, newspapers and magazines. The international interest in brand-name clothes and shoes, fast food and branded soft drinks and beers, pop music and major sports stars has never been greater. However, cultural transmission is not a one-way process. The influence of Islam has increased considerably in many Western countries, while Asian, Latin American and African cuisine can be found in many different parts of the world.
Linguistic	English has clearly emerged as the working language of the 'global village'. Of the 1.9 billion English speakers, some 1.5 billion people around the world speak English as a second language. In a number of countries there is great concern about the future of the native language.
Political	The power of nation-states has been diminished in many parts of the world as more and more countries organise themselves into trade blocs. The European Union is the most advanced model for this process of integration, taking on many of the powers that were once the sole preserve of its member nation-states. The United Nations has intervened militarily in an increasing number of countries in recent time, leading some writers to talk about the gradual movement to 'world government'. On the other side of the coin is the growth of global terrorism.
Demographic	The movement of people across international borders and the desire to move across these borders has increased considerably in recent decades. More and more communities are becoming multicultural in nature.
Environmental	Increasingly, economic activity in one country has had an impact on the environment in other nations. The long-range transportation of airborne pollutants is the most obvious evidence of this process. The global environmental conferences in Rio (1992) and Johannesburg (2002) are evidence that most countries see the scale of the problems as so large that only coordinated international action can bring realistic solutions.

Figure 4 *The dimensions of globalisation.*

The development of globalisation

Globalisation is a recent phenomenon (post-1960) which is very different from anything the world had previously experienced. It developed out of **internationalisation**.

A key period in the process of internationalisation occurred between 1870 and 1914 when:

- transport and communications networks expanded rapidly
- world trade grew significantly with a considerable increase in the level of interdependence between rich and poor nations
- there were very large flows of capital from European companies to other parts of the world.

International trade tripled between 1870 and 1913. At this time the world trading system was dominated and organised by four nations: Britain, France, Germany and the USA. However, the global shocks of the First World War and the Great Depression put a stop to this period of phenomenal economic growth. It was not until the 1950s that international interdependence was back on track.

Today's globalisation is very different from the global relationships of 50 or a 100 years ago. Peter Dicken makes the distinction between the 'shallow integration' of the pre-1914 period and the 'deep integration' of the present period. The global economy is more extensive and complicated than it has ever been.

Until the post-1950 period the production process itself was mainly organised within national economies. This has changed rapidly in the last 50 years or so with the emergence of a **new international division of labour (NIDL)** reflecting a change in the geographical pattern of specialisation with the fragmentation of many production processes across national boundaries. The NIDL divides production into different skills and tasks that are spread across regions and countries rather than within a single company. Other factors responsible for economic globalisation are:

- the increasing complexity of international trade flows as this process has developed
- major advances in trade liberalisation under the World Trade Organisation – economic and legal barriers to world trade (tariffs, quotas and regulations) are much lower today than in the past
- the emergence of fundamentalist free-market governments in the USA (Ronald Reagan) and the UK (Margaret Thatcher) around 1980 – the economic policies developed by these governments influenced policy-making in many other countries
- the emergence of an increasing number of newly industrialised countries
- the integration of the old Soviet Union and its Eastern European communist satellites into the capitalist system – now, no significant group of countries stands outside the free market global system
- the opening up of other economies, particularly those of China and India
- the deregulation of world financial markets, allowing a much greater level of international competition in financial services
- the 'transport and communications revolution' that has made possible the management of today's complicated networks of production and trade.

Which are the major global economies?

Figure 5 shows the relative size of the top 20 global economies according to the traditional measure, gross domestic product (GDP). However, more and more organisations such as the UN and the IMF are publishing GDP data at purchasing power parity (PPP). Once

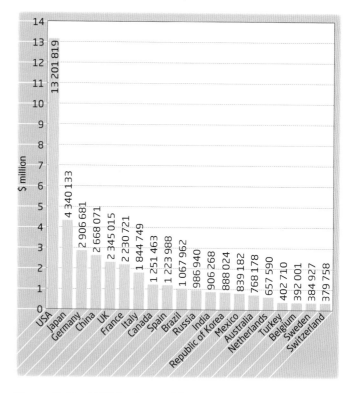

Figure 5 *Total GDP for the top 20 global economies, 2006.*

The fall of the Berlin Wall – the beginning of the integration of Eastern Europe into the free market system. The photo on the left shows a remaining part of the wall, the photo on the right marks the position where the wall once was.

Discussion point

What is the difference between the phases of internationalisation and of globalisation?

differences in the local purchasing power of currencies are taken into account, China's economy moves firmly into second place behind the USA (Figure 6). The other major emerging economy whose relative importance increases significantly once output is measured on a PPP basis is India.

Globalisation indices

There are a number of ways of measuring globalisation. Two of the most prominent methods are the KOF Index provided by the KOF Swiss Institute of Technology Zurich and the A.T. Kearney index published in *Foreign Affairs* magazine, a US publication. Another interesting analysis is produced by the Centre for the Study of Globalisation and Regionalisation (CSGR), based at the University of Warwick.

Activities

1 Define the term 'globalisation'.
2 **a** Describe the data presented in Figure 1.
  b Suggest reasons for the changes indicated in Figure 1.
3 Define the terms:
  a 'capitalism'
  b 'anti-capitalism'.
4 Comment briefly on the views of globalisation presented in Figure 2.
5 Study Figure 3.
  a List the main components of the global economy.
  b Briefly comment on the relationships between them.
6 Define the terms:
  a 'transnational corporation'
  b 'global shift'.
7 **a** What are newly industrialised countries (NICs)?
  b Describe and explain the different generations of newly industrialised country shown in Table 1.
8 Explain the 'new international division of labour' (NIDL).
9 Briefly discuss the factors responsible for economic globalisation.
10 **a** Describe the data presented in Figure 5.
  b Why do the amounts and rankings in Figure 6 differ from those in Figure 5?

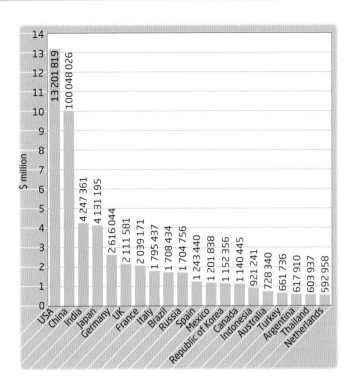

Figure 6 *Purchasing power parity (PPP) GDP for the top 20 global economies, 2006.*

The KOF Index of Globalisation

The KOF Index of Globalisation measures globalisation on economic, social and political dimensions. It was first published in 2002. The KOF Index defines globalisation as:

> the process of creating networks of connections among actors at multi-continental distances, mediated through a variety of flows including people, information and ideas, capital and goods. Globalisation is conceptualised as a process that erodes national boundaries, integrates national economies, cultures, technologies and governance and produces complex relations of mutual interdependence.

The KOF Index measures globalisation on a scale of 1 to 100 with the underlying variables entered in percentiles. Higher values denote greater globalisation. The weightings for calculating the sub-indices are determined using principal components analysis. Under this method the impact of extreme data points is reduced, also ensuring fewer fluctuations over time.

Table 2 (on pages 8–9) shows the rankings of the top 50 countries for 2009 which are based on 2006 data. The second column shows the figures for the total globalisation index,

Country	Globalisation index	Country	Economic globalisation	Country	Social globalisation	Country	Political globalisation
1. Belgium	91.51	1. Singapore	96.67	1. Luxembourg	93.87	1. France	98.03
2. Ireland	91.02	2. Luxembourg	93.43	2. Switzerland	93.85	2. Italy	97.04
3. Netherlands	89.92	3. Ireland	92.63	3. Ireland	91.96	3. Belgium	97.01
4. Switzerland	89.87	4. Malta	92.63	4. Antigua and Barbuda	91.90	4. Austria	96.85
5. Austria	89.14	5. Belgium	91.63	5. Cyprus	91.72	5. Sweden	96.64
6. Sweden	88.68	6. Netherlands	91.30	6. Puerto Rico	90.66	6. Spain	95.22
7. Denmark	87.37	7. Estonia	90.35	7. Singapore	90.65	7. Switzerland	95.11
8. Canada	86.32	8. Hungary	90.22	8. Austria	90.62	8. Canada	94.90
9. Luxembourg	86.28	9. Bahrain	88.37	9. Grenada	88.53	9. USA	94.05
10. Hungary	85.15	10. Sweden	88.11	10. Belgium	88.12	10. Poland	93.88
11. Czech Republic	84.65	11. Cyprus	86.74	11. Malta	87.99	11. Netherlands	93.61
12. New Zealand	84.55	12. Czech Republic	86.58	12. New Zealand	87.24	12. Egypt, Arab Rep.	93.35
13. Finland	84.19	13. Denmark	85.49	13. Canada	87.22	13. Denmark	93.13
14. Singapore	84.07	14. Chile	85.48	14. Slovenia	86.51	14. Germany	92.80
15. Portugal	83.92	15. New Zealand	85.20	15. Netherlands	86.37	15. Argentina	92.78
16. France	83.68	16. Portugal	84.96	16. Denmark	85.81	16. Greece	92.20
17. Estonia	83.45	17. Israel	84.96	17. Sweden	84.52	17. Brazil	92.15
18. Spain	82.94	18. Finland	84.69	18. Estonia	84.13	18. Portugal	92.11
19. Cyprus	82.70	19. Slovak Republic	84.13	19. UK	83.65	19. Turkey	91.72
20. Slovenia	82.40	20. Austria	83.04	20. Bahamas, The	82.97	20. India	91.65
21. Norway	82.27	21. Iceland	82.90	21. Iceland	82.72	21. Hungary	91.63
22. Germany	81.75	22. Switzerland	82.73	22. New Caledonia	82.59	22. Romania	90.88
23. Malta	81.24	23. Latvia	82.60	23. Croatia	82.57	23. Australia	90.65
24. Slovak Republic	81.24	24. Panama	81.65	24. Germany	82.37	24. Nigeria	89.95
25. Croatia	80.61	25. Spain	80.95	25. Norway	81.98	25. Finland	89.92
26. Australia	80.49	26. Canada	80.29	26. Latvia	81.73	26. Japan	89.42
27. UK	79.31	27. Slovenia	80.26	27. French Polynesia	81.24	27. Norway	89.26
28. Italy	78.80	28. Lithuania	80.24	28. France	81.22	28. Morocco	89.25

1 Measuring global interactions

Table 2 2009 KOF Index of Globalisation – top 50 countries.

Country	Score	Country	Score	Country	Score	Country	Score
29. Lebanon	78.56	29. UK	79.30	29. Czech Republic	80.43	29. Pakistan	88.81
30. Poland	77.96	30. Jamaica	78.51	30. Finland	80.29	30. Czech Republic	88.53
31. Lithuania	77.24	31. Norway	78.37	31. United Arab Emirates	79.80	31. Chile	87.23
32. Greece	77.00	32. Croatia	78.28	32. Lebanon	78.49	32. Bulgaria	87.16
33. Malaysia	76.24	33. Australia	78.04	33. Portugal	78.03	33. Senegal	87.09
34. Latvia	76.14	34. Malaysia	78.03	34. Spain	77.62	34. Tunisia	87.00
35. Iceland	76.12	35. France	77.57	35. Slovak Republic	77.44	35. South Africa	86.90
36. Jordan	75.51	36. Bulgaria	76.08	36. Seychelles	77.16	36. Ireland	86.72
37. Chile	74.99	37. Poland	74.93	37. Australia	76.89	37. Korea, Rep.	86.64
38. USA	74.93	38. Germany	74.50	38. Brunei Darussalam	76.53	38. China	86.36
39. Bulgaria	74.85	39. Italy	74.37	39. Samoa	76.46	39. Jordan	85.50
40. Israel	74.69	40. Kazakhstan	73.98	40. Hungary	76.27	40. Peru	85.28
41. Bahrain	72.89	41. Greece	73.54	41. Lithuania	76.13	41. Algeria	85.28
42. Panama	70.88	42. Jordan	73.25	42. Barbados	75.98	42. Kenya	84.60
43. Bosnia and Herzegovina	70.81	43. Trinidad and Tobago	72.71	43. Maldives	75.94	43. Russian Federation	84.60
44. Romania	70.58	44. Oman	72.30	44. Kuwait	75.72	44. Indonesia	84.59
45. Antigua and Barbuda	70.52	45. Moldova	71.31	45. Qatar	75.69	45. Uruguay	84.52
46. Jamaica	69.76	46. Botswana	70.57	46. Mauritius	75.64	46. Philippines	84.17
47. Ukraine	69.30	47. Bosnia and Herzegovina	70.50	47. Macao, China	74.40	47. Malaysia	83.73
48. United Arab Emirates	69.26	48. Uruguay	69.93	48. Bahrain	74.31	48. Ghana	83.30
49. Mauritius	69.26	49. Costa Rica	69.64	49. Macedonia, FYR	74.03	49. Ukraine	83.14
50. Uruguay	69.14	50. Thailand	69.43	50. Italy	72.38	50. Slovak Republic	82.81

Source: KOF Index of Globalisation 2009

with the first five positions occupied by Belgium, Ireland, Netherlands, Switzerland and Austria. The first countries of significant population size to appear in the ranking are France in 16th position and Germany in 22nd place.

The remaining columns of Table 2 give the top 50 positions for economic, social and political globalisation which are combined to arrive at the overall Index of Globalisation. All countries in the top 50 have an index of over 69.0 for the overall index. Indonesia, which is ranked 100th, and Nepal, 150th, have respective figures of 57.66 and 39.65. The bottom five ranking countries in order of lowest first are Myanmar, Democratic Republic of the Congo, Burundi, Niger and Rwanda. Figure 7 contrasts the 15 most and least globalised countries in the world. The graphs show the relative contributions of the three measures of globalisation.

There are significant variations between the columns. Singapore is in 14th position on the overall globalisation index, but ranks first for economic globalisation, 7th for social globalisation and only 125th for political globalisation. The UK ranks 27th on the overall index, 29th for economic, 19th for social and 77th for political. For both Singapore and the UK, their political rankings are very different from their other rankings. In contrast, the

European Parliament building, Brussels: Belgium is the most globalised country in the world according to the KOF Index.

USA ranks 9th for political globalisation, 56th for social globalisation and 59th for economic globalisation. This gives the USA an overall globalisation index ranking of 38th.

The lowest levels of globalisation under the KOF Index are in Africa, the Middle East, South and South-east Asia, and Latin America (with the exceptions of Chile and Argentina).

Table 3 shows the indices and variables used to assess the three dimensions of globalisation. Economic globalisation is characterised as long-distance flows of goods, capital and services, as well as information and perceptions that accompany market exchanges. Economic globalisation is subdivided into

- actual flows

- restrictions.

Actual economic flows include data on trade, **foreign direct investment (FDI)** and portfolio investment. Each measure is given a weighting according to its perceived importance. Economic restrictions on trade and capital include hidden import barriers, mean tariff rate, taxes on international trade and an index of capital controls. For example, a country with higher tariffs than another country is less globalised.

Social globalisation is expressed as the spread of ideas, information, images and people. Three categories are employed here:

- personal contacts

- information flows

- cultural proximity.

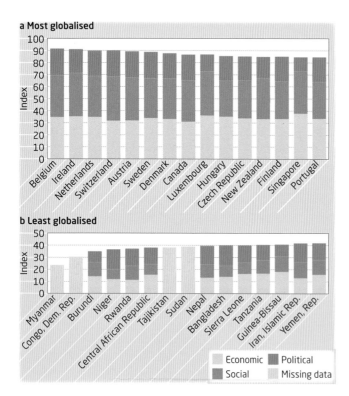

Figure 7 *The world's 15 most globalised and 15 least globalised countries.*

Indices and variables	Weights (%)
A Economic globalisation	**37**
i Actual flows	*50*
Trade (% of GDP)	19
Foreign direct investment, flows (% of GDP)	20
Foreign direct investment, stocks (% of GDP)	24
Portfolio investment (% of GDP)	17
Income payments to foreign nationals (% of GDP)	20
ii Restrictions	*50*
Hidden import barriers	22
Mean tariff rate	28
Taxes on international trade (% of current revenue)	27
Capital account restrictions	22
B Social globalisation	**39**
i Data on personal contact	*33*
Telecoms traffic	26
Transfers (% of GDP)	3
International tourism	26
Foreign population (% of total population)	20
International letters per capita	25
ii Data on information flows	*36*
Internet users per 1000 people	36
Television per 1000 people	36
Trade in newspapers (% of GDP)	28
iii Data on cultural proximity	*31*
Number of McDonald's restaurants per capita	43
Number of IKEA outlets per capita	44
Trade in books (% of GDP)	12
C Political globalisation	**25**
Membership in international organisations	25
Embassies in country	28
Participation in UN Security Council Missions	22
International treaties	25

Table 3 *2009 KOF Index – indices and variables.*

The personal contacts category attempts to capture direct interaction among people living in different countries. It includes international telecoms traffic, the incoming and outgoing tourism of a country, transfer payments between countries, the foreign population as a percentage of total population, and the number of international letters sent and received.

The information flows category attempts to measure the potential flow of ideas and images. It includes the proportion of Internet users, the number of households with a television set and volume of international newspapers traded. Together, these variables illustrate people's potential for receiving news from other countries which contributes to the global spread of ideas.

The concept of cultural proximity is more difficult to calculate. It is important to use measures for which data is widely available. Thus the indicators used by KOF are:

- the number of McDonald's restaurants located in a country per capita; this major US brand has become synonymous with the process of globalisation
- the number of IKEA outlets per capita, with the same rationale as for McDonald's
- imported and exported books relative to GDP; this is used as an indicator of the extent to which beliefs and values move across national borders.

Political globalisation is characterised by the diffusion of government policies. Membership of international organisations is considered the most important of the four measures used in this aspect of globalisation. This is followed by the number of embassies in a country because of the importance of face-to-face contact between

Shoppers outside on IKEA store in Beijing.

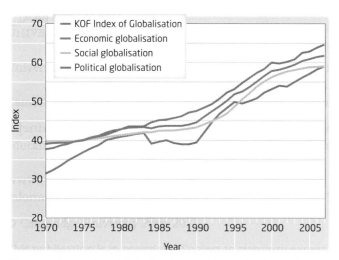

Figure 8 *KOF Index of Globalistation worldwide, 1970–2007.*

government officials of different countries. Also included are participation in UN Security Council Missions and the number of international treaties signed by a country.

Figure 8 shows how the levels of globalisation according to KOF have changed since 1970. In recent decades economic globalisation has been above the general index of globalisation while social and political globalisation have been below. The overall upward trend was relatively slow between 1970 and 1990 compared with the post-1990 period.

Some critics have argued that the KOF Index is constructed by making some problematic assumptions about the measurement, normalisation and weighting of the variables included in the Index. Small countries with successful economies figure very prominently in the rankings. As a result some writers feel that larger economies may be undervalued in terms of their true contributions to globalisation. Perhaps naturally, many economists feel that the economic component of globalisation should be given more prominence in the rankings, but experts from other disciplines often have alternative viewpoints.

Hong Kong has experienced phenomenal economic growth since the 1960s.

Moneygram, international money transfer: remittances are a major source of income for many developing countries.

Activities

1 Discuss the factors used by the KOF Index to measure globalisation.
2 Describe the data shown in Table 2 (pages 8-9). Suggest reasons for the differences in ranking in the columns globalisation index and economic, social and political globalisation.
3 **a** Where are the least globalised countries according to the KOF Index?
  b What are the reasons for their low globalisation status?
4 Look at Figure 8. Describe how the worldwide level of globalisation changed between 1970 and 2007.

Review

Examination-style question

1 a Describe how one prominent index measures global interaction.

   b How effective is this measure in comparing the level of global interaction of different countries?

Websites

www.atkearney.com
A.T. Kearney global management consultants

www.ifg.org
International Forum on Globalization

www.worldbank.org
World Bank

www.oecd.org
Organisation for Economic Cooperation and Development

www.opendemocracy.net
Open Democracy

www.freetheworld.org
Economic Freedom Network

Key terms

Globalisation the growing interdependence of countries worldwide through the increasing volume and variety of cross-border transactions in goods and services and of international capital flows, and through the more rapid and widespread diffusion of technology.

Capitalism the social and economic system which relies on the market mechanism to distribute the factors of production (land, labour and capital) in the most efficient way.

Anti-capitalism a broad term which can cover any challenge to capitalism as the best or only way to organise the world. It was given media prominence during the 1999 WTO summit in Seattle where a wide range of organisations protested against the workings of the international economic system.

Transnational corporation (TNC) a firm that owns or controls productive operations in more than one country through foreign direct investment.

Global shift the large-scale filter-down of economic activity from developed countries to NICs and developing countries.

Newly industrialised countries (NICs) nations that have undergone rapid and successful industrialisation since the 1960s.

Internationalisation the extension of economic activities across national boundaries. It is essentially a quantitative process which leads to a more extensive geographical pattern of economic activity. The phase preceding globalisation.

New international division of labour (NIDL) this divides production into different skills and tasks that are spread across regions and countries rather than within a single country.

Foreign direct investment (FDI) overseas investments in physical capital by transnational corporations.

02 Global core and periphery

KEY QUESTIONS

- Where are the core areas at the focus of global interaction?
- Where are the global peripheries and areas relatively unaffected by these interactions?

People living in an abandoned railway carriage: shelter takes many different forms in poor countries.

The application of **core–periphery** theory at the global scale identifies the developed countries of the world as the **economic core** of the global economic system and the developing countries as the **economic periphery**. This correlates with the general distinction made between the developed 'North' and the developing 'South'. These terms were first used in *North–South: A Programme for Survival* published in 1980, a significant exercise in international diplomacy oriented towards global reform (Figure 1). This publication was produced by a distinguished international commission and is generally known as the 'Brandt Report' after its chairperson Willy Brandt, former chancellor of the then West Germany. Here, the South was taken to be Latin America, Africa and the Middle East, and Asia (with the exception of Japan and the Asiatic region of Russia). Other terms used to distinguish between the richer and poorer nations are:

- developed and developing countries
- more economically developed countries (MEDCs) and less economically developed countries (LEDCs).

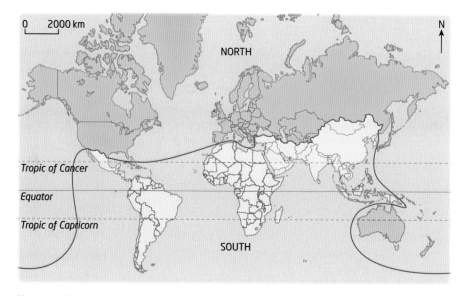

Figure 1 *The North–South divide.*

While a useful classification at the time, the **North–South divide** is now seen as rather simplistic. Undoubtedly it overestimated the strength of the economies of the former Soviet Union and its Eastern European satellites. It was not really until the fall of the Berlin Wall and the Iron Curtain that the fragility of these economies became apparent. It also failed to take note of those newly industrialised countries that had already made significant progress by 1980, namely the four 'Asian tigers'. A **tiger economy** is one that grows rapidly in a short period of time.

Buckingham Palace, UK; the UK is one of the richest countries in the world (part of the core) and Queen Elizabeth II is one of the richest individuals.

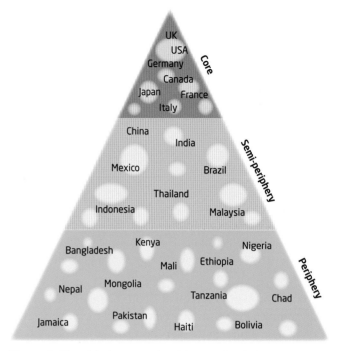
Figure 2 The global core, semi-periphery and periphery examples of countries in each grouping.

However, in recent decades the world economy has become much more complex. It is now more accurate to distinguish between:

- the core
- the semi-periphery and
- the periphery.

The semi-periphery occupies a position between the core and periphery. In this tripartite system countries can move from one level to another, with most changes being in an upward direction. Figure 2 gives examples of countries currently at each level. The semi-periphery is the location of the world's newly industrialised countries. The number of newly industrialised countries has increased significantly over the past 50 years. Undoubtedly, more countries will move from the periphery to the semi-periphery in the future.

Immanuel Wallerstein with his **world-systems theory** was arguably the first academic to make this distinction between the different types of world region and to attempt to explain the interactions between them.

A beggar in Vienna, Austria – poverty amidst wealth in rich countries.

World-systems theory: Wallerstein

New approaches to an issue or subject are often stimulated by the shortcomings of previous theorising. The breakthrough of world-systems theory in the mid 1970s, popularised by Immanuel Wallerstein and others, was at least partly a response to the deficiencies of earlier

Discussion point

Why is poverty such a significant problem in many countries in the global core? What is the evidence of such poverty?

approaches, such as those of W.W. Rostow (modernisation theory) and A.G. Frank (dependency theory).

The world-systems approach asserts that a capitalist world economy has been in existence since the 16th century. Before this, global interdependence did not exist. Instead the world was made up of a number of relatively independent mini-systems. From then on capitalism incorporated a growing number of previously more or less isolated and self-sufficient societies into a complex system of functional relationships. A small number of core states transformed a much larger external area into a periphery. In between core and periphery, semi-peripheries existed which played a key role in the functioning of the global system. The semi-periphery is an economic condition to which parts of the periphery may rise or parts of the core may fall.

Within the system a division of labour operated, with the core countries as industrial producers and the peripheral areas as agricultural and other raw materials producers. The terms of trade were heavily skewed in favour of the core, particularly with regard to the periphery but also to a lesser extent in relation to the semi-periphery. The process of underdevelopment started with the incorporation of a particular external area into the world system. As the system expanded, first Eastern Europe, then Latin America, Asia and Africa, in that order, were peripherised.

The semi-peripheral countries/regions form the most dynamic part of the system, characterised by an increase in the relative importance of industrial production. The rising semi-peripheries of the present, the NICs, are ambitious, competing to varying degrees for core status. Thus the world-systems approach has a degree of optimism lacking in dependency theory, recognising that some countries can break out of the state of underdevelopment. However, Wallerstein (1979) acknowledges that rapid change is not easy and that there are indeed 'limited possibilities of transformation within the capitalist world economy'.

The rise and fall of major economic powers forms part of the cyclical movements of the world system, movements that are basically influenced by economic long waves. Thus the world system has periods of expansion, contraction, crisis and structural change, paving the way to renewed expansion.

The criticisms of Wallerstein's approach include:

- too high a level of eurocentricity by underrating the sophistication of other early trading systems, particularly with regard to China, Japan and elsewhere in Asia

- too great a degree of simplicity in assuming a universal one-way flow of resources from the periphery to the core

- failing to recognise the high level of competition between core nations by suggesting that they organise the world economy in order to maintain a clearly defined core club.

Recent favela development in Manaus, Brazil.

The Clark-Fisher model

This model (Figure 3) shows how, over time, the relative importance of the sectors of employment change. In the pre-industrial phase the primary sector dominates, as it did in Britain prior to the Industrial Revolution. The proportion of the workforce employed in manufacturing

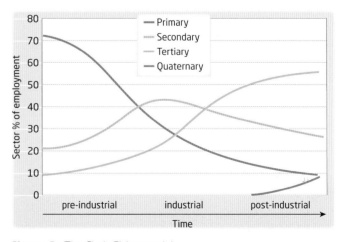

Figure 3 *The Clark–Fisher model.*

increases as a country's economy diversifies away from heavy reliance on the primary sector. This usually begins with low-technology industries based on locally available raw materials. Over time the manufacturing base widens. To support the increasing number of industries and the demands of a more affluent population, a growing range of services is required, leading to the expansion of tertiary employment.

Geographical skill

Look at Figure 3. To what extent is the Clark-Fisher model useful in distinguishing between countries that are in the core, semi-periphery and periphery?

Changes in the sectors of employment can happen quite quickly. In 1900, 40% of employment in the USA was in the primary sector. However, the mechanisation of farming, mining, forestry and fishing drastically reduced the demand for labour in these industries. As these jobs disappeared, people moved to urban areas where most secondary, tertiary and quaternary employment is located. Less than 4% of employment in the USA is now in the primary sector.

Human labour has steadily been replaced in manufacturing too. In more and more factories, robots and other advanced machinery handle assembly-line jobs that were once done by large numbers of people. In 1950, the same number of Americans were employed in manufacturing as in services. By 1980, two-thirds were working in services.

The tertiary and quaternary sectors are also changing. In banking, insurance and many other types of business, computer networks have reduced the number of people

Theory of Knowledge

The Clark-Fisher model (Figure 3), like all models, is a simplification of reality. The actual changes that have occurred in some countries might have varied significantly from the model. To what extent can the model be simultaneously both a help and a hindrance to our thinking? How typical is this of models in other subjects that you have studied?

required. But elsewhere service employment is rising, such as in health, education and tourism.

Globalisation has been a significant factor in the changing importance of the sectors of employment in many countries. Such change has occurred most rapidly in the newly industrialised countries, the success story of globalisation. In the least developed countries, those nations that have been largely bypassed by the rapidly evolving global economy, there is still heavy reliance on the primary sector.

Activities

1 Define the terms:
   a 'economic core'
   b 'economic periphery'.
2 Why is it now thought to be more accurate to think in terms of core, semi-periphery and periphery rather than core and periphery?
3 Look at Figure 2 (page 15). For each subdivision give the names of two more countries.

Identifying core nations

Many attempts have been made to identify the core nations in the global economic system. There is a high correlation between these classifications, with the only differences occurring at the margins. The agreed core is:

- the USA and Canada
- the European Union, EFTA (Iceland, Norway and Liechtenstein) and Switzerland
- Japan
- Australia and New Zealand.

The debate is generally over:

- the first generation of newly industrialised countries – South Korea, Singapore, Hong Kong, Taiwan
- the oil-rich Arab states
- Israel.

Some of these countries have GDP per capita figures far in excess of some of the less well-off members of the acknowledged global core. In any classification it is very easy for inconsistencies to occur. Also, it seems that the fortunes of countries can change more rapidly now than at virtually any time in the past.

Harvard University – high quality education is an important element of development.

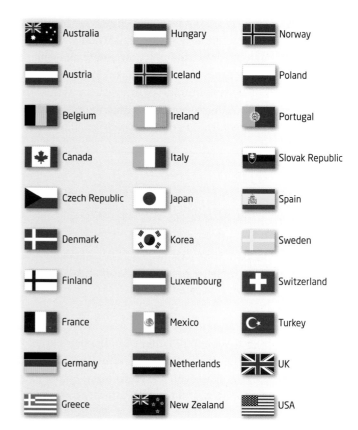

Figure 4 *The OECD countries.*

The Organisation for Economic Cooperation and Development (OECD)

The OECD is a grouping of the world's most advanced economies (Figure 4). It is one way of identifying the global economic core. The OECD currently has 30 members, but a number of other countries are in the process of applying for membership. The OECD states that its aim is to bring together the governments of countries committed to democracy and the market economy from around the world to:

- support sustainable economic growth
- boost employment
- raise living standards
- maintain financial stability
- assist other countries' economic development
- contribute to growth in world trade.

The OECD provides a setting where governments compare policy experiences, seek answers to common problems, identify good practice and coordinate domestic and international policies.

In January 2010 it was announced that Chile was to become the 31st member of the OECD, once its parliament had ratified the agreement. Chile will be the first member from South America in this prestigious organisation. The Chilean President Michelle Bachelet stated: 'Chile is leaving underdevelopment behind and is walking steadily towards becoming a developed nation in a few more years.'

The OECD has been in discussions with a number of other countries over their future membership at various points in time. These countries include Russia, Israel, Brazil, China, Indonesia and South Africa.

The global city network

Of course, while a country as a total entity might not be advanced enough to be considered as part of the global core, its main cities may be of considerable importance to the global economic system. One way of looking at the world's economic core is to identify its global cities.

A **global city** is one that is judged to be an important nodal point in the global economic system. The term 'global city' was first introduced by Saskia Sassen in her book *The Global City*, published in 1991. Initially referring to New York, London and Tokyo, Sassen described global cities as ones that play a major role in global affairs in terms of politics, economics and culture. The number of global cities has increased significantly in recent decades as the process of globalisation has deepened.

The Globalisation and World Cities (GaWC) Research Network at Loughborough University has identified various levels of global city. Figure 5 shows what are termed the 'Alpha' cities in 2008, subdivided into four categories. Only New York and London are placed in the highest, Alpha++ category under this classification. The cities in the second-ranking, Alpha+ category are Beijing, Shanghai, Hong Kong, Tokyo, Paris, Singapore and Sydney. The GaWC analysis also recognises four lower levels of urban area around the world. The results are based upon the office networks of 175 advanced producer service firms in 526 cities in 2008.

In 2008, the American journal *Foreign Policy* published its Global Cities Index. The rankings are based on 24 measures over five areas:

- business activity
- human capital
- information exchange
- cultural experience
- political engagement.

Foreign Policy noted that 'the world's biggest, most interconnected cities help set global agendas, weather transnational dangers, and serve as the hubs of global integration. They are the engines of growth for their countries and the gateways to the resources of their regions.'

Activities

1   **a** What is the OECD?
    b To what extent is it reasonable to think of the OECD as a grouping of core nations?
2   **a** What is a global city?
    b Describe the spatial distribution of global cities shown in Figure 5.
3   Why is London considered to be one of the world's major global cities?

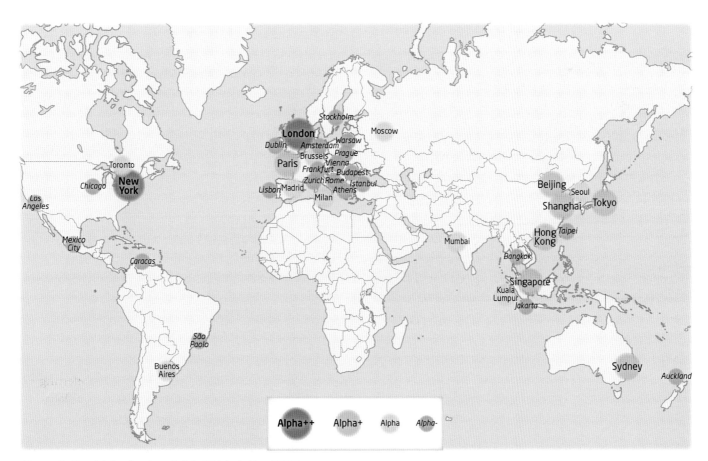

Figure 5 *Spatial distribution of global 'Alpha' cities, 2008.*

Case study

Business and financial services in the City of London

London is considered one of the world's major global cities for a number of reasons, but the most important factor by far is what happens right at the centre of this large urban area – in the City of London. London is one of the big three financial centres in the world, along with New York and Tokyo. Often called 'The Square Mile' because of its geographical size, the City is run by the City of London Corporation. Among the important buildings here are the Bank of England, the London Stock Exchange and Lloyd's of London (insurance).

The City of London is the most important concentration of tertiary industry in the UK and arguably in the world. With a resident population of fewer than 3,000 its workforce is just under 300 000, 75% of whom work in banking, finance, insurance and business services.

The City of London is a major part of London's central business district (CBD). Most employment in London's CBD is in the tertiary sector. The West End specialises in

City of London
- $1359 billion foreign exchange turnover each day (34% of global share)
- 53% of the global foreign equity market (stocks and shares)
- World's leading market for international insurance
- $1686 billion pension fund assets under management
- 75% of the world's largest 500 companies located in London, most in the City
- 254 foreign banks in London, most in the City
- 692 foreign companies listed on the London Stock Exchange

Figure 6 *City of London factfile.*

retailing while the City specialises in business and financial services. Canary Wharf is part of the London Docklands development. It has extended London's CBD to the east, adding much needed office and retail space. Other important tertiary functions in London's CBD are major public buildings, theatres, cinemas, hotels, universities, hospitals and restaurants.

To remain in such a formidable position, continuing investment is vital. The Corporation of London's Economic Development Unit is responsible for maintaining London's global position. The Unit's objectives are:

- to ensure that all the leading companies in global finance and commerce are in the City and that they have the professional support to function efficiently
- to enhance the quality of the working and living environment within the City
- to ensure an efficient infrastructure and a high-quality workforce by working closely with the property and training sectors
- to market the attributes of the City and of London as a whole on a worldwide basis
- to achieve an orderly property market by using its influence as both planning authority and landowner.

City of London emblem marking the boundary of the City of London, one of the world's great financial centres.

Challenges to the existing order

The rapid growth of newly industrialised countries has brought about major changes in the economic strength of countries. An article in The *Sunday Telegraph* (3 January 2010) entitled 'Developing nations emerge from shadows as sun sets on the West' charted the financial problems that beset the West in the first decade of the new millennium, culminating with the impact of the global recession 2008/10. It highlighted the poor decisions made by Western policy-makers, contrasting this with the powerful economic growth figures of countries such as China, India and Brazil. For example:

- China's Shanghai Composite Index of leading shares gained 140% 2000–09.
- India's Sensex 30, the main index on the Mumbai Stock Exchange, was up 249% in the same period.
- Brazil's Bovespa index of leading shares rose by 301%.
- Russia's Micex index increased by a massive 802%.

Together, these four formidable economies are known as the BRICs (Brazil, Russia, India and China). Their substantial growth rates are a serious threat to the established economic order. These four countries, along with other high-growth nations outside of the established core group of nations, are known as **emerging markets**.

While the developed world (the core) grew by an average of 2.1% a year in the first decade of the 21st century, the emerging markets expanded by 4.2%. The International Monetary Fund (IMF) estimates that the figures for 2010 will be 1.3% and 5.1% respectively, and for 2011–14 the respective growth rates will be 2.5% and 6.4% a year. These are very significant differences indeed.

The 'Sugarloaf', Rio de Janeiro. Brazil is one of the BRIC nations.

In 1990 the developed world controlled about 64% of the global economy as measured by GDP. This fell to 52% by 2009 – one of the most rapid economic changes in history! Most of this global shift occurred in the last decade. Such a huge global economic change has had major political consequences, with the emerging economies exerting much more power than they had previously in international negotiations.

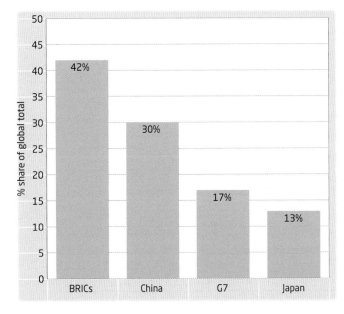

Figure 7 *Foreign exchange reserves.*

Many major investors are turning their backs, at least in part, on Western nations and seeking out opportunities in the faster-growing emerging markets. Figure 7 shows the distribution of the world's foreign exchange reserves. The G7 countries (USA, Canada, Japan, Germany, UK, France and Italy) now only hold 17% of the global total between them. Japan is the only significant creditor nation in this group. In contrast the BRICs hold 42%. China alone holds 30%. It is not so long ago that the USA was the world's biggest creditor. Today the USA is by far the world's biggest debtor. Much of the money borrowed by the USA and other Western economies has come from the reserves built up in emerging markets. The West no longer dominates the world's savings and as a result no longer dominates global investment and finance.

Figure 8 shows the extent to which the global share of GDP has changed since 1980. The data here is at purchasing power parity. The decline in the share of the EU has been particularly sharp over this time period. In contrast the share of the BRICs has been very significant indeed.

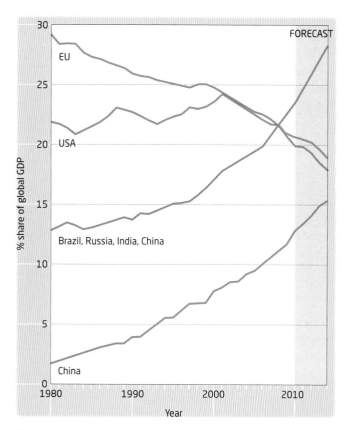

Figure 8 *Global share of GDP.*

The periphery and the global financial crisis

The global economic downturn has had a major impact on developing countries. Significant falls in investment, production and trade are now undermining the progress that has been made over the last decade or so in lifting people out of poverty. Recent reports have highlighted these problems:

- In early 2009 the World Bank estimated that over 2 million children could die as a result of the global recession.
- The *Global Monitoring Report* published by UNESCO in March 2009 estimates that the 390 million poorest Africans will suffer an income decline of about 20% – a much sharper fall than in developed countries.
- The IMF has said that the world's 22 poorest countries might need an additional $25 billion in 2009 to cope with the financial crisis.
- In March 2009 the President of the World Bank urged G20 leaders to deal with protectionism as their 'first stop' to prevent a social and humanitarian crisis in developing countries.

Figure 9 summarises the initial problems and the resultant effects that have caused such distress in developing countries.

Initial problems	Primary effects	Secondary effects
Sharp fall in commodity prices as demand falls in developed countries and NICs in particular	Sharp decline in government revenues/ royalties from primary products	Government spending cuts in health, education and other sectors in an attempt to balance the budget
Significant decrease in foreign direct investment as TNCs reduce international spending as demand for products declines	Business closures; plans to expand curtailed; critical decline in business confidence	Rising unemployment and underemployment; growing uncertainty about the future - increasing potential for social unrest?
Large international banks require assistance and curtail lending; banks in developing countries too small to provide the level of support required	Governments, businesses and individuals find it more and more difficult to obtain loans; internal financial organisations increasingly nervous about lending	Some banks and businesses default; business transactions decline due to concerns about the ability of customers to pay for goods/services
Fall in value of many currencies in developing countries against main international currencies	Rising inflation in many developing countries; high energy and food prices a particular problem	A decline in the terms of trade which causes a decrease in national income; balance of payment problems
Squeeze on bilateral and multilateral aid due to financial problems in developed countries	Aid projects under threat as aid contributions from a number of key donors fall	Major setback to achieving Millennium Development Goals: numbers living in poverty increase; rises in malnutrition, infant/child mortality
Charitable NGOs under pressure as donations drop	NGOs have had to reduce activities or pull out of some countries	Poorest communities in developing countries suffer most from decline of carefully targeted aid projects
Increasingly protectionist measures in some developed countries	Reduced export opportunities for developing countries	Increased financial pressures on economies of developing countries

Figure 9 *Developing countries and the global financial crisis.*

Case study

Mongolia: part of the global periphery

Mongolia is very much part of the global periphery and is one of the poorest countries in Asia. Sandwiched between Russia and China, Mongolia covers 1.5 million km², an area three times the size of France. It has a population of only 2.7 million of which 40% of live in the capital, Ulaanbaatar. The rest of the population is spread over vast, often inaccessible areas. Mongolia is a land of natural contrasts comprising large areas of rolling steppe, a continuation of Siberian alpine meadows to the north, snow-capped mountains in the west and the Gobi Desert in the south. The country endures a harsh climate with temperatures well below freezing during the winter. In 2007 the lowest recorded temperature in the country was –53°C while the highest was +44°C.

Camels in the harsh environment of the Gobi Desert: part of the global periphery.

Between 1923 and 1990 Mongolia was under communist rule, supported largely by the Soviet Union. In 1990, following the collapse of the Soviet Union, Mongolia went through a transition from communist rule to democracy. From 1923 the country's economy was heavily subsidised by the Soviet Union, with its infrastructure and industry developed using Russian expertise and investment. Mongolia enjoyed high levels of literacy, basic education and health care, and full employment. The speed of the collapse of the Soviet Union and the loss of financial support that followed led to significant economic problems in Mongolia.

Much of the country remains poor. The National Statistics Office of Mongolia reports that 35 out of every 100 people in Mongolia live in poverty. In Ulaanbaatar, more than 50% of the population live in poor ger (traditional nomadic tent dwellings) districts on the outskirts of the city. The ger districts suffer from a high level of pollution, particularly during the winter as families living in gers burn coal and other materials to fight the severe temperatures that regularly fall below –30°C.

Mongolia is in many ways a typical developing country. Like many such countries Mongolia is highly **primary product dependent** so the collapse of mining revenues as a result of the global financial crisis, in particular for copper, has caused acute financial problems for the country. Mongolia has become more dependent on mining revenues in recent years although the traditional agricultural economy based on herding remains important – about a third of the population live as nomadic herders on sparsely populated grasslands. In recent years, droughts and unusually cold and snowy winters have decimated livestock, destroying the livelihood of hundreds of thousands of households. Many have moved to Ulaanbaatar where they live in impoverished conditions.

% of total revenue in 2008

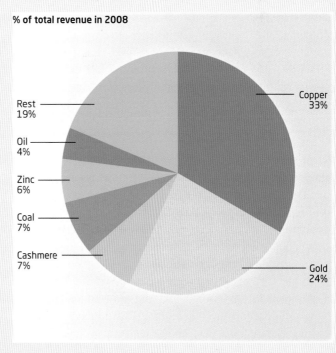

Copper 33%

Rest 19%

Oil 4%

Zinc 6%

Coal 7%

Cashmere 7%

Gold 24%

Figure 10 *Mongolia's export revenues are dominated by a small number of commodities.*

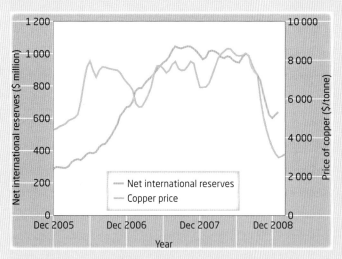

Figure 11 *Recent decline in Mongolia's international reserves.*

The global economic crisis has meant a considerable fall in demand for most commodities, resulting in significantly lower prices. The fall in the price of copper in particular has hit Mongolia very hard. The considerable decrease in price for Mongolia's main mineral exports began in mid 2008. From then until the end of January 2009 the copper price fell by 64% (Figure 11). The prices of other commodities have also dropped sharply. Other key raw material exports include coal, zinc and crude oil. Government revenue depends on a royalty of 5% paid by the mines.

Mongolia relies heavily on the export of commodities for foreign exchange. This valuable foreign exchange allows it to pay for the range of imports it requires. Mongolia's reserves of foreign currency have fallen rapidly to a worryingly low level – by $365 million between July and December 2008, which is a very large fall for a country with such a small population.

Government revenue has declined significantly, with falling commodity prices. The rapid decline in export earnings has resulted in the trade balance swinging from positive to negative, creating balance of payments problems. Considerable government spending cuts are already being implemented, but many cuts will have a disproportionate impact on the poorest sections of society. Commercial external financing is expensive and difficult to acquire as international banks and other financial organisations are restricting lending. The domestic banking system has a very limited capacity to finance the government due to its small size.

International financial help is urgently required. The Mongolian government has asked the IMF for help. The country has also approached China for a large loan. The World Bank and several bilateral partners have shown willingness to provide financial support for a programme agreed to with the IMF.

The value of private remittances from Mongolians working abroad has fallen as the economies of the countries concerned have contracted. This has reduced the flow of vital income for many families with the inevitable impact on local economies. An increasing number of Mongolians working abroad have been returning home. The problem for them is that they have returned to a domestic situation of rising unemployment and underemployment.

Livestock herders have been badly affected by falling prices of cashmere and other livestock-originated raw materials. The fall in the price of cashmere has been particularly sharp. An added concern is that loans to the livestock sector have come under pressure. Herders have become increasingly worried about getting 'essential' bank loans which in the past have generally been forthcoming. Banks are restructuring loans, but problems remain. The poor government financial situation is a threat to the sustainability of programmes that have been set up to improve the lives of herders. These programmes have focused on:

- livestock insurance to protect herders from losses incurred in the extreme winters that occur every few years
- expansion of mobile phone coverage throughout the countryside
- expansion of rural education.

In the Mongolian countryside, herders live in gers and do not have houses to put up as collateral against loans. Instead, many herders have put up their livestock as collateral. The economic situation has seen demand for expensive cashmere products decline, leading to a 33% fall in cashmere prices in Mongolia in 2008. The fall in demand and prices means many herders have struggled to repay loans they have taken out. Some herders are now forced by banks to sell their livestock to repay the loans.

The *Wall Street Journal* reported that the effect of the financial crisis on rural Mongolia was a *zud*. *Zud* is the Mongolian term for the devastating winters, characterised by heavy snowfalls, that decimate livestock. These *zuds* caused large numbers of people to migrate to Ulaanbaatar's poor ger districts looking for work.

Least developed countries

The least developed countries (LDCs) are the most marginalised in the world and have been relatively unaffected by the interactions between global core and periphery. Where effects have been felt they are as likely to have been negative as positive. Figure 12 shows the 49 nations currently designated as LDCs.

The list of LDCs is reviewed every three years by the United Nations Economic and Social Council. The criteria for the latest review in March 2009 were:

- the 'low income' criterion, based on a three-year average estimate of the gross national income (GNI) per capita, with a threshold of $905 for addition to the list, and a threshold of $1086 for graduation from LDC status
- the 'human assets weakness' criterion, involving a composite index based on indicators of (a) nutrition, (b) health, (c) school enrolment and (d) literacy
- the 'economic vulnerability' criterion, involving a composite index based on indicators of (a) natural shocks, (b) trade shocks, (c) exposure to shocks, (d) economic smallness and (e) economic remoteness.

The problems of LDCs are so deeply entrenched that even with UN support they find it hard to make substantial progress. Only two countries have so far graduated from LDC status: Botswana in 1994 and Cape Verde in 2007. However, in 2009 it was recommended that Equatorial Guinea be graduated from the list, with the same process potentially happening to Samoa and Maldives in the next few years. After a recommendation to graduate a country has been endorsed by the Economic and Social Council, the graduating country is granted a three-year grace period before graduation effectively takes place.

Traditional housing in Botswana, which is no longer an LDC.

Look at www.unctad.org to find out the latest information about the least developed countries (LDCs).

1 What are (a) the BRICs and (b) emerging markets?
2 a Describe the data illustrated in Figure 7 (page 21).
  b What are the reasons for the BRICs holding such a high share of foreign exchange reserves?
3 Describe the changes shown in Figure 8 (page 22).
4 Discuss the impact of the global financial crisis on peripheral nations.
5 Why can Mongolia be considered to be a vulnerable country?
6 Why have the least developed countries been relatively unaffected by the process of globalisation?

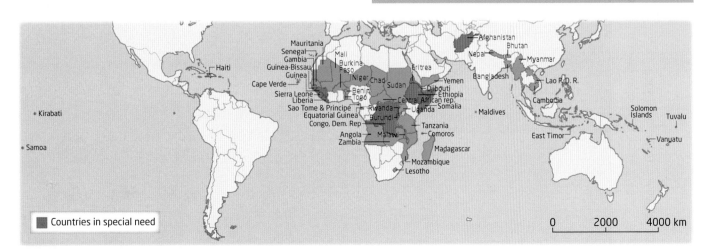

Figure 12 *The least developed countries.*

Review

Examination-style questions

1 a Describe and explain the location of global core and peripheral areas.
  b Examine the possible changes that might occur in this division of the world in future.

Websites

www.oecd.org
Organisation for Economic Cooperation and Development

www.cityoflondon.gov.uk
City of London Corporation

www.mol.mn
Mongolia Online

www.lboro.ac.uk
Loughborough University, UK

www.unctad.org
UN Conference on Trade and Development

Key terms

Core-periphery the concept of a developed core surrounded by an undeveloped periphery. The concept can be applied at various scales.

Economic core the global economic core consists of the most advanced countries in the world which exhibit very high levels of investment in infrastructure and other economic and social activities. The populations of these countries enjoy the highest living standards in the world.

Economic periphery the global economic periphery is made up of countries with a much lower level of infrastructure and economic activity than the core. Per capita incomes is these countries are considerably lower than in the core countries.

North-South divide the simple division set out in 1980 between developed countries (mainly in the North) and developing countries (mainly in the South).

Tiger economy an economy that grows very rapidly in a short period of time.

World-systems theory an approach based on the history of the capitalist world economy since its formation in the 16th century. Countries fall into three economic levels – core, semi-periphery and periphery – and can move from one level to another if their contribution to the world economy changes.

Global city a global city is one that is judged to be an important nodal point in the global economic system.

Emerging markets developing countries that are experiencing the fastest rate of growth in the global economy.

Primary product dependent countries that depend on one or a small number of raw materials for the majority of their export earnings.

03 Time–space convergence and the reduction in the friction of distance

KEY QUESTIONS

- How has the reduction in the friction of distance resulted in time-space convergence?
- What have been the relative changes in the speed and capacity of two types of transport responsible for the flow of goods, materials and people?

Sea planes, Vancouver Island, Canada.

The conceptual basis

The transport and communications revolution

Major advances in transport and telecommunications systems have significantly reduced the geographical barriers separating countries and peoples. **Transport systems** are the means by which materials, products and people are transferred from place to place. **Communications systems** are the ways in which information is transmitted from place to place in the form of ideas, instructions and images. Before the development of electric technology in the 19th century, information could only move at the same speed as the transport system carrying it. The development of first the telegraph and then the telephone broke this link to establish a new era. Figure 1 shows some of the main milestones in the history of transport and communications which have helped bring the world closer together in various ways. As time has progressed, the **diffusion** of new ideas has speeded up so that a technical breakthrough in one part of the world has had an impact on other parts of the world much more quickly than ever before.

In terms of communications, television has brought people all round the world images and knowledge of a large number of other places. This occurs not just in factual programmes but also in fiction. The number of television sets worldwide is approaching 2 billion. Even if people do not actually own a television set, there is a good chance that they have at least temporary access to one in their community. There have also been dramatic increases in the number of people with access to fixed line and mobile phone links. Even in very poor countries mobile phone sales are rising fast.

Many newspapers and magazines have a much more global flavour than they had even 20 years ago. Books written in one country may now be translated into many different languages. There are very few communities that are so isolated they do not have a reasonable knowledge about what is going on in the outside world. However, it has been the Internet that has had the greatest impact on communications in modern times at both the business and personal scales. Articles can be translated on the Internet, making them accessible to a much wider number of people.

In terms of transport, advances in aircraft technology have significantly reduced both the time and costs associated with flying. Developments in ocean freight have had a substantial impact on the movement of goods around the world. Here it is the development of container transport that has had the greatest impact. There have also been significant improvements in road, rail and pipeline transportation. **Intermodal transportation** means that containers can be moved quickly between ship, road and rail. High-speed train networks have brought about dramatic reductions in travel

Date	Event
*c.*60 000 BC	Homo sapiens' colonisation of Australia implies the construction of seaworthy boats
*c.*2900 BC	Egyptian hieroglyphic script fully developed
*c.*2500 BC	Chariots in Mesopotamia, skis in Scandinavia
*c.*1200 BC	Phoenician alphabet of 22 letters invented
*c.*220	Three-masted ships in Greece
271	Magnetic compass invented in China
*c.*650	Chinese scholars develop technique for printing texts from engraved wooden blocks
1403	Movable metal type first used for printing in Korea
1522	Spanish ships returning from Magellan's voyage complete the first circumnavigation of the world
1807	First steamboat service begins operation on Hudson river, USA
1825	Stockton-Darlington railway, Britain, opens with locomotive designed by George Stephenson
1843	SS *Great Britain* is first propeller-driven ship to cross the Atlantic
1866	First transatlantic cable is successfully laid
1876	Telephone is invented by US scientist Alexander Graham Bell
1878	First electric railway is demonstrated in Germany by Werner von Siemens
1886	Four-wheeled petrol-powered automobile is built by German engineer Gottlieb Daimler
1901	Marconi transmits radio signals across the Atlantic
1903	Wright brothers make first sustained flight of powered aircraft
1908	Mass production of cars begins with Model T Ford in USA
1927	First public broadcast of television is transmitted in Britain
1941	First flight of jet-powered plane, with engine designed by British engineer Frank Whittle, takes place
1951	US engineers build UNIVAC I, the first commercial computer
1957	Soviet Union launches an artificial satellite – *Sputnik I*
1962	US communications satellite *Telstar* is launched
1964	Japanese railways begin running high-speed 'bullet' trains
1970	Boeing 747 enters service
1975	A personal computer (PC) in kit form goes on sale in the USA
1984	A mobile phone network is launched in Chicago, USA
1994	World Wide Web is created
1997	Mobile Internet technologies emerge (WAP)

Figure 1 *Transport and communications milestones.*

times in a number of countries, including France, Japan and China. All these developments have reduced the real cost of transport in terms of moving both people and goods.

The friction of distance

The **friction of distance** is a traditional concept in geography which has been affected in a big way by modern developments in transport and communications.

Research idea

Find out more about two of the transport and communication milestones listed in Figure 1. Other people in the class could do the same. Produce a bullet-point report to present to your class.

Trans-Siberian Railway, Russia.

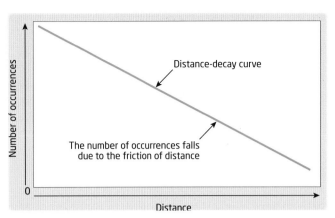

Figure 2 *Distance-decay curve.*

Communication is vital to the transmission of knowledge. However, there is considerable debate about the effectiveness of various types of communication in the transmission of knowledge, understanding and skills. Has ready access to vast amounts of digitised information devalued the importance of conceptual frameworks and deeper understanding?

The friction of distance refers to the reduced likelihood of people using a service the greater the distance that they live from it. Distance is seen to be a disadvantage due to the time and cost involved to overcome it. The effect of the friction of distance is to create a **distance decay** in the use of the service. Distance decay is thus the reduction in the amount of movement or spatial interaction between two places, the greater the distance they are apart (Figure 2). Examples of the friction of distance and distance decay are:

- the reduction in commuting with increasing distance from a city
- the decrease in support for a sports team as the distance from the stadium increases
- the decline in the use of a newsagent's with distance from it.

Testing the strongly related concepts of the friction of distance and distance decay has been a popular choice for many geographical enquiries at different levels of the school curriculum in the past.

While both concepts are useful, they are affected by the uneven distribution of phenomena in the real world. For example, the friction of distance is far less in a lowland region with high-level transport systems than in a rugged highland area where transport routes are few and far between. Thus the friction of distance in relation to a particular place may vary according to direction if there are significant variations in the physical and human landscape. In some directions **accessibility** may be high, but in other directions it may be much reduced. In general the friction of distance is less in rich countries than in poor countries due to the usually poorer level of accessibility in the latter. It also tends to be less in urban areas than in rural areas.

Stonehenge, Wiltshire, UK. The giant stones were transported up to 400 km to Stonehenge about 4000 years ago. How do you think this was done?

Time-space convergence

Globalisation is altering the way in which time–space operates and is perceived. The concept of **time–space convergence**, in which 'the travel time required between places decreases and distance declines in significance', was developed by D.G. Janelle in 1968 to examine the changing nature of spatial relationships. Time–space convergence means that the friction of distance is being reduced.

Figure 3 illustrates the way in which time–space convergence has resulted in a shrinking world. It is likely that you have travelled much more than your parents did when they were your age, and far more still than your grandparents at your age!

Figure 4 shows the role of time–space convergence in the process of spatial reorganisation. Time–space convergence

is a direct consequence of transport innovation. This may be in terms of the mode of transport itself or improvements in transport infrastructure that allow the mode of transport to operate more efficiently. Time–space convergence can have an array of consequences for a city, region or country, some positive and some negative. A particular improvement in transport may stimulate demands for even greater improvements in accessibility. People are more aware than ever of what is possible because of their improved knowledge of events elsewhere in the world.

Janelle illustrated how time–space convergence can be calculated. In one illustration of the subject, Janelle used the example of the travel time between Los Angeles and Santa Barbara in the USA, which took 500 minutes in 1901 and only 100 minutes in 2001. This gives a time–space convergence of 400 minutes or an average rate of convergence of 4 minutes per year. Another example researched by Janelle is the distance between Edinburgh and London in the UK. He concluded that the two cities had converged at an average rate of 30 minutes per year over a 200-year period.

Figure 5 provides a hypothetical example of the reduction in travel time between two cities, A and B. The relationship is shown as a curve rather than a straight line because in reality the improvements in transport that would reduce the travel time to such an extent would have occurred at particular points in time, for example on the opening of a motorway or a new rail link.

The last two centuries have witnessed phenomenal rates of time–space convergence. This has been particularly the case since the 1960s with jet air travel and advanced

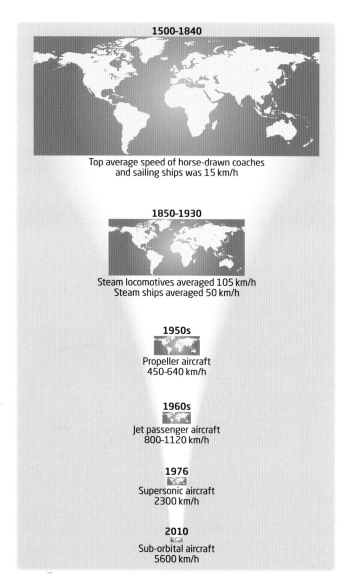

1500–1840

Top average speed of horse-drawn coaches and sailing ships was 15 km/h

1850–1930

Steam locomotives averaged 105 km/h
Steam ships averaged 50 km/h

1950s
Propeller aircraft
450–640 km/h

1960s
Jet passenger aircraft
800–1120 km/h

1976
Supersonic aircraft
2300 km/h

2010
Sub-orbital aircraft
5600 km/h

Figure 3 *Global shrinkage.*

Greyhound bus, USA.

Geographical skill

Study Figure 5. Produce another example of your own to illustrate time-space convergence. Make sure that you include a calculation to show the average time-space convergence.

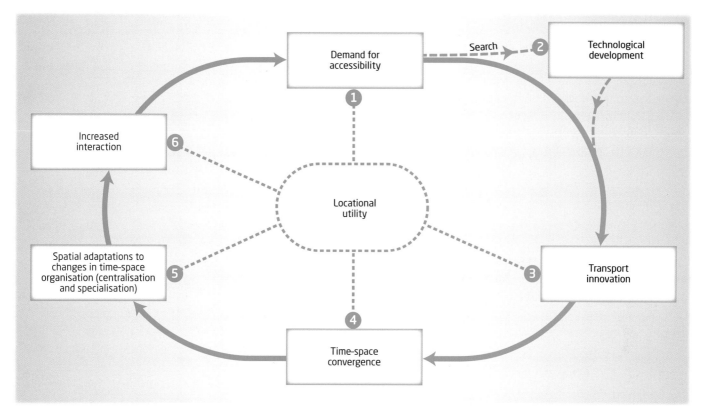

Figure 4 *A process of spatial reorganisation.*

telecommunications. However, the assumptions of continuing time–space convergence may need to be questioned in a future of almost certain high energy costs. It is also relevant to note the restrictions that societies place on time–space convergence, for example speed limits on motorways and air traffic control limitations. High usage of infrastructure can lead to congestion and increasing travel times, or **time–space divergence**, which can have an impact on different activities and social groups.

Time–space convergence is sometimes viewed in terms of cost rather than time. Figure 6 shows the world measured in terms of the cost of a minute-long phone call from the USA in 2000. The map shows considerable spatial differentiation. For example, London and Tokyo are shown as being 'closer' to the USA than Mexico City. This is perhaps not surprising as New York, London and Tokyo are the world's three most important financial centres with a huge volume of communication between them.

About 60% of the world's population now have mobile phone subscriptions, showing that mobile phones are the communications technology of choice. Figure 7 shows how much fixed-line and mobile subscriptions increased between 2002 and 2008. Mobile subscriptions increased from 1 billion to 4.1 billion over this short time period. This information from a UN report noted that the great surge in

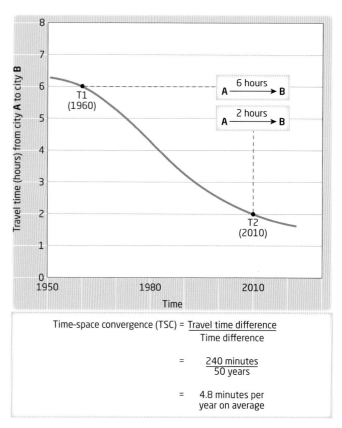

Figure 5 *Time–space convergence.*

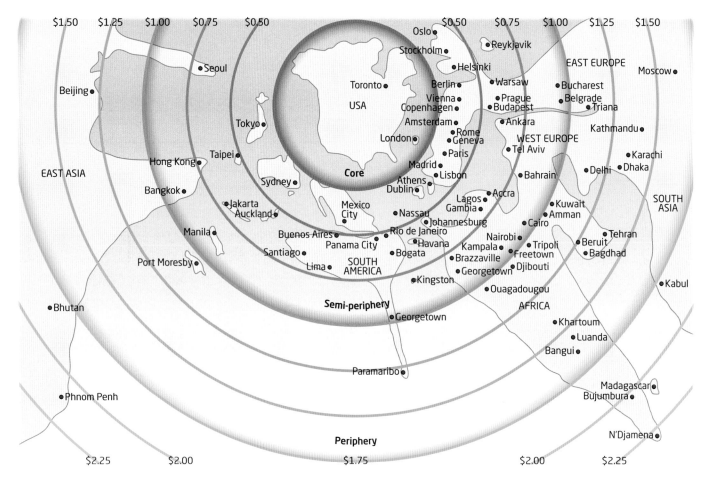

Figure 6 *Time–space convergence and divergence – the cost of a minute-long phone call from the USA, 2000.*

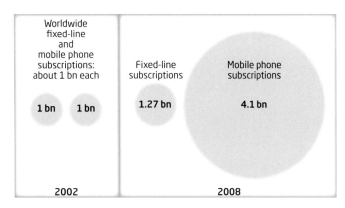

Figure 7 *Worldwide fixed-line and mobile subscriptions, 2002 and 2008.*

the uptake of mobile phones was most marked in developing countries where they are now an invaluable tool among poor people. In 2008, 28% of people in Africa had a mobile phone compared with just 2% in 2000. Developing countries now account for around two-thirds of mobile phones in use compared with less than half in 2002. An important reason is money transfer services which allow people without bank accounts to send money by text message.

Activities

1. What do you understand by the terms (a) 'transport systems' and (b) 'communications systems'?
2. What is diffusion?
3. Explain (a) friction of distance and (b) distance decay.
4. Give two examples of how distance decay might operate in the region in which you live.
5. Define 'accessibility'.
6. Describe the information presented in Figure 3 (page 30).
7. **a** Define 'time–space convergence'.
   b Explain the role of time–space convergence in the process of spatial reorganisation shown in Figure 4 (page 31).
8. Under what circumstances might time–space divergence take place?
9. Look at Figure 6. To what extent is the cost of a minute-long phone call from the USA related to distance from the USA? Suggest reasons for your answer.
10. Explain the two different trends shown in Figure 7.

Changes in the speed and capacity of transport

Transport is one of the world's largest industries. Its elements range from taxis and trucks to aircraft, trains, ships, barges, pipelines, warehouses and logistical services. For example, in its various forms it directly employs about 4.5 million Americans and accounts for more than 10% of America's economic activity. Transport is a major land use. Between its terminals and its routes it has a major impact on the environment.

The cost of transport has two components: fixed (terminal) costs and line-haul costs. Fixed costs are accrued by the equipment used to handle and store goods, and the costs of providing the transport system. Line-haul costs refer to the cost of actually moving the goods and are largely composed of fuel costs and wages. In Figure 8 the costs of the main methods of freight transport are compared. While water and pipeline transport have higher fixed costs than rail and road their line-haul costs are significantly lower. Air transport, which suffers from both high fixed and line-haul costs, is only used for high-value freight or for goods such as flowers which are extremely perishable. Other factors affect the cost of transport too:

- The type of load carried – perishable and breakable commodities which require careful handling are more costly to move than robust goods such as iron ore and coal.

- Journeys that involve transferring cargo from one mode of transport to another are generally more costly than those using the same mode of transport throughout.

- There are varying degrees of competition within and between the competing modes of transport.

Although once a major locational factor, the share of industry's total costs accounted for by transport has fallen steadily over time. For most manufacturing firms in developed countries, transport now accounts for less than 4% of total costs. The main reasons for this reduction are:

- major advances in all modes of transport
- great improvements in the efficiency of transport networks
- technological developments moving industry to the increasing production of higher-value/lower-bulk goods.

Advances in international **logistics** such as multi-modal transport technology, electronic documentation and streamlined customs procedures have greatly expanded the scope for international trade in goods and services. This has resulted in the significant reshaping of **supply chains** in recent decades, a trend that is almost certain to continue.

Broken bridge – maintaining transport links is difficult in many poor countries.

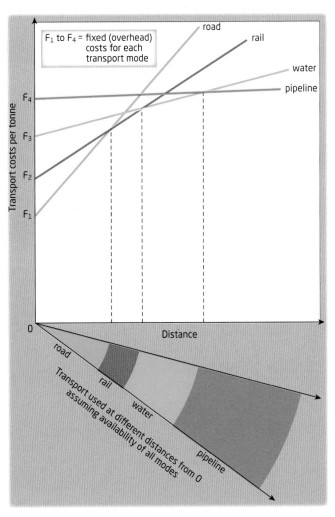

Figure 8 *Transport costs and distance.*

The increase in size of transport carriers has helped meet the growing demand for higher levels of transport capacity in recent years. However, in some cases it seems that limits might already have been reached. For example, the advent of mega lorries has generated considerable controversy and varied responses from different countries. In the USA and much of Europe, lorries travelling on motorways are generally limited to 40 tonnes, meaning that 60 tonne mega lorries are not permitted. However, in Canada and Australia lorries up to 70 tonnes can operate.

In some countries the speed of transport development has been very rapid indeed. For example:

- China had only about 200 km of motorways in 1989. By the beginning of 2008, it had more than 50 000 km of motorways, second in terms of length only to America's Interstate Highway system (75 600 km).

- The Chinese government unveiled a $586 billion economic stimulus package in November 2008 that is largely earmarked for roads, railways and airports. Major projects include a $17.6 billion passenger rail line in north-west China; a $22 billion network of freight rail lines in north-central China; and a $24 billion high-speed passenger railroad from Beijing to Guangzhou.

Figure 9 illustrates the factors influencing the development of a transport system. Historical legacy is an important factor as this often provides the basis for future improvements. For example, in the UK many

Port of Felixstowe is the largest container port in the UK.

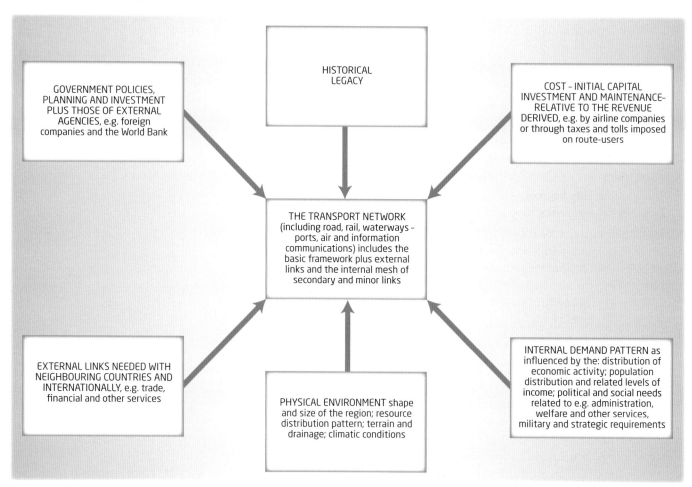

Figure 9 *Factors influencing the development of a transport system.*

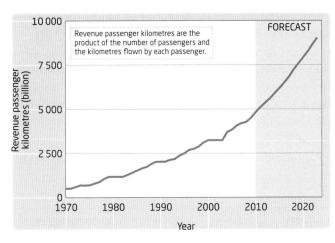

roads follow routes of old Roman roads. As transport technology has advanced, more barriers presented by the physical environment have been overcome, but often at considerable cost. An important factor that has to be borne in mind in relation to transport networks is the cost of maintenance. Even very rich countries sometimes struggle with the high costs involved in maintaining advanced transport networks. This is particularly so in times of economic difficulty.

Discussion point

How many different types of transport have you used in the last month? What were the reasons for using different modes of transport?

Air transport

Air transport, and the advances that have taken place in this mode of travel, has been a major catalyst in the globalisation process. Although commercial air travel is barely 90 years old it has had a phenomenal influence on interactions within and between countries. It has helped to reduce the differences between cultures and had a major impact on shrinking the previously sea-bound world. Figure 10 shows the trend in air passenger transport since 1970 with a projection until 2020. Air transport has been expanding at a faster rate than any other form of transport.

Air China at Beijing airport.

Figure 10 *Revenue passenger kilometres for air transport, 1970–2025.*

In 2007 the aircraft manufacturer Boeing estimated that about 26 000 new passenger and cargo airplanes would be delivered to airlines in the next 20 years. About 25% of these will replace retiring airplanes, while 75% will add to the extension of the global aircraft fleet. The actual expansion of the aircraft fleet during this period will depend very much on economic trends. The global air transport network:

- is a highway for world commerce, particularly in the movement of business people, but increasingly for high-value/low-bulk freight
- is closely interlinked with global economic growth as face-to-face contact is still perceived to be of high importance for many types of business
- has been fundamental to the development of tourism in many parts of the world
- contributes 3% of global GDP
- carried 4.8 billion passengers and 89 million tonnes of freight in 2007
- recorded more than 76 million aircraft movements in 2007
- is a major employer.

While the overall trend in air transport is clearly upward, economic fluctuations can have a distinct impact. This has been very evident with the recent global financial crisis. According to the International Civil Aviation Organisation (ICAO), world airline passenger traffic fell 3.1% in 2009, the biggest drop in aviation industry history. This was a direct consequence of the global financial downturn. Total passenger traffic fell in all regions except the Middle East, which recorded 10% growth. All other regions recorded negative growth, with Africa hardest hit with a fall of 9.6% overall.

The ICAO predicted a moderate recovery of 3.3% growth for the airline industry in 2010, in line with improving economic conditions around the world. For 2011, it forecast a return to the traditional 5.5% yearly growth rate in airline passenger traffic. Forecast air traffic growth is the highest for any mode of transport.

Table 1 shows the 20 largest airports in the world. Hartsfield-Jackson Atlanta International Airport, located 11 km south of the CBD of Atlanta, Georgia, is the world's busiest airport by passenger traffic, serving 90 million passengers a year. It is also the world's busiest airport in terms of landings and take-offs. Atlanta has 151 domestic and 28 international gates and is the main **airline hub** of Delta Air Lines, Air Tran Airways and Atlantic Southeast Airlines. The creation of hub airports has been an important concept in extending the connectivity of air transport. If all of the traffic for London's five airports were added together, then London would be the busiest airport in the world.

The Dubai World Central International Airport is currently under construction. It is due to be fully operational in 2017 and will have a larger capacity than any other currently operating airport in the world. It will have 6 runways, 16 cargo terminals capable of handling 12 million tonnes a year, and will be capable of handling 120 million passengers a year.

Very large aircraft (VLA) are steadily increasing in number. VLA are defined as planes with seating for more than 400 passengers. The Airbus 21st-century flagship A380 is the largest example, with Boeing's 747-8 also placed in this category. A recent forecast by Airbus predicts 1283 VLA globally by 2026.

Business trips once accounted for the majority of air travel. However, today tourism is the major source of demand, accounting for over 70% of air travel globally. Half of international tourists outside Europe travel by air. Nevertheless airlines derive the bulk of their profits from business travel.

Although the proportion of freight carried by air is relatively low compared with other modes of transport, the rate of increase has been very significant. Air transport is very important for key modern industries whose high-cost/low-bulk products can accommodate air freight charges.

Today the cost of air travel is generally perceived to be at its lowest ever. Intense competition between airlines has been driving ticket prices down which, in turn, sustains air traffic growth. The budget airlines such as Ryanair and easyJet have led to a small revolution in air transport. They have had a major impact on ticket prices as the traditional carriers have sought to retain as much of their market share as possible. Where flying was previously unaffordable for some people, lower ticket prices have now made it possible for them to use this mode of transport. Although large new aircraft grab most media attention, it will be smaller aircraft run by low-cost airlines that will dominate the global market over the next few decades.

Ryanair, founded in 1986, has expanded its network rapidly, often having a considerable impact on new airports and regions to which it flies. Figure 11 shows

Airport	Total passengers (millions)	
	2001	**2008**
Hartsfield-Jackson Atlanta International Airport	75.9	90.0
O'Hare International Airport, Chicago	67.4	69.4
London Heathrow	60.7	67.1
Tokyo International	58.7	66.8
Paris Charles de Gaulle	48.0	60.9
Los Angeles International	61.6	59.5
Dallas-Fort Worth International	55.2	57.1
Beijing Capital International	27.2*	55.9
Frankfurt	48.6	53.5
Denver International	36.1	51.2
Madrid-Barajas	34.0	50.8
Hong Kong International	32.5	47.9
JFK International, New York	29.3	47.8
Schiphol Airport, Amsterdam	39.5	47.4
McCarron International, Las Vegas	35.2	43.2
George Bush Intercontinental, Houston	34.8	41.7
Phoenix International, Arizona	35.4	39.9
Suvarnabhumi, Bangkok	30.6	38.6
Singapore Changi Airport	28.1	37.7
Dubai International	N/A	37.4
* 2002 figure		
N/A = not available		

Table 1 *The 20 largest airports in the world, 2008 and 2001.*

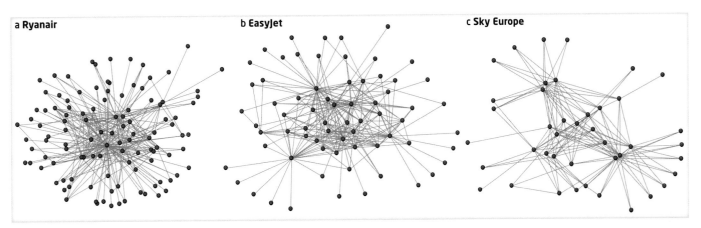

a Ryanair **b EasyJet** **c Sky Europe**

Figure 11 *Airline route networks for three budget airlines.*

Research idea

Look at the website for one of the airlines shown in Figure 11. Find a map showing the destinations of the airline. Find out how the airline has expanded its destinations over time. Does the airline have any plans to expand its network in the future?

route networks for three relatively young budget airlines which all started with a very basic route structure but have matured into more complex networks.

One of the most important changes in air transport has been the gradual **deregulation** of airlines from international and government control. Until the early 1980s fares and standards of service were largely controlled by the International Air Transport Association. Deregulation has resulted in a higher level of competition and lower fares in real terms. This has been followed by government deregulation. For example, in 1993 the European Commission deregulated EU flights leading to more competition on European routes.

However, increases in fuel prices and tax may well push ticket prices up again. Many environmental groups argue that the cost of air travel must rise to an extent that it deters people from flying and to compensate developing countries for the damage it does to the environment. All the political signs are that air travel is too cheap. Over the long term, the biggest concern for the air transport industry is the cost of fuel.

The air transport industry suffers from a poor image. It is a target for environmentalists and those who oppose the process of globalisation. Historically, noise has been the main

concern and this has led to many campaigns against the expansion of existing airports and the building of new ones. Today, emissions from aircraft has become a major issue. For 15% of European airports, environmental issues are limiting factors. On the positive side, manufacturers are producing:

- cleaner aircraft to help reduce emissions
- better navigation systems
- improved use of on-board energy
- optimisation systems for taxiing and descending.

However, the impact of these advances is strongly dependent on the renewal rate of airline fleets.

The expansion of London's Heathrow airport

Heathrow, located 21 km west of central London, is the world's busiest international airport. More than 90 airlines fly to over 170 international destinations from this important hub airport. In 2007 almost 68 million passengers passed through the airport's terminals on 476 000 flights. Heathrow accounts for almost 30% of all UK air passenger traffic. More than 35% of Heathrow's passengers are business travellers. Heathrow is the second busiest airport in the world for cargo. It accounts for 55% of all UK air freight by volume.

Recently a fifth terminal was opened at Heathrow which drew a number of protests, but the really big issue is the proposed third runway which would substantially expand the number of flights using Heathrow.

The main arguments against the further expansion of the airport are:

- the considerable increase in the number of people who will be affected by aircraft noise

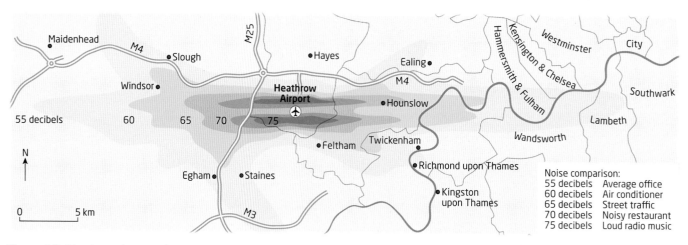

Figure 12 *Heathrow airport and surrounding noise levels.*

- the increased noise levels for many people already affected by aircraft noise
- rising air pollution levels due to an increase in flights
- a significant increase in road traffic generated by the extra flights
- the impact on wildlife.

Figure 12 shows the area currently affected by aircraft noise from Heathrow. This map was originally published by the Department for the Environment, Food and Rural Affairs in late 2007. The area stretches from the southern outskirts of Maidenhead in the west to the edge of Camberwell in the east, and 600 000 people are affected by noise levels of 55 decibels or over. People living close to the airport are affected by noise levels up to 75 decibels. Significant annoyance from aircraft noise begins at 50 decibels.

Campaigners against the expansion of Heathrow argue that plans to increase the number of flights from 420 000 a year to 700 000 will bring far more people within the area affected by aircraft noise. A recent study has highlighted the link between exposure to noise and ill health, noting in particular the relationship between night-time aircraft noise and high blood pressure. The latter can lead to heart attacks and strokes.

However, the economic importance of Heathrow to the local region, to London as a whole and to the national economy cannot be underestimated:

- Heathrow is a huge direct employer with 72 000 working at the airport. It has been estimated that Heathrow supports another 100 000 further jobs in the UK. Nearly half of all those employed at Heathrow live in the five boroughs directly surrounding the airport. Heathrow is the biggest single site employer in the UK.

- A large number of independent firms depend on Heathrow for much of their business. Examples are in-flight catering and security services.
- Many companies say that relatively easy access to Heathrow was an important factor in locating in the surrounding region. Heathrow provides access to virtually every major city in the world. The airport has been described as 'the UK's gateway to the global economy'.
- There is a strong relationship between Heathrow and the financial services industry operating in the City of London.
- Supporters of the airport's expansion argue that if the third runway is not built, Heathrow will lose business to competing airports such as Paris and Amsterdam.

Activities

1. **a** On an outline map of the world, use a graphical technique to illustrate the data in Table 1 (page 36).
   b Describe and explain the spatial distribution shown on your map.
   c Calculate the percentage change in passenger traffic for each airport between 2001 and 2008.
2. Discuss the role of budget airlines such as Ryanair and easyJet in the global expansion of air transport.
3. What are the main factors that will influence trends in air transport in the future?
4. Look at Figure 12. Describe the area currently affected by noise from Heathrow airport.
5. Detail the arguments against a third runway at Heathrow.
6. Outline the arguments for building a third runway at Heathrow.

Ocean transport

Water transport is the cheapest way of moving heavy and bulky goods such as iron ore, coal and grain. The volume and flow patterns of water transport to a significant extent reflect the locations of supply and demand for raw materials, semi-processed products and manufactured goods. Figure 13 shows the world's major shipping lanes. There is a significant concentration in the northern hemisphere focusing on North America, Europe and East Asia. Movement is considerably lower for South America, Africa, South Asia and Australasia.

Bulk cargo is a commodity that is transported unpackaged in large quantities. The size of bulk carriers rose steadily in the 20th and early 21st centuries. In 2009 the largest bulk carrier in the world was the 364 768 tonne iron ore carrier *Berge Stahl* which carries iron ore between Brazil and Rotterdam, where it calls once every five weeks. Rotterdam is the only European port that can accommodate a ship of such size and it takes four or five days to unload it. The busiest bulk cargo port in the world is the Port of South Louisiana near New Orleans.

Italian port – ships and containers.

The container has been the major development in intermodal transportation. It has changed the movement of goods so much that the term 'container revolution' has been used to describe the massive change in freight movement brought about by the use of containers. Containers are boxes made of steel or aluminium into which goods are packed. They are 2.4 metres high, 2.4 metres wide and can be 3, 6, 9 or 12 metres long.

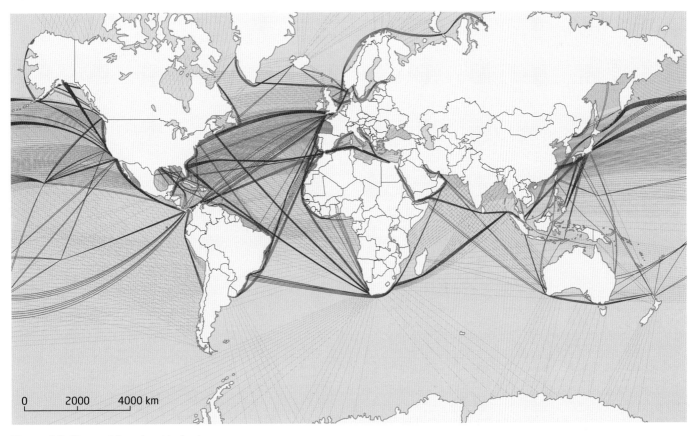

0   2000   4000 km

Figure 13 *The world's major shipping lanes.*

They can be carried on railway flat-cars, lorries, aircraft, barges and ships, and moved quickly from one to another. The general use of standard-sized containers began in the early 1960s and now all major transport terminals have container facilities. Containerisation is tightly linked to roll-on roll-off facilities. Lorries with their loads can be driven onto a ship and then driven off at the other end of the sea journey. The diffusion of container technology around the world has been rapid.

Table 2 shows the twelve busiest container ports in 2008 and also their container traffic in 2002. All ports recorded higher levels of container traffic in 2008 than in 2002, and in most cases the increase has been very substantial indeed. There have been some changes in ranking, with Hong Kong recording most container traffic in 2002 and Singapore in 2008. Nine of the twelve busiest container ports in 2008 were in Asia, illustrating the growing importance of this continent in world trade.

Ultra-large container vessels (ULCV) are making increasing inroads into the container market. In 2009 the first 13 800 TEU vessel was launched (TEU stands for '20-foot equivalent unit', the standard unit for measuring container volume). One forecast is that there may be 200 vessels of this size operating around the world by 2013. Shipbuilders are already planning to scale up to 16 000 and 22 000 TEU. Advocates of these larger vessels argue that they could reduce average transport costs by up to 40%. However, potential disadvantages are that:

- larger ships are more vulnerable to a decline in world trade because they have much higher financial break-even points
- infrastructure limits such as the size of canals and ports may mean that they are unable to function on some important routeways.

Widening of the Panama Canal

The Panama Canal (Figure 14) has long been a crucial link in the global supply chain. However, since the 1970s an increasing number of ships have been too big to pass through it. The largest container ships today can carry more than 12 000 containers, whereas the biggest that can fit in the canal at its current size carry only 4500. Since the mid 1990s it has become obvious that the canal will need to be widened.

The upgrading of the canal to accommodate more and larger vessels will result in a major improvement in global shipping movement. Completion of a third set of ship locks in 2014, at a cost of $5.25 billion, will provide many of the world's largest ships with a crucial intercontinental shortcut. As well as reducing costs for such ships it will result in increased trade opportunities for a number of seaports in the western hemisphere.

Port	Country	Container traffic (thousand TEU*)	
		2002	**2008**
Singapore	Singapore	16 941	29 918
Shanghai	China	8620	27 980
Hong Kong	Hong Kong	19 144	24 248
Shenzhen	China	7614	21 414
Busan	South Korea	9436	13 425
Dubai	United Arab Emirates	4194	11 827
Ningbo	China	1860	11 226
Guangzhou	China	2180	11 001
Rotterdam	Netherlands	6515	10 784
Qingdao	China	3410	10 320
Hamburg	Germany	5374	9737
Kaohsiung	Taiwan	8493	9677
* TEU = 20-foot equivalent units			

Table 2 *The world's busiest container ports.*

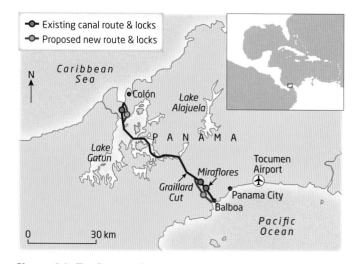

Figure 14 *The Panama Canal.*

Energy pathways

The long-running tensions that exist in the Middle East have at times caused serious concerns about the vulnerability of oilfields, pipelines and oil tanker routes. The destruction of oil wells and pipelines during the Iraq War showed all too clearly how energy supplies can be disrupted. Middle East oil exports are vital for the functioning of the global economy.

Most Middle East oil exports go by tanker through the Strait of Hormuz, one of the world's major **energy pathways**. It is a relatively narrow body of water between the Persian Gulf and the Gulf of Oman. The strait at its narrowest is 55 km wide. Roughly 30% of the world's oil supply passes through the strait, making it one of the world's strategically important **chokepoints**. Iran has at times indicated that it could block this vital shipping route in the event of serious political tension. This could cause huge supply problems for many importing countries. Another potential chokepoint of concern to China and other Asian countries is the Strait of Malacca between Malaysia and the Indonesian island of Sumatra. A huge volume of ocean transport passes through this narrow body of water.

A new age of piracy?

Piracy is something that most of us learn about in school history lessons. However, it seems to have made something of a comeback in recent years, particularly off the coast of Somalia in East Africa. Piracy in this region has been a threat to international shipping since the beginning of the Somali Civil War in the early 1990s. A significant number of international vessels have been captured with ransom money demanded for their release. A number of countries, including China, Japan and the UK, have sent warships to the area to protect commercial shipping.

Impact of the global financial crisis

Firms that operate the container ships that traverse the world's oceans saw a dramatic reduction in business during the global financial crisis. Intense competition and empty ships created a sharp drop in shipping prices. Ports suffered a large decline in arrivals. In March 2009, the number of massive container ships sitting idle globally was estimated at an all-time high of 453 vessels. This was in stark contrast to a few years earlier when demand for shipping was very high.

Activities

1. With reference to Figure 13 (page 39), describe and explain the routes taken by the world's major shipping lanes.
2. Define (a) 'bulk cargo' and (b) 'intermodal transportation'.
3. **a** Describe a container.
   b Why has the widespread development of container transportation become known as the 'container revolution'?
4. On an outline map of the world show the locations of the world's busiest container ports. Use an appropriate graphical technique to illustrate the changes in traffic between 2002 and 2008.
5. Why is the widening of the Panama Canal already being described as one of the most important global infrastructure projects of the 21st century?
6. **a** Why is ocean transport so important to the movement of oil around the world?
   b Using an example, explain the concept of a chokepoint.
7. What was the impact of the global financial crisis of 2008–09 on ocean transport?

Review

Examination-style questions

1 a Explain the concept of the friction of distance.

   b How has a reduction in the friction of distance resulted in time–space convergence?

2 a Why is transportation so important to global interaction?

   b Describe and explain the changes in the speed and capacity of one type of transport.

Websites

www.dft.gov.uk
Department for Transport, UK

www.iata.org
International Air Transport Association

www.unece.org
United Nations Economic Commission for Europe

Key terms

Transport systems the means by which materials, products and people are transferred from place to place.

Communications systems the ways in which information is transmitted from place to place in the form of ideas, instructions and images.

Diffusion the spread of a phenomenon over time and space.

Intermodal transportation transporting freight by using two or more transportation modes. This is made possible by transportation terminals linking different modes of transport.

Friction of distance as the distance from a place increases, the interactions with that place decrease, usually because the time and costs involved increase with distance.

Distance decay the reduction in the amount of movement or spatial interaction between two places the greater the distance they are apart.

Accessibility a measure of the ease with which an individual can reach features in the wider environment.

Time-space convergence this process concerns the changing relationship between time and space, and notably the impacts of transportation improvements on such a relationship. It is closely related to the concept of speed, which indicates how much space can be travelled over a specific amount of time.

Time-space divergence when the journey time between places increases due to congestion, lower speed limits or other limiting factors.

Logistics the management of the flow of goods, information and other resources, including energy and people, between the point of origin and the point of consumption in order to meet the requirements of consumers.

Supply chain the movement of products from a manufacturer to a distributor to a retailer and any points in between.

Airline hub an airport that an airline uses as a transfer point to get passengers to their intended destinations.

Deregulation the lifting of government controls over an industry which usually results in greater competition and lower prices for consumers.

Bulk cargo a commodity that is transported unpackaged in large quantities.

Energy pathways supply routes between energy producers and consumers; they may be pipelines, shipping routes or electricity cables.

Chokepoint a point at which traffic or other movement can easily become blocked.

04 Extension and density of networks

The Internet has a key role in the transmission of images for worldwide business.

The expansion of the Internet

The **Internet** is basically a group of protocols by which computers communicate. It involves innumerable servers and cables. The concept was developed in 1970 at the University of California, Los Angeles. Originally, the Internet was only used by the government and universities. Research scientists used the Internet to communicate with other scientists at different labs and to access powerful computer systems at distant computing facilities. However, its use soon became more widespread. It is the fastest-growing mode of communication ever. It took 38 years for radio to reach 50 million users, 13 years for television to reach this mark, but just 4 years for the Internet.

Internet café in Bangkok, Thailand.

The Internet and its content have grown rapidly. Figure 1 provides information for seven major countries for 2002, 2004, 2006 and 2008. Internet traffic is expanding by about 50% a year, with video and music streaming increasing at the fastest rate. The fastest rates of overall growth have been in emerging economies. In 2002 there were 167 million Internet users in the USA compared with 46 million in China and 7 million in India. By 2008 the number of users in the USA had risen to 220 million while in China it had grown to a phenomenal 253 million users. In India the number of Internet users had risen to 60 million by 2008. China now has 17% of the world's Internet users compared with 15% in the USA. However, per capita usage remains much higher in developed countries: 72.5% of the population in the USA is connected to the Internet compared with 19% in China. In India it is still only 4% and this is highly concentrated in key urban areas.

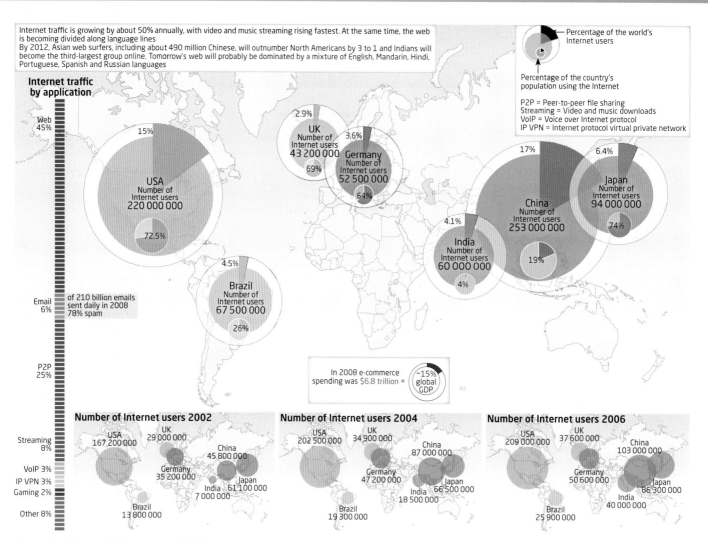

Figure 1 *The exploding Internet, 2008.*

World regions	Population (2009 est.)	Internet users 31 Dec. 2000	Internet users latest data	Penetration (% popn)	Growth 2000–09 (%)	Users % of table
Africa	991 002 342	4 514 400	86 217 900	8.7	1 809.8	4.8
Asia	3 808 070 503	114 304 000	764 435 900	20.1	568.8	42.4
Europe	803 850 858	105 096 093	425 773 571	53.0	305.1	23.6
Middle East	202 687 005	3 284 800	58 309 546	28.8	1 675.1	3.2
North America	340 831 831	108 096 800	259 561 000	76.2	140.1	14.4
Latin America/ Caribbean	586 662 468	18 068 919	186 922 050	31.9	934.5	10.4
Oceania/ Australia	34 700 201	7 620 480	21 110 490	60.8	177.0	1.2
World total	**6 767 805 208**	**360 985 492**	**1 802 330 457**	**26.6**	**399.3**	**100.0**

Table 1 *World Internet usage by region.*

In 2008, global use of the Internet included:

- 1.58 billion users
- 210 billion emails per day
- $6.8 trillion in e-commerce spending, amounting to 15% of global GDP
- online advertising spending of $65 billion.

Table 1 shows world Internet use by region. The highest rates of growth between 2000 and 2009 were in the Middle East and Africa. The **Internet penetration rate** as a percentage of the population is far lower in Africa than in any other world region. In 2009 only 8.7% of the population was connected to the Internet, accounting for only 4.8% of the world total. The lowest rate of growth (140.1%) between 2000 and 2009 was in North America. Perhaps this is not surprising as North America has the highest rate of Internet penetration at 76.2%.

Figure 2 highlights the relative isolation of East Africa, one of the last places on Earth without fibre-optic Internet links. Until recently the region was only linked by satellite connection resulting in very slow and costly linkage. The countries in the region hope that modern Internet connection will provide a considerable stimulus to economic development. It should provide a range of opportunities that simply have not been viable until now. However, the advantages will not just be economic but also social and political. Certain levels of infrastructure are vital if international business is to be attracted to a country or region on a significant scale.

It is not just Internet connection in itself but also the speed of connection that is becoming increasingly important,

Mobile phone advertisement.

Africa

A new telecoms revolution in the offing

June 2009

The Horn of Africa is one of the last populated bits of the planet without a proper connection to the world wide web. Instead of fibre-optic cable, which provides for cheap phone calls and YouTube-friendly surfing, its 200 million or so people have had to rely on satellite links. This has kept international phone calls horribly overpriced and internet access equally extortionate and maddeningly slow.

But last week, in the Kenyan port of Mombasa, a regional communications revolution belatedly got under way when Kenya's president, Mwai Kibaki, plugged in the first of three fibre-optic submarine cables due to make landfall in Kenya in the next few months. They should speed up the connection of Burundi, Rwanda, Tanzania and Uganda, as well as bits of Somalia, Ethiopia and Sudan, to the online world. Laying the cable cost $130 million, mostly at the Kenyan government's expense; Mr Kibaki hailed the event for bringing 'digital citizenship' to his countrymen.

The new cable will compete with the other two to be welcomed onshore, perhaps later this year. The hope is that the high bandwidth and fierce competition between the three cables will slash costs and help create new business. With a mass of young English-speakers only an hour or two ahead of Europe's time zones, East Africa should, with luck, be well placed to compete with India and Sri Lanka for back-office work for Western companies. Broadband, say its promoters, will transform the lives of millions in countries such as Kenya and Sudan, almost as dramatically as mobile telephones have done – all the more so because of the parlous state of East Africa's more old-fashioned infrastructure, especially roads and railways.

A few call centres have already got a toehold in the market and expect to expand fast when the cables arrive. Security experts say cybercrime and junk mail may increase too. Still, mobile telephones, not internet cafés, will continue to grow the fastest. The number and quality of handsets should rise. In a couple of years even fairly poor East Africans may be getting knowledge, news and entertainment on robust versions of existing Apple iPhone and Palm Pre models. That, in turn, may prove to be a political as well as economic boon, as information gets shared 'horizontally' among people rather than 'vertically' via media outlets run by the political and commercial elites.

Figure 2 'East Africa gets broadband', *The Economist, 2009.*

particularly for business use. Figure 3 shows how average advertised broadband speeds vary in OECD countries. In September 2008, Japan, South Korea and France had significantly higher average broadband speeds than other OECD countries. The remaining countries on the graph not only have considerably lower broadband speeds but also have a much smaller range of speeds between them.

A recent report in the USA voiced concern that the country was significantly behind a number of competitor countries in broadband speed and making only slow progress in reducing the gap. The report argued that continued job growth, innovation and regional development require high-speed, universal networks. Data shows that for every $5 billion invested in broadband infrastructure to create these networks, 97 500 new jobs in the telecommunications, computer and IT sectors will be created. A national broadband plan is due to be published in the USA in 2010. It will lay out a policy road map for ensuring that all Americans have access to an affordable high-speed Internet service.

ICT masts on a Chicago skyscraper.

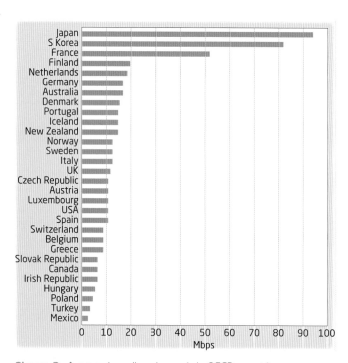

Figure 3 *Average broadband speeds in OECD countries.*

As Internet usage spreads around the world, the web is becoming divided along language lines. Until relatively recently the English language has dominated the web, but this has been changing markedly in the first decade of the new century. By 2012, the number of people in Asia on the

Internet will outnumber North Americans by 3 to 1. In the coming years the Internet will probably be dominated by a mixture of English, Mandarin, Hindi, Portuguese, Spanish and Russian languages. Some experts are concerned that language changes will accelerate national fragmentation of the Internet. In terms of content, several, million web pages are added each day according to Google, which says that its systems had registered a trillion unique pages.

Research idea

Talk to the ICT department in your school to find out the extent to which ICT has developed in the school over the last 15 years.

The Internet has resulted in what can be described as the creation of a new community or communities among users, known as **cyberspace**. This is where people meet in online communities as opposed to having face-to-face contact. Some people put a very high value on this form of social contact, but sceptics see such relationships as shallow and superficial, and no substitute for traditional personal relationships. The main concern of this group is that spending too much time online is taking many people increasingly away from face-to-face contact. Various studies have shown that communication within families can suffer as a result.

The **digital divide** is a term used to refer to inequalities in access to ICT. Such inequality can be seen between:

- developed and developing countries
- urban and rural areas
- ethnic and socio-economic groups in the same country
- different age groups
- males and females.

Figure 4 looks at who the Internet 'have-nots' are most likely to be. Some of these groups are making more progress than others in terms of connection to the Internet. As about 60% of the material on the Internet is in English, a lack of reasonable English may be a hindrance depending on an individual's use of the web. If the non-English speakers concentrate on local and national websites, language should not be a problem. However, if access to international websites is desired, an inability to read English may prove to be a major barrier.

A reasonable disposable income is a big factor in gaining home Internet access, although computers and Internet packages have been steadily falling in cost in real terms. In many countries, access in libraries, Internet cafés and other sources may be available as an alternative to home use. Some of these sources may provide free access, but most will require payment. A low disposable income affects an individual's ability not only to buy a computer and Internet package but also to undertake financial transactions on the web. An inability to undertake the latter may reduce the incentive to become connected in the first place.

Although the proportion of 'silver surfers', or Internet users aged over 60, is rising in most countries, a significant number in this age group are resistant to this form of technology and are disadvantaged in various ways as a result. Many products and services are offered at lower prices online compared with being purchased in a shop, which can put older people on lower incomes at a disadvantage.

In many countries there is an Internet gender divide. In some parts of the UK, for example, males outnumber females in Internet connectivity. Differences between urban and rural areas are also significant, tending to be greatest in the poorest countries. This is in part related to income differentials, but other factors are also relevant. Many of the poorest countries lack a universal electricity supply which is a major factor in lack of connectivity.

A study published in 2009 by the University of Alabama at Birmingham in the USA regarding gender differences among children using mobile phones found that boys had

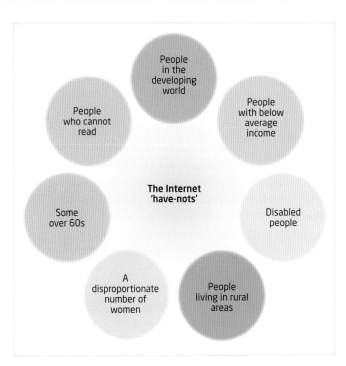

Figure 4 *The Internet 'have-nots'.*

higher usage rates than girls for using their phones to play games, share pictures and videos, listen to music and/or send emails. Girls, on the other hand, used the phone as a phone book or contact list more often than boys did.

All aspects of Internet use are increasing in importance. Digital music sales accounted for more than a quarter of the music industry's global income in 2009, for the first time ever. A total of £2.6 billion was generated from the 27% of worldwide music revenues accounted for by digital downloads. This was a 12% increase on the previous year. In 2009, CDs still made up the remaining 73% of total revenues. Over the five-year period ending in 2009, there had been a 940% rise in revenues from digital sales. The industry's revenues as a whole fell by 30% during the same period. The use of the Internet for music sales is even more age sensitive than general Internet use, with teenagers and young adults dominating this section of the market.

Theory of Knowledge

What are the advantages and disadvantages of the Internet compared with more traditional information sources, such as libraries (for example Wikipedia versus encyclopedias)? Are print materials more reliable than electronic ones?

The Internet and the environment

It is easy to think that the Internet has no obvious impact on the environment. However, one estimate is that it takes 152 billion kilowatt-hours a year to power the data centres that keep the Internet running. The energy used by all computers worldwide and peripherals linked to them must also be considered. With everything taken together, computers and the Internet could be responsible for as much as 2% of all human-made carbon dioxide emissions. At this level it would be on a par with the aviation industry.

Discussion point

Suggest why there is so little debate about the impact of ICT on the environment compared with the environmental consequences of the aviation industry.

Activities

1. **a** What is the Internet?
   b When and where was the concept of the Internet developed?
2. Compare the development of the Internet in the seven countries illustrated in Figure 1 (page 44).
3. Look at Table 1 (page 44).
   a Describe the growth in Internet use by world region between 2000 and 2009.
   b What do you think are the main reasons for such significant differences?
   c Comment on the proportionate use of the Internet by world region.
4. **a** What is the 'digital divide'?
   b Look at Figure 4. Briefly explain why each of the groups shown is part of the Internet 'have-nots'.
   c Comment on the findings of the University of Alabama, Birmingham, relating to mobile phone use among children.
5. **a** Assess the impact of the Internet on the environment.
   b What is being done to try to reduce this impact?

Environmentalists are now beginning to make people more aware of the impact of using their computers. One thousand Internet searches produces the same carbon dioxide emissions as a car driving 1 km. The Climate Group, an international environmental coalition, estimates that total emissions from computers will rise by 280% by 2020. This will be equivalent to 1.4 gigatonnes of carbon dioxide.

However, technical advances are reducing the environmental impact of computers and the Internet. An increasing number of organisations are using **green data centres** which are much more efficient at cooling computers compared with traditional data centres. With green data centres the energy needed to send each megabyte of data across the net is about 30% less per year.

IBM states that it is developing carbon-neutral data centres. These will use a new form of water cooling that uses the heat given off by computer chips to provide warmth for nearby offices and homes.

The role of ICT in civil society

Global civil society has become an important focus of the literature concerning the process of globalisation. Anheier, Glasius and Kaldor identify four interpretations of this term:

- protest groups who act as a counterweight to capitalism – their aim is to 'civilise' globalisation
- the human infrastructure that is needed for the spread of democracy and development
- the efforts of groups like Save the Children and Médecins sans Frontières to provide humanitarian assistance, and other signs of global solidarity with the poor or oppressed
- the growing connectedness of citizens around the world.

The role of civil society in global governance has expanded rapidly in the last two decades. Civil society representatives have played a major role in directing international attention to the importance of a range of global issues. A United Nations publication recognised a number of different types of civil society groupings:

- Mass organisations – formally constituted organisations which represent the interests of particular population groups. The most important of these within the UN system are organisations representing women, children and young people, peasants, the unemployed, indigenous people, the elderly, and disabled people.

- Trades-related organisations – membership organisations representing people through the profession or means of employment they pursue. Many of these organisations are known as trade unions.

- Faith-based organisations – mostly membership-based religious organisations dedicated either to worship or to the advancement of a creed.

- Academic organisations – communities of scholars, researchers, intellectuals and other academics.

- Public benefit NGOs – organisations formed to provide a benefit to the general public or the world at large, either through the provision of specific services or through advocacy. Examples include: organisations involved in environmental, developmental, volunteering, human rights or reproductive rights issues; consumer groups and cooperatives; disarmament organisations; anti-corruption watchdog organisations; and international networks of like-minded NGOs.

- Social movements and campaign networks – mass and loose associations of people who share common experiencees and who elect to work together to redress identified wrongs. Examples include landless peasant movements, the anti-globalisation movement and the feminist movement. There is overlap in this category with mass organisations and public benefit NGOs.

Oxfam – an important civil society organisation.

Developments in ICT have been vital to the expansion of civil society both within and between countries. ICT has allowed cheap, reliable and almost instantaneous communications around most of the world, permitting the sharing of information on an unprecedented scale. Civil society organisations (CSOs) are steadily and successfully applying ICT to the promotion of improved human development. Well-designed websites have made policy documents available online and allowed the formation of virtual communities of like-minded individuals, enabling them to communicate by email and chatrooms.

The ICT revolution means that what was once largely a one-way flow of information from government to people is much more evenly balanced than it ever was before. Some writers have used terms such as 'e-democracy' and 'e-government' to explain the changes brought about by ICT. Others argue that they are overstating the case in terms of the current situation and looking more towards possibilities for the future. Steven Clift has defined e-democracy as 'the use of information and communications technologies and strategies by "democratic sectors" within the political processes of local communities, states/regions, nations and on the global stage'. The democratic sectors identified by Clift are governments, elected officials, media, political parties and interest groups, civil society organisations, international governmental organisations and citizens.

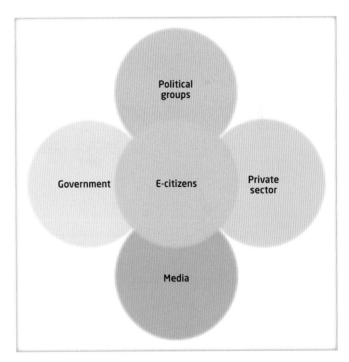

Figure 5 *E-democracy conceptual model.*

Figure 5 is a simplified model illustrating e-democracy activities as a whole. Its main areas and relationships are:

- governments providing information and interacting electronically with citizens

- political groups running online advocacy campaigns and parties increasingly campaigning online
- media and portal search sites which play a significant role in providing news and online navigation
- the private sector, representing commercially driven connectivity, software and technology.

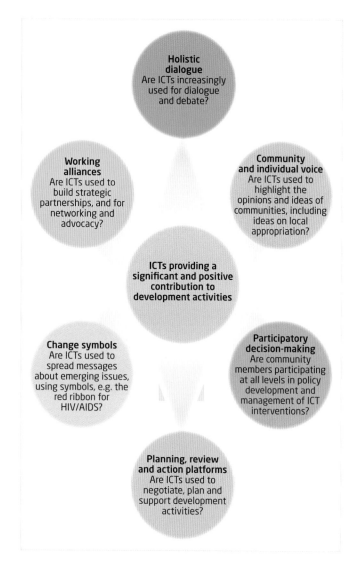

Figure 6 *The contribution of ICT to development activities.*

ICT use in remote communities, such as this veterinary practice in Tanzania, is an important part of local development processes.

Figure 6 shows how advances in ICT have provided a significant contribution to development activities. The diagram poses a series of key questions for both local communities and the organisations that are attempting to help them. The quality of life of communities, particularly those that are relatively isolated, can be much improved when ICT becomes part of the community's livelihood system. Increasingly CSOs are integrating ICT into the fabric of development programmes and projects. As local skills in this sector develop, people are more equipped to find employment and develop small business opportunities. Greater communication within communities themselves and with the outside world is becoming increasingly recognised as an essential part of the development process.

Political participation

The role of the Internet and modern communications in general in the fall of the 'Iron Curtain' which divided Europe into East and West has been well documented. Demolition of the Iron Curtain started in Hungary during the summer of 1989 when, on 11 September, thousands of East Germans began to emigrate to West Germany via Hungary, foreshadowing the fall of the Berlin Wall in November 1989. Prior to the modern communications revolution it was difficult for most people in the former communist countries of the East to:

- organise opposition towards their authoritarian governments
- communicate with people in the outside world
- know what was happening in the outside world.

Modern communications technology has played a significant role in political change in other countries since then.

Some authoritarian governments have worked to restrict the use of ICT by civil society in recent years. The objective has been to suppress democratic movements by placing restrictions on free speech and political involvement. The military government in Burma imposes major restrictions on access. A new wave of obstacles were imposed on Internet usage, and two American journalism teachers were expelled on 6 May 2009. It is getting steadily harder for Burmese people to send emails or access websites, while all means of communication around opposition leader Aung San Suu Kyi's home were cut on 14 May 2009. The military government tries to isolate Burma whenever there is political tension. The government is fearful of the use of the Internet to coordinate dissent within the country itself and of the impact of connections with the outside world. Other countries that place significant restrictions on Internet use by their citizens include China, Iran and Saudi Arabia.

Social networking

Table 2 shows the rapid rise in the popularity of social networking sites. Facebook, with 11.8 million daily visitors in the UK in 2009, recorded an increase of 54% in a year. The micro-blogging site Twitter is expanding much faster, but at present it is on a significantly smaller scale than Facebook. As social networking sites have grown in popularity, they have generated increasing attention from the advertising industry. Facebook is keen on what are termed 'engagement' advertisements which allow the user to choose whether to look at the advert and, if they like it, put it in their personal 'news feed' so that their friends will see it.

Fan clubs are major users of social networking sites. Nike has 1.8 million fans on Facebook and Burberry 800 000. McDonald's recently conducted a poll on whether its burgers were better with the gherkin in or out! As more advertising money is spent on social networking sites, it increases the competition for other forms of media.

However, social networking sites are not without their problems. Identity thieves often scour such sites to acquire security information about individuals that they may be able to target. There can also be wider security implications. In January 2010 Britain's Ministry of Defence admitted 16 instances of sensitive information being leaked on social networking websites in the past 18 months. This was in response to a Freedom of Information request.

Research idea

Find the most up-to-date information on social networking sites. What is the current situation compared with the data presented in Table 2?

	Average UK visitors per day (million)	Average minutes per user per month	Annual % change in average UK monthly visitors	UK ad display impressions per month (billion)	
Facebook	11.86	356.1	+54	Facebook	12.52
Bebo	1.03	113.0	-37	Microsoft	4.95
MySpace	0.40	16.6	-33	Yahoo!	2.63
Twitter	0.38	23.4	+1783	Google	2.19
LinkedIn	0.30	14.8	+269	eBay	2.01

Table 2 *Changes in use of major social networking sites in the UK.*

Response to natural disasters

Media coverage, which increasingly involves the Internet, is a major factor in the scale of response in terms of public donations. In the wake of the Indian Ocean tsunami in December 2004, technology had a major impact on the way in which people pledged their support. A survey for the Charities Aid Foundation in the UK found that 61% of people who gave online did so for the first time, and 41% of those who used a debit or credit card to donate by telephone were also doing so for the first time.

The large increase in Internet use has helped to a certain extent to overcome two significant constraints on the traditional mass media in terms of maintaining public awareness of emergencies. These are:

- space constraints due to the need to cover other stories
- time constraints as high-interest news stories move off the front pages to less prominent positions.

The Internet has helped to maintain awareness over longer time periods, often through the personal accounts of local people and through the steady transmission of moving images. It is now commonplace for websites to be established by organisations involved in emergencies. The Internet allows emergencies to be linked to related campaigns and programmes. Such websites often have particularly relevant use in schools in subjects such as geography, social studies and religious education. In the UK, for example, geography syllabuses often include natural disasters and responses to them.

Civil society, ICT and finance

ICT has transformed the way in which many people manage their personal finances. The following are some of the most important ways in which personal finance has changed for many people, particularly in developed countries, but also increasingly in developing countries:

- An increasing number of people manage their bank account online and often no longer receive paper bank statements. Money can be transferred from one account to another online.
- Money is taken out at cash machines rather than face to face inside a bank itself.
- Bills and taxes can be paid online.

- Many large businesses no longer accept cheques, but require payment by cash or card instead.
- ICT has made trading in shares much more accessible to ordinary people so more people are shareholders today than 20 years ago.
- Money can be transferred by mobile phone. An increasing number of migrant workers send money back to their home country in this way.
- The use of comparison websites means that people can compare quotes from different companies very quickly to try to find the best deal available.
- Online shopping can often offer lower prices than buying in a store. Tuesday 15 December 2009 was the biggest sales day in the history of online retailing, says web measurement firm comScore Inc. On that day global e-retail sales totalled $913 million, making it the first day ever to top the $900 million mark. This was the last day that many online retailers would guarantee free delivery in time for Christmas.

ICT and sedentary lifestyles

A report published in the *British Medical Journal* in January 2010 described how the sedentary lifestyle of the 'computer generation' has led to a rise in cases of rickets among children. Spending too much time on indoor pursuits and not enough time outdoors can result in too little vitamin D, the main source of which is sunlight. A contributory factor is that modern diets often contain less vitamin D than in the past. Insufficient vitamin D is the predominant cause of rickets, a condition in children characterised by retarded growth and bow legs. Rickets is one of a number of health problems being associated with too much time spent on electronic pursuits to the detriment of a more active lifestyle.

Activities

1. What do you understand by the term 'global civil society'?
2. How has ICT helped civil society to organise more effectively?
3. Comment on the data presented in Table 2.

The UK and China: contrasts in the use of ICT

China

Internet use in China expanded rapidly in the first decade of the present century. Table 3 shows that the number of Internet users increased from 22.5 million in 2000 to 384 million in 2009. In 2000 only 1.7% of China's population used the Internet, but by 2009 this had risen to 28.7%, an extremely rapid rate of increase.

In 2009 the proportion of Chinese Internet users aged 10–19 was 33% (Figure 7), the highest of any age group. The next most important age group, 20–29, accounted for 29.8% of users. In contrast, people over 50 years of age only made up 5.7% of total Internet users in China. However, there has been a trend towards maturity in recent years, with the most significant increase in the 30–39 age group. In terms of gender, 55.8% of rural Internet users in 2009 were male while 44.2% were female (Figure 8). The male/female Internet gap is much more pronounced in rural areas than in urban environments. In terms of the three major regions in China – eastern, central and western – recent growth has been fastest in the more remote western provinces which record the lowest absolute rates of connection. Average incomes are highest in the eastern region, lower in the central region, and lower still in the western region.

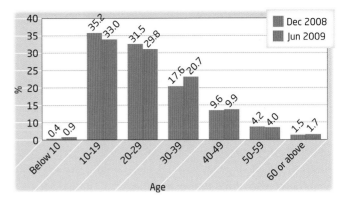

Figure 7 *Comparison of the age structure of Internet users in China, 2009.*

In rural areas with low household Internet penetration rates, Internet cafés play a particularly important role. Rural people who have migrated to urban areas for work have been an important influence on increasing Internet penetration. When they return to their villages on either a temporary or permanent basis they often bring with them computing skills acquired in urban areas. ICT is bringing about important changes in rural China.

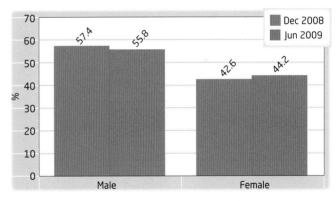

Figure 8 *Comparison in the gender structure of rural Internet users in China, 2009.*

Alongside the data given in Figure 8, China Internent Information Centre's (CNNIC's) *24th Statistical Report on Internet Development in China* also noted the following:

- By June 2009, the number of mobile Internet users had reached 155 million, up 32.1% within six months. This was linked to a certain extent to the particularly fast penetration of mobile phones into rural areas.

- The number of users shopping online rose to 87.9 million, an increase of nearly 14 million within six months.

Year	Users	Population	% penetration
2000	22 500 000	1 288 307 100	1.7
2001	33 700 000	1 288 307 100	2.6
2002	59 100 000	1 288 307 100	4.6
2003	69 000 000	1 288 307 100	5.4
2004	94 000 000	1 288 307 100	7.3
2005	103 000 000	1 289 664 808	7.9
2006	137 000 000	1 317 431 495	10.4
2007	162 000 000	1 317 431 495	12.3
2008	253 000 000	1 330 044 605	19.0
2009	384 000 000	1 338 612 968	28.7

Table 3 *Internet usage in China, 2000–09.*

Has the growth in virtual relationships, through developments such as social networking, produced a qualitative shift in the way people relate to each other in the real world?

The report also noted that recent data shows that the most frequent online practices included listening to music, reading news, and doing searches. While China's Internet users are engaged more in recreational activities, they are shifting to consumption-related practices, including tourism reservations, online stock playing, and e-banking.

Although there is still a significant disparity in Internet use between the urban and rural areas, Internet users in rural areas reached 106.8 million by the end of 2009, an increase of 26.3% from 2008. A government-funded project to sell household electrical appliances in rural areas at lower prices contributed to more Internet coverage in rural areas. The Chinese government is anxious that the quality-of-life gap between urban and rural areas does not get any wider.

In January 2010 Google announced that it was considering pulling out of China due to the government's increasingly high level of censorship. Under these conditions many of Google's services are blocked by the Chinese government. In June 2009 the government publicly criticised Google, claiming that it was helping to spread pornography in China. Google was forced to apologise and to disable a function that lets the search engine suggest terms to search for.

An international group of academics concluded in 2005 that China has 'the most extensive and effective legal and technological systems for Internet censorship and surveillance in the world'. The increase in restrictions recently has brought more condemnation both from within China and internationally. Many of the comments on Chinese message boards support the US government's call for China to lift restrictions on the Internet. The issue has become a source of friction between the two governments, particularly because Google is an American company.

The UK

About 70% of the UK's population is connected to the Internet, compared with China's 29%. In 2009, the UK's Prime Minister, Gordon Brown, stated that a fast Internet connection is now seen by most people as an essential service, alongside water, gas and electricity. What is now concerning politicians, educationalists and other interested parties is the 30% of households still lacking Internet access. Many of this group comprise the most socially and economically vulnerable people in UK society.

A number of reports have highlighted the link between social and digital exclusion. Nineteen out of twenty adults with a degree or equivalent qualification live in a household with Internet access. This falls to just over half (52%) for people with no formal qualification. As more public and private services are delivered online, it can become a significant disadvantage for those without access. As in most countries, there are distinct regional differences. London has the highest level of access at 80%, while Scotland and the North East have the lowest levels of access at 62% and 66% respectively.

The UK government has focused on ICT as an important skill in gaining access to employment. In 2008 Gordon Brown announced plans to set aside £300 million to provide every schoolchild with broadband Internet access at home. Parents would be offered vouchers to buy computers and Internet connection for the 1.4 million children in homes without a computer.

About 3 million homes in the UK in 2009 had broadband speeds of less than two megabits per second (2 Mbps) according to research commissioned by the BBC. The report stated that so-called 'notspots' were not limited to rural communities, with many in suburban areas and even streets in major towns. Slow connections can effectively prevent a number of Internet activities and make working from home, so-called flexible working, impractical.

In 2009 the government published the *Digital Britain Report* which set out a strategic vision to ensure that the UK is at the leading edge of the global digital economy. An important element of the strategy is to digitise certain areas of government services by 2012. By this time the government plans to have 2 Mb high-speed broadband Internet available to the whole of the UK. It is hoped that this will be a significant cost-cutting measure as 80% of government interactions with the public take place with the bottom 25% of society. The government has appointed a Digital Inclusion Champion to help push its plans forward. Part of this role is recognising that it is not just a lack of money and skills that prevents people going online – some people simply choose not to do so. The Digital Inclusion Champion will try to break down the perceived irrelevance of the Internet in these cases.

Telecommunications mast in the UK.

There is increasing concern that:

- many shops and businesses offer their cheapest prices online, making them unavailable to poorer households without Internet access
- an increasing number of businesses will only accept online applications for jobs
- more and more jobs require basic computing skills.

A study published in 2009 revealed that only half of people over 50 have Internet access compared with almost 82% in the 25–49 age group. This leaves 10 million people over 50 on the wrong side of the digital divide. There is a significant drop in Internet user rates among people in their late 50s and another drop among people in their late 60s. This is partly attributable to lower incomes among pensioners, but is also due to a lack of ICT skills and mistrust of the Internet.

Similarities and differences in Internet access in the UK and China

- The level of Internet access is much higher in the UK than in China. However, the rate of growth is much greater in China than in the UK.
- Regional differences in Internet access are more significant in China than in the UK. However, the regional digital divide is narrowing at a faster rate in China.
- Both countries have very significant differences in Internet use by age group.
- Socio-economic status is a very significant factor in Internet access in both countries.
- Both governments have developed policies to improve Internet access, recognising how important this is in an increasingly knowledge-based world.

Theory of Knowledge

The financial cost of accessing the Internet can be considerable. There is no such thing as absolutely 'free' access to information. Should the ability to pay be the only constraint on accessing material via the Internet?

Activities

1. Look at Table 3 (page 53). Describe the increase in Internet usage in China between 2000 and 2009.
2. With reference to Figures 7 and 8, describe and explain how Internet usage varies by age and gender.
3. Discuss the variations in Internet usage in the UK.

Review

Examination-style questions

1 a Describe the differences in Internet penetration rates by global geographic region.

  b Explain the reasons for such differences.

2 a For a country you have studied, describe the age structure of Internet users.

  b What are the reasons for the significant differences in Internet use by age and what is being done to narrow the gap?

Websites

www.cnnic.nett.cn
China Internet Information Centre

www.internetworldstats.com
Internet World Stats: Usage and Population Statistics

www.statistics.gov.uk
UK National Statistics

www.internationalcommunicationsjournal.com
Journal of International Communications

www.fcc.gov
US Federal Communications Commission

Key terms

Internet a global system of interconnected computer networks.

Internet penetration rate the percentage of the population in a country or world region with access to the Internet.

Cyberspace the virtual shared universe of the world's computer networks; it has come to describe the global information space.

Digital divide refers to the gap between people with effective access to digital and information technology and those with very limited access to it, or none at all.

Green data centres data centres that are much more efficient at cooling computers compared with traditional data centres.

Global civil society all movements, associations or individual citizens, independent from the state, whose aim is to transform policies, standards or social structures through communal efforts at a national or international level.

05 Financial flows

KEY QUESTIONS

- How important are loans, debt repayment, development aid, remittances, foreign direct investment and repatriation of profits in the transfer of capital between the developed core areas and the peripheries?
- What is the influence of governments, world trading organisations and financial institutions (such as the World Trade Organisation, International Monetary Fund and World Bank) in the transfer of capital?

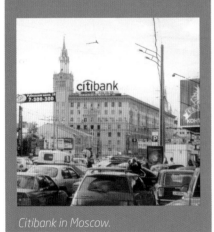

Citibank in Moscow.

International capital flows can be of great benefit to the global economy. Flows of money and **investment** from the developed core areas to the periphery of the world economy allow investors in the capital-rich core to earn higher rates of return than they would do otherwise, and allow workers in the resource-rich periphery access to the fixed and working capital they need to increase their productivity and wages.

Historically, the movement of capital has been from rich to poor nations. However, the situation has been changing significantly over the last two decades with the advent of more globalised markets. The developing world now exports capital to the developed world. In 1997 the balance was even. According to the United Nations, in 2002 there was a net flow to the developed world of $229 billion; this increased to $784 billion in 2006.

A major reason for this is that many countries have felt the need to increase their hard currency reserves. These are important to cover foreign debts or to use in case of emergencies. Since 1990, the world's developing countries have increased their reserves on average from about three months' worth of imports to more than eight months'. They have done this because of the increased uncertainties in a more globalised economy. China and many other countries maintain their reserves to a considerable extent in US Treasury bills (T-bills), which have long been viewed as being totally secure. However, when developing countries buy US Treasury bills they are in effect lending the USA money. This has enabled America to maintain low interest rates and accumulate big deficits. Although T-bills are very secure, the interest earned on them is low. Critics argue that this money could earn higher returns invested elsewhere or it could be used to fund education, health and other desirable projects in developing countries.

The USA owes more money to the rest of the world than any other country. Some other rich countries such as the UK and France also owe substantial

The 'Three Towers', Docklands – an important part of London's financial centre.

amounts. However, these countries have huge assets against which they can borrow, so their debts are thought to be manageable. Debt repayment by rich countries is very different to the immense struggle that poor countries have in trying to pay their debts.

Transnational corporations and foreign direct investment

Major TNCs and FDI flows

Investment involves expenditure on a project in the expectation of financial (or social) returns. Transnational corporations (TNCs) are the main source of foreign direct investment (FDI). TNCs invest to make profits and are the driving force behind economic globalisation. They are capitalist enterprises that organise the production of goods and services in more than one country. As the rules regulating the movement of goods and investment have been relaxed in recent decades, TNCs have extended their global reach. As the growth of FDI has expanded, the sources and destinations of that investment have become more and more diverse. FDI is not dominated by flows from core to periphery in the same way that it was even 20 years ago. Investment flows from newly industrialised countries such as South Korea, Taiwan, China, India and Brazil have increased markedly. The investment flow network is more complex today than it has ever been.

There are now few parts of the world where the direct or indirect influence of TNCs is not important. In some countries and regions their influence on the economy is huge. Apart from their direct ownership of productive activities, many TNCs are involved in a web of collaborative relationships with other companies across the globe. Such relationships have become more and more important as competition has become increasingly global in its extent.

TNCs have a substantial influence on the global economy in general and in the countries in which they choose to locate in particular. They play a major role in world trade in terms of what and where they buy and sell. A not inconsiderable proportion of world trade is intra-firm, taking place within TNCs. The organisation of the car giants exemplifies intra-firm trade, with engines, gearboxes and other key components produced in one country and exported for assembly elsewhere. Table 1 shows the world's largest TNCs by revenue according to *Global 500*

published by Fortune in July 2009. The list is led by Royal Dutch Shell, Exxon Mobil and Wal-Mart Stores. All three companies recorded revenue in excess of $400 billion. Exxon Mobil recorded the largest profit of any company in the world at $45 billion. However, it should be noted that 11 of the top 50 corporations actually made a loss.

Rank	Corporation	Revenues ($ million)	Profits ($ million)
1	Royal Dutch Shell	458361	26277
2	Exxon Mobil	442851	45220
3	Wal-Mart Stores	405607	13400
4	BP	367053	21157
5	Chevron	263159	23931
6	Total	234674	15500
7	ConocoPhillips	230764	−16998
8	ING Group	226577	−1067
9	Sinopec	207814	1961
10	Toyota Motor	204352	−4349
11	Japan Post Holdings	198700	4208
12	General Electric	183207	17410
13	China National Petroleum	181123	10271
14	Volkswagen	166579	6957
15	State Grid	164136	664
16	Dexia Group	161269	−4868
17	ENI	159348	12917
18	General Motors	148979	−30860
19	Ford Motor	146277	−14672
20	Allianz	142395	−3577
21	HSBC Holdings	142049	5728
22	Gazprom	141455	29864
23	Daimler	140328	1973
24	BNP Paribas	136096	4422

Table 1 *The world's 50 largest TNCs, 2009.*

25	Carrefour	129 134	1 862
26	E.ON	127 278	1 853
27	PDVSA	126 364	7 451
28	ArcelorMittal	124 936	9 399
29	AT&T	124 028	12 867
30	Siemens	123 595	8 595
31	Pemex	119 235	−10 056
32	Hewlett-Packard	118 364	8 329
33	Valero Energy	118 298	−1 131
34	Petrobras	118 257	18 879
35	Banco Santander	117 803	12 992
36	Statoil Hydro	116 211	7 664
37	Bank of America Corp.	113 106	4 008
38	Royal Bank of Scotland	113 087	−43 167
39	Citigroup	112 372	−27 684
40	Samsung Electronics	110 350	5 027
41	Berkshire Hathaway	107 786	4 994
42	McKesson	106 632	823
43	Société Générale	104 378	2 942
44	Nippon Telegraph & Telephone	103 684	5 362
45	International Business Machines	103 630	12 334
46	Crédit Agricole	103 582	1 499
47	Assicurazioni Generali	103 103	1 260
48	Nestlé	101 565	16 670
49	J.P. Morgan Chase & Co.	101 491	5 605
50	Metro	101 217	590

Table 1 (continued) *The world's 50 largest TNCs, 2009.*

General Motors world headquarters, Detroit, Michigan.

Research idea

Find out the countries of origin of the 50 largest global corporations shown in Table 1.

According to the World Investment Report 2009, there are 82 000 TNCs worldwide, with 810 000 foreign affiliates. The 100 largest TNCs represent a significant proportion of total global production. Over the three years from 2006 to 2008, they accounted for, on average, 9%, 16% and 11% respectively of estimated foreign assets, sales and employment of all TNCs. Their combined value-added accounted for about 4% of global GDP.

Global FDI inflows reached a historic high of $1979 billion in 2007 (Figure 1), although this declined by 14% in 2008 with the onset of the global financial crisis. The crisis has changed the geography of investment, with the share of developing and 'transition economies' in global FDI flows rising sharply to 43% in 2008. The transition economies are those in south-east Europe and the Commonwealth of Independent States (CIS). They have been given the term 'transition economies' by the World Investment Report to recognise that they are still in the process of change from centrally planned communist economies to full members of the capitalist global economy. In 2008, FDI inflows into developing and transitional economies reached record levels, accounting for 37% and 7% respectively of global FDI.

In 2008 FDI flows to structurally weak economies including least developed countries, landlocked developing countries and small island developing states increased by 29%, 54% and 32% respectively. This has been a very welcome trend, but there are concerns that the global financial crisis will wipe out the benefits gained from this trend.

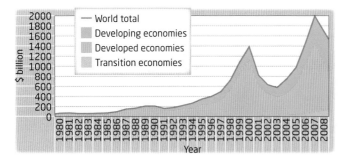

Figure 1 *FDI inflows, global and by groups of economies, 1980–2008.*

Figure 2 shows the shares of the three major groups of economies in global FDI inflows for the period 1990–2008. The developed countries recorded the highest share for the entire period but the gap has been narrowing. Three distinct periods of convergence can be recognised in Figure 2. In 1990, the developed economies accounted for over 80% of global FDI inflows. By 2008 this had fallen below 60%. The developing economies accounted for only about 16% of global FDI inflows in 1990, but have got up to or close to 40% during the three periods of convergence. The share of the transition economies was extremely low until the new millennium, but it is now rising at a significant rate.

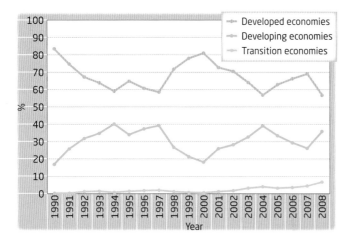

Figure 2 *Shares of the three major groups of economies in global FDI inflows, 1990–2008.*

Figure 4 shows the top 20 countries in the world for both FDI inflows and outflows in 2007 and 2008. In 2008 the leading FDI inflow nations were the USA, France, China, the UK and Russia. The leading outflow countries were the USA, France, Germany, Japan and the UK. In terms of FDI inflow, 10 of the top 20 countries could be viewed as not being part of the traditional global core. For FDI outflow, only 4 out of 20 would be in this category.

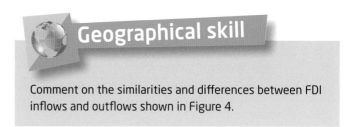

Comment on the similarities and differences between FDI inflows and outflows shown in Figure 4.

Figure 3 illustrates net capital flows to developing countries between 2000 and 2009. The impact of the recent global financial crisis is clear to see. Foreign direct investment has been the most important source of net capital flows throughout this time period, while the other three sources of capital have changes in rank at certain times. The latest data shows that **official development assistance (ODA)** is currently the second most important source of capital flowing into developing countries.

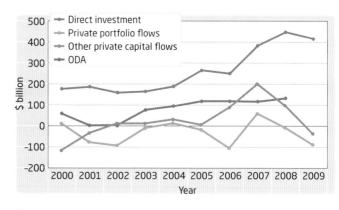

Figure 3 *Net capital flows to developing countries, 2000–09.*

Capital flow can help developing countries with economic development by furnishing them with necessary capital and technology. However, capital flow from developed countries to developing countries has been skewed, with some countries far more favoured than others. Most Sub-Saharan African countries, which have urgently needed foreign capital for economic betterment, have been

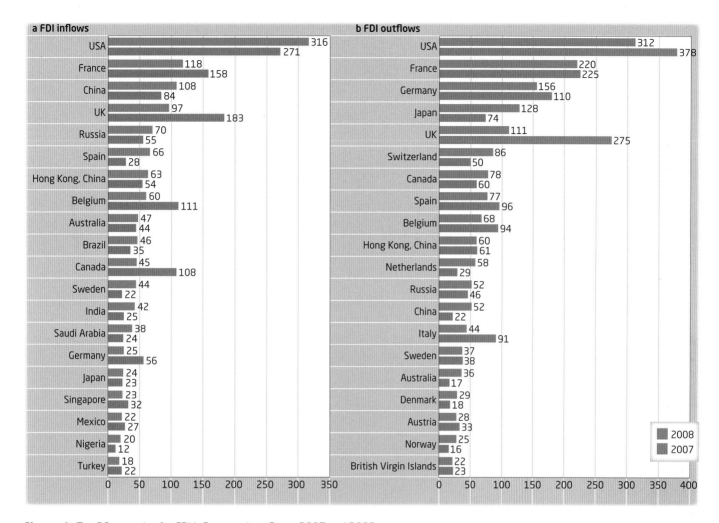

a FDI inflows

Country	2008	2007
USA	316	271
France	118	158
China	108	84
UK	97	183
Russia	70	55
Spain	66	28
Hong Kong, China	63	54
Belgium	60	111
Australia	47	44
Brazil	46	35
Canada	45	108
Sweden	44	22
India	42	25
Saudi Arabia	38	24
Germany	25	56
Japan	24	23
Singapore	23	32
Mexico	22	27
Nigeria	20	12
Turkey	18	22

b FDI outflows

Country	2008	2007
USA	312	378
France	220	225
Germany	156	110
Japan	128	74
UK	111	275
Switzerland	86	50
Canada	78	60
Spain	77	96
Belgium	68	94
Hong Kong, China	60	61
Netherlands	58	29
Russia	52	46
China	52	22
Italy	44	91
Sweden	37	38
Australia	36	17
Denmark	29	18
Austria	28	33
Norway	25	16
British Virgin Islands	22	23

Figure 4 *Top 20 countries for FDI inflows and outflows, 2007 and 2008.*

largely excluded from globalised investment in the past although there is evidence that this is beginning to change. While controlling for other social and economic factors, democratised developing countries appear to attract more foreign capital than undemocratic countries because their democratic institutions can provide a secure and profitable environment for investment with protection of property rights and social spending on human capital.

Discussion point

Is there any evidence of FDI in the region in which you live? If the answer is yes, what form does this take? If the answer is no, why do you think FDI is lacking?

New York stock exchange.

Repatriation of profits

Profit repatriation can be defined as 'returning foreign-earned profits or financial assets back to the company's home country'. For example, when the Volkswagen Group earns profits anywhere in the world, it takes a share back home to Germany, after converting it into euros; this 'taking profits back home' process is called profit repatriation.

Clearly, host countries in receipt of FDI will want to keep as much of the profits made by foreign TNCs reinvested in the local economy as possible. However, they will be aware that TNCs will want to repatriate a certain proportion of profits to justify the original reasons for the investment. In addition, a host country can tax profits, but will still want to remain an attractive location for investment. Thus a situation where there is a good balance of benefits for both the host country and the investing company is the most desirable. However, many host countries complain that large TNCs are so powerful that the balance of benefits is invariably distorted in their favour.

The repatriation of profits represents an outflow of a host country's limited foreign exchange resources and has a negative impact on the country's balance of payments. The poorest developing countries are usually the worst affected because they will often offer very favourable tax exemptions and financial incentives to attract foreign investment.

Not all FDI is beneficial

Any serious analysis of FDI has to look at its targets. It is the quality of FDI rather than the quantity that brings net benefits to the receiving country. To bring such benefits FDI needs to be channelled into productive rather than speculative activities. The power of governments to influence the quality of investment has been steadily declining. It is a fact that a significant proportion of FDI is made up of companies:

- buying out state firms
- purchasing equity in local companies
- financing mergers or acquisitions.

Over the last decade or so a relatively new phenomenon has gathered pace – alliances of capital. This involves a great variety of negotiated arrangements: cross-licensing of technology among corporations from different countries, joint ventures, secondary sourcing, offshore production of components, and cross-cutting equity ownership. All these actions can result in substantial benefits for the companies concerned but may be of little benefit to the regions and countries where the investment occurs.

Financial speculation

Prior to the relatively recent deregulation of global financial markets, the activities of banks, insurance companies and investment dealers had been confined largely within national boundaries. With the removal of regulations the financial sector scanned the globe for the best returns. In this new relaxed atmosphere, finance capital became a destabilising influence on the global economy, with an increasing level of speculation as opposed to 'firm' investment. Nervous short-term investors who withdraw capital at the first hint of a problem can cause a vicious downward spiral to a country's economy which can be very difficult for a government to counter. Figure 5 illustrates what happened in East Asia in the mid to late 1990s. This crisis was a major blow to the promise of economic globalisation. The East Asian crisis added to the other perceived problems of globalisation, and led to the mass public protests in Seattle (1999) and Prague (2000). Critics of globalisation often use the term 'global casino' to refer to the rapid movement of speculative money around the world.

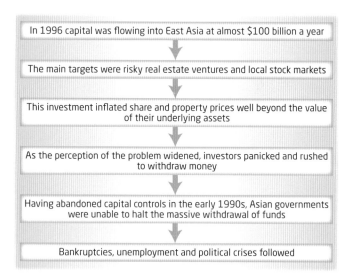

Figure 5 *The East Asian financial crisis.*

Loans and debt repayment

Experts from a variety of different disciplines blame the rules of the global economic system for excluding many countries from its potential benefits. Many single out **debt** as the major problem for the world's poorer nations. Many poor countries are currently paying back large amounts in debt

Activities

1. Look at Table 1 (pages 58 and 59). List the ten largest corporations in terms of profit.
2. Describe the trends shown in Figure 1 (page 60).
3. Analyse the changes illustrated in Figure 2 (page 60).
4. Describe and suggest reasons for the changes shown in Figure 4 (page 61).
5. **a** What is meant by the term 'profit repatriation'?
   b Why is this sometimes a controversial issue?
6. What are the dangers of financial speculation to the global economy?

repayments to banks, lending agencies and governments in developed countries while at the same time struggling to provide basic services for their populations. An ever increasing proportion of new debt is used to service interest payments on old debts. While supporters of globalisation argue that economic growth through trade is the only answer, critics say that developed countries should do more to help the poor countries through debt relief and by opening their markets to exports from developing countries.

The total external debt of the poorest countries of the world (the 'low-income countries') was $375 billion in 2006. During 2006 these countries paid over $34 billion to the developed world to service their debts. These payments averaged $94 million a day. When a country has to use a high proportion of its income to service debt, this takes money away from what could have been spent on education, health, housing, transport and other social and economic priorities.

Loans can help countries to expand their economic activities and set up an upward spiral of development if used wisely. However, many of the loans that burden the world's poorest countries were given under dubious circumstances. Critics argue that banks frequently lent irresponsibly to governments known to be corrupt. Often such loans led to little tangible improvement in the quality of life for the majority of the population, but instead saddled them with long-term debt. If such countries had been companies they would have been declared bankrupt. However, international law offers no 'fresh start' to countries in such a situation.

In recent years much of the debt has been 'rescheduled' and new loans have been issued. However, new loans have frequently been granted only when poor countries agreed to very strict conditions under 'structural adjustment programmes' which have included:

- agreeing to **free trade** measures which have opened up their markets to intense foreign competition
- severe cuts in spending on public services such as education and health
- the privatisation of public companies.

Figure 6 shows international lending to developing countries by region from 2000 to 2007. In 2000 and 2001, the highest lending went to Latin America and the Caribbean. Thereafter Europe and Central Asia became the focus of lending, with Latin America and the Caribbean in second place. Despite the disadvantages that many countries have suffered over the medium and long term from improper lending, it is a vital component of the global economic system.

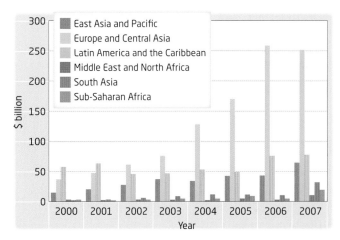

Figure 6 *Gross cross-border bank lending to developing countries, by region 2000–07.*

Figure 7 is a Christian Aid newspaper advertisement illustrating the plight of Haiti, one of the world's poorest countries, after the devastating earthquake of January 2010. Other organisations such as Oxfam, CAFOD and Islamic Relief have mounted similar campaigns to cancel debt.

The Heavily Indebted Poor Countries (HIPC) initiative

The HIPC initiative was first established in 1996 by the IMF and the World Bank. Its aim is to provide a comprehensive approach to debt reduction for heavily indebted poor countries. To qualify for assistance countries have to pursue IMF and World Bank supported adjustment and reform programmes. By early 2008, debt reduction packages had been approved for 33 countries, 27 of them in Africa. Eight additional countries are eligible for HIPC initiative assistance.

THE ONLY THING STILL STANDING IS THE DEBT.

The suffering in Haiti is extraordinary. Tens of thousands dead. Many more injured and homeless. The British public have donated over £38m to the DEC to get emergency aid to the people suffering on the ground. It's been a fantastic response.

But when the emergency response teams have done their work, the Haitians will still face an uphill battle. Haiti has debts of over $800m. No wonder 80% of the population lives in poverty. As part of our ongoing fight against systems that keep people poor, Christian Aid is lobbying Chancellor Alistair Darling (the UK's representative at the IMF) to lead the world in making sure that all of Haiti's debt is cancelled. You can help us.

Sign the petition online to drop the debt. Visit www.christianaid.org.uk

POVERTY   christian aid

Figure 7 *Christian Aid Haiti campaign, 2010.*

Research idea

Look at the Jubilee Debt Campaign website (www. jubileedebtcampaign.org.uk) to see what the charities involved want governments to do with regard to the debt of poor countries.

Development aid

Aid is assistance in the form or grants or loans at below market rates. In 2008, total net ODA from members of the Development Assistance Committee (DAC) of the Organisation for Economic Cooperation and Development

(OECD) rose by 10.2% in real terms to $119.8 billion (Figure 8). This is the highest figure ever recorded. Bilateral development projects and programmes have been on a rising trend in recent years; they rose significantly by 12.5% in real terms in 2008 compared with 2007, indicating that donor countries are substantially scaling up their core aid programmes.

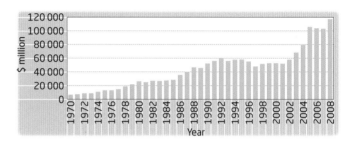

Figure 8 *OECD Development Assistance Committee aid, 1970–2008.*

At the UN General Assembly in 1970 the rich donor governments promised to spend 0.7% of Gross National Income (GNI) on international aid. The deadline for reaching the target was the mid 1970s. However, the reality has been that almost all donor countries have consistently failed to reach this target. International aid is more of a priority in some countries than others. The largest donors in 2008, by volume, were the USA, Germany, the UK, France and Japan. However, only five countries exceeded the UN target of 0.7% of GNI: Denmark, Luxembourg, the Netherlands, Norway and Sweden.

Figure 9 shows that most ODA goes to Africa and Asia. In Europe and Oceania it is the poorest countries that are in receipt of aid. Table 2 shows the top ten recipients of ODA in 2006. Nigeria and Iraq were by far the largest beneficiaries of ODA.

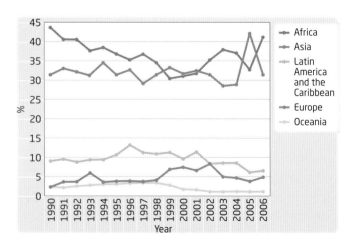

Figure 9 *Regional share of total ODA, 1990–2006.*

Country	$ (million)	%
1 Nigeria	11 434	11
2 Iraq	8 661	8
3 Afghanistan	3 000	3
4 Pakistan	2 147	2
5 Sudan	2 058	2
6 Congo, Dem. Rep.	2 056	2
7 Ethiopia	1 947	2
8 Vietnam	1 846	2
9 Tanzania	1 825	2
10 Cameroon	1 684	2
Other recipients	68 633	65
Total	**105 292**	**100**

Table 2 *Top ten recipients of ODA, 2006.*

Figure 10 shows the different types of international aid. The basic division is between official government aid and voluntary aid:

- Official government aid is where the amount of aid given and who it is given to is decided by the government of an individual country. The Department for International Development (DFID) runs the UK's international aid programme.

- Voluntary aid is run by non-governmental organisations (NGOs) or charities such as Oxfam, ActionAid and CAFOD. NGOs collect money from individuals and organisations. However, an increasing amount of government money goes to NGOs because they have the expertise to run aid efficiently.

Official government aid can be divided into (a) bilateral aid which is given directly from one country to another and (b) multilateral aid which is provided by many countries and organised by an international body such as the United Nations. Aid supplied to poorer countries is of two types. Short-term emergency aid is provided to help cope with unexpected disasters such as earthquakes, volcanic eruptions and tropical cyclones. Long-term development aid is directed towards the continuous improvement in the quality of life in a poorer country.

Critics of international aid argue that:

- too often aid fails to reach the very poorest people and when it does the benefits are frequently short-lived

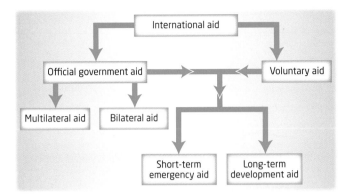

Figure 10 *The different types of international aid.*

- a significant proportion of foreign aid is 'tied' to the purchase of goods and services from the donor country and often given for use only on jointly agreed projects

- the use of aid on large capital-intensive projects may actually worsen the conditions of the poorest people

- aid may delay the introduction of reforms, for example the substitution of food aid for land reform

- international aid can create a culture of dependency.

Remittances

Remittances sent back to their home nation by migrants represent the largest source of external capital in many developing countries. The World Bank estimated worldwide remittances at $251 billion in 2007 (Figure 11). This represents more than twice the level of international aid. If remittances through informal channels are taken

Aid project, Port-au-Prince, Haiti, 2010.

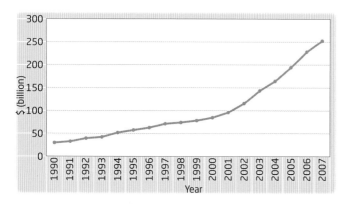

Figure 11 *Remittances to developing countries, 1990–2007.*

Activities

1 What is debt?
2 Why are loans important for developing countries?
3 Suggest reasons why a significant number of developing countries have had difficulties repaying loans they have taken out in the past.
4 What is the HIPC initiative?
5 Describe the data shown in Figure 6 (page 63).
6 Look at Figure 7 (page 64). Suggest why progress has been so limited on cancelling the debt of poor countries.
7 a Define 'official development assistance'.
   b Comment on the changes shown in Figure 8 (page 64).
8 With reference to Figure 9, describe the changes to regional shares of total net ODA.
9 Use Figure 10 (page 65) to describe the different types of international aid.
10 a What are remittances?
   b Describe the distribution of remittance flow to developing countries shown in Table 3.

into account, the figure may be up to 50% higher (World Bank, 2006). Remittances are much less concentrated in certain countries than foreign direct investment, which tends to focus on particular countries. The global financial crisis has seen a distinct fall in remittances which is having a very noticeable impact in some countries.

One-third of global remittances originate in the USA. Most of the rest is sent from Europe and the Middle East. An increasingly significant volume of remittance money also circulates within the developing world. Latin America and the Caribbean is the region receiving the highest level of remittances per capita. The money sent to the region has risen tenfold in real terms over the past 20 years. In Latin America and the Caribbean, remittances totalled over $66.5 billion in 2007. This represents more than the sum of foreign direct investment and official development aid combined. In seven Latin American and Caribbean countries remittances account for more than 10% of GDP.

Table 3 shows remittances to developing countries by region. In Zimbabwe the government tried to persuade its citizens working abroad to channel their remittances through formal transfer agencies, in a bid to boost foreign exchange reserves. For the majority of Somalis, money sent back by relatives and friends working abroad has been the single most important source of income since the country's economy collapsed in the 1990s.

Research projects have shown that higher remittance flows are associated with lower poverty, better health and higher levels of education in the developing world. However, there is a downside to remittance flows. Households and national economies that rely on remittances become vulnerable to distant events and trends. Also, many countries dependent on remittances see their working-age adult population shrink. Family members left behind may stop working and develop a culture of dependency.

The influence of governments and major international institutions

Governments

Along with TNCs, national governments are the major players in the global economy. National governments exert their influence through national policies and membership of major international organisations. They influence the transfer of capital to developing countries in a number of ways, which include the following:

- Tariffs, quotas and regulations with regard to imports from developing countries. Most development economists argue that trade is more important than aid and that developed countries should do more to open their markets to exports from poorer nations. The fact that Sub-Saharan Africa is the poorest region of the world is strongly linked to its very small share of world trade. Money gained from selling goods and services to richer countries brings in valuable foreign exchange.

- The level of ODA. Only a handful of countries give the 0.7% of GDP to ODA which was the objective set

$ billion	2002	2003	2004	2005	2006	2007	2008e*
Developing countries	**116**	**144**	**164**	**195**	**229**	**281**	**305**
East Asia and Pacific	30	35	39	47	53	65	70
Europe and Central Asia	14	16	22	31	38	50	53
Latin America and Caribbean	28	37	43	50	59	63	63
Middle East and North Africa	15	20	23	24	26	31	34
South Asia	24	30	29	33	40	52	66
Sub-Saharan Africa	5	6	8	9	13	19	20
Growth rate (%) Developing countries	21	25	14	18	17	23	9
East Asia and Pacific	47	20	10	19	13	23	7
Europe and Central Asia	11	13	43	41	23	31	5
Latin America and Caribbean	15	31	18	16	18	7	0
Middle East and North Africa	4	34	13	5	6	22	8
South Asia	26	26	−6	15	20	31	27
Sub-Saharan Africa	8	19	34	17	37	44	6
World ($ billion)	**170**	**207**	**235**	**268**	**307**	**371**	**397**

* e = estimate

* Including the revision to Nigeria data in 2007. Excluding that, remittance flows to Sub-Saharan Africa would have experienced a more modest growth rate of 14.4%, and to developing countries 22%, in 2007.

Authors' calculation based on data from IMF *Balance of Payments Statistics Yearbook 2008* and data releases from central banks, national statistical agencies and World Bank country desks. Remittances are defined as the sum of workers' remittances, compensation of employees, and migrant transfers. See www.worldbank.org/prospects/migrationandremittances for data definitions and the entire dataset.

Table 3 *Remittances to developing countries by region.*

for the world's richer nations at the UN in 1970. Well-targeted assistance can help countries help themselves in the long term.

- Taxation and regulations affecting the work of non-governmental agencies abroad. For example, in the UK the Gift Aid scheme means that money given to charities is exempt from taxation. This has led to an increase in money available to charities in the UK. Some of this is spent in the UK, but a significant amount goes to projects in developing countries. Charities that have benefited from the Gift Aid scheme include WaterAid, Oxfam and CAFOD.
- The number of foreign workers allowed into a country. This is the main factor affecting the flow of remittances. Developing countries argue that more labour migration

should be allowed between the developing and developed worlds.

- Taxation and regulations affecting investment abroad by companies and individuals. This can vary significantly from country to country.
- Advocacy in multinational institutions. Some countries such as the UK have been major advocates for the cancellation of the debts of the world's poorest countries. The major economies in particular have a big influence on the World Trade Organisation, the World Bank and the International Monetary Fund.

Some books and articles on globalisation and linked topics give the impression that the days of the nation-state are limited. Although considerable changes have occurred with the formation of trade blocs and more

Headquarters of the International Monetary Fund, Washington DC.

powerful international institutions than previously existed, nation-states, particularly the more powerful ones, retain considerable muscle. Look at Figure 13 to see one viewpoint on this!

The International Monetary Fund and the World Bank

The International Monetary Fund (IMF) and the World Bank were brought into being at a conference designed to plan a new economic structure for the post-war period, held at Bretton Woods, New Hampshire, USA, in 1944. The role of the World Bank was to assist in the funding of reconstruction in the countries decimated by war, while the IMF would ensure that the process would take place in a stable economic climate. A country running short of foreign currency reserves that it needed to maintain its currency exchange rate could turn to the IMF for help. IMF funds come from the contributions or 'quotas' of its member countries. Voting power on the IMF is in proportion to the size of a country's quota, with the USA holding 17% of the total votes. As any major change to IMF policy requires 85% backing, the USA is able to block by itself any proposed change it might not like.

Countries usually apply for funding from the IMF when they are unable to obtain it from other sources. IMF money is designed to prevent the disruption to the international financial system that would occur through a country failing to meet its commitments to other nations. Along with funding, the IMF is also able to renegotiate the terms of debt on behalf of nations in financial difficulties. To prevent the situation reoccurring the IMF will usually impose conditions, in the form of a 'stabilisation programme', on its financial assistance. The objective is 'structural adjustment', changing the fundamental conditions of the economy to make it more competitive and less likely to return to a position of crisis. It is the nature of these conditions that has caused so much controversy about the way in which the IMF operates.

The International Bank for Reconstruction and Development, commonly known as the World Bank, borrows between $20 billion and $30 billion a year in a variety of currencies. This money has provided financing for more than 4000 development projects in 130 countries, through $300 billion in lending. When the reconstruction of Europe was complete the World Bank increasingly turned its attention to developing countries.

While the IMF focuses primarily on the international financial transactions of a country, the World Bank deals mainly with internal investment projects. For most recipient countries lending is at market rates of interest. However, in 1960 a branch of the World Bank known as the International Development Association (IDA) was formed. The IDA lends only to nations with a very low per capita income. For such countries, loans are interest free and allow long repayment periods.

The World Bank has many critics. The US-based Heritage Foundation examined economic growth rates in the 85 countries that received IDA loans in the 1980s and 1990s and found that:

- rather than helping the recipient countries, the loans pushed many into further debt, with new loans often being used to pay off old ones – the classic vicious circle
- recipient countries were more likely to experience a drop in per capita wealth than to achieve significant economic growth.

In spite of adverse publicity such as this, the World Bank is highly sought after by global investors who buy bonds and in doing so provide the funds that the Bank distributes to development projects. However, the World Bank Bonds Boycott campaign is trying to deter investors from continuing their support of the World Bank, arguing that the conditions attached to World Bank loans have:

- crippled economic growth in recipient countries
- hindered development
- promoted dependency and
- increased poverty.

Critics argue that the rich nations use the World Bank to run other countries for the benefit of their merchant banks. Many countries and organisations are calling for the reform of the World Bank and the IMF. Others go further and argue for the abolition of these agencies and a complete restructuring of the world financial system.

The World Trade Organisation

The view that the protectionist policies of the 1930s should not be allowed to reoccur led to the establishment of another important international institution in 1947, the General Agreement on Tariffs and Trade (GATT). The objective of GATT was to gradually lower the barriers to trade, with free trade as its conceptual objective. This was the first multilateral accord to lower trade barriers since Napoleonic times. In 1995 the GATT was replaced by the World Trade Organisation (WTO). Unlike the loosely organised GATT, the WTO was set up as a permanent organisation with far greater powers to arbitrate trade disputes.

Although agreements have been difficult to broker at times, the overall success of GATT/WTO is undeniable: today average tariffs are only a tenth of what they were when GATT came into force and world trade has been increasing at a much faster rate than GDP. However, in some areas **protectionism** is still alive and well, particularly in clothing, textiles and agriculture. In principle, every nation has an equal vote in the WTO. In practice, the rich world shuts the poor world out from key negotiations.

The WTO exists to promote free trade. The fundamental issue is: does free trade benefit all those concerned or is it a subtle way in which the rich nations exploit their poorer counterparts? Most critics of free trade accept that it does generate wealth but they deny that all countries benefit from it. The non-governmental organisation Oxfam is a major critic of the way the present trading system operates. Figure 12 shows the main goals of its 'Make Trade Fair' campaign.

1 End the use of conditions attached to IMF-World Bank programmes which force poor countries to open their markets regardless of the impact.

2 Improve market access for poor countries and end the cycle of subsidised agricultural overproduction and export dumping by rich countries.

3 Change WTO rules so that developing countries can protect domestic food production.

4 Create a new international commodities institution to promote diversification and end oversupply in order to raise prices for producers and give them a reasonable standard of living.

5 Change corporate practices so that companies pay fair prices.

6 Establish new intellectual property rules to ensure that poor countries are able to afford new technologies and basic medicines.

7 Prohibit rules that force governments to liberalise or privatise basic services that are vital for poverty reduction.

8 Democratise the WTO to give poor countries a stronger voice.

Figure 12 *Some aims of Oxfam's 'Make Trade Fair' campaign.*

The most vital element in the trade of any country is the terms on which it takes place (the **terms of trade**). If countries rely on the export of commodities that are low in price and need to import items that are relatively high in price, they need to export in large quantities to be able to afford a relatively low volume of imports. Many poor nations are primary product dependent – that is, they rely on one or a small number of primary products to obtain foreign currency through export. The world market prices for primary products are in general very low compared with those for manufactured goods and services. Also, the price of primary products is subject to considerable variation from year to year, making economic and social planning extremely difficult. The terms of trade for many developing countries are worse now than they were a decade ago. It is not surprising,

Lamy's lament on trade liberalisation

Davos: There may be the will to build global institutions to run the world economy, but let's get real: nation states still rule.

As Pascal Lamy, the director general of the World Trade Organisation noted yesterday, business and finance have gone global but international governance dates back to the Treaty of Westphalia, which created the modern system of nation states. 'The only way you can force a country to do something in a Westphalian system is through war,' Lamy said.

It's easy to understand Lamy's frustration. For the past eight and a bit years, he has been trying to get the WTO's 150-odd members to sign off a new round of trade liberalisation. The process has been long and fiendishly complex. Few people understand the details of the talks, and every attempt by world leaders to break the logjam has quickly foundered in a morass of detail.

The closest comparison from literature is the case of Jarndyce v Jarndyce in *Bleak House*, which goes on for years, is utterly baffling and ends with nobody – apart from the lawyers, naturally – gaining a penny. Lamy remains hopeful that Geneva's version of Jarndyce v Jarndyce will have a happier ending. Some participants are not so sure.

Now, the WTO is not universally loved. If the Doha finally collapsed from exhaustion, its critics would say 'good riddance'. But there is a wider point here.

The WTO is the only modern attempt at creating a new global body that has the teeth to impose discipline on its members. Countries that break WTO rules can be brought to book. Sanctions can be imposed.

Even then, it has proved impossible to get WTO members – all of whom say they want a deal – to make the compromises needed to get the Doha round signed off.

Nothing remotely as permanent and robust exists for the other big global issues currently under discussion. Where is the mechanism that would discipline countries that reneged on commitments to cut climate change? How can the rest of the world force China to revalue its currency or the Americans to stop living beyond their means?

The reality is that power still resides with nation states, or groups of nation states, as in the case of the European Union. For the foreseeable future, it will be these states – answerable to their own populations – who will be taking the decisions that matter.

therefore, that so many nations are struggling to get out of poverty.

By July 2008, the WTO had 153 members. Russia is the only major economy not a member. Russia wants to join, but it must first convince the EU and the USA that it has reformed its business practices.

There is currently an impasse over a long-awaited global trade deal intended to cut subsidies, reduce tariffs and give a fairer deal to developing countries (Figure 13). Discussions on this – the so-called Doha round of talks – began in 2001. But a breakthrough has proved elusive, with rows emerging among the WTO's key players over agricultural tariffs and subsidies.

Trade deficits

Because the terms of trade are generally disadvantageous to poor countries, many developing countries have very high **trade deficits** (Figure 14). Among lower-income countries the average trade balance is a deficit of 12.3% of GDP. Such a level is a rarity among developed nations.

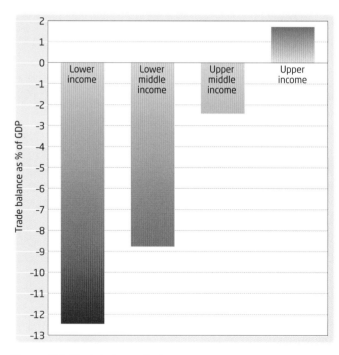

Figure 14 *Trade balances by income group.*

Figure 13 *An article from* The Guardian, *January 2010.*

Activities

1 What are the functions of (a) the World Bank and (b) the International Monetary Fund?
2 What are the objectives of the World Trade Organisation?
3 Discuss Oxfam's criticisms of the way the WTO operates.
4 Produce a brief bullet-point summary of Figure 13.
5 Describe and explain the data presented in Figure 14.

Theory of Knowledge

How do we decide something is fair or is not fair? Think about how the word is used in different contents (at home, on the sports field, in terms of intellectual property or in global trade).

Review

Examination-style questions

1 a Discuss the role of FDI and repatriation of profits in the transfer of capital between the developed and developing worlds.

b Examine the role of remittances in the global transfer of capital.

2 a Discuss the differences between bilateral, multilateral and humanitarian aid.

b Why are net debt forgiveness grants so important to the future development of many of the world's poorest countries?

Websites

www.islamic-relief.com
Islamic Relief Worldwide

www.nber.org
The National Bureau of Economic Research

www.imf.org
International Monetary Fund

www.money.cnn.com
CNN Money.com

www.unctad.org
UN Conference on Trade and Development

www.worldbank.org
World Bank

Key terms

Investment expenditure on a project in the expectation of financial (or social) returns.

Official development assistance (ODA) aid given by governments and other agencies to support the economic, social and political development of developing countries.

Profit repatriation returning foreign-earned profits or financial assets back to the company's home country.

Debt money owed by a country to another country, to private creditors (e.g. commercial banks) or to international agencies such as the World Bank or IMF.

Free trade a hypothetical situation whereby producers have free and unhindered access to markets everywhere.

Loan money borrowed that is usually repaid with interest.

Remittance a transfer of money by a foreign worker to his/her home country.

Protectionism the institution of policies (tariffs, quotas, regulations) that protect a country's industries against competition from cheaper imports.

Terms of trade the price of a country's exports relative to the price of its imports, and the changes that take place over time.

Trade deficit when the value of a country's exports is less than the value of its imports.

06 Labour flows

KEY QUESTION

- What are the causes and effects of the large flow of labour between Mexico and the USA?

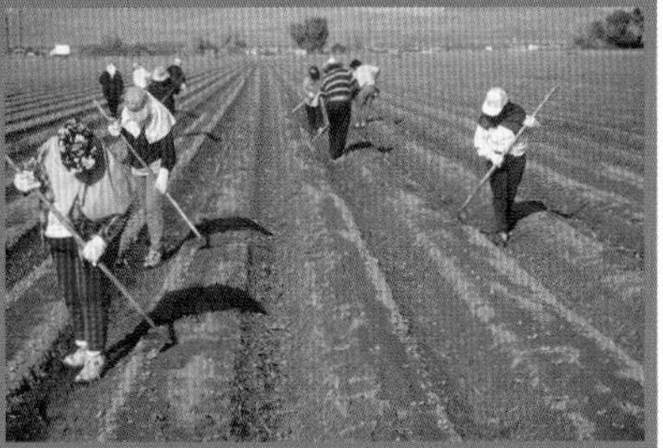

Migrant Mexican workers on a large estate, Arizona, USA.

The causes and effects of the flow of labour from Mexico to the USA

One of the largest **labour migrations** in the world has been from Mexico to the USA – a rare example where a developed country borders a developing country. This movement has largely been the result of a very large gap in:

- average income: the income gap has been a powerful stimulus to movement, and emigration has tended to surge during periods of wage decline in Mexico
- unemployment rates: weak growth in Mexico's labour demand has resulted in high levels of unemployment and **underemployment**
- the growth of the labour force: with significantly higher population growth in Mexico than in the USA
- the overall quality of life: in virtually every aspect of quality of life, conditions are better in the USA than in Mexico.

About 30% of legal immigrants in the USA and an estimated half of all unauthorised foreigners in the country are from Mexico. The ties between the two countries go back to the 19th century, when what is now the south-western USA was part of Mexico. However, there was only very limited movement across the US/Mexican border until the 20th century. In fact most migration has taken place in the last three decades. Although previous surges occurred in the 1920s and 1950s, persistent **mass migration** between the two countries did not take hold until the late 20th century. Figure 1 summarises the main push and pull factors influencing migration from Mexico to the USA. Mexico is Latin America's major emigration country, sending up to 500 000 people – half of its net population increase – to the USA each year. Most make unauthorised entries.

Type of migrant	Demand-pull	Supply-push	Network/other
Economic	Labour recruitment (guest workers)	Unemployment or underemployment; low wages (farmers whose crops fail)	Job and wage information flows
Non-economic	Family unification (family members join spouse)	Low income, poor quality of life, lack of opportunity	Communications; transport; assistance organisations; desire for new experience/adventure
Note: All three factors may encourage a person to migrate. The relative importance of pull, push and network factors can change over time.			

Figure 1 *Factors encouraging migration from Mexico, by type of migrant.*

Early and mid 20th-century migration

In the early part of the 20th century the American government allowed the recruitment of Mexican workers as **guest workers**. Young Mexican men, known as 'braceros', were allowed into the USA legally between 1917 and 1921 and then later between 1942 and 1964. Figure 3 shows the number of Mexican immigrants admitted to the USA on a permanent basis between 1942 and 1965, while Figure 4 shows the number of braceros admitted annually during the same period.

In the mid to late 1950s the number reached almost 450 000 a year.

Both guest worker programmes began when US farms faced a shortage of labour during periods of war. US farmers were strong supporters of allowing the entry of Mexican labour as the increased supply of labour kept wages low and this contributed to higher land prices. Trade unions and many religious groups were against the programmes. Congress agreed with what was then a common view in the USA – that the inflow of Mexican workers was holding down the wages of US farm workers – and ended the programme.

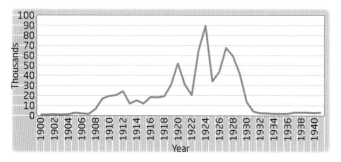

Figure 2 *Number of Mexican immigrants admitted to the USA, 1900–41.*

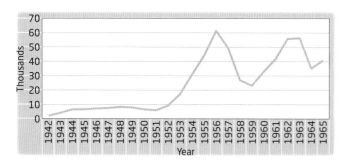

Figure 3 *Number of Mexican immigrants admitted to the USA, 1942–65.*

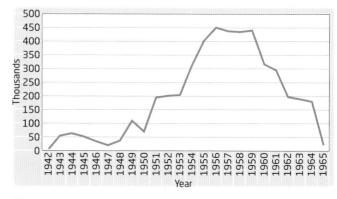

Figure 4 *Number of braceros admitted to the USA annually, 1942–65.*

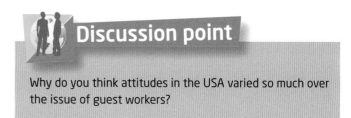

Discussion point

Why do you think attitudes in the USA varied so much over the issue of guest workers?

The end of the bracero programme

The end of the bracero programme saw farm wages rise, along with the increasing mechanisation of US agriculture. Re-adjusting the labour market in America after several decades of significant dependence on Mexican workers was not easy. On the other side, the loss of US jobs and wages was a difficult adjustment for many Mexican workers. Under the bracero programme American farmers were required to pay for the transportation of Mexican workers from the US/Mexican border. This was an incentive for many Mexicans to move to the border area in the hope of being selected for work in the USA. When the programme ended they returned to border communities in Mexico where unemployment was extremely high.

Maquiladoras

The US and Mexican governments made changes to their trade laws to allow the establishment of **maquiladoras**. These are factories in Mexico that import components and use Mexican labour to assemble them into goods such as televisions for export to the USA. The logical location for the maquiladoras was in towns just over the border in Mexico so that they were as close to their US markets as possible. As the number of factories grew, more Mexicans migrated from other parts of the country to the border towns to be in competition with returning braceros for jobs. The establishment of maquiladoras only solved the returning bracero problem to a certain extent as many of the jobs in the factories went to women.

Increase in illegal migration

Although many rural Mexicans had become dependent on US employment, there was very little illegal migration from Mexico to the USA in the 1960s and 1970s. However, high population growth and the economic crisis in the early 1980s resulted in a considerable increase in illegal migration across the border. Networks were soon established between Mexican communities and US employers. At this time no penalties were placed on American employers who knowingly hired illegal migrants. During this period Mexican workers spread out more widely in the USA than ever before. They were employed mainly in agriculture, construction, various manufacturing industries and low-paid services jobs. The US border patrol was responsible for apprehending illegal workers, but their numbers were limited and they only had a modest impact on the spread of illegal workers. Figure 5 shows the number of Mexican immigrants to the USA between 1966 and 1999.

Mexican soldiers patrol the Santa Fe Bridge between Ciudad Juarez, Mexico and El Paso, Texas.

As attitudes in America again hardened against illegal workers, Congress passed the Immigration Reform and Control Act (IRCA) of 1986. This imposed penalties on American employers who knowingly hired illegal workers. The objective was to discourage Mexicans from illegal entry. Much of the opposition of the unions to

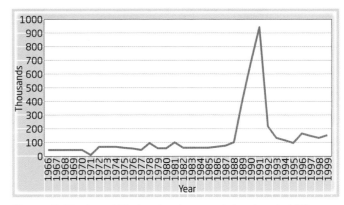

Figure 5 *Number of Mexican immigrants admitted to the USA, 1966–99.*

guest workers was because they saw the process creating 'bonded workers' with very limited rights.

However, the Act also legalised 2.7 million unauthorised foreigners. Of this number, 85% were Mexican. The legalisation substantially expanded network links between Mexican workers and US employers.

The formation of the North American Free Trade Agreement (NAFTA) lowered barriers to trade and investment flow between Mexico, the USA and Canada. At the time, the Mexican government expected Mexico's export trade to increase and Mexico–US migration to fall due to NAFTA. However, this proved not to be the case and migration from Mexico to the USA increased. Labour migration continued at a high rate even after economic and employment growth in Mexico improved in the late 1990s.

Table 1 shows the number of Mexican guest workers in the USA under H-2 visas from 1998 to 2006. The H-2 programme was created in the 1980s to revise the guest worker programme. The H-2A visa is granted for agricultural work, and the H-2B visa for non-agricultural work.

2000 and beyond

The US Census in 2000 found an estimated 8.4 million, mostly Mexican, unauthorised foreigners. This stimulated new attempts to regulate migration between the two countries. George Bush, elected President in 2000, stated that he favoured a guest worker programme to permit more Mexicans to work in America. In 2001 Mexican President Vicente Fox pressed the US government to endorse what was known as the 'whole enchilada'. This would involve legalisation for unauthorised Mexicans in the USA, a new guest worker programme, improved conditions along the border, and exempting Mexico from

	1998	1999	2000	2001	2002	2003	2004	2005	2006
H-2A	21594	26069	27172	21569	12846	9924	17218	1282	40283
H-2B	10727	18927	27755	41852	52972	65878	56280	89184	89184
Total	32321	44996	54927	63421	65818	75802	73498	90466	129467

Table 1 *Mexican guest workers in the USA under H-2 visas, 1998–2006.*

immigrant visa ceilings. These discussions were halted by the 11 September 2001 terrorist attacks.

Legal and illegal migration from Mexico continued as before. By 2006 there were an estimated 12 million Mexican-born people living in the USA. This amounted to around 11% of people living in USA. With their children also taken into account the figure increased to more than 20 million. This was equivalent to almost a fifth of the population of Mexico. The next four leading countries of origin were the Philippines, India, China and Vietnam, with between 1.1 and 1.6 million people each. This illustrates the size and impact of Mexican immigration into the USA. In 2005 the median income for Mexicans in the USA was $21000, a little more than half that for US-born workers. However, it was still far in excess of the median income in Mexico itself.

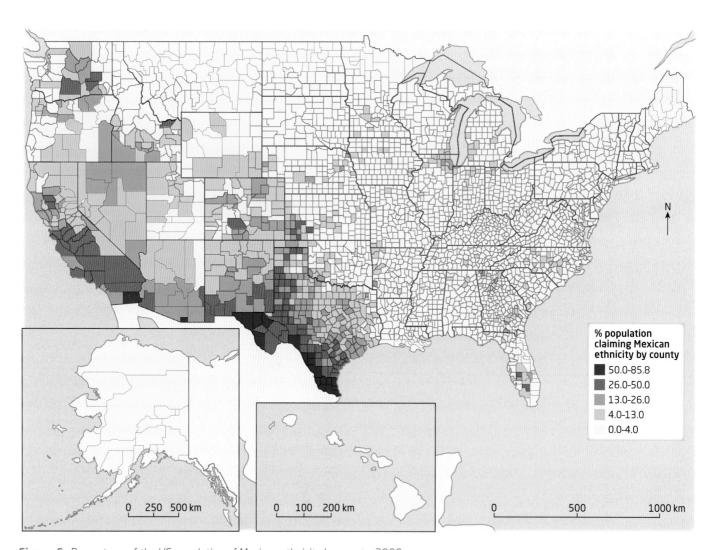

Figure 6 *Percentage of the US population of Mexican ethnicity by county, 2000.*

A poor Mexican rural community.

Geographical skill

Look at Figure 6. Describe the geographical pattern of the Mexican population living in the USA. Use an atlas so that you can refer accurately to states and regions. Comment on areas of high, moderate and low density.

Figure 6 shows the distribution of the Mexican population in the USA by county. Counties are subdivisions of states in the USA. There is a very strong concentration of the US Mexican population in the four states along the Mexican border: California, Arizona, New Mexico and Texas. The concentration is particularly strong in California and Texas. Other western states, including Washington, Oregon, Colorado, Nevada and Idaho, also have above average concentrations. The main reasons for this spatial distribution are:

- proximity to the border
- the location of demand for immigrant farm workers
- urban areas where the Mexican community is long established.

Figure 7 shows the distribution of the Mexican population in the Los Angeles region. Within the urban area itself the Mexican population is concentrated in areas of poor housing and low average income. In more peripheral areas the Mexican population is concentrated in low-cost housing areas where proximity to farm employment is an important factor.

Mexican culture has had a sustained impact on many areas in the USA, particularly urban areas close to the border. As a result many Mexican migrants find reassuring similarities between the two countries. One study on labour migration from Mexico to the USA stated: 'Many Mexicans find adapting to Los Angeles as easy as navigating Mexico City.'

There is no doubt that the Mexican population in the USA has undergone a process of **assimilation** over time. There are three facets to assimilation:

- economic
- social
- political.

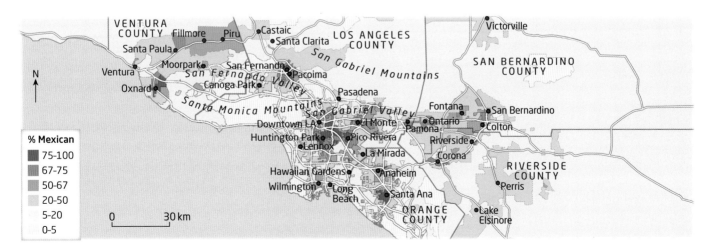

Figure 7 *Distribution of the Mexican population in the Los Angeles region.*

Assimilation tends to occur in the order presented above, with economic assimilation occurring first. While most migrants from Mexico would be in the low-skills category, their children and grandchildren usually aspire to, and gain, higher qualifications and skills. Such economic mobility inevitably results in greater social contact with the mainstream population. Eventually more people from migrant populations get involved in politics and the migrant community gains better political representation.

The demography of Mexican migration to the USA

In an article entitled 'The demography of Mexican migration to the US', G.H. Hanson and C. McIntosh highlight the fact that with the US baby boom peaking in 1960, the number of US native-born people of working age actually declined in the 1980s. In contrast high levels of fertility continued in Mexico in the 1960s and 1970s. The sharp increase in Mexico–US relative labour supply coincided with the stagnation of Mexico's economy in the 1980s, after significant economic progress in the 1960s and 1970s. This created ideal conditions for an emigration surge.

However, the conditions behind recent emigration from Mexico are unlikely to be sustained. Today Mexico's labour supply growth is converging to US levels. Between

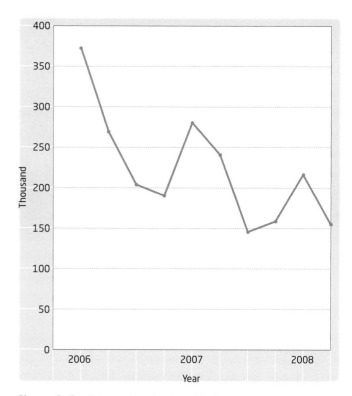

Figure 9 *Declining emigration from Mexico.*

1965 and 2000, Mexico's **total fertility rate** fell from 7.0 to 2.5, close to the US rate of 2.1. Thus labour supply pressures for emigration from Mexico peaked in the late 1990s and are likely to fall in coming years.

Figure 8 is a simulation of migration from Mexico to the USA based on differences in labour supply and wage differentials between the two countries. Population projections are used to estimate future labour supply. Hanson and McIntosh's analysis correlates with recent census data published by the Mexican government (Figure 9) which showed 226 000 fewer people emigrating from Mexico during the year that ended in August 2008 than during the previous year, a decline of 25%. All but a very small fraction of emigration from Mexico is to the USA.

Hanson and McIntosh conclude that 'while Mexico's labour force growth is slowing, Central America's is not, meaning that in coming decades Mexico may face conditions on its southern border similar to what the US has just seen'.

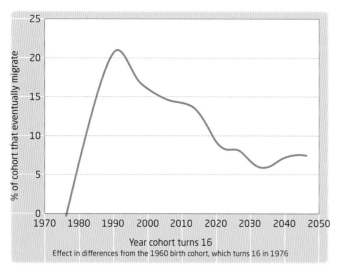

Figure 8 *Labour supply pressures for Mexican migration to the USA.*

Opposition to Mexican migration into the USA

In the USA the Federation for American Immigration Reform (FAIR) argues that unskilled newcomers:

- undermine the employment opportunities of low-skilled US workers
- have negative environmental effects
- threaten established US cultural values.

The recent global economic crisis saw unemployment in the USA rise to about 10%, the worst job situation for 25 years. Immigration always becomes a more sensitive issue in times of high unemployment. FAIR has also highlighted the costs to local taxpayers of illegal workers in terms of education, emergency medical care, detention and other costs that have to be borne.

Those opposed to FAIR see its actions as uncharitable and arguably racist. Such individuals and groups highlight the advantages that Mexican and other migrant groups have brought to the country.

Marchers showing support for Mexican immigrants, Los Angeles, 2008.

The impact on Mexico

Sustained large-scale labour migration has had a range of impacts on Mexico, some of them clear and others debatable. Significant impacts include:

- the high value of remittances, which totalled $25 billion in 2008; as a national source of income, this is only exceeded by oil exports

- reduced unemployment pressure, as migrants tend to leave areas where unemployment is particularly high
- lower pressure on housing stock and public services
- changes in population structure with emigration of young adults, particularly males
- loss of skilled and enterprising people
- migrants returning to Mexico with changed values and attitudes.

Activities

1. With reference to Figure 1 (page 73), discuss the factors that encourage migration from Mexico by type of migrant.
2. Describe the trends illustrated in Figures 2–5 (pages 74–75).
3. Draw a graph to represent the data shown in Table 1 (page 76).
4. Describe the distribution of the Mexican population in Los Angeles shown in Figure 7 (page 77).
5. Describe and explain the information presented in Figure 8.
6. Analyse the trends shown in Figure 9.

Theory of Knowledge

Labour migration is often an emotive subject. Yet it is one that has many dimensions. Some of the best and brightest people from LEDCs are recruited to work in the public services such as health or the business sectors of MEDCs, sometimes adversely affecting their own countries, yet attention is far more often focused on the migration of unskilled or low-skilled workers. Why do you think this is?

Research idea

Read the following case study and find out about the location and characteristics of the Mexican population in another city in the USA.

Case study

San Agustin in Mexico and Poughkeepsie in the USA

A. Mountz and R. Wright (1996) presented an interesting **ethnographic** account of the transnational migrant community of San Agustin, a village in the Mexican state of Oaxaca, and Poughkeepsie, a city in New York state. The link between the two communities began with the migration of a lone Oaxacan to Poughkeepsie in the early 1980s. In classic network fashion the Mexican population of Poughkeepsie, predominantly male, grew to well over 1000 over the next decade. Most Oaxacans found employment as undocumented workers in hotels, restaurants and shops and as building workers and landscapers. Their remittances transformed village life in their home community.

What struck Mountz and Wright most was the high level of connectedness between San Agustin and Poughkeepsie, with the migrant community keeping in daily contact with family and friends via telephone, fax, camcorders, videotape and VCRs: communications technology that was rapidly being introduced to San Agustin. Rapid migration between the two communities was facilitated by jet travel and systems of wiring payments. In effect the community of San Agustin had been geographically extended to encompass the Oaxacan enclave in Poughkeepsie. This is a classic example of **time–space distanciation** – the stretching of social systems across space and time.

Migrant remittances were used not only to support the basic needs of families but also for home construction, the purchase of consumer goods and for financing fiestas. The last provided an important opportunity for migrants to display continued village membership. However, as out-migration became more established, tensions began to develop between some migrants and the home community. The main point of conflict was over the traditional system of communal welfare that requires males to provide service and support to the village. Where this could not be done in terms of time, a payment could be substituted. This was increasingly resented by some migrants who saw 'their money as their own'. However, this was not the only way that traditional village structures were coming under threat. Mountz and Wright identified six groups of people who were challenging traditional village attitudes: dissenters, 'los irresponsables', female migrants, Seventh Day Adventists, practical questioners, and wife robbers (elopement). The traditionalists in the village cited migration as the major cause of the decline of established values and attitudes.

The researchers found that a **migrant culture** had now become established in San Agustin, as it has in so many other Mexican communities, for four main reasons:

- economic survival
- rite of passage for young adult males
- the growing taste for consumer goods and modern styles of living
- the enhanced status enjoyed by migrants in the home community.

What started out as an exception was now well on the way to becoming the rule for San Agustin's young males.

Review

Examination-style questions

1 **a** Why has global labour migration increased in recent decades?

   b Explain the causes and effects of one major flow of labour between two countries that you have studied.

Websites

www.globalworkers.org
Global Workers Justice Alliance

www.foreignpolicy.com
Foreign Policy magazine

www.migrationinformation.org
Migration Policy Institute

www.ilo.org
International Labour Organization

Key terms

Labour migration migration from one country to another when the primary purpose is to seek employment.

Underemployment a situation where people are working less than they would like to and need to in order to earn a reasonable living.

Mass migration the migration of a large group of people from one geographical area to another.

Guest worker a foreigner who is permitted to work in a country on a temporary basis, for example a farm labourer.

Maquiladoras assembly plants in Mexico, especially along the border between the USA and Mexico, to which foreign materials and parts are shipped and from which the finished products are returned to the original market.

Assimilation the process of becoming integrated into mainstream society.

Total fertility rate the number of children an average woman would have, assuming that she lives her full reproductive lifetime.

Ethnographic an ethnography is a type of case study that focuses upon the cultural patterns that develop within a group.

Time-space distanciation the stretching of social systems across space and time.

Migrant culture the attitudes and values of a particular society to the process of migration.

07 Information flows

KEY QUESTION

- What has been the role of ICT in the growth of international outsourcing?

Dublin's International Financial Services Centre (IFSC) is a major outsourcing location.

Outsourcing (also known as offshoring) is the concept of taking internal company functions and paying an outside firm to handle them. It is a form of subcontracting. Outsourcing is done to save money, improve quality or free company resources for other activities. It became a significant part of business activity in the 1980s as companies considered different ways to reduce costs and become more competitive. It has been the revolution in information and communications technology (ICT) that has enabled outsourcing to develop so rapidly into a major global industry. As higher-level ICT has spread down the global economic hierarchy from core to periphery, more and more countries have been competing for this valuable business.

The overall outsourcing market globally was worth about $500 billion in 2008, making it a huge business sector. The bulk of offshore outsourcing to date has been among large organisations, defined as those with more than $1 billion in annual revenue, but recently there has been stronger growth from small and medium-sized businesses. This is because they want a variable cost model for their business, rather than the fixed costs that hiring an in-house IT department or other costly business facility would involve. All sizes of business use outsourcing for specialised skills that they do not have in-house, particularly when they only need such skills occasionally.

When the concept was first introduced during the 1970s, it was mainly manufacturing companies that contracted out some of their job functions to other companies. Then – as it is now – the biggest reason to outsource was to save money. Wanting to expand, yet realising the cost implications of hiring new personnel and creating new departments, companies simply thought of contracting out their low-level yet still important requirements to outside businesses.

Figure 1 shows a typical relationship between clients, a client company and an outsourcing provider. Imagine you are a client (customer) of a European insurance company (the client company) and you are making a claim. You telephone the claims department which has been outsourced to a company in Bangalore, but you can also directly contact the company headquarters in Europe, by phone or email, if you feel the need to do so.

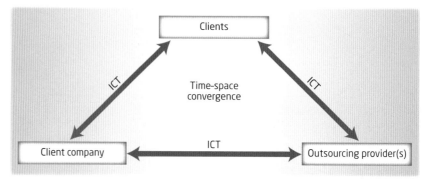

Figure 1 *Relationship between clients, client company and an outsourcing provider.*

The components of businesses typically outsourced include:

- information technology
- human resources
- facilities
- real estate management and
- accounting.

Many companies also outsource customer support and call centre functions like telemarketing, CAD drafting, customer service, market research, manufacturing, designing, web development, print-to-mail, ghostwriting and engineering.

Logistics has become a vitally important aspect of manufacturing businesses which have seen a rapid growth in outsourcing. The information age, with its introduction of sophisticated databases that can track inventory levels and shipments on a global basis via the Internet, has created vast transport and logistics efficiencies. As a result, supply chain technology has been one of the fastest-growing segments in the information field. The rapid adoption of outsourcing has led many companies, when shipping is vital to their business, to turn to logistics services providers for many different types of shipping support, including warehousing, scheduling and distribution services. The sectors of transport, **supply chain management (SCM)** and logistics services are permanently intertwined, creating efficiencies once undreamed of in the transportation arena.

Outsourcing allows companies to focus on their core business. Acquiring logistics expertise internally can be very expensive and time-consuming. Using a logistics provider can reduce capital expenditure considerably. For example, there is no longer the need to purchase and maintain a transportation fleet, equipment and distribution centre. High-quality ICT gives manufacturers the ability to see their inventory as it moves through the supply chain. Good logistics is increasingly about managing information efficiently.

Research idea

Find out if your school and local authority (council) outsource any of the services they need and provide. If this is indeed the case, what is provided by outsourcing companies and why has this process occurred?

The leading global outsourcing centres

A survey published in October 2009 recognised six Indian cities among the top eight global destinations for outsourcing (Table 1). The fourth Global Services-Tholons top 50 emerging outsourcing destinations survey placed Bangalore, Delhi, Mumbai, Chennai, Hyderabad and Pune among the leading outsourcing destinations (Figure 2). The remaining two top outsourcing destinations are Manila and Dublin.

Outsourcing has developed into such big business that **outsourcing city clusters** have started to develop. These city clusters are based on human talent and other infrastructural advantages, such as rapid transportation, within the wider region. The globalisation of services has now reached such a level of maturity that it has the capability to influence the development of city regions.

Rank	City	Country
1	Bangalore	India
2	Delhi NCR	India
3	Mumbai	India
4	Manila NCR	Philippines
5	Dublin	Ireland
6	Chennai	India
7	Hyderabad	India
8	Pune	India
NCR = National capital region		

Table 1 *The top eight outsourcing cities, 2009.*

In national terms, the top five offshore nations according to the Global Services-Tholons survey were India, the Philippines, China, Ireland and Brazil. The next five countries in rank order were Canada, Russia, Mexico, Vietnam and Poland.

India continues to top the list with revenues of $40 billion in IT-BPO (business processing outsourcing) export services in 2008. Indian IT-BPO export services have recorded 35% year on year growth rates in the last five years. The Philippines increased outsourcing revenues by 25% from $4.8 billion in 2007 to $6 billion in 2008 while increasing

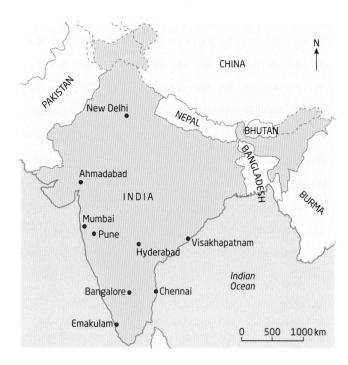

Figure 2 *Major outsourcing centres in India.*

industry employment by 33% to an estimated 400 000 employees.

India's FDI inflows recorded the largest increase globally at 46% in 2008, from $25 billion to $46 billion even as

global FDI flows decreased from $1.9 trillion to $1.7 trillion and several developing economies struggled to acquire investments from client nations. Avinash Vashistha, CEO of Tholons, says that 'finding a Centre of (Outsourcing) Excellence is more than just lower cost. It must consider location, risk mitigation for business, cultural affinity and scalability of the skilled workforce.'

The survey also identified the top destinations by function:

- Business analytics: Delhi NCR, Mumbai, Bangalore, Chennai, Krakow
- Finance and accounting: Mumbai, Bangalore, Manila NCR, Krakow, Shanghai
- Human resources: Prague, Bucharest, Bangalore, Makati City, Budapest
- Legal services: Manila NCR, Mumbai, Chennai
- Contact centre–English: Delhi NCR, Manila NCR, Dublin, Mumbai, Bangalore
- Contact centre–multilingual: Mexico City, Cairo, Krakow, Buenos Aires, Dalian
- Product development: Bangalore, Moscow, Chennai, Shanghai, Ho Chi Minh City
- Application development and maintenance: Bangalore, Mumbai, Hyderabad, Chennai, Dublin

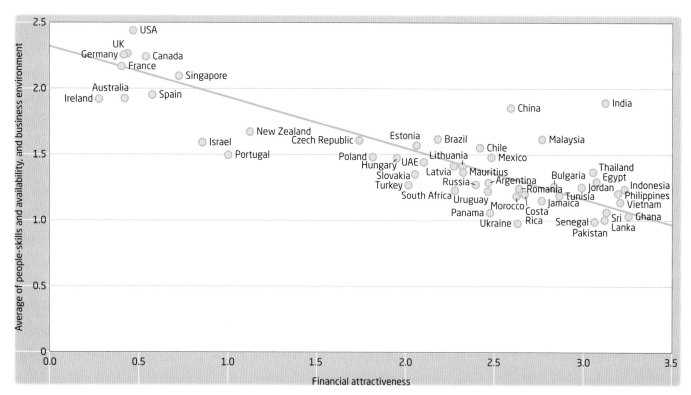

Figure 3 *Outsourcing attractiveness.*

Rank	Country	Financial attractiveness	People-skills and availability	Business environment	Total score
1	India	3.13	2.48	1.30	6.91
2	China	2.59	2.33	1.37	6.29
3	Malaysia	2.76	1.24	1.97	5.98
4	Thailand	3.05	1.30	1.41	5.77
5	Indonesia	3.23	1.47	0.99	5.69
6	Egypt	3.07	1.20	1.37	5.64
7	Philippines	3.19	1.17	1.24	5.60
8	Chile	2.41	1.20	1.89	5.50
9	Jordan	2.99	0.91	1.59	5.49
10	Vietnam	3.21	1.02	1.24	5.47
11	Mexico	2.48	1.50	1.45	5.43
12	Brazil	2.18	1.83	1.37	5.39

Table 2 *A.T. Kearney Global Services Location Index, 2009.*

- Testing: Bangalore, Chennai, Hyderabad, Ho Chi Minh City, Toronto, Shanghai

- Engineering services: Bangalore, Chennai, Pune, St Petersburg, Guangzhou

- R&D: St Petersburg, Bangalore, Moscow, Shanghai, Dublin

- Animation/game development: Shanghai, Beijing, Moscow, São Paulo

- Health care services: Hyderabad, Bangalore, Warsaw, Prague, St Petersburg, Mumbai

- Infrastructure management services: Bangalore, Dublin, Kuala Lumpur, Delhi NCR, Toronto.

An alternative analysis by the major US consulting company A.T. Kearney confirms India as the most attractive outsourcing country in the world, followed by China, Malaysia, Thailand and Indonesia (Table 2). It is not surprising that the rankings of the two surveys are different because of variations in the criteria used. Figure 3, from the A.T. Kearney analysis, shows how India and China in particular are such attractive environments for outsourcing, scoring very highly on both variables shown on the graph. Table 3 shows the criteria used by A.T. Kearney to rank the world's major outsourcing locations.

A growing number of countries are competing for the increasingly valuable global outsourcing business. For example, Egypt was praised recently as 'by far the

Middle Eastern country currently best positioned to take advantage of the boom in outsourcing', in a report by the Yankee Group. Cairo was also placed 7th in a study prepared by Global Services-Tholons of the top 50 emerging outsourcing cities in 2008. In addition, A.T. Kearney placed the country 13th in its 2007 Global Services Location Index. The growing list of multinationals investing in Egypt includes Vodafone, Wipro, Satyam, IBM and Microsoft.

Toronto's central business district – Canada is in the top thirty of outsourcing countries.

Category	Subcategories	Metrics
Financial attractiveness (40%)	Compensation costs	• Average wages • Median compensation costs for relevant positions (call-centre representatives, BPO analysts, IT programmers and local operations managers)
	Infrastructure costs	• Rental costs • Commercial electricity rates • International telecom costs • Travel to major customer destinations (New York, London, Tokyo)
	Tax and regulatory costs	• Relative tax burden • Corruption perception • Currency appreciation and depreciation
People-skills and availability (30%)	Remote services sector experience and quality ratings	• Size of existing IT and BPO sectors • Contact centre and IT centre quality certifications • Quality ratings of management schools and IT training
	Labour force availability	• Total workforce • University-educated workforce • Workforce flexibility
	Education and language	• Scores on standardised education and language tests
	Attrition risk	• Relative IT and BPO sector growth and unemployment rates
Business environment (30%)	Country environment	• Investor and analyst ratings of overall business and political environment • A.T. Kearney Foreign Direct Investments Confidence Index • Security risk • Regulatory burden and employment rigidity • Government support for the ICT sector
	Infrastructure	• Overall infrastructure quality • Quality of telecom, Internet and electricity infrastructure
	Cultural exposure	• Personal interaction score from A.T. Kearney Globalisation Index
	Security of intellectual property	• Investor ratings of IP protection and ICT laws • Software piracy rates • Information security certifications

Table 3 *Criteria used by A.T. Kearney to rank major outsourcing locations.*

Geographical skill

a What is the extent of the relationship between the two variables in Figure 3 (page 84)?

b What statistical technique could you use to arrive at a mathematical answer to the question?

c How would you go about extracting the necessary data from Figure 3 for this type of analysis?

Activities

1 Define 'outsourcing'.
2 Describe and explain the relationships illustrated in Figure 1 (page 82).
3 What are outsourcing city clusters?
4 Comment on the location of India's main outsourcing centres shown in Figure 2 (page 84).
5 Briefly discuss the factors used to compile the A.T. Kearney Global Services Location Index.
6 What are the reasons for the growth of 'periphery to periphery' outsourcing?

Theory of Knowledge

Some people describe outsourcing as 'job exporting'. The image is of the job going abroad to the (cheaper) worker, rather than of the worker coming to the job. Is outsourcing a 'mirror image' of labour migration, or are there important differences, for example in the costs and benefits to both the 'partner' countries involved?

Cairo – Egypt is a rapidly growing outsourcing centre.

Periphery to periphery outsourcing

The structure of global outsourcing has become much more complex in recent years. It is now not just about developed countries outsourcing to developing countries; the latter are now outsourcing to each other:

- For decades, Egypt has supplied skilled migrant labour to the oil-rich nations of the Persian Gulf. Now that improved telecommunications allow for remote delivery, some of these skilled workers can deliver their services without leaving Egypt.

- Mauritius is a growing service exporter to Europe, particularly to France. Several Mauritius companies that provide BPO services to France have opened up their own offshore centres in nearby Madagascar. Here the services of French-speaking workers are acquired at much lower costs.

India: global leader in outsourcing

The transformation of the Indian economy over the last two decades has been led by the service sector. Outsourcing has been a major aspect of the rapid development of the service sector in India, leading to its recognition as a third generation newly industrialised country from the late 1980s / early 1990s. The country has a large number of highly qualified professionals whose skills are in demand in other countries, particularly in the English-speaking world. Demand and supply have been united by developments in telecommunications and by worker migration.

A milestone in India's economic progress was reached in 1999 when Infosys Technologies, a software exporter, became the first Indian company to list on a US stock market. It was soon joined by ICICI, the first Indian financial institution to undergo a US audit, and Satyam Infoway, an Internet service provider.

India's software and ICT services sector has been at the forefront of the country's economic growth. India's ICT sector has benefited from the filter down of business from the developed world. Many European and North American companies which previously outsourced their ICT requirements to local companies are now using Indian companies. Outsourcing to India occurs because:

- labour costs are considerably lower
- a number of developed countries have significant ICT skills shortages
- India has a large and able English-speaking workforce (there are about 50 million English speakers in India)
- the perceived early success of outsourcing to India has had a cumulative effect resulting in more and more outsourcing business coming into the country.

In 1999 India established a Ministry of IT. The Ministry's main task was to increase software and ICT services revenue for the country. From low-technology beginnings, Indian companies are migrating to high-value software services, e-commerce, business consultancy and technology research. This is all to maximise India's real cost advantage which is in brainpower and not manpower.

A number of the financial journals describe India as the 'back office of the world'. Such functions go well beyond ICT services to encompass a wide range of office skills that richer economies are only too eager to outsource to much lower-wage nations. The term 'IT-enabled services' is often used to describe such functions.

India's **back office industry** has two sections:

- 'Captive' operations of large Western companies seeking to cut back office costs: for example, GE Capital Services opened India's first international call centre in the mid 1990s, which now employs over 5000 people. Other companies that operate major back office facilities in India include American Express, British Airways and Swissair. Western companies often save 40–50% by shifting work to India. Call centres often give their staff American or European pseudonyms, a practice that has become something of a national joke.
- 'Shorter-term' contracts between Western companies and subcontractors in India, often brokered by

middlemen: an important element in this sector is medical transcription, in which companies convert dictation by doctors in America into written records. India has about 200 medical transcription companies employing 10 000 transcribers. Intense competition between them has driven down costs which may attract other developed countries to make greater use of such services.

India's teleworking industry can be divided into five sectors:

- data entry and conversion, for example medical transcription
- rule-set processing – here a worker might decide, under an airline's rules, whether a passenger qualifies for an upgrade
- problem solving, for example deciding if an insurance claim should be paid
- direct customer interaction – here the teleworker handles more elaborate transactions with the client's customers
- expert 'knowledge services', which require specialists (e.g. engineers and lawyers) using databases.

The development of rural outsourcing

A company called Rural Shores has set up outsourcing offices in rural areas, saying that it makes more sense to take jobs to where people live rather than expecting them to migrate to major urban centres. Some businesses like Rural Shores have begun looking to rural India for an untapped pool of eager and motivated office workers. With much lower rent and wages than other similar centres in cities, the company says it can do the same jobs as many outsourcing companies at half the price. A majority of the workers are the children of farmers and often the first generation to finish high school. For many, a job at an outsourcing centre is seen as a major opportunity.

Discussion point

What are the benefits of rural outsourcing to both rural and urban areas?

Case study

Bangalore

Bangalore is the most important individual centre for the software and ICT services industry. The city is known as the Silicon Valley of India. It is the home of three big service providers – Infosys, TCS and Wipro – along with many other companies, some long established, others relatively new.

Business outsourcing centre, Bangalore.

In the 1980s Bangalore became the location for the first large-scale investment in high technology in India when Texas Instruments selected the city above a number of other possibilities. Other multinationals soon followed as the reputation of the city grew. Bangalore's pleasant climate (moderated by its location on a plateau over 900 metres above sea level) is a significant attraction to foreign and domestic companies alike. The city claims that US and European companies can make savings of 70% by outsourcing to Bangalore.

Apart from ICT industries, Bangalore is also India's most important centre for aerospace and biotechnology. Its economic strength has made the city a significant destination for rural–urban migrants.

Bangalore has developed from low-end ITO and BPO such as coding and data-entry processes to high-end ITO and BPO such as embedded systems and voice-based technical support. Banglaore's ITO client list includes Intel, Microsoft, Oracle, SAP, Cisco, Google, Yahoo, HP, Motorola, Siemens and Samsung. In the BPO/KPO (knowledge process outsourcing) sector, companies include Citi, Reuters, HSBC, Goldman Sachs, Dell and JP Morgan.

Relatively recent companies to choose Bangalore as a location are:

- Simbiosys Bio, the US-based biotechnology firm
- HP's subsidiary Global e-business operations which provide finance accounting solutions with a focus on HR, supply chain and business analytics
- Blue Vector, which provides appliances using radio frequency identification technology
- Visionet which has a mortgage-processing centre in the city catering to major US banks.

Q&A: Mukesh Aghi, Chairman and CEO, Steria (India)

How do you perceive Bangalore as an outsourcing destination?

Even when outsourcing hadn't taken off in India, Bangalore was known for its excellence in education and infrastructure. Moreover, the city has an added advantage of defense support. The presence of institutions like IIS (Indian Institute of Science) and DRDO (Defence Research and Development Organization) adds value to the talent pool in the city.

What are the other factors that signify the city as a 'talent and IT hub'?

The cosmopolitan culture in Bangalore is incredible. It's an awesome cosmopolitan city. The youth is attracted to the city because of its lively pub culture and amazing weather, any time of the year. I believe that the people in the city are more adaptable as compared to big cities like Delhi. It would be unfair not to mention the safety of women in Bangalore. The female workforce is more than willing to do night shifts in a city like Bangalore because of the low crime rate. Thus, highly efficient labour is easily available and enthusiastic to work.

However, the city needs to keep pace with the increasing crowd by handling its infrastructure carefully. Otherwise, it is anticipated that there will be a trend to invest in smaller Indian cities instead.

By Diksha Dutta

Figure 4 *'Awesome cosmopolitan city'.*

Figure 4 emphasises some of the main attractions of Bangalore to both foreign companies and to skilled Indian workers. As competition for highly skilled workers increases, the quality of life of a major business centre has become an increasingly important factor in attracting and retaining high-quality labour.

The future of outsourcing in India

The Shifting Geography of Offshoring, by A.T. Kearney in 2009, stated: 'In just one decade India has transformed and reinvented the outsourcing industry several times over, staying ahead of all trends.' Continual investment in ICT infrastructure and upgrading the skills of its workforce have been pivotal to India maintaining its position as the number one outsourcing country in the world. However, India's position is not unchallenged, with three main concerns identified in *The Shifting Geography of Offshoring*. These are (a) currency movements, (b) terrorism and (c) corporate scandals (Figure 5).

Activities

1 What are the main reasons for the large-scale development of outsourcing in India?
2 How has the nature of outsourcing changed in India over time?
3 Discuss the reasons for the emergence of Bangalore as India's most important outsourcing location.
4 Briefly consider the factors covered in Figure 5 that might prove to be obstacles to the continuing development of outsourcing in India.

There is no debate around India's leading position in offshoring, yet recent events have highlighted that even India is vulnerable. Currency movements, terrorism and a major corporate scandal have made some executives uneasy with India.

Currency movements. Starting in late 2006, the rupee began strengthening against the dollar, trading at 37 rupees per dollar in 2007 as opposed to 47 rupees in 2006. The across-the-board cost increase of almost 30 percent, in dollar terms, created much concern and questions about the sustainability of the Indian offshoring industry.

Starting in 2008 the trend reversed when the rupee returned to normal levels – a trend reinforced by the economic crisis as investors flee to safer currencies and the rupee trades at record lows. Although this is good news for the Indian offshoring industry, the currency developments in 2007 show how fast a cost advantage can erode. India will remain cost-competitive for U.S. companies, but its advantage may come under attack from cheaper locations.

Terrorism. While terrorism has been a fact of life in India for a long time, the attacks in Mumbai in November 2008 drove home the risks of operating in India, especially for Western companies. Western interests were deliberately attacked, raising fears that corporate interests could be next on the target list.

Though the overall risk may or may not have changed in India, the perception and risk equation in the minds of executives has changed. Continued cross-border tension with Pakistan has not helped. The search for alternative locations to complement the Indian centers has accelerated and there is an opportunity for countries with lower exposure to terrorism, such as China, to capture market share.

Corporate scandals. Adding to the worries, the confidence in India took a hit following the unveiling of a large-scale accounting fraud at Satyam. Much like the Enron debacle shook confidence in corporate America, the Satyam scandal has put the spotlight on Indian corporate governance practices. Given the reliance on Indian outsourcing partners, India will have to reestablish trust in its regulatory environment to prevent such scandals from happening again.

In addition, there have been recent examples of companies abandoning India, returning customer service functions to domestic locations. The world's largest airline, Delta Airlines, announced in April 2009 that it would close its contact centers in India and return these functions to the United States in an effort to improve customer service.

Similar centers in Jamaica and South Africa are not affected by the decision. Delta competitor United Airlines announced in February 2009 the relocation of its customer-facing functions from India to Chicago and Hawaii. In a similar move, Dell is now offering a premium technical-support subscription, which guarantees American customers they can talk to customer service representatives in the United States as opposed to India.

Still, India remains indispensable in offshoring and no country or combination of countries can replace it – at least not yet. Nonetheless, these events illustrate India's vulnerabilities and the challenges to staying on top.

Figure 5 *Is India vulnerable?* Source: The Shifting Geography of Offshoring by A.T. Kearney

Review

Examination-style questions

1 In what ways has ICT facilitated the growth in international outsourcing?
2 Examine the development of one major outsourcing centre.

Websites

www.tholons.com
Tholons financial advisory consultant

www.globalservicesmedia.com
Global Services: global sourcing of IT and BPO services

www.atkearney.com
A.T. Kearney global management consultants

www.computerweekly.com
Computer Weekly online magazine

Key terms

Outsourcing the concept of taking internal company functions and paying an outside firm to handle them.

Supply chain management (SCM) the control of materials, information and finances as they move in a process from supplier to manufacturer to wholesaler to retailer to consumer.

Outsourcing city clusters the spread of outsourcing from the main city in a region to neighbouring urban areas linked by high-level transport and communications systems.

Back office industry offices of a company handling high-volume communications by telephone, electronic transaction or letter. Such low- to medium-level functions are relatively footloose and have been increasingly decentralised to locations where space, labour and other costs are relatively low.

08 Degradation through raw material production

KEY QUESTIONS

- What have been the effects of agro-industrialisation and changes in international production and consumption on the physical environment?
- What have been the environmental consequences of the increasing international demand for soybeans?
- How important is the concept of food miles and what are the environmental consequences of increasing volumes of air freight?

Tate and Lyle sugar mill on the banks of the River Thames, London.

Major issues associated with raw material production

The diffusion of agro-industrialisation

Agro-industrialisation or industrial agriculture is the form of modern farming that refers to the industrialised production of livestock, poultry, fish and crops. This type of large-scale, capital-intensive farming originally developed in Europe and North America and then spread to other parts of the developed world. It has been spreading rapidly in many developing countries since the beginning of the **Green Revolution**. Industrial agriculture is heavily dependent on oil for every stage of its operation. The most obvious examples are fuelling farm machinery, transporting produce, and producing fertilisers and other farm inputs.

The characteristics of agro-industrialisation include:

- very large farms
- concentration on one (monoculture) or a small number of farm products
- a high level of mechanisation
- low labour input per unit of production
- heavy usage of fertilisers, pesticides and herbicides
- sophisticated ICT management systems
- highly qualified managers
- often owned by large agribusiness companies
- often vertically integrated with food processing and retailing.

Not all farms and regions involved in agro-industrialisation will display all these characteristics; for example, intensive market gardens may be relatively small although the capital inputs are extremely high.

Regions where agro-industrialisation is clearly evident on a large scale include:

- the Canadian Prairies
- the corn and wheat belts in the USA
- the Paris Basin
- East Anglia in the UK
- the Russian steppes
- the Pampas in Argentina
- Mato Grosso in Brazil
- the Murray-Darling Basin in Australia.

Large-scale wheat harvesting, Montana, USA.

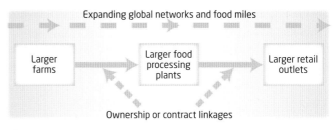
Expanding global networks and food miles

Larger farms → Larger food processing plants → Larger retail outlets

Ownership or contract linkages

Figure 1 *Agro-industrialisation: increasing vertical integration.*

Agro-industrialisation is a consequence of the globalisation of agriculture, the profit ambitions of large agribusiness companies and the drive for cheaper food production. Over the last half-century every stage in the food industry has changed in the attempt to make it more efficient (in an economic sense). Vertical integration has become an increasingly important process with growing linkages between the different stages of the food industry (see Figure 1). Agro-industrialisation is led by huge companies. For example:

- Global trade in food commodities is dominated by a small number of companies.

- The top ten seed firms control 30% of the global market.

- The top ten agrochemical corporations control 84% of the global market.

- A dozen supermarket chains dominate food sales in the USA and Europe.

- Over 80% of the world's biotech patents are held by five companies – Monsanto, DuPont, Syngenta, Dow Chemicals and Avents.

- In the USA, only 8% of farms account for 72% of agricultural sales.

Farming and food production around the world is becoming increasingly dominated by large biotechnology companies, food brokers and huge industrial farms. The result is a complex movement of food products around the world. The food products, both fresh and processed, available in a typical supermarket have a much wider global reach than they did 20 years ago. People's expectations in terms of variety and quality of food have never been higher, which has increased the pressure that the large food retailers have placed on suppliers. Large supermarkets and other bulk purchasers are generally able to switch suppliers faster than ever before, in some cases buying from a different continent. The falling real cost of transport has been an important factor in this trend.

Large agricultural companies are continually seeking to produce new products, increase market share and reduce costs in order to increase their competitiveness. An increasing percentage of agricultural land in the developing world has come under the control of outside influences either directly or indirectly. Direct ownership by TNCs invariably means the cultivation of crops for export at the expense of food production for the domestic population. But even when farms are not foreign-owned, IMF policies may dictate that land is used to produce for the export market. This may not always be a bad thing but if a country is undergoing food shortages at the same time it is an ironic situation.

However, there has been an increasing reaction to high-input farming as more and more people have become concerned about the use of fertilisers, pesticides, herbicides and other high-investment farming practices which are

Terraced mountain sides, Pakistan – over farming has led to soil degradation.

having a significant impact on the environment. The main evidence of this concern is the growth of the organic food market and the increasing sale of food resulting from more 'gentle' farming practices.

The environmental impact of capital-intensive farming

There is a growing realisation that the modes of production, processing, distribution and consumption that prevail – because in the short to medium term they are the most profitable – are not necessarily the most healthy or the most environmentally sustainable. In many parts of the world agro-industrialisation is having a devastating impact on the environment, causing:

- deforestation
- land degradation and desertification
- salinisation and contamination of water supplies
- air pollution
- increasing concerns about the long-term health of farmworkers
- landscape change
- declines in biodiversity.

The industrialised farmlands of today are all too frequently lacking in the wild flowers, birds and insects of the past. These sterilised landscapes provide relatively cheap food, but at high environmental cost. These costs are typically borne by the citizens of the countries concerned rather than by the producers. About a third of the world's farmland is already affected by salinisation, erosion or other forms of degradation.

It has been estimated that food production and consumption accounts for up to twice as many greenhouse gas emissions as those from road vehicles. Figure 2 shows US data published in the *New Scientist*. The average US household's footprint for food consumption is 8.1 tonnes of carbon dioxide equivalent compared with 4.4 tonnes from road vehicles. Figure 3 illustrates the footprint of individual products in a shopping basket. The meat at 4800 g has the highest footprint, with the cheese, eggs and milk also recording high figures. In comparison the footprint of most of the fruit and vegetables is low except for the tomatoes grown in a greenhouse.

Some supermarkets have already initiated pilot programmes to label food products with their carbon footprint. The Carbon Trust, an environmental organisation based in London, is working on a standardised

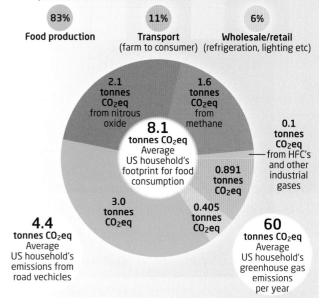

Figure 2 *Comparison of household greenhouse gas emissions from food and from road vehicles.*

system that companies can follow to calculate the footprint of any products. The impact of food on the environment includes:

- methane and nitrous oxide emissions due to meat and dairy product: methane remains in the atmosphere for up to 15 years and traps heat 21 times as effectively as carbon dioxide, so methane production is a major issue; nitrous oxide is released by manure and fertiliser and remains in the atmosphere for over 100 years – it is 296 times more effective at trapping heat than carbon dioxide
- the emissions of transporting produce to wholesalers and then on to retailers
- refrigeration of produce at the wholesale, retail and home consumption stages
- consumers driving to and from food stores
- cooking food which in developed countries requires the burning of fossil fuels; in the world's poorest countries burning fuelwood causes deforestation and indoor air pollution.

The most emission-intensive foods are red meat and dairy products. Livestock in total accounts for 18% of 'man-made' greenhouse gas emissions – 9% of all carbon dioxide, 35–40% of methane and 65% of nitrous oxide (mainly through fertiliser). The amount of grain required for the production of each kilogram of meat is:

- 2.3 kg for chicken
- 5.9 kg for pork
- 13 kg for beef.

However, there is some debate about the accuracy and value of such calculations. For example, regional differences in farming practices can have a big impact on the final figure.

The global cattle population is currently around 1.5 billion. The pasture required amounts to about a third of all the world's agricultural land. A further third of this land is taken up by animal feedcrops. An estimated 1.3 billion people are employed in the livestock industry. The balance between livestock and grass is sustainable at present, but as the demand for meat increases, the pressures that cattle put on the land may well soon exceed supply. More cattle means more manure. Manure is often used to restore depleted soil, but can lead to pollution by heavy metals such as cadmium, nickel, chromium and copper.

In 2000, annual global meat consumption was 230 million tonnes. The forecast for 2050 is 465 million tonnes. There is a strong relationship between meat consumption and rising per capita incomes (Figure 4) although anomalies do occur due to cultural traditions. It is no coincidence that many committed environmentalists are vegetarian.

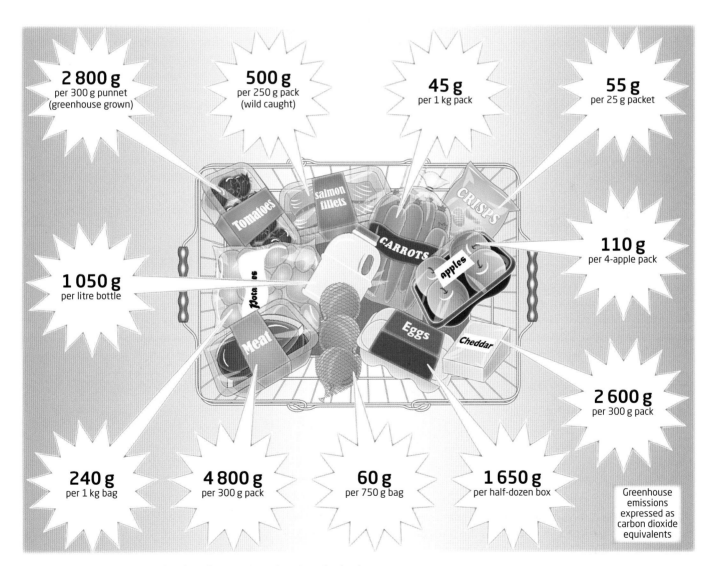

Figure 3 *Carbon footprint of various food products in a shopping basket.*

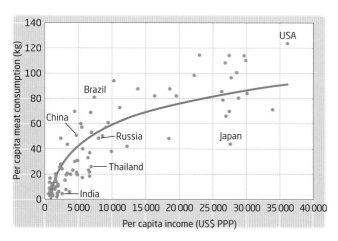

Figure 4 *Meat consumption and income.*

A study at the University of Chicago calculated that a person changing from the average American diet to a vegetarian one could cut their annual emissions by almost 1.5 tonnes of carbon dioxide.

Geographical skill

Describe and explain the relationship between per capita income and per capita meat consumption illustrated in Figure 4. Suggest reasons for significant anomalies. What statistical technique could you use to assess the relationship between these two variables?

Figure 5 examines a growing aspect of agro-industrialisation known as 'vertical food-chain integration'. This process is designed to ensure as far as possible consistent quality in a food product. Major retailers such as Tesco and McDonald's are the final destinations of vertical food-chain integration.

The use of genetically modified (GM) feeds is not the only concern sceptics have about this process:

- Critics of the meat industry point out that current methods of producing animal meat are very inefficient. Only 5–25% of the nutrients, depending on the animal, are converted into edible meat. A possible alternative is 'in vitro meat' where the animal is eliminated from the production process and the meat is grown in a vat. Here the meat could be cultivated from muscle stem cells from cows, pigs and sheep. The cells are attached to either small edible spheres or a 3D scaffold and then cultured in a liquid nutrient broth until the clusters of

The economics of livestock production have seen the implementation of a process known as 'vertical food-chain integration'. This is where a single bull, whose genes perform well across a range of criteria, is selected to suit a particular product line, such as a supermarket's brand of beef. The supermarket then employs farmers to rear that bull's offspring in isolation in such a way that they consistently produce meat with reliable marbling and taste, so that what the customer buys off the shelf in, say, Edinburgh in 2009 will be more or less identical in every respect (including genetically) to beef another customer might buy in Essex in 2015.

One notable successful example of this in cattle breeding is a bull known as Lorabar Mighty Prince, who belongs to Genus Breeding in north Wales. Prince is an Aberdeen Angus, and nearly all of his children's valuable back ends end up in Tesco's Finest range, while their front ends end up as McDonalds's Angus burger patties.

In Brazil, vertical integration is becoming the norm; tens of thousands of cattle are reared, finished and slaughtered on the same farm. The theory of vertical integration is agriculturally essential – with so many mouths to feed, guaranteed high-quality genes improve productivity for farmers and welfare for the cattle. But the effect is that we will one day find ourselves all feeding from the same carcass. Add to this the fact that the majority of intensive cattle feeds used in Europe (maize and soy) are genetically modified, and the picture of our increasingly factory farmed diet is complete: what goes into our bellies has been 'improved' in a lab.

Figure 5 *Vertical integration,* Geographical, *April 2009.*

muscle cells are large enough to harvest. The first In Vitro Meat Symposium was held at the Norwegian Food Research Institute near Oslo in April 2008. Advocates say that while in vitro meat will not be greenhouse gas emission free, its impact will be considerably less than conventional meat production.

- Large-scale farming has been expanding geographically into a number of fragile environments, particularly into areas of rainforest (Figure 6). *The State of the World's Forests 2007,* published by the UN Food and Agricultural Organization (FAO), reported that between 1990 and 2005 the world's total forest area was reduced by 3%. This is a rate of 7.3 million hectares a year.

- Mainly because of the uniformity required by large food companies, important breeds of livestock are becoming extinct. The FAO's *State of the World's Animal Genetic Resources 2007* report stated that at least one livestock

Meat firms sued over illegal deforestation

Brazilian authorities investigating illegal deforestation have accused the suppliers of several UK supermarkets of selling meat linked to massive destruction of the Amazon rainforest. Firms that supply Tesco, Asda and Marks & Spencer are among dozens of Brazilian companies named by prosecutors, who are seeking hundreds of millions of pounds in compensation.

The move follows a three-year investigation by Greenpeace into the trade in cattle products such as meat and leather traced to illegal farms across the Amazon region The Greenpeace report, revealed in the Guardian earlier this month, showed that a handful of major Brazilian processors exported products linked to Amazon destruction to dozens of blue-chip companies across the world.

Daniel Cesar Avelino, the public prosecutor handling the cases, brought by Brazil's public prosecution office (MPF), said: 'We know that the single biggest driver of deforestation in the Amazon is cattle. We want all companies who are part of this destructive economic chain to be responsible for their economic crimes.'

> **'We know that the single biggest driver of deforestation in the Amazon is cattle'**

The MPF has started legal action against 21 farms and slaughterhouse companies including Bertin, which supplies Tesco and Princes Food with processed beef. The MPF said the Brazilian companies could be to blame for illegal deforestation across 150 000 hectares. It is seeking £630m compensation for 'environmental crimes against Brazilian society'.

The accused farms include the Espirito Santo farm in Para state, which the Guardian visited in an undercover investigation with Greenpeace last month. Bertin said it was 'analysing the content of the [legal] action to respond later'. The MPF has also warned a further 69 firms said to have bought products associated with illegal deforestation, including JBS, which supplies Princes Foods, Asda and M&S.

Figure 6 *From* The Guardian, *June 2009.*

breed a month had been lost over the previous seven years. Food scientists are concerned about this trend as genetic resources are the basis of food security.

- Agro-industrialisation is characterised by large areas of monoculture which, among other things, leaves crops more vulnerable to disease due to the depletion of natural systems of pest control. Monoculture results in reliance on pesticides which creates a downward environmental cycle.

Land degradation in Brazil's Centre-West.

The environmental impact of the Green Revolution

Much of the global increase in food production in the last 50 years can be attributed to the Green Revolution which took agro-industrialisation to the developing world on a large scale. India was one of the first countries to benefit when a high-yielding variety seed programme (HVP) commenced in 1966–67. In terms of production it was a turning point for Indian agriculture which had virtually reached stagnation. The HVP introduced new hybrid varieties of five cereals: wheat, rice, maize, sorghum and millet. All were drought resistant with the exception of rice, were very responsive to the application of fertilisers, and had a shorter growing season than the traditional varieties they replaced. Although the benefits of the Green Revolution are clear, serious criticisms have also been made, many linked to the impact on the environment:

- High inputs of fertiliser and pesticide have been required to optimise production. This is costly in both economic and environmental terms.

- The problems of salinisation and waterlogged soils have increased along with the expansion of the irrigated area, leading to the abandonment of significant areas of land.

- High chemical inputs have had a considerable negative effect on biodiversity.

- Some people suffer ill health due to contaminated water and other forms of agricultural pollution.

In the early 1990s nutritionists noticed that even in countries where average food intake had risen, incapacitating diseases associated with mineral and vitamin deficiencies remained commonplace and in some instances had actually increased. The problem is that the high-yielding varieties introduced during the Green Revolution are usually low in minerals and vitamins. Because the new crops have displaced the local fruits, vegetables and legumes that traditionally supplied important vitamins and minerals, the diet of many people in the developing world is now extremely low in zinc, iron, vitamin A and other micronutrients.

In India's Punjab, yield growth has flattened since the mid 1990s. Over-irrigation has resulted in a steep fall in the water table, now tapped by 1.3 million tube wells. Since the beginning of the Green Revolution in Asia, the amount of land under irrigation has tripled.

The Green Revolution has been a major factor enabling global food supply to keep pace with population growth, but with growing concerns about a new food crisis, new technological advances may well be required to improve the global food security situation.

Organic farming

Organic farming does not use manufactured chemicals and thus is practised without chemical fertilisers, pesticides, insecticides and herbicides. Instead animal and green manures are used along with mineral fertilisers such as fish and bone meal. Thus organic farming requires a higher input of labour than mainstream farming. Weeding is a major task with this type of farming. Organic farming is less likely to result in soil erosion and is less harmful to the environment in general. For example, there will be no nitrate runoff into streams and much less harm to wildlife.

Organic farming tends not to produce the 'perfect' potato, tomato or carrot but because of the increasing popularity of organic produce it commands a substantially higher price than mainstream farm produce. However, organic farming doesn't always mean lower emissions.

For example, battery-farmed poultry are reared in such cramped conditions that more of their food energy is likely to be converted into protein in comparison with free range poultry.

Food market, Morocco – much of this local produce is organic, largely because poor farmers can't afford to purchase fertiliser.

Food waste and packaging

An astounding amount of edible food is thrown away each day in rich countries. In the UK, the government-funded Waste and Resources Action Programme estimates that 20 million tonnes of food is thrown away each year. This is equivalent to £50 of the average family's shopping bill. The marketing strategies of retailers such as 'buy one, get one free' are partly to blame for this. Some retailers are now trialling 'buy one now, get one free next time' schemes.

More food, particularly fruit and vegetables, is sold with packaging compared with even 20 years ago. For food retailers this is a way of 'adding value' or charging more for the product. However, packaging has to be disposed of and is now a considerable environmental issue. Very recently there has been a movement to reduce packaging following the success of the reduction in plastic bag usage at supermarkets.

Research idea

Keep a log of the food your family wastes over a two-week period. If you keep the till receipts from your supermarket or other food stores you should be able to estimate the value of the food wasted.

The future

Grave concerns already exist about the environmental impact of global agriculture. How much worse will the situation be when world population reaches 9 billion in the latter part of the century? It will take significant changes in the way we grow crops and keep livestock just for the environmental impact to plateau. The biggest issue may well be GM crops which have been presented by some agricultural scientists as the next agricultural revolution. GM crops in theory require fewer pesticides. An FAO report on GM farming in China certainly supports this assertion. The area planted with GM crops is expanding by about 15% per year. Most of the world's soybeans are already grown as GM crops.

Consumer awareness of the problems of modern agriculture is greater today than at any time in the past. This is having an effect on government policies and companies behaviour. The question is, will it be too little too late? Examples are:

- Reforms to the European Union's Common Agricultural Policy (CAP): each stage of change has reflected a greater need to protect the environment.

'Wheel' irrigation, Idaho, USA.

- Community support agriculture (CSA) in the USA: this is a consumer-driven movement emphasising proximity, food security, self-reliance and sustainability. Only a relatively small number of farms are involved at present, but the number is rising.
- Cuba has switched to organic farming more quickly and on a larger scale than any other country as a result of a radical change in government policy. After a period of food shortages, Cuba became largely self-sufficient in food by the late 1990s.
- China has strongly promoted organic farming in recent years, partly by setting up bodies such as the Organic Food Development Centre.

Activities

1   a What is agro-industrialisation?
    b List its main characteristics.
2   Briefly discuss the main environmental consequences of agro-industrialisation.
3   Describe the data illustrated in Figure 2.
4   Explain the differences in greenhouse gas emissions of the food products shown in Figure 3.
5   With reference to Figure 5 explain why vertical food-chain integration is increasing in importance.
6   Discuss the environmental impact of Green Revolution farming.
7   Describe the characteristics of organic farming.
8   With world population projected to rise to 9 million in the latter part of the century, what is the likelihood that (a) the environmental impact of agriculture will get worse (b) new policies and technical advances will effectively combat the environmental impact of agriculture?

Soybeans

The environmental consequences of increasing international demand

The global demand for soybeans has been rising rapidly due to the increasing world population and rapidly rising meat consumption. Soybeans are a major source of cattle feed. Global meat consumption rose from 44 million tonnes in 1950 to 280 million tonnes in 2009, a six-fold increase.

Soybean production has risen from 17 million tonnes in 1950 to 250 million tonnes in 2009, a more than 14-fold increase. Soybeans are produced for three main purposes:

- 10% is consumed directly as food (tofu, meat substitute, soy sauce etc.)
- 20% is used to extract oil for cooking
- 70% is used as meal for livestock and poultry.

McDonald's, Berlin. Fast food outlets are the end of the 'food chain' for much soybean production.

Farmers in eastern China domesticated the soybean about 3000 years ago, while the first soybeans were planted in North America in the 1760s. By 1970 the USA was producing three-quarters of global soybean production and providing most of the world's exports of this product. A greater area of cropland in the USA is currently devoted to soybeans than wheat, the former exceeding the latter from the mid 1990s (Figure 7). Only corn now covers a larger land area in the USA. The land area used for soybean production has been rising significantly in other key producing countries too (Figure 8). Soybeans dominate agriculture in both Brazil and Argentina.

A key development was the discovery in the mid 20th century that combining one part soybean meal with four parts grain significantly increased the efficiency with which livestock and poultry converted grain into animal protein. It was this advance that propelled the soybean to become one of the world's leading crops alongside rice, corn and wheat.

In the 1970s the USA placed an embargo on soybean exports in an attempt to contain domestic food price inflation due to a considerable rise in global grain and soybean prices. Leading soybean importers such as

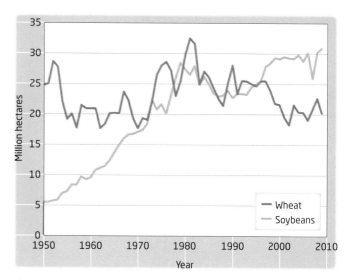

Figure 7 *Area harvested for wheat and soybeans in the USA, 1950–2009.*

Japan looked for alternative suppliers at a time when Brazil was looking for new crops to export. The area devoted to soybeans in Brazil rose rapidly in response to an increasingly lucrative export market. Today the area planted with soybeans is greater than that devoted to all the grain crops combined. A similar process occurred in Argentina. The increasing area of land devoted to soybean production is having a serious impact on the environment, particularly in terms of rainforest destruction. The impact is being felt most intensely in the Amazon where the impact on biodiversity has been devastating (Figures 6 and 9).

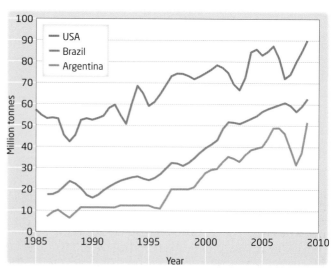

Figure 8 *Soybean production in the USA, Brazil and Argentina, 1985–2009.*

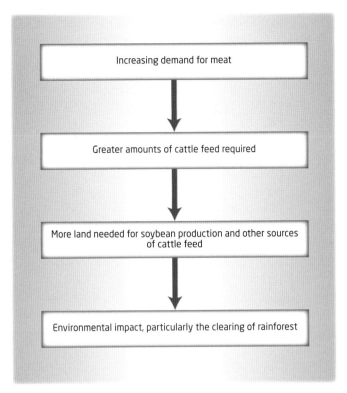

Figure 9 *Environmental impact of the increasing demand for meat.*

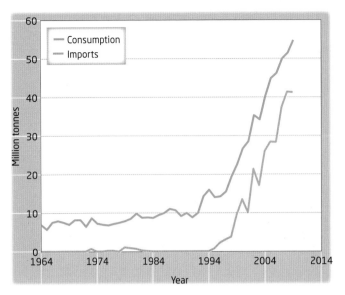

Figure 10 *Soybean imports and consumption in China, 1964–2009.*

Brazil became the world's leading exporter of beef in the middle of the first decade of the new millennium. The country's beef exports have tripled since the late 1990s. Brazil now has 200 million cattle on nearly one-tenth of the country's available agricultural land. Almost a third of this land, 13 million hectares, was once part of the Amazon rainforest. About two-thirds of deforestation in the Amazon is the result of clearing for cattle ranches, but forest clearance for soybean cultivation has increased considerably over the last decade. Brazil's soybeans are an important source of cattle feed in Europe and China. Increasing demand from countries such as China pushes up prices which in turn increases pressure for greater production. Demand for soybeans in China has been fuelled by rising incomes as an increasing number of people move up the food chain, eating more meat, eggs, milk and farmed fish. Soybean consumption in China reached 55 million tonnes in 2009, of which almost 75% was imported (Figure 10). About half of all global soybean exports are destined for China.

Soybeans have had a particularly serious environmental impact because agricultural scientists have not had the same success in increasing yields for soybeans as they have for grain crops. Since 1950 corn yields have risen four-fold while yields of soybeans have only doubled. This means that more and more land has been required for soybean production to keep up with demand.

In 2006, Greenpeace published a report entitled 'Eating up the Amazon' which led to a moratorium on cutting rainforest for new soybean cultivation. The moratorium extended to July 2009. The Greenpeace report particularly criticised three large US commodities firms for the rapid expansion of soybean production in Brazil and the environmental consequences that followed. It blamed Archer Daniels Midland, Bunge, and Cargill for supplying the seeds, pesticides, mills and port facilities to make soybean production possible on such a large scale in the Amazon rainforest. Greenpeace also criticised Maggi, the Brazilian soybean exporter which is owned by the governor of Mato Grosso state.

As a result of the actions of Greenpeace and other environmental organisations, a number of companies stopped buying Brazilian soybeans. However, even with the moratorium in place, soybean planting has proved very difficult to monitor. The fact is that much of Brazilian-grown animal feed still comes from illegal producers. Another weakness in the legislation is that the moratorium does not extend to forest clearance for cattle farming. Thus soybean farmers have been buying up ranchland and converting it to soybean production.

In a 2010 update from the Earth Policy Institute, Lester Brown stated that saving the Amazon rainforest now depends on curbing the growth in demand for soybeans by stabilising population worldwide as soon as possible and reducing the amount of meat eaten globally.

Case study

Agricultural and environmental change in the Pampas, Argentina

Traditionally, cattle rearing has dominated farming in the Pampas of Argentina. The Pampas is one of the world's great grasslands. It is a flat prairie with deep, fertile topsoil. The landscape is dotted with 'estancias', large ranches which have practised extensive commercial cattle rearing. The estancias and the gauchos (cowboys) who work them are an important part of the country's identity and tradition.

However, rapid change is underway as crop production replaces cattle rearing over significant areas of the Pampas. According to the Argentine Rural Society, 10 million hectares of the Pampas have been ploughed up in the last 15 years. This is an area roughly two and a half times the size of Switzerland. There are undoubted benefits to this process as farmers are responding to changing patterns of global demand. But there are also risks involved in such a considerable change in land use.

More profitable soybeans and corn are replacing cattle on the grassy plains of the central Pampas. Global demand, particularly from China, has pushed up world prices considerably. In 2006 Argentina exported $9 billion of soybeans and soybean products, amounting to almost a fifth of the country's total exports. Argentina is the world's third largest soybean exporter after the USA and Brazil.

The world-famous cattle of the Pampas are being driven to the harsher swamps and scrubland in the north of Argentina. This is a major agricultural migration. In these northern landscapes cattle have to contend with drought, flooding, poisonous snakes, vampire bats and piranhas. In 2007 it is estimated that 40 000 cattle died either through starvation or because of infected wounds from piranha bites. Temperatures can reach 40°C in the far north. The north of Argentina now contains more than a third of the country's cattle, compared with less than 10% in 2002.

The change from pastoral to arable farming has considerably increased chemical input onto the land. This is having a significant impact on the ecosystem. The World Wide Fund for Nature (WWF) is concerned that the Pampas is now being over-farmed. This is endangering wildlife, including South American ostriches, pumas and wildcats. The WWF is also concerned about the widespread destruction of native grasses.

Activities

1 For what purposes are soybeans produced?
2 To what extent has global soybean production increased?
3 Describe the trends illustrated in Figures 7 and 8 (page 100).
4 Describe and explain the relationship between the trends indicated in Figure 10.
5 Why has there been such environmental concern about the extension of soybean production in Brazil?
6 Describe the location of the Pampas.
7 Suggest why the Pampas developed into an important cattle rearing region.
8 Explain why so much of the grassland in the Pampas has been turned over to crop production.
9 What are the environmental concerns about such large-scale agricultural change?

Food miles and increasing air freight: environmental consequences

The term 'food miles' was first used in the 1990s by Dr Tim Lang, professor of food policy at London's City University, as part of the debate on sustainable agriculture. **Food miles** can be defined as the distance food travels from the farm where it is produced to the plate of the final consumer. It is an indication of the environmental impact of food consumption. In the UK, 95% of the fruit eaten and half the vegetables are imported. Increasingly these food imports have been transported by plane. Air transport emits more carbon dioxide per unit of transport than any other form of transport. Although food carried by air makes up less than 1% of total UK food miles, it accounts for about 11% of the total carbon dioxide emissions from UK food transport. Transport by air generates 177 times more greenhouse gases than water transport.

Most supermarkets now provide a home delivery service.

In the UK cars account for 20% of carbon dioxide emissions from food transport as consumers drive to and from supermarkets and other food stores. Sometimes food may be produced very close to the point where it is consumed, but because it may have to pass through a supermarket's national distribution system the food miles incurred may be far in excess of the straight-line distance between the points of production and consumption (Figure 11). Supermarket distribution now frequently operates on the 'just-in-time' principle, allowing the maximum possible floorspace to be used for sales and keeping storage areas to the minimum. The result is a high volume and complex network of vehicle deliveries. Such a system has pushed up the food miles total considerably.

The growing volume of air freight has resulted in increasing emissions of various pollutants, in particular carbon dioxide and nitrogen oxides. Fruit and vegetables are the main food products transported by air, but other food products such as animal feed are increasing in volume. Due to rising public concern, some large retailers now label fresh food transported by air with an airplane sticker.

Between 1961 and 1999 there was a four-fold increase in the amount of food exported. This considerable increase in food miles has a significant environmental impact. Trade-related transportation is one of the fastest-growing sources of greenhouse gas emissions.

However, it is important to remember that many other processes contribute to the carbon footprint of food, including:

- farming methods
- processing and packaging
- refrigeration.

For example:

- A 2005 Defra report in the UK found that it can be more energy efficient to import tomatoes from Spain by lorry than to grow them in a heated greenhouse in the UK.

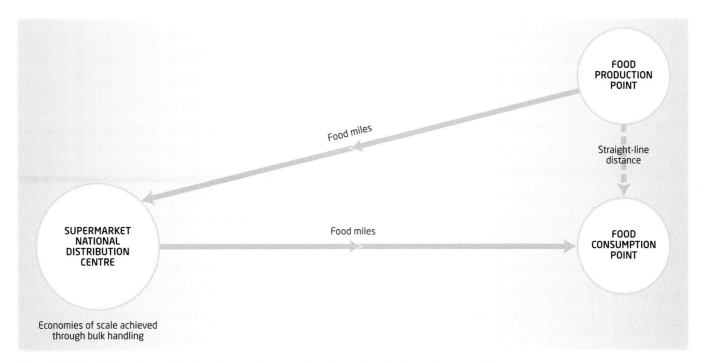

Figure 11 *Food miles – the straight-line distance between the points of production and consumption.*

- Lincoln University in New Zealand calculated that rearing and distributing British lamb produces more carbon dioxide emissions than the UK importing the meat 18 000 km by sea exporting from New Zealand.

Calculating the total environmental impact from point of production to point of consumption is known as the **life cycle**.

Although the concept of food miles has clear limitations as it is only one component of the life cycle of food, it has done much to stimulate the debate about the carbon footprint of food. In the UK, Tesco is working with the Carbon Trust to map the carbon footprint of various foods. The amount of food air freighted into the UK more than trebled between 1992 and 2008.

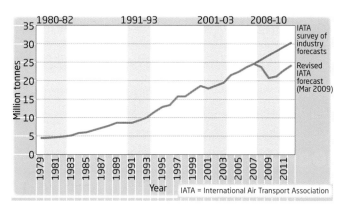

Figure 12 *International air freight, 1979–2009.*

Figure 12 shows the increase in international air freight from 1979 to 2009. The volume of freight flown internationally has risen more than five-fold since 1979. If domestic air freight is also included, global air freight reached a peak of 88.55 million tonnes in 2007 before a pronounced drop due to the global financial crisis. By

Market gardening in Egypt for both domestic consumption and for export.

value this amounted to 35–40% of world trade. Figure 13 shows how air freight rates have fallen since the mid 1950s as carriers have been able to achieve increasing **economies of scale**. This has been largely due to the expansion of long-haul passenger services providing significant bellyhold capacity for cargo. Other factors include the liberalisation of world trade and the change in the composition of world trade to lighter products. The most significant drop came in the early part of the period, illustrated by Figure 13. However, as concern grows about the environmental impact of air transport, the trend of falling rates may not continue.

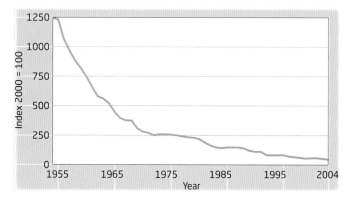

Figure 13 *Air freight rates, 1954–2004.*

Despite the fall in rates shown by Figure 13, air transport remains high cost relative to other modes of transport. Thus its use tends to be limited to specific categories of cargo:

- High value – products that are also usually low weight and where the cost of transport is relatively low compared with the value of the cargo. Examples include pharmaceuticals and high-value electrical equipment.

- Limited life cycle – for perishable goods such as fish and flowers, reducing transit time to a minimum is essential to ensure that goods arrive at their market in optimal condition.

- Process-critical – products required urgently, such as medicines and spare machinery parts.

Air freight falls into two categories:

- freight that uses the bellyhold capacity of scheduled passenger flights

- freight that is carried in dedicated freighters on routes with high volumes.

Global supply chains are often multimodal with freight changing between air and other forms of transport.

Multimodal supply chains and transshipment (goods loaded from one aircraft to another) mean that the distance freight travels may greatly exceed the distance between origin and destination.

In the UK, Defra has calculated the impact of dedicated air freighter emissions per tonne km as up to 10 times those of road transport and up to 43 times those of rail transport. The environmental impact of air freight is not uniform, but very much concentrated around key freight airports. In the UK, Heathrow handled 1.4 million tonnes of freight in 2008, 50% of the UK total.

The other main environmental issue, apart from air pollution, is noise which has become more and more of a contentious issue around major airports. The noise generated by air freight at night is a particular problem. Many freighter aircraft are converted passenger aircraft and generally older than those used for passenger services from UK airports. As such they tend to generate higher noise levels than their more modern equivalents. A recent study has highlighted the link between exposure to noise and ill health, noting in particular exposure to night-time aircraft noise and high blood pressure. The latter can lead to heart attacks and strokes.

Activities

1 Define the term 'food miles'.
2 Which other factors apart from food miles contribute to the life cycle of a food product?
3 How is it possible for the carbon footprint of a food product transported from Australia to the UK to be less than a similar product produced and consumed in the UK?
4 Explain the concept shown in Figure 11 (page 103).
5 Describe the growth in international freight transport illustrated in Figure 12 (page 104).
6 Describe and give the main reasons for the fall in air freight rates shown in Figure 13 (page 104).
7 What are the environmental problems associated with the substantial increase in air freight?

Review

Examination-style questions

1 **a** What are the reasons for the rapid growth of agro-industrialisation?

  b Discuss the environmental consequences of increasing international demand for one raw material.

2 **a** Why has the volume of air freight increased considerably in recent decades?

  b Discuss the environmental consequences of increasing volumes of air freight.

Websites

www.newscientist.com
New Scientist magazine

www.fao.org
Food and Agricultural Organization of the United Nations

www.geographical.co.uk
Geographical magazine

www.rainforestrelief.org
Rainforest Relief

www.panna.org
Pan North America Pesticide Network

Key terms

Agro-industrialisation the form of modern farming that refers to the industrialised production of livestock, poultry, fish and crops. It is typically large scale and capital intensive.

Green Revolution the introduction of high-yielding seeds and modern agricultural techniques in developing countries.

Organic farming the process of producing food naturally, avoiding the use of synthetic chemical fertilisers, pesticides, herbicides and genetically modified organisms to influence the growth of crops.

Food miles the distance food travels from the farm where it is produced to the plate of the final consumer.

Life cycle (of food) aggregate of emissions, waste and the resource use from soil to kitchen per unit of different food items.

Economies of scale the reduction in unit cost as the scale of an operation increases.

09 The effects of transnational manufacturing and services

Industrial factory emitting pollution.

The global shift of polluting industries

Transnational manufacturing and service companies have been relocating operations from developed to developing countries since the 1950s, but on a more significant scale over the past 30 years. There have been a number of reasons for such a global shift with the search for lower costs and cheaper labour in particular at the forefront of this activity. But as environmental legislation has become stricter and more costly to comply with in developed countries, this factor has become an increasingly important reason in global shift for polluting industries.

The process of global shift (or filter-down) has been detailed by W.R. Thompson and others. Economic core regions have long been vulnerable to the migration of labour-intensive manufacturing to lower-wage areas of the periphery. The filter-down process is based on the notion that corporate organisations respond to changing critical input requirements by altering the geographical location of production to minimise costs and thereby ensure competitiveness in a tightening market.

The economic core has monopolised invention and innovation, and has thus continually benefited from the rapid growth rates characteristic of the early stage of an industry's **product life cycle**, one of exploitation of a new market. Production is likely to occur where the firm's main plants and corporate headquarters are located. Figure 1 indicates that, in the early phase, scientific-engineering skills at a high level and external economies are the prime location factors. In the growth phase, methods of mass production are gradually introduced and the number of firms involved in production generally expands as product information spreads. At this stage management skills are the critical human inputs. Production technology tends to stabilise in the mature phase. Capital investment remains high and the availability of unskilled and semi-skilled labour becomes a major locating factor. As the industry matures into a replacement market the production process becomes rationalised and often routine. The high wages of the innovating area, quite consistent with the high-level skills required in the formative stages of the learning process, become excessive when the skill requirements decline and the industry, or a section of it, 'filters-down' to smaller, less industrially sophisticated areas where cheaper labour is available, but which can now handle the lower skills required in the manufacture of the product. On a global scale, large transnational companies have increasingly operated in this way since the 1950s by moving routine operations to the developing world.

How does the product life cycle help explain the global shift of manufacturing industry from developed to developing countries?

It has been the revolution in transport and communications that has made such substantial filter-down of manufacturing to the developing world possible. Containerisation and the general increase in scale of shipping have cut the cost of the overseas distribution of goods substantially, while advances in telecommunications have made global management a reality. In some cases whole industries have virtually migrated, as shipbuilding did from Europe to Asia in the 1970s. In others the most specialised work gets done in developed countries by skilled workers, and the simpler tasks elsewhere in the global supply chain.

Many of the manufacturing industries that have filtered down to developing countries have been significant polluters. While developing countries have reaped the economic benefits of global shift they have suffered the environmental consequences. At first the movement of polluting industries from developed to developing countries was mainly coincidental with lower labour costs. However, in the last 30 years or so with increasingly strict environmental legislation in developed countries, an increasing number of companies have made the 'global shift decision' more and more on environmental

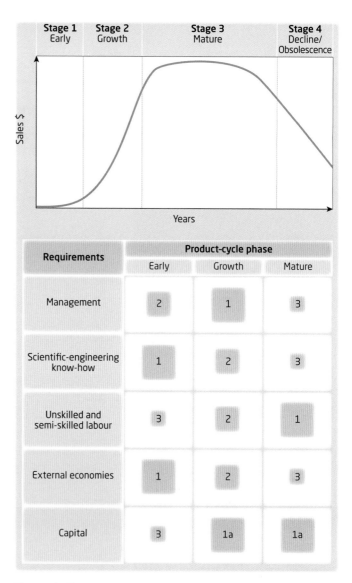

Requirements	Product-cycle phase		
	Early	Growth	Mature
Management	2	1	3
Scientific-engineering know-how	1	2	3
Unskilled and semi-skilled labour	3	2	1
External economies	1	2	3
Capital	3	1a	1a

Figure 1 *The product life cycle.*

grounds to avoid the often high costs of complying with environmental legislation in developed countries. Most developing countries have had weaker environmental legislation which has also often been poorly enforced.

Considering the intense use of energy and materials, levels of **pollution** are relatively low in the developed world because of global shift but also because industry has spent increasing amounts on research and development to reduce pollution – the so-called 'greening of industry'. Added to this has been the increasing concentration on service industries in developed economies, the so-called 'tertiarisation' of the economy.

Therefore the expectation is that after a certain stage of economic development in a country the level of pollution will decline. Figure 2 shows what has happened in many

Iron and steel works on the banks of Lake Michigan, USA.

countries as GDP increases. In the early and middle stages of industrialisation there is a strong positive correlation between rising GDP and pollution. However, as the population of a country becomes more affluent and begins to look beyond income to the wider aspects of the quality of life, and as pollution becomes more and more of a problem, the government will act to contain and eventually reduce pollution. Complying with stricter environmental legislation can be a costly affair for business. One consequence is that companies engaged in the most polluting activities frequently look to developing economies where environmental controls and safety regulations are weaker. As this usually also coincides with lower wages, there is often a powerful incentive to move.

Types and amounts of pollution change with economic development. In low-income economies where primary industries frequently dominate, pollution related to agriculture and mining often predominates. As countries industrialise, manufacturing industries, energy production and transport become major polluters. The focal points of pollution will be the large urban-industrial complexes. The newly industrialised countries of the world are in this stage. In contrast, the developed countries have experienced **deindustrialisation** as many of their major polluting industries have filtered down or relocated to NICs. This has resulted in improved environmental conditions in many developed countries in general, although pollution from transportation has often increased.

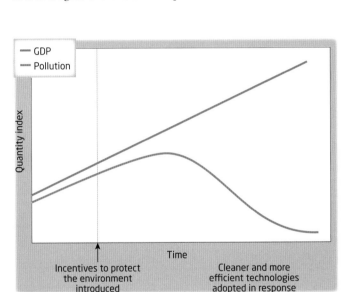

Figure 2 *Theory of the relationship between GDP and pollution.*

The **Kuznets curve** is a graph representing Simon Kuznets's theory. It was originally developed to show how inequality in a country changes over time. Economic inequality increases at first as a country develops. Then, after a critical average income is reached, inequality begins to decrease. However, the curve has also been applied to environmental degradation (Figure 3). The rationale for the environmental Kuznets curve is as follows:

- In the early stages of industrialisation the focus is on economic development with little concern for the environment. Pollution levels increase rapidly.

- After a certain standard of living is reached and pollution is at its highest, attitudes to pollution change and there is now a general desire to tackle the problem.

- With increasing environmental investment, pollution levels fall.

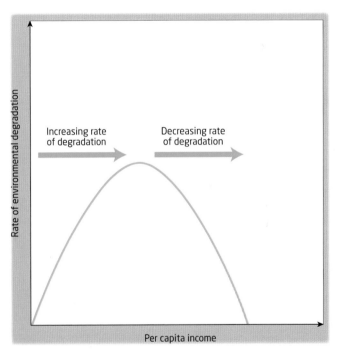

Figure 3 *The environmental Kuznets curve.*

Theory of Knowledge

The Kuznets curve is an example of a theory that has had its application expanded over time. Initially developed to show how economic inequality in a country changes over time, it has also been applied to environmental degradation. Can you think of examples where models that were developed in one sphere have been applied elsewhere?

Derelict factory in France – a legacy of deindustrialisation.

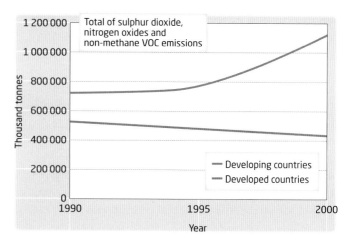

Figure 4 *Air pollution trends in developed and developing countries, 1990–2000.*

In the USA and the UK the proportion of workers employed in manufacturing has fallen from around 40% at the beginning of the 20th century to less than half that now. Even in Japan and Germany, where so much industry was rebuilt after 1945, manufacturing's share of total employment has dropped below 25%. Not a single developed country has bucked this trend, the causal factors being:

- technological change enabling manufacturing to become more capital intensive and more mobile
- the filter-down of manufacturing industry from developed countries to lower-wage economies, such as those of South-east Asia
- the increasing importance of the service sector in the developed economies.

There can be little surprise in the decline of manufacturing employment for it has mirrored the previous decline in employment in agriculture in the developed world.

Figure 4 shows changing air pollution trends in developed and developing countries between 1990 and 2000. It shows a slow but steady decline in developed countries and a very significant rise in developing countries from the mid 1990s. This is partly due to the relocation of industries from developed countries, but also due to indigenous industrial development at a range of scales, and to rapid urbanisation.

The threat to human health

Virtually every substance is toxic at a certain dosage. In many parts of the developing world levels of **toxicity** are alarmingly high. The most serious polluters are the large-scale processing industries which tend to form agglomerations as they have similar locational requirements (Figure 5). The impact of a large industrial agglomeration may spread well beyond the locality and region to cross international borders. As heavy industrial agglomerations have declined in the developed world they have become

Modern business park in Gurgaon, India – most employment is now in the service sector.

Industrial sector	Examples
Fuel and power	Power stations, oil refineries
Mineral industries	Cement, glass, ceramics
Waste disposal	Incineration, chemical recovery
Chemicals	Pesticides, pharmaceuticals, organic and inorganic chemicals
Metal industries	Iron and steel, smelting, non-ferrous metals
Others	Paper manufacture, timber preparation, uranium processing

Figure 5 *The most polluting industries.*

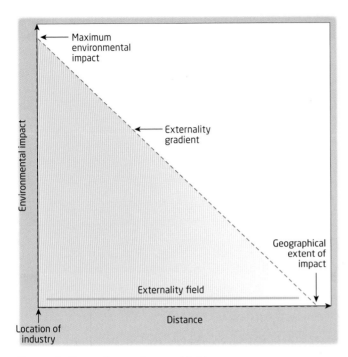

Figure 6 *Externality gradient and field.*

Heavy pollution in Seoul, South Korea.

causing activities, declining with distance from such concentrations (Figure 6). For some sources of pollution it is possible to map the **externality field** and gradient. In general, health risk is greatest immediately around the source of pollution and the risk decreases with distance from the source. However, atmospheric conditions and other factors can complicate this pattern.

Exposure to pollution can result in health effects (Figure 7) that range from fairly minor to severe. These include:

- skin irritation
- nose irritation
- fatigue
- breathing problems

more prevalent in developing countries, bringing with them a range of advantages and disadvantages. Many newly industrialised countries have huge industrial agglomerations illustrating horizontal and vertical linkages such as the proximity of oil storage, oil refining and petrochemicals.

Pollution is the major **externality** of industrial and urban areas. It is at its most intense at the focus of pollution-

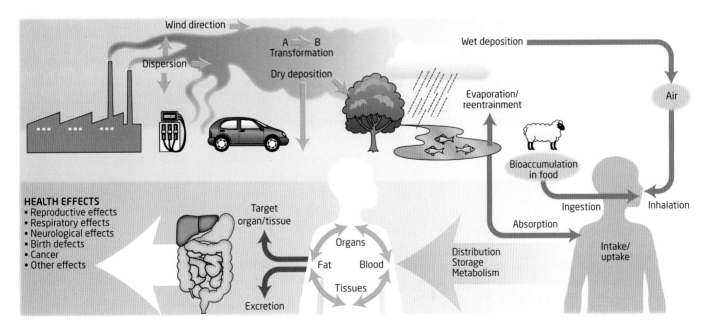

Figure 7 *How exposure to pollution can affect human health.*

- changes in behaviour
- changes in immune system response
- headaches
- blood disorders
- cancer.

Cancer is an example of a delayed health problem that may be a result of long-term exposure to a chemical. In poorer countries the link between polluting industry and ill health is often not recognised until a substantial number of people have been affected.

China: growth and pollution

The Chinese economy has now attained such a size and is growing so rapidly that it is being called the 'new workshop of the world', a phrase first applied to the UK during the height of its Industrial Revolution in the 19th century. China's rapid economic growth has led to widespread environmental problems. In the last 20 years China has been in receipt of a very high level of foreign direct investment. Much of this has gone into manufacturing and China is now undertaking many industrial tasks that were once commonplace in the developed world.

The Pearl river delta region, an area the size of Belgium in south-east China, is the focal point of a massive wave of foreign investment. The Pearl river drains into the South China Sea. Hong Kong is located at the eastern limit of the delta, with Macau situated at the western entrance. Within the region the main centres of industrial expansion are Shunde, Shenzhen, Dongguan, Zhuhai, Zhongshan and Guangzhou. The region's manufacturing industries employ more than 30 million people but this will undoubtedly increase in the future. There is increasing concern over environmental pollution. The entire delta is heavily polluted, with the worst problems around Guangzhou.

The three major environmental problems in the Pearl river delta are air and water pollution and deforestation. In 2007, eight out of every ten rainfalls in Guangzhou were classified as acid rain. The high concentration of factories and power stations is the source of this problem, along with the growing number of cars in the province. The city has the worst acid rain problem in the province of Guangdong. The province's environmental protection bureau has reported that two-thirds of Guangdong's 21 cities were affected by acid rain in 2007. Overall, 45% of the province's rainfall in 2007 was classified as acid rain.

Research idea

Find out more about the mix of industries in the Pearl river delta and what is being done to tackle the pollution problem.

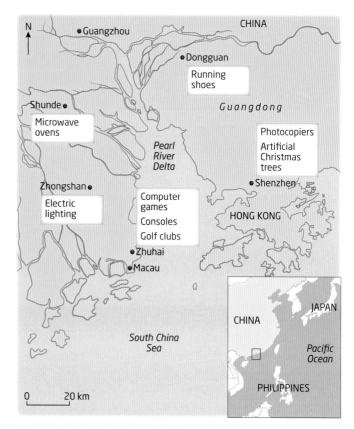

Figure 8 *The Pearl river delta, China.*

Pollution problems are so severe in some areas of China that the term 'cancer villages' has become commonplace. In the village of Xiditou south-east of Beijing the cancer rate is 30 times the national average. This has been blamed on water and air contaminated by chemical factories. Tests on tap water have found traces of highly carcinogenic benzene that were 50% above national safe limits. In the rush for economic growth, local governments eagerly built factories, but they had very limited experience of environmental controls.

A World Bank study of air quality found that 16 of the 20 most polluted cities in the world are in China. The State Environmental Protection Administration has stated that

Linfen has the worst air quality in the country. Levels of sulphur dioxide and other particulates are many times higher than limits set by the World Health Organization. Figure 9 shows the top ten most polluted locations in the world according to a report published by the Blacksmith Institute in September 2007.

The Chinese government admits that 300 million people drink polluted water. This comes from polluted rivers and groundwater. Thirty thousand children die of diarrhoea or other water-borne illnesses each year. The river Liao is the most polluted, followed by waterways around Tianjin and the river Huai.

Pollution in China is still increasing, but it is hoped that concerted action will cause pollution levels to fall in the future. The scale of pollution in China has a global impact. China is already the world's second biggest producer of greenhouse gases, due largely to the burning of fossil fuels in industry and energy production. China and other major greenhouse gas emitters are coming under strong pressure to reduce emissions. All countries agree that this is necessary, but at the recent Climate Change Conference in Copenhagen (December 2009) they found it difficult to agree exactly how this should be done.

Site name and location	Major pollutants and sources	Scope of the problem and human health impact	Clean-up status
Sumgayit, Azerbaijan	Organic chemicals and mercury, from petrochemical and industrial complexes	Dated technologies, a lack of pollution controls and improper disposal of industrial waste have left the city contaminated.	Various multilateral development agencies, international banks and governments have invested money to do the clean-up.
Linfen, China	Particulates and gases from industry and traffic	Expanding and unregulated industry based on local coal and other resources has resulted in the worst air quality in China. There are high incidences of respiratory and skin diseases and lung cancer.	The local government plans to shut down more than 200 factories by the end of 2007 and replace them with clean and better regulated facilities.
Tianying, China	Heavy metals and particulates; industry	Average lead content in the air and soil are up to ten times higher than national standards. Children suffer from birth defects and developmental challenges.	The State Environmental Protection Administration has ordered all lead processing firms to be shut down until they address environmental impacts.
Sukinda, India	Hexavalent chromium; chromite mines	Waste rock and untreated water from the mines pollutes local water supplies. The air and soils are also heavily affected. Residents suffer from gastrointestinal bleeding, tuberculosis and asthma. Infertility and birth defects are common.	Some piecemeal actions have been taken by mining companies but the scale of the problems is 'beyond the means of the State to solve'.
Vapi, India	Wide variety of industry effluents; industrial estates	More than 50 industrial estates discharge heavy metals, pesticides and chemical waste. Mercury in the groundwater is 96 times higher than WHO standards. Very high incidences of cancer and birth complications have resulted.	A number of waste facilities have been constructed but serious problems persist, despite pressure from environmental agencies and NGOs. No comprehensive plan for the area has been proposed.
La Oroya, Peru	Lead and other heavy metals; mining and metal processing	Metal mining and smelting over 80 years has caused significant lead contamination. Blood lead levels for children average 33.6 g/dl, triple WHO limits.	The current owner, Doe Run, has made some investments in the operating plant but the legacy issues have not been addressed.

Figure 9 *The top ten most polluted locations in the world. (Continued overleaf.)*

Site name and location	Major pollutants and sources	Scope of the problem and human health impact	Clean-up status
Dzerzhinsk, Russia	Chemicals and toxic by-products, lead; chemical weapons and industrial manufacturing	A major site for Cold War era manufacturing where industrial chemicals have been discharged into the local water supplies. Life expectancy is short and the death rate is significantly higher than Russia's average.	A number of isolated efforts have been undertaken in individual villages but no major clean-up activity has been undertaken.
Norilsk, Russia	Heavy metals, particulates; mining and smelting	Mining and smelting operations have devastated the area with particulates and heavy metal pollution. Norilsk Nickel is the biggest air polluting industrial enterprise in Russia.	Norilsk Nickel has begun to implement plans for some emissions controls. There is as yet little visible improvement.
Chernobyl, Ukraine	Radioactive materials; nuclear reactor explosion	The legacy of this most infamous of nuclear disasters lingers and has resulted in thousands of cancer deaths. Respiratory, ear, nose and throat diseases are common ailments.	Most residents have moved and some remediation projects have been implemented. Future health impacts are possible.
Kabwe, Zambia	Lead; mining and smelting	Unregulated lead mining and smelting operations resulted in lead dust covering large areas. Children's blood lead levels average between 50 and 100 g/dl – up to ten times the recommended maximum.	The World Bank has begun a $40 million remediation programme with the government of Gambia, initiated with Blacksmith involvement.

Note: Sites are not ranked, but in alphabetical order of country.

Figure 9 (continued) *The top ten most polluted locations in the world.*

Activities

1   Explain the trends illustrated in Figure 2 (page 109).
2   **a** Describe the data presented in Figure 4 (page 110).
    b To what extent does Figure 4 correspond to the environmental Kuznets curve shown in Figure 3 (page 109)?
3   With reference to Figure 5 (page 110), identify the industries that contribute most to pollution.
4   Discuss the ways in which exposure to pollution can affect human health.
5   Select four of the industrial locations identified in Figure 9. For each location discuss (a) the causes of pollution, (b) the scope and impact of the problem and **c** what is being done to reduce the environmental impact.

Waste disposal: dumpers and dustbins

Transboundary dumping of hazardous waste refers to the export, often illegal, of hazardous waste by developed and industrialised countries to developing nations. Increasingly the Sub-Saharan African countries have become the focus of this activity. Hazardous waste is the inevitable by-product of industrial development and several manufacturing processes. It is costly to process and an unpopular activity in affluent nations.

As environmental legislation has tightened in the developed world, many poorer countries have become dustbins for unwanted waste. In 1990 the UN estimated that one-tenth of the waste produced worldwide each year was being shipped from the developed world to the developing world, with Asia the main recipient. Legislation has tightened in many developing countries since then and a number of important international agreements have been signed, but illegal movements still continue because of the amount of money involved. Not all countries have signed up to the Basle Convention (1989) and the Basle Ban Amendment (1995), which ban the export of hazardous materials, and those that have signed up continue to find ways to circumvent the provisions. This has led to an increase in the environmental problems associated with the export of hazardous waste.

Urban waste pollution in Accra, Ghana.

Greenpeace has identified four reasons for the increasing export of hazardous waste to Sub-Saharan Africa:

- Poverty – Guinea Bissau, one of the poorest countries in the world, was to be paid $600 million for storing and disposing of imported hazardous waste. At the time of the offer, the amount was twice the country's foreign debt.

- Lack of stringent environmental regulations – toxic waste treatment and disposal facilities can be built relatively cheaply and without considerations for adverse human health and environmental effects. In Dakar, Senegal, the hazardous waste landfill is built very close to the water table thereby posing a threat to the drinking water supply of the estimated 2.5 million residents of the country's capital city.

- High level of corruption – government officials can easily be bribed to surreptitiously import toxic waste into their country. The unregulated dumping of toxic waste on Kassa Island in Guinea involved the collaboration of a Guinean company and the complicity of some officials of the country's Ministry of Trade.

- Lack of technical expertise – exporting companies are aware of this and often disguise hazardous wastes as useful commodities that are relatively harmless. Within this context, the wastes are often shipped or labelled as recyclables, liquid fertilisers, road construction or brick-making materials.

In many Sub-Saharan countries there is a general lack of awareness of the effects of hazardous waste and its residue. There have been examples of people using the empty containers of illegally dumped hazardous waste for domestic purposes, including the storage of drinking water. Adverse health effects of improperly managed hazardous waste may be exacerbated because of the high prevalence of infectious diseases and low nutritional status which may reduce people's physiological defence against toxic substances. In addition, many countries lack adequate health care facilities and the personnel that are necessary for the diagnosis and treatment of health problems related to hazardous waste. Apart from the health effects, the dumping of hazardous waste in Sub-Saharan Africa has moral undertones, an issue that some African leaders have taken up at international conferences.

Discussion point

What are your views on the transfer of waste from developed to developing countries?

E-waste

E-waste often ends up dumped in countries with little or no regulation of its recycling or disposal. Historically this has taken place in Asia, but recently the trade has spread to other regions, particularly West Africa.

Greenpeace, 2008

ICT has been an important development tool in many countries, but there is a downside: e-waste. Modern electronics contain up to 60 different elements, many valuable, some hazardous, and some both. E-waste is a growing problem in all countries because of the rapid spread of ICT. E-waste includes items such as printers, mobile phones, pagers, laptop computers, toys and televisions. Technological advance is so rapid that there is a high and ever increasing turnover of products with an escalating amount of equipment becoming obsolete. The lifespan of computing equipment decreased from 4–6 years in 1997 to 2–4 years in 2005.

A report released by the UN Environment Programme (UNEP) in February 2010 revealed that developing nations such as China, India, South Africa and Morocco are experiencing a growing pile of e-waste issues with the rise in popularity of electronics. The consequences could be damaging to public health and the local environments if not addressed correctly. Currently, over 40 million tonnes of e-waste is being generated globally per year. This rising figure has caused UN experts to warn countries that action must be taken to prevent disastrous consequences. The UNEP predicts that in India e-waste from old computers will have risen by 500% by 2010 compared with 2007 levels. In South Africa and China this increase is predicted to be between 200% and 400%.

The report was revealed at the newly opened three-day meeting of the Basle Convention. The report said China produced about 2.3 million tonnes of e-waste domestically a year, second only to the USA with 3 million tonnes. More e-waste is expected to pile up in developing countries in the wake of rapidly rising sales and aggressive marketing of mobile phones and other electronic appliances. Basle Action Network say around 50–100 containers of e-waste arrive at Chinese ports each year, many from the USA. The network tracked nine containers of hazardous e-waste from an e-waste collection facility in the USA and found the containers were shipped to Indonesia, but it managed to foil the attempt by contacting the Indonesian authorities (Figure 10). The containers were then sent back to the USA.

In August 2008, the environmental organisation Greenpeace highlighted Ghana as a major recipient of foreign e-waste in an article entitled 'Poisoning the Poor – Electronic Waste in Ghana'. Previously Greenpeace had brought the attention of the world to similar practices in China, India and Nigeria. The Ghana analysis was based on samples and observations taken at two e-waste scrapyards.

Containers filled with e-waste arrived from Germany, Korea, Switzerland and the Netherlands under the false label of 'second-hand goods'. Exporting e-waste from Europe is illegal but exporting old electronics for 'reuse' allows unscrupulous traders to profit from dumping old electronics in Ghana. The majority of the containers' contents end up in Ghana's scrapyards to be crushed and burned by unprotected workers. This waste is often laden with toxic chemicals such as lead, mercury and brominated flame retardants. Most workers, many of them children, wear no protective clothing or equipment. Boys were observed burning electronic cables and other components to melt the plastic and reclaim the copper wiring, releasing

RI congratulated for rejecting e-waste from US
Tuesday, February 23, 2010

Nusa Dua, Bali (ANTARA News) – The Basel Action Network has praised Indonesia for turning down nine containers of e-waste (electronic waste) from the United States last November 2009.

'Last night, I congratulated the Indonesian environmental affairs minister for the Indonesian authorities' diligent action,' Jim Puckett, coordinator of Basel Action Network (BAN), said here on Monday.

Old computer monitors in the nine containers are considered hazardous e-waste for containing lead, he said when speaking to journalists attending a United Nations Environment Program (UNEP) Workshop on 'Reporting Green – Environment as News'.

He said e-waste was a problem which could poison the people. Some children working in electronic companies have lead in their blood which later could damage their brain. A similar problem could be found in China, India and Nigeria, he said.

The e-waste coming from Massachusetts was about to enter Semarang, Central Java, last November. But, thanks to a tip-off from BAN, the Indonesian authorities managed to foil the smuggling attempt.

In accordance with Indonesia's law, hazardous import was banned, while for the US, which has not yet ratified the Basel Convention, the export was legal, he said.

Besides the US, Afghanistan and Haiti are yet to ratify the Basel Convention.

An attempt was made to dump used computer monitors in Indonesia because it was cheaper to export than recycle them, he said.

Figure 10 *News from Indonesia.*

toxic chemicals in the process. Plastic and other materials perceived to be of no value were either burned or dumped. Some samples contained toxic metals as much as 100 times above background levels. A significant number of samples contained chemicals known to interfere with sexual reproduction. Other samples contained chemicals that can affect brain development and the nervous system.

The e-waste problem is becoming particularly serious in developing countries due to:

- a lack of legislation and enforcement
- a lack of controlled take-back systems
- informal sector dominance in recycling

- a lack of awareness by government, institutions and the general public
- illegal importation of e-waste from developing countries, often using false documentation
- the increasing outsourcing of ICT from developed to developing countries.

Discussion point

How much e-waste does your class create during the course of a year?

Chemical and nuclear waste

In 2008, Ahmedou Ould-Abdallah, the UN envoy for Somalia, confirmed to news organisations that the UN had 'reliable information' that European and Asian companies were dumping toxic waste, including nuclear waste, off the Somali coastline. Allegations of the dumping of toxic waste in this region have circulated since the early 1990s. The lack of effective government in Somalia over the last two decades has made it a relatively easy target for the dumpers. The UN envoy stated that the dumping of waste helped fuel the 18-year-old civil war in Somalia as companies were paying Somali government ministers to dump their waste, or to secure licences and contracts. Waste has been traced back to Swiss and Italian shipping firms. There have been claims that the Italian mafia controls an estimated 30% of Italy's waste disposal companies, including those that deal with toxic waste.

The UNEP reported that the tsunami of 2004 had washed up rusting containers of toxic waste along the Somali coastline. Nick Nuttall, a UNEP spokesman, said:

> European companies found it to be very cheap to get rid of the waste, costing as little as $2.50 a tonne, where waste disposal costs in Europe are something like $1000 a tonne. There is uranium radioactive waste. There is lead, and heavy metals like cadmium and mercury. There is also industrial waste, and there are hospital wastes, chemical wastes – you name it.

George Monbiot has recently highlighted another example of the dumping of toxic waste in Africa (Figure 11). The country affected in this case is Ivory Coast (Côte d'Ivoire).

Tell people something they know already and they will thank you for it. Tell them something new and they will hate you for it.

The Trafigura scandal is just one of thousands of cases of the rich world's fly-tipping.

It was revolting, monstrous, inhumane – and scarcely different from what happens in Africa almost every day. The oil trading company Trafigura has just agreed to pay compensation to 31 000 people in Cote d'Ivoire, after the Guardian and the BBC's Newsnight obtained emails sent by its traders. They reveal that Trafigura knew that the oil slops it sent there in 2006 were contaminated with toxic waste. But the Ivorian contractor it employed to pump out the hold of its tanker dumped them around inhabited areas in the capital city and the countryside. Tens of thousands of people fell ill and 15 died. It is one of the world's worst cases of chemical exposure since the gas leak at the Union Carbide factory in Bhopal. But in all other respects the Trafigura case is unremarkable. It's just another instance of the rich world's global fly-tipping.

The Trafigura story is a metaphor for corporate capitalism.

The effort of all enterprises is to keep the profits and dump the costs on someone else. Price risks are dumped on farmers, health and safety risks are dumped on subcontractors, insolvency risks are dumped on creditors, social and economic risks are dumped on the state, toxic waste is dumped on the poor, greenhouse gases are dumped on everyone.

By George Monbiot.

Figure 11 *Toxic assets,* The Guardian, *2009.*

Monbiot classes this example as one of the worst cases of chemical exposure in recent decades. The crisis began in 2006 when a ship unloaded 500 tonnes of petrochemical waste into a number of trucks which then dumped it in at least 15 sites around Abidjan, the West African country's largest city with about 5 million inhabitants.

The waste contained a mixture of petroleum distillates, hydrogen sulphide, mercaptans, phenolic compounds and sodium hydroxide. The symptoms of those people affected included nosebleeds, nausea and vomiting, headaches, skin and eye irritation and respiratory symptoms. During the first days after the waste was dumped, the most severely affected patients presented respiratory distress, dehydration and intestinal bleeding. Following a formal request from the Ivorian government, UNEP conducted an investigation through the Secretariat of the Basle Convention on the Transboundary Movement of Hazardous Wastes and their Disposal, which it administers.

Nuclear waste has always been one of the main issues in a country's decision to introduce or continue with nuclear energy as a source of power. Until a few years ago the future of nuclear power looked bleak with a number of countries apparently 'running down' their nuclear power stations and many other nations firmly set against the idea of introducing nuclear electricity. However, heightened fears about oil supplies, energy security and climate change have brought this controversial source of power back onto the global energy agenda. This means the nuclear waste issue is right back at the forefront of the global environmental agenda.

Most concern is over the small proportion of 'high-level waste'. This is so radioactive it generates heat and corrodes all containers. It would cause death within a few days to anyone directly exposed to it. As an example in the UK this type of waste amounts to about 0.3% of the total volume of all nuclear waste; however, it accounts for about half the total radioactivity. No country has yet implemented a long-term solution to the nuclear waste problem. The USA and Finland have plans to build waste repositories deep underground in areas of known geological stability.

Activities

1   Discuss the reasons identified by Greenpeace for the increasing export of hazardous waste to Sub-Saharan Africa.
2   Why has e-waste become a major global environmental problem?
3   Discuss the causes and consequences of the dumping of chemical and nuclear waste in developing countries.

Review
Examination-style questions

1 Look at Figure 12.

  a Describe the locational change taking place in the global chemical industry.

  b Discuss the reasons for and consequences of this relocation.

2 **a** Why is domestic production of e-waste in developing countries increasing at such a rapid rate?

  b Discuss the causes and consequences of the dumping of e-waste in developing countries by more affluent nations.

The chemical industry has been growing rapidly for more than 50 years. The fastest-growing sectors have been in the manufacture of synthetic organic polymers used as plastics, fibres and elastomers. The chemical industry has until now been concentrated in three parts of the world: North America, Western Europe and Japan. The EU remains the largest producer area, followed by the USA and Japan.

The traditional dominance of chemical production by the countries in these regions is now being challenged by changes in materials availability and price, labour cost, energy cost, differential rates of economic growth and environmental pressures. The changing structure of the global chemical industry has also been influenced by economic growth in China, India, Korea, South-east Asia, Indonesia, Nigeria, the Middle East, Trinidad, Thailand, Brazil and Venezuela.

Figure 12

Key terms

Product life cycle the pattern of sales in the life of a product usually divided into four stages: early, growth, maturity and decline.

Pollution contamination of the environment. It can take many forms – air, water, soil, noise, visual and others.

Kuznets curve a graph with measures of increased economic development on the horizontal axis, and measures of income inequality on the vertical axis. Hypothesised by Kuznets in 1955, it has an inverted U-shape. The environmental Kuznets curve shows the rate of environmental degradation on the vertical axis.

Deindustrialisation the long-term absolute decline of employment in manufacturing.

Toxicity a measure of the degree to which something is poisonous. It is often expressed as a dose–response relationship.

Externality the side-effects, positive and negative, of an economic activity that are experienced beyond its site.

Externality field the geographical area within which externalities are experienced.

Websites

www.recycle.co.uk
Recycle.co.uk

www.timesonline.co.uk
Times Online

www.world-nuclear.org
World Nuclear Association

www.greenpeace.org
Greenpeace International

www.eoearth.org
The Encyclopedia of Earth

4 Environmental change

10 Transboundary pollution

KEY QUESTIONS

- To what extent did the Chernobyl nuclear accident affect its country of origin and other countries?
- What were the consequences of and response to this major pollution event?
- How has environmental awareness increased as a result of Chernobyl and other major pollution events?
- What has been the role of Greenpeace in fostering improved environmental management?

Polluting factory in Maine, USA - close to the border with Canada.

Of all types of pollution, air pollution has the most widespread effects on human health. Air pollution affects people at a range of scales from local to global. In many parts of the developing world indoor air pollution is more severe than that experienced outdoors. This is the result of the use of biomass fuels for cooking and heating.

The methods of exposure to pollutants are:

- breathing in chemical vapours and dust (inhalation)
- drinking or eating the chemical (ingestion)
- absorbing the chemical through the skin (absorption).

The Great Wall of China – visibility is often impaired due to pollution from industrial areas.

It is important to consider the different impact on health between one-off pollution incidents (**incidental pollution**) and longer-term pollution (**sustained pollution**). The former is mainly linked to major accidents caused by technological failures and human error. Causes of the latter include ozone depletion and global warming. Some of the worst examples of incidental pollution are shown in Figure 1.

Major examples of incidental pollution such as Chernobyl and Bhopal can have extremely long-lasting consequences which are often difficult to determine in the earlier stages. The effects of both accidents are still being felt more than two decades after they occurred.

Location	Causes and consequences
Seveso, Italy	In July 1976 a reactor at a chemical factory near Seveso in northern Italy exploded, sending a toxic cloud into the atmosphere. An 18 km² area of land was contaminated with the dioxin TCDD. The immediate after-effects – a small number of people with skin inflammation – were relatively mild. However, the long-term impact has been much worse. The population is suffering increased numbers of premature deaths from cancer, cardiovascular disease and diabetes.
Bhopal, India	A chemical factory owned by Union Carbide leaked deadly methyl isocyanate gas during the night of 3 December 1984. The plant was operated by a separate Indian subsidiary which worked to much lower safety standards than those required in the USA. It has been estimated that 8000 people died within two weeks and a further 8000 have since died from gas-related diseases. The NGO Greenpeace puts the total fatality figure at over 20 000. Bhopal is recognised as the world's worst industrial disaster.
Chernobyl, Ukraine	The world's worst nuclear power plant accident occurred at Chernobyl, Ukraine, in April 1986. Reactor number four exploded, sending a plume of highly radioactive fallout into the atmosphere which drifted over extensive parts of Europe and eastern North America. Two people died in the initial explosion and over 336 000 people were evacuated and resettled. In total 56 direct deaths and an estimated 4000 extra cancer deaths have been attributed to Chernobyl. The estimated cost of $200 billion makes Chernobyl the most expensive disaster in modern history.
Harbin, China	An explosion at a large petrochemical plant in the north-east Chinese city of Harbin released toxic pollutants into a major river. Benzene levels were 108 times above national safety levels. Benzene is a highly poisonous toxin which is also carcinogenic. Water supplies to the city were suspended. Five people were killed in the blast and more than 60 injured. Ten thousand residents were temporarily evacuated.

Figure 1 *Major examples of incidental pollution.*

It is usually the poorest people in a society who are exposed to the risks from both incidental and sustained pollution. In the USA the geographical distribution of minority race groups and the poor has been found to be highly correlated to the distribution of air pollution, municipal landfills and incinerators, abandoned toxic waste dumps, and lead poisoning in children. The race correlation is even stronger than the class correlation. Unequal environmental protection undermines three basic types of equity:

- procedural equity – the extent that planning procedures, rules and regulations are applied in a non-discriminatory way
- geographical equity – the proximity of communities to environmental hazards and locally unwanted land uses such as smelters, refineries, sewage treatment plants and incinerators
- social equity – the role of race and class in environmental decision making.

Ironically some government actions have created and exacerbated environmental inequity. More stringent environmental regulations have driven noxious facilities to follow the path of least resistance towards poor, overburdened communities where protesters lack the financial clout and professional skills of affluent areas, or where the prospects of bringing in much needed jobs justifies the risks in the view of some residents.

Research idea

When was the last significant pollution incident in the country in which you live? What happened and what was done to try to reduce the effects of this incident?

Activities

1 Define 'pollution'.
2 What are the three methods of exposure to pollutants?
3 Explain the difference between incidental pollution and sustained pollution.
4 Why are poor people more likely to live close to polluting activities than middle- and higher-income people in the same country?

The nuclear disaster at Chernobyl, Ukraine

Although there have been many more recent pollution events affecting more than one country, none has been as serious than the world's worst nuclear accident which occurred on 26 April 1986. This was when testing of reactor number four in the Chernobyl power plant triggered a meltdown of the reactor's core, leading to the only Level 7 event on the International Nuclear Event Scale. The result was a severe release of radioactivity following a massive explosion that destroyed the reactor. Figure 4 explains exactly what happened in more detail. Most fatalities from the accident were caused by radiation poisoning.

An aerial view of the destroyed nuclear reactor at Chernobyl.

The V.I. Lenin Memorial Chernobyl Nuclear Power Station is located in Ukraine (Figure 2), near the town of Pripyat, which had been built to house power station employees and

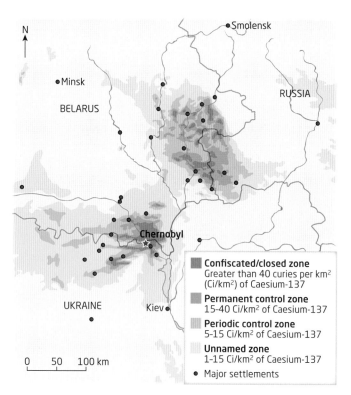

Figure 2 *Location of Chernobyl and radiation hotspots in Ukraine, Belarus and Russia.*

their families. The power station is near the Ukraine–Belarus border, approximately 18 km north-west of the city of Chernobyl and 100 km north of Kiev, the capital of Ukraine. The border with Russia is about 150 km to the north-east. Ukraine also has borders with Poland, Slovakia, Hungary, Romania and Moldova. At the time of the accident Ukraine was part of the Soviet Union. It became independent in 1991 when the Soviet Union was dissolved.

The Chernobyl nuclear power station housed four nuclear reactors which produced about 10% of Ukraine's electricity. Construction of the plant began in the late 1970s, with reactor number one commissioned in 1977. This was followed by number two in 1978, number three in 1981, and number four in 1983. Each reactor had a capacity of 1 gigawatt (GW) of electricity. When the accident occurred in 1986, two other nuclear reactors, also with a capacity of 1 gigawatt each, were under construction.

The radioactive plume resulting from the accident drifted over large parts of eastern, western and northern Europe, with some nuclear rain falling as far west as Ireland. Radionuclides were measurable in all countries of the northern hemisphere. Large areas in Ukraine, Belarus and Russia were badly contaminated, resulting in the evacuation and resettlement of more than 336 000 people.

It has been estimated that about 60% of the radioactive fallout landed in Belarus. The accident caused serious social and psychological disruption in the lives of those affected and vast economic losses over the entire region. Many economic sectors were affected, but agriculture was particularly badly hit. Figure 2 shows the radiation hotspots in the three worst-affected countries. The two main concentrations of very high-level radiation straddled (a) the Ukraine–Belarus border and (b) the Belarus–Russian border. Figure 3 illustrates the wider European impact of radiation from Chernobyl. A significant number of other countries were affected. At the time of the accident there was great uncertainty about the scope and extent of radiation from Chernobyl. Certainly the worst-case scenarios did not materialise.

The very large differences in the deposition of radioactive materials were due mainly to variations in meteorological conditions during and after the accident and were especially influenced by patterns of rainfall. In some cases, high deposition levels necessitated the introduction of restrictions on the distribution and consumption of foodstuffs. Figure 4 details the levels of exposure of individuals.

One hundred times more radiation was released than by the atomic bombs dropped over the Japanese cities of Hiroshima and Nagasaki in August 1945. Of 600 workers present at the power plant during the early morning of 26 April 1986, 134 received high doses of radiation (0.7–13.4 Gy) and suffered from radiation sickness. Twenty-eight of these workers died in the first three months and another 19 died between 1987 and 2004 of various causes not necessarily associated with radiation exposure. During 1986 and 1987 around 450,000 recovery operation workers received radiation doses of between 0.01 and 1 GY. This group is at potential risk of later consequences such as cancer.

Today, the 19-mile exclusion zone around the reactor remains uninhabitable. Over 5 million people currently live in the affected areas of Ukraine, Russia and Belarus which have been classified as 'contaminated' with radionuclides from the accident. Within this area, skin lesions, respiratory

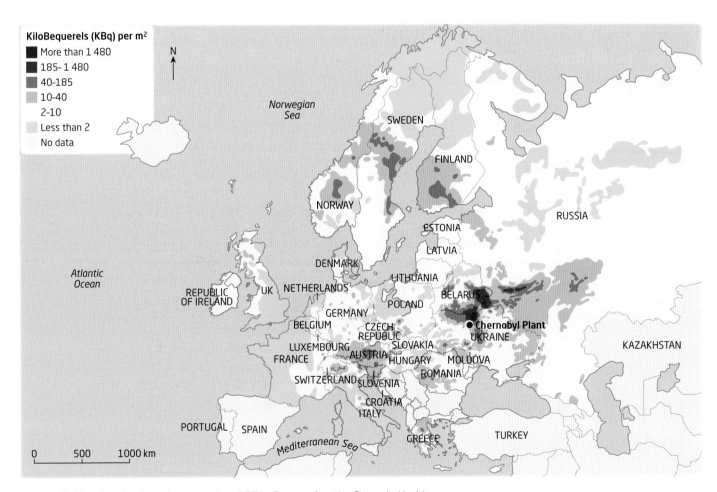

Figure 3 *Map showing deposits of caesium-137 in Europe after the Chernobyl incident.*
Source: EUR 16733, Bureau de la Communaute europeenne, Luxembourg, 1996. Adapted from Le Monde Diplometique, July 2000.

The Chernobyl accident

The accident at the Chernobyl reactor happened during an experimental test of the electrical control system as the reactor was being shut down for routine maintenance. The operators, in violation of safety regulations, had switched off important control systems and allowed the reactor to reach unstable, low-power conditions. A sudden power surge caused a steam explosion that ruptured the reactor vessel, allowing further violent fuel-steam interactions that destroyed the reactor core and severely damaged the reactor building. Subsequently, an intense graphite fire burned for ten days. Under those conditions, large releases of radioactive materials took place.

The radioactive gases and particles released in the accident were initially carried by the wind in westerly and northerly directions. On subsequent days, the winds came from all directions. The deposition of radionuclides was governed primarily by precipitation occurring during the passage of the radioactive cloud, leading to a complex and variable exposure pattern throughout the affected region, and to a lesser extent, the rest of Europe.

Exposure of individuals

The radionuclides released from the reactor that caused exposure of individuals were mainly iodine-131, caesium-134 and caesium-137. Iodine-131 has a short radioactive half-life (eight days), but it can be transferred to humans relatively rapidly from the air and through consumption of contaminated milk and leafy vegetables. Iodine becomes localised in the thyroid gland. For reasons related to the intake of those foods by infants and children, as well as the size of their thyroid glands and their metabolism, the radiation doses are usually higher for them than for adults.

The isotopes of caesium have relatively longer half-lives (caesium-134 has a half-life of 2 years while that of caesium-137 is 30 years). These radionuclides cause longer-term exposures through the ingestion pathway and through external exposure from their deposition on the ground. Many other radionuclides were associated with the accident, which were also considered in the exposure assessments.

Average effective doses to those persons most affected by the accident were assessed to be about 120 mSv for 530 000 recovery operation workers, 30 mSv for 116 000 evacuated persons and 20 mSv during the first two decades after the accident to those who continued to reside in contaminated areas. Maximum values of the dose may be an order of magnitude higher. Outside Belarus, Russia and Ukraine, other European countries were affected by the accident. Average doses there were at most 1 mSv in the first year after the accident with progressively decreasing doses in subsequent years. The dose over a lifetime was estimated to be 2–5 times the first-year dose. These doses are comparable to an annual dose from natural background radiation and are, therefore, of little radiological significance.

Figure 4 *Release of radionuclides and exposure of individuals.*

ailments, infertility and birth defects became commonplace in the years after the accident. There are plans for the 19-mile exclusion zone to be opened for restricted industrial uses, but an environmental impact assessment will have to be carried out first and an integrated radioactive waste management programme put in place.

While a huge amount of radiation was released into the atmosphere during the disaster, much has remained trapped within the power plant. How much exactly remains is uncertain, but one estimate is that more than 100 tonnes of uranium and other radioactive products such as plutonium could be released if there were another accident. The derelict power plant is also thought to contain about 2000 tonnes of combustible materials. There are concerns that cracks in the structure have allowed rainwater and fuel dust to form a toxic liquid that may be contaminating groundwater.

Ukraine, Russia and Belarus have been left with continuing and substantial decontamination and health care costs. It is difficult to know exactly how many deaths were caused by the Chernobyl accident, as over time it becomes harder to determine whether a death has been caused by exposure to radiation. A 2005 report prepared by the Chernobyl Forum, led by the International Atomic Energy Agency and World Health Organization, attributed 56 direct deaths to the accident. This comprised 47 accident workers, and 9 children with thyroid cancer. The report also estimated that there may be 4000 extra cancer deaths among the approximately 600 000 most highly exposed people. Although the Chernobyl Exclusion Zone and certain limited areas remain off limits, the majority of affected areas are now considered safe for settlement.

The nuclear accident at Chernobyl, following the serious incident at the Three Mile Island nuclear power plant in

Pennsylvania, USA, in 1979, brought any growth in the nuclear industry to a virtual halt. For example, no new nuclear power plants have been ordered in the USA since then although other countries such as China and India, deeply concerned about their ability to satisfy demand for electricity, have gone ahead with nuclear power programmes in recent years.

Activities

1 Describe the location of the Chernobyl nuclear power plant.
2 With reference to Figure 4 discuss in detail the cause of the accident.
   a Describe the location of radiation hotspots in Ukraine, Belarus and Russia (Figure 2) resulting from the accident.
   b To what extent did radiation from Chernobyl vary across the rest of Europe?
   c Explain the reasons for such variations in levels of radiation.
3 How has the accident affected Ukraine, Belarus and Russia in the long term?

Greenpeace International

Greenpeace is arguably the most well-known international civil society organisation working to improve environmental management around the world. Greenpeace has 2.8 million members worldwide and many millions more who generally support its views. Greenpeace states that it is 'an independent global campaigning organisation that acts to change attitudes and behaviour, to protect and conserve the environment and to promote peace'.

Discussion point

How active is Greenpeace in the country in which you live? What other environmental organisations have a significant presence?

Greenpeace has been campaigning against environmental degradation since 1971 when it was founded in Vancouver, British Columbia, Canada. The origins of Greenpeace lie in the Peace Movement and the Campaign for Nuclear

Headquarters of Greenpeace UK in London.

Disarmament generally. Bill Darnell has received the credit for combining the words 'green' and 'peace', thereby giving the organisation its globally recognisable name.

Also in 1971, a small boat of volunteers and journalists sailed into Amchitka, an area north of Alaska, where the US government was conducting underground nuclear tests. The tests were not prevented, but the voyage laid the groundwork for Greenpeace's later activities. This action began the tradition of 'bearing witness' in a non-violent manner, a tactic that Greenpeace has used with increasing frequency over the years. Greenpeace has a presence in 40 countries across Europe, the Americas, Asia, Africa and the Pacific. In order to maintain its independence, Greenpeace does not accept donations from governments or corporations but relies on contributions from individual supporters and foundation grants.

Greenpeace aims to achieve its overall objectives by specific means:

• Catalysing an energy revolution to address climate change, the main threat facing the planet. Greenpeace campaigns against fossil fuels and the use of coal in particular. It is urging governments to invest more in renewable energy. Greenpeace scores electronics brands on chemical and electronic waste, and on new energy criteria. Greenpeace is urging electronics companies to clean up their products by eliminating hazardous substances, and to take back and recycle their products responsibly once they become obsolete. The two issues are connected: the use of harmful chemicals in electronics products prevents their safe recycling once the products are discarded.

- Defending the oceans by challenging wasteful and destructive fishing, and creating a global network of marine reserves. It aims to build on a protection and recovery system established to manage land-based over-exploitation. Marine Reserves are the ocean equivalent of National Parks. They are a scientifically developed and endorsed approach to managing the oceans sustainably. Greenpeace campaigns in particular against industrial fishing, by-catch and unfair fisheries.

- Protecting the world's ancient forests and the animals, plants and people that depend on them. Forest destruction produces about one-fifth of global greenhouse gas emissions, more than that emitted from all the cars, planes and trains in the world. Recent successes achieved by Greenpeace and other environmental groups include (a) timber certification and a moratorium on soya crops that are grown in deforested areas in the Brazilian Amazon and (b) the protection of the Canadian Great Bear rainforest in 2009 after a decade-long campaign by Greenpeace, Sierra Club and ForestEthics.

- Working for disarmament and peace by tackling the causes of conflict and calling for the elimination of all nuclear weapons. As well as the potentially devastating impacts of nuclear war, over 2000 nuclear weapons tests have left a legacy of global and regional contamination. People living near the test sites have suffered from cancers, stillbirths, miscarriages and other health effects – and are still suffering today.

- Creating a toxic-free future with safer alternatives to hazardous chemicals in today's products and manufacturing. Greenpeace argues that the production, trade, use and release of many synthetic chemicals is a global threat to human health and the environment. Yet the world's chemical industries continue to produce and release thousands of chemical compounds every year, in most cases with no or very little testing and understanding of their impacts on people and the environment.

- Campaigning for sustainable agriculture by rejecting genetically engineered organisms, protecting biodiversity and encouraging socially responsible farming. Greenpeace says that genetically modified organisms (GMOs) should not be released into the environment since there is not an adequate scientific understanding of their impact on the environment and human health. The organisation is working to

Greenpeace Action Day – Vienna, Austria.

replace destructive chemical-intensive agriculture with methods that work with nature, not against it.

Arguably the most controversial issue involving Greenpeace occurred in 1985 when the Greenpeace ship *Rainbow Warrior* entered the waters surrounding Moruroa atoll, the site of French nuclear testing. Although it sounds unbelievable today, the French secret service bombed the ship in a New Zealand harbour on orders from the President, François Mitterrand. A Dutch photographer, Fernando Pereira, was killed as a result of this action. The attack brought international condemnation for France, after it was quickly exposed by the New Zealand police. The French government in 1987 agreed to pay New Zealand compensation of NZ$13 million and formally apologised for the bombing. The French government also paid 2.3 million French francs in compensation to the family of the photographer who died in the explosion.

In the UK, Greenpeace has been campaigning against plans to build a third runway and sixth terminal at London's Heathrow airport. Figure 5 details one rather unusual tactic in this battle. The expansion of Heathrow is an issue that could drag on for some time because of such opposing views.

Despite its founding in North America, Greenpeace has achieved much more success in Europe, where it has more members and generates most of its funds. Like any large campaigning organisation, Greenpeace is not without its critics. Some former members left to join more radical organisations, viewing Greenpeace's non-violent approach as too timid.

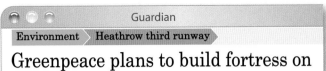

Greenpeace plans to build fortress on Heathrow runway site

Environmental activists have invited some of the UK's leading architects to design an 'impenetrable fortress' to be built on land earmarked for the third runway at Heathrow.

Greenpeace plans to build the winning design at the centre of the site where airport operator BAA hopes to construct a £7 bn runway and a sixth terminal.

The charity bought the parcel of land in 2009 and then distributed ownership to more than 60 000 supporters around the world.

Organisers say the small individual plots will create a legal headache for any government trying to push ahead with expansion plans.

Figure 5 *Greenpeace campaign at Heathrow airport: extract from the* Guardian, *January 2010.*

Activities

1. When was Greenpeace founded and which activity did it first protest against?
2. What is the organisation's overall objective?
3. Explain Greenpeace's tradition of 'bearing witness'.
4. Briefly discuss each of the six global issues that Greenpeace is campaigning to improve.
5. How and why have the actions of Greenpeace been criticised?

The growth of environmental awareness

A combination of the actions of prominent environmental groups and serious pollution accidents has made the global population more environmentally aware than at any time in the past. Environmental policies that were at the margin of politics 30 or 40 years ago have become mainstream, with today's main political parties advocating many of the policies presented by environmental groups several decades ago.

Gaining knowledge and understanding of the environment is now an important part of the school curriculum in most countries, and often the younger generation feel passionately about environmental issues. There is no doubt at all that increased knowledge about the environment has resulted in changing attitudes to a whole range of environmental issues,

and this in turn has galvanised politicians into producing much improved environmental policies (Figure 6).

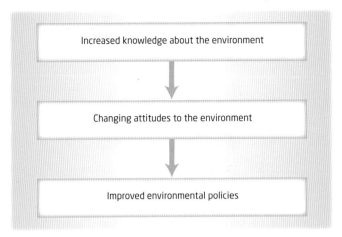

Figure 6 *Environmental knowledge, attitudes, policies.*

However, this is not always an easy process, as various studies of the relationship between greater environmental knowledge and changing attitudes have shown. Attitudes can be difficult to change and this can vary considerably with the issues under consideration. The prevalence of other pressing issues at the time can have a substantial impact. At times of economic crisis or when there are major political or social concerns, people may downgrade environmental issues on their personal agendas. Some of the most obvious examples have been government campaigns designed to try to change people's behaviour where progress has usually been slower than originally anticipated.

Although there are significant differences in environmental awareness between countries, the Internet and the mass media in general have done much to reduce this gap. Many

Theory of Knowledge

Environmental organisations are sometimes criticised because (a) their policies do not always follow what is generally thought to be the best available knowledge and (b) they sometimes develop a stance based on incomplete knowledge. Such organisations would respond by saying that information can be interpreted in different ways and that waiting for a more complete knowledge base may prevent solutions being put in place in sufficient time to solve a problem. How can we decide who is right in situations like this? Is it just a matter of weighing one kind of risk against another?

Students discuss Earth Force environmental project an Earth Day, Alexandria, Virginia.

of the major environmental organisations like Greenpeace are international in nature. They campaign against environmental degradation wherever it occurs and attempt to involve local people in appreciating the need to challenge activities that have an adverse impact on the environment.

The link between economic development and environmental awareness is well established although significant variations can still occur. For example, the Scandinavian countries have generally shown greater concern for environmental issues than other affluent nations.

It is not possible for governments and companies today to take the types of decision that can result in adverse environmental consequences that they would have taken even two decades ago. People are much more questioning today, both as individuals and as members of various civil society organisations.

In the UK, Defra published the results of a survey across a range of issues relevant to the environment. Figure 7 (opposite) shows the responses to a range of statements. More than half of all respondents agreed with the first five

statements which were expressed in a broadly positive way towards the environment. Table 1 (page 130) compares responses between 2007 and 2009. The majority of responses show an improved attitude towards environmental issues, but the responses to some questions will have disappointed environmental groups. However, the fact that people in the UK, as elsewhere in the world, were concerned about the global financial crisis may have influenced the results.

Urban bicycle scheme, Stockholm, Sweden.

Geographical skill

Look at Figure 8.
a Describe the differences between the 2007 and 2009 surveys.
b Suggest reasons for the differences you have identified.

Activities

1 a Discuss the logic of Figure 6.
  b Why is the sequence of events shown in Figure 6 difficult to achieve?
2 Comment on the responses presented in Figure 7.
3 Look at Table 1. To what extent did attitudes to environmental issues change between 2007 and 2009?
4 How do you think attitudes to environmental issues will change in the future? Give reasons for your answer.

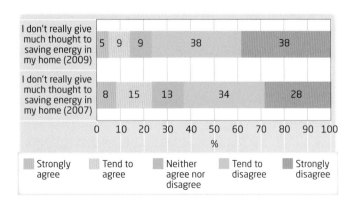

Figure 8 *Extent of thought about saving energy in the home.*

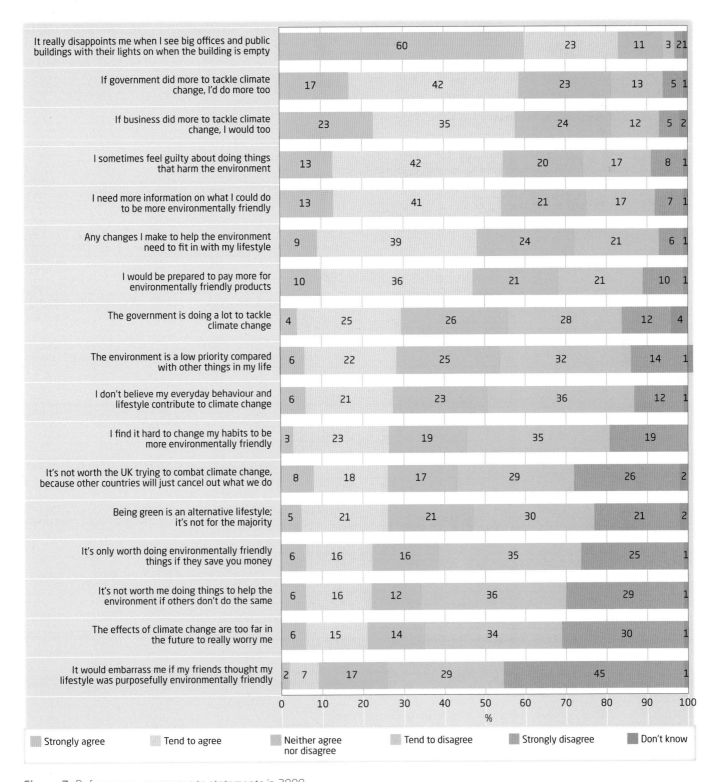

Figure 7 *Defra survey – responses to statements in 2009.*

	Agree (2009) %	Agree (2007) %	Disagree (2009) %	Disagree (2007) %	*Change in balance of opinion (- indicates an increase in disagreement) %
Being green is an alternative lifestyle; it's not for the majority	26	30	51	30	−25
I find it hard to change my habits to be more environmentally friendly	26	33	54	42	−19
It's not worth the UK trying to combat climate change, because other countries will just cancel out what we do	26	36	55	46	−19
It's not worth me doing things to help the environment if others don't do the same	22	28	65	56	−15
I need more information on what I could do to be more environmentally friendly	55	63	24	18	−14
The government is doing a lot to tackle climate change	29	24	40	47	12
I sometimes feel guilty about doing things that harm the environment	55	59	24	16	−12
It would embarrass me if my friends thought my lifestyle was purposefully environmentally friendly	8	10	74	71	−5
If government did more to tackle climate change, I'd do more too	58	60	17	14	−5
The effects of climate change are too far in the future to really worry me	21	21	64	61	−3
Any changes I make to help the environment need to fit in with my lifestyle	48	46	27	28	3
It's only worth doing environmentally friendly things if they save you money	22	20	61	61	2
I don't believe my everyday behaviour and lifestyle contribute to climate change	28	28	48	46	−2
The environment is a low priority compared with other things in my life	28	27	47	47	1
I would be prepared to pay more for environmentally friendly products	46	44	31	29	0
If business did more to tackle climate change, I would too	58	–	17	–	N/A
It really disappoints me when I see big offices and public buildings with their lights on when the building is empty	83	–	5	–	N/A

Base: All respondents (2009 adults surveyed in 2009/3618 adults surveyed in 2007)

Note: Change in balance of opinion has been calculated for each statement by looking at both the change in the level of agreement and the change in the level of disagreement, then adding these together for each statement. This has been used to rank responses as it provides an indication of overall change in opinion. While the change in the level of agreement could have been used to rank responses, this would not have revealed where the largest overall changes in opinion had occurred.
The biggest change between the 2007 and 2009 surveys can be seen in the responses to 'Being green is an alternative lifestyle; it's not for the majority'.

Table 1 *Defra survey – comparisons between 2009 and 2007.*

Review

Examination-style questions

1 **a** Describe one major pollution event affecting more than one country.

  b Examine the consequences of aid responses to this event.

2 **a** Describe the role of one international civil society organisation working to improve environmental management.

  b How has this organisation helped to change public attitudes over time?

Websites

www.iaea.org
International Atomic Energy Agency

www.unscear.org
UN Scientific Committee on the Effects of Atomic Radiation

www.greenpeace.org
Greenpeace International

Key terms

Incidental pollution a one-off pollution incident.

Sustained pollution pollution that occurs over a significant period of time.

11 Homogenisation of landscapes

KEY QUESTION

- To what extent have urban landscapes become more uniform in terms of common commercial activity, structures, styles of construction and infrastructure?

Urban sprawl: Cairo, Egypt – urban sprawl is a common characteristic of cities in both the developed and developing world.

In the 19th and early parts of the 20th centuries geographical analysis was very much about the uniqueness of places. For many people this was what made the subject fascinating and today this remains the focus of publications such as *National Geographic* and *Geographical,* as well as being the theme of numerous television documentaries. However, the process of globalisation that has brought the peoples of the world closer together has had a radical impact on the differences between places, with greater similarity the dominant theme. This trend has been gathering pace since the 1950s and is most readily apparent in urban areas which are rapidly changing all over the world.

Globalisation has undoubtedly had a significant impact on the **homogenisation of landscapes**:

- Agro-industrialisation has had a huge impact on farming landscapes around the world as capital-intensive agriculture has made substantial inroads into more and more countries.

- Transportation landscapes have also witnessed increasing uniformity for similar reasons.

- Major tourist destinations have become more and more alike as international tourists have increasingly expected similar standards from hotels and other tourism infrastructure.

- The economies of scale necessary for both heavy and light industries to survive in an increasingly competitive global market have resulted in the growing uniformity of industrial landscapes.

Urbanisation, in its extent and intensity, is one of the most homogenising of all major human activities. Cities homogenise the physical environment because they are built to meet the relatively narrow needs of just one species, humanity. Thus urbanisation has been viewed by many as a driving force for the increased homogenisation of flora and fauna.

As early as 1970, A. Toffler in *Future Shock* argued that the evolution of transport and communications technologies and the resultant intensified flows of people have led to a situation where 'place is no longer a primary source of diversity'. Figure 1 attempts to illustrate this point. Rem Koolhaas has used the term 'generic city' to describe the development of common characteristics in urban areas, the result of the operation of broadly similar processes.

Figure 1 *Homogenised destinations.*

Many aspects of globalisation combine to create homogeneity, but locally specific history and geography is a powerful influence on the urban landscape. W.E. Murray in his book *Geographies of Globalization* sees the subsequent interaction between the two leading to hybridised or 'glocalised' outcomes in culture, economy and politics. To a certain extent this will be reflected in the form of the urban landscape (Figure 2).

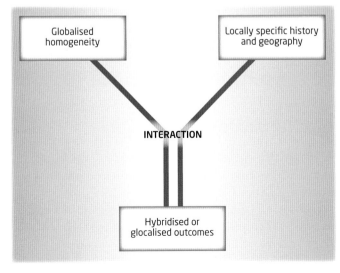

Figure 2 *Interaction between global and local forces.*

Research idea

Search the Internet and other sources to find images of London, Tokyo and New York. Select key images that show both the similarities and differences between these three global cities. Discuss the images you have selected.

World cities

To be classed as a world city a major urban area has to meet a range of criteria to prove its international importance. This will undoubtedly increase its similarities to a certain degree to other world cities. However, it will still remain distinctive in many aspects and city governments and populations are anxious that this should be so. Although a world city is an important node on a network, it is still a distinctive place. Much of this of course is based on its historical legacy and this is an important reason for international tourism. How distinctive would London be without:

- The Houses of Parliament and Big Ben?
- Buckingham Palace?
- The Tower of London and Tower Bridge?
- Trafalgar Square?
- Piccadilly Circus?
- St Paul's Cathedral?

If these and other important historical buildings and locations were not there, much of the uniqueness of London as a place would not exist. It would lose much of its fascination and appeal. Certainly fewer tourists would

Theory of Knowledge

Perceptions about places can be heavily influenced by key images such as some of those discussed above. Sometimes people will know hardly anything else about a country. This can also apply to the people of a country, of whom a perceived characteristic (which may not be accurate) may be how the population is viewed in another country or group of countries. Some people think that this process, known as stereotyping, is inevitable (a kind of mental shorthand). Under what circumstances can it become harmful?

visit. But what impact would this have on London as a business location? Would a much more bland London result in a lower level of business investment?

The unique characteristics of the centre-points of many capital cities are immediately recognised: Red Square, Moscow, and the Eiffel Tower, Paris.

Urban landscapes

Figure 3 illustrates the main ways in which common urban characteristics have diffused around the world. Many developments will of course also encompass local traits, but the strong global elements will be clear to see.

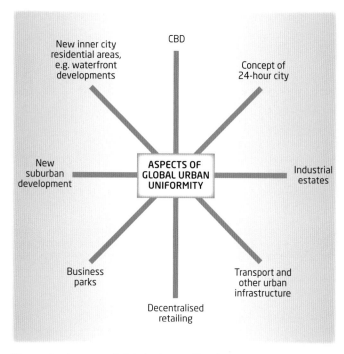

Figure 3 *Aspects of global urban uniformity.*

Central business districts

Similar land uses concentrate in central business districts worldwide because, at least in theory, the **central business district (CBD)** is the most accessible location in a city. The two dominant land uses in a CBD of a large urban area are the offices of major national and international companies and a wide range of retail outlets. Intense competition for space resulting from maximum **accessibility** leads to the highest land prices in the urban area and substantial vertical development. Thus tall office blocks are a familiar and expected part of the urban landscape of the CBD. Such blocks will house familiar international banks and other businesses. Modern architecture has done much to make new high-rise buildings distinctive and some cities now may be as recognisable by their modern architecture as by their historic buildings. Examples are the Petronas Towers in Kuala Lumpur and the three main tower buildings in London's Docklands.

Global retailing has become increasingly dominated by leading brands in terms of both the retailers themselves and the goods on sale. Visit large department stores in Beijing, Moscow and London and there will be little difference in the range of products on sale. It is the smaller, independent retailers that provide so much of the character of a CBD, particularly where similar functions congregate in certain areas, either in formal shop premises or in street markets.

Indoor shopping centre, Toronto – most big cities now have large indoor shopping centres.

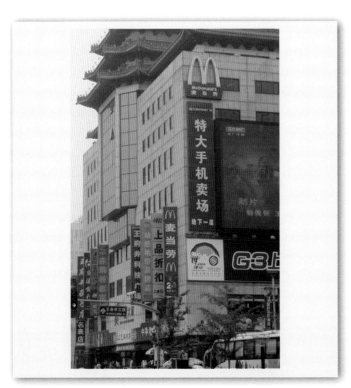
CBD, Beijing – CBDs around the world have so much in common!

Fast food restaurants are similar the world over and characterised by the presence of international names such as McDonald's, KFC and Pizza Hut. Although such companies often make some effort to tailor their meals to local traditions, the feeling of homogeneity is all-pervading. However, indigenous restaurants can do much to illustrate the distinctiveness of national culture and are often a major part of the experience of visiting a town or city. Indoor shopping centres are now a familiar element of CBDs in

both the developed and developing worlds, along with **pedestrianised precincts**, multi-storey and underground car parks, and the sight-seeing tower present in so many capital cities. The main hotels in major urban areas are increasingly owned by transnational companies offering a uniformity of standard worldwide. Visual recognition is an important marketing element for some hotel chains. Although local cuisine will be available in their restaurants you will also find standard 'international food'.

As CBDs in the developing world become more like their developed world counterparts, fewer people actually live in central areas as the demand for commercial land use increases. Commercial land uses can outbid all but the richest residential land users. The uniqueness of a CBD

Hilton hotel, Cairo, Egypt – the major hotel groups are present in most large cities.

is provided to a large extent by its historic buildings: government offices, royal residences, churches, mosques and temples, art galleries and museums, universities, theatres and other buildings with distinctive architecture.

Outer retail areas

Within the CBD land is restricted in area, very expensive and not very accessible to all parts of the urban area. It is therefore not surprising that significant retailing functions can be found outside the CBD. A now common characteristic of most developed cities and a growing number of developing cities is the **retail park**. These are clusters of retail functions which require considerable floorspace and which usually provide free parking as an incentive to customers. Accessibility is a key locational characteristic, so retail parks are often found along important arterial and ring roads. The photo below shows the Reading Gate Retail Park which was built in conjunction with the Madejski Stadium, home of Reading Football Club.

Retail park, Reading, UK.

Superstores and shopping malls located at the edge of cities or in the **rural–urban fringe** have also become common characteristics in many cities. The rural–urban fringe is the boundary zone where urban and non-urban land meet and is an area of transition from agriculture and other rural activities to urban use. The rural–urban fringe is characterised by a mixture of land uses, most of which require large areas of land. With similar processes operating in most large urban areas the characteristics of the rural–urban fringe show considerable global homogenisation.

Planning regulations can have a substantial impact on the pattern of land use in the rural–urban fringe and of course on all the zones within the urban area itself. Regulations in some countries are much stricter than in others and may have been in operation for a longer period of time.

Transport and other urban infrastructure

Large urban areas cannot function effectively without reasonably efficient systems of transportation. Although solutions to the urban transport problem are not entirely uniform, for most large urban areas the similarities are all too readily apparent. Logic is an obvious cause of uniformity. Common transport characteristics include:

- Multi-lane arterial roads linking the CBD to suburban areas and other towns and cities in the wider region: the one-way systems popular in the central areas of North American cities have been applied in many other large cities around the world.

- Inner and outer city ring roads: designed to keep the CBD and inner city as congestion-free as possible, ring roads are inevitably used in most large cities because of their proven efficiency.

- Underground railway mass transit systems: due to the very large investment required for underground mass transit systems, these are found only in the largest cities of both the developed and developing worlds.

- Urban bus networks and tram systems: surface public transport systems are vital and illustrate common characteristics the world over.

- Increasing air transport connections: as the importance of an airport (or airports) to major urban areas has grown over time, the functions that agglomerate close to major airports are very similar all over the world. However, modern airport design has produced some very distinctive airports around the world, another example of the architect's battle against uniformity.

Urban transport, Basle, Switzerland – public transport is an essential element in all major urban areas.

The metro, Beijing.

Various international agreements have brought greater uniformity in road signs, primarily for safety reasons. Many road signs around the world use easy-to-decipher symbols, intended to assist visitors who do not speak the native tongue. In 1968, European countries signed the Vienna Convention on Road Traffic treaty, with the aim of standardising traffic regulations in participating countries in order to facilitate international road traffic and increase road safety. Part of the treaty was the Vienna Convention on Road Signs and Signals which defined the traffic signs and signals. As a result, in Western Europe the traffic signs are all standardised. Motorway signage has generally followed the North American model. Thus what began in Europe and North America has gradually spread around the world.

The visual signs of other urban infrastructure have also become more uniform, although in some cities designers have very successfully made a difference.

Residential areas

The old distinction between developed and developing cities in terms of the location of richer and poorer residents is now not as clear as it once was. In developed cities the contrast between relatively poorer inner cities and more affluent suburbs provides a general model for urban analysis. In developing cities the more affluent have tended to live in close proximity to the CBD, with the majority of the poor living in peripheral squatter settlements. Poor transport infrastructure and often the location of former colonial housing adjacent to the CBD were added incentives for the more affluent to live close to their businesses or government offices

in the CBD. However, as transport infrastructure has improved and land developers have constructed middle- and higher-income suburban areas, there has been a certain movement of the more affluent to such areas.

Urban sprawl is a global phenomenon brought about by rural–urban migration and the extension of urban transport systems. The differences between cities are often mainly in terms of population density. Building by craftsmen on an individual basis has been increasingly replaced by large-scale development by major companies using international standards of design and build. The suburban life of North America in particular has become the standard to which so many people aspire around the world.

The rural urban fringe of Vancouver, Canada.

However, it must not be forgotten that the majority of the populations of developing cities live in poverty in parts of urban areas that most visitors do not see. The wealth gap between these people and the much smaller numbers on middle and higher incomes is rising in most countries. For many of the poor there has been little change in their immediate urban landscape and any thought of greater uniformity with Western cities must seem like a dream. In some newly industrialised countries the urban housing situation has changed rapidly, but for most poorer developing countries shanty-style sub-standard housing is the norm for many people.

Land use zoning and other planning regulations have generally converged in an international sense, with what has been perceived as good practice in one country being followed by many others. For example, the UK's New Towns have served as a model for new urban development in many other countries. The development of London's

Docklands, using the derelict site of the old London docks, has provided a model for waterfront development in many other cities.

In most developed world cities there is clear evidence of the **cycle of urbanisation** which shows the stages of urban change from the growth of a city to **counterurbanisation** through to **reurbanisation.** Since the beginning of the 1970s counterurbanisation has been a significant process in all developed countries as people have moved out of the largest urban areas to urban areas further down the urban hierarchy and its rural areas. In more recent years the phenomenon of reurbanisation has been recognised in a growing number of cities as the attractions of inner urban areas in particular have regained popularity.

 **Discussion point**

Think about the largest urban area near to you. How is it similar and different from other large urban areas around the world?

Industrial areas and business parks

Urban planning in most countries has sought to separate housing and industry, with the development of industrial estates a key element in this strategy. The location of industrial estates along major transport routes characterises all large urban areas.

However, in cities in many developing countries small-scale industry remains an important activity in residential areas and this shows little sign of changing. The urban pollution that was once so characteristic of developed cities is now a major problem in most developing cities.

As the economies of developed countries have become more and more dominated by tertiary industry, business parks rather than industrial estates have become more familiar sights in and around towns and cities. The characteristics are frequently similar although architects, as they have done with other urban construction, have tried to impart a certain degree of individuality.

A gradient of homogenisation?

Urban ecologists have noted a **gradient of homogenisation** in terms of flora and fauna from the urban core to the periphery. Is this also true of the human urban landscape, with greatest homogenisation in the CBD with all its obvious signs of globalisation, but with a decline towards the edge of the urban area? This is a trend that can certainly be recognised in some urban areas, but it is not so obvious in others. It can be argued that the gradient of homogenisation is less in newly industrialised countries where investment has not just been concentrated in the CBD and other key areas, but has spread more widely to many parts of the city, and is greater in poorer developing countries.

 Activities

1 **a** What common characteristics would you expect to find in the CBDs of large cities all around the world?
   b What are the reasons for such similarities?
2 Describe and explain other characteristics of urban areas which have become more uniform in recent decades.
3 Explain the meaning of a 'gradient of homogenisation'.

Limits of homogenisation

There is no doubt that the homogenisation of urban landscapes has occurred and is continuing to happen. However, it is important not to overestimate this process and to continue to be aware of the ways in which places remain distinctive. This is a key role for the geographer.

 Theory of Knowledge

Is the homogenisation of landscapes a model of the whole process of globalisation - everything becomes essentially more alike (following a Western model), apart from ornamental, largely insignificant, local variations? Or is this a misrepresentation of the true picture?

Case study

The city of Gurgaon, India

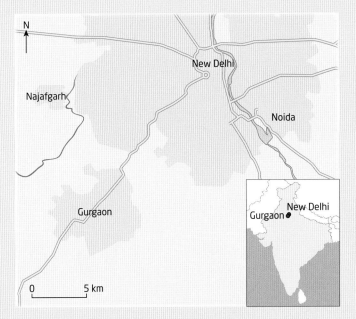

Figure 4 *Location of Gurgaon.*

Gurgaon is one of Delhi's four major satellite cities and is part of the National Capital Region (NCR) of India. With a population of 228 820 recorded by the 2001 Census, Gurgaon is 32 km south-west of Delhi. It is an important centre in ancient Hindu mythology. A significant number of transnational companies have located there since GE did so in 1997. Gurgaon has been labelled 'the call centre

High-tech industry, Ericsson headquarters in Gurgaon, India.

capital of the world'. A survey by *Business Today* rated Gurgaon as the best Indian city to both work and live in. It has the third highest per capita income in the country after Chandigarh and Mumbai.

In an article entitled 'A 21st Century Urban Landscape: the Emergence of New Socio-Spatial Formations in Gurgaon', Seth Schindler describes how Gurgaon in the north Indian state of Haryana has undergone profound changes since the early 1990s. The catalyst has been the rapid rate of growth of the Indian economy in recent years. Gurgaon has taken on a number of aspects of modern global urban uniformity including:

- wide boulevard-type streets
- modern entertainment plazas
- futuristic glass office towers
- luxurious gated residential complexes
- a skyline replicated in urban areas around the world.

Much of the development has been completed by large construction companies such as DLF and Unitech. Both companies have made a point of branding their developments as cosmopolitan and global, distinguishing areas of new construction from 'Old Gurgaon'. This is reflected in the names of new developments which include: The Park Place, Sahara Mall, World Spa and The Summit. The last is advertised as being 'in tune with international benchmarks'. Figure 5 (page 140) shows what is on offer at a recent residential development along the Sohna Road.

Retailers in the new developments use global visual imagery and say they subscribe to global service standards. Schindler argues that this is the expected norm when you locate a business in 'global space'. Businesses operating in such locations are not just selling a product, they are selling the image of globalisation.

What has happened in Gurgaon is an interaction between social and spatial change. In a relatively short period of time many people in the city are spending their leisure time in new ways, altering their diet and behaving in other ways which broadly fit in with the international model of globalisation based on consumerism. Here the value of people and places is increasingly determined by visual signs and symbols. Access to space in terms of where people live, which restaurants they eat in, where they buy clothes and where they engage in other activities is one of the main ways that the affluent in Gurgaon differentiate themselves from one another.

Original booking open for 'Unitech sunbreeze' Sector-69, Sohna Road Gurgaon

Unitech has launched an affordable residential project called Unitech Sun Breeze at Sohna Road, Gurgaon. Unitech Sun Breeze Gurgaon is spread over a huge lush green garden of 18 acres (total land is much more) and it comprises 2 bedrooms, hall and kitchen, 3 bedrooms, hall and kitchen and 4 bedrooms, hall and kitchen spacious apartments.

Key Features:

- Located near Sohna Road, 3 km from Rajiv Chowk
- 15 minutes drive to IGI Airport New Delhi
- 0 km from the nearest metro station (proposed metro route connected to South Delhi and Central Delhi)
- Reputed school, shopping malls & major hospital in close vicinity

Unitech Sun Breeze Amenities:

Badminton Court, Volley Ball Court, Kids Play Area, Table Tennis Court, Gymnasium, Club House, Multipurpose Hall, Medical Facilities, Swimming Pool, Community Centre, Convenience Store, Bank Branches and ATM Centre.

Figure 5 *Unitech Sun Breeze residential development.*

Schindler is also at pains to illustrate the uniqueness of Gurgaon and the huge gap between rich and poor by saying, 'Although actually less than a kilometre, the figurative distance between slum and global space is vast.' He argues that because of the changes that have taken place, the city defies classification as either Indian or Western, being undeniably linked with the global economy yet still exhibiting strong local forms in many parts of the city.

Activities

1   Describe the location of Gurgaon.
2   How and why has Gurgaon become more globally uniform in recent decades?

Review

Examination-style questions

a Describe how urban landscapes have become more uniform in recent decades.

b What are the reasons for this trend?

Websites

www.gurgaon.co.in
Gurgaon, India

www.worldcities.com.sg
World Cities Summit 2010

www.uwm.edu/Library/digilib/cities
University of Wisconsin Library, Cities of the World

Key terms

Homogenisation of landscapes the process whereby different landscapes in a country increasingly resemble those found in other countries because similar processes of change are at work.

Central business district (CBD) the major commercial centre of an urban area, usually centrally located at the point of maximum accessibility.

Accessibility the degree to which a location is accessible to as many people as possible.

Pedestrianised precincts urban areas where vehicles are totally banned or very strictly controlled to allow total access to people on foot.

Retail park a grouping of retail functions requiring large floorspaces and offering many parking spaces, usually without charge. Usually located on major roads.

Rural-urban fringe the boundary zone where urban and non-urban land meet, and an area of transition from agriculture and other rural activities to urban use.

Planning regulations the conditions that govern existing and new building.

Cycle of urbanisation the stages of urban change from the growth of a city to counterurbanisation through to reurbanisation.

Counterurbanisation the process of population decentralisation as people move from large urban areas to smaller urban settlements and rural areas.

Reurbanisation when, after a clear period of decline, the population of a city, in particular the inner area, begins to increase again.

Gradient of homogenisation the thesis that homogenisation is at its most intense at the core of an urban area and declines towards the periphery.

12 Cultural diffusion: the process

Ceramic statue from the Tajin culture, Mexico.

Culture can be defined as the total of the inherited ideas, beliefs, values and knowledge which constitute the shared basis of social action. It is the way of life of a particular society or group of people. Culture is important in interpreting and making sense of the world. It can determine people's attitudes to the issues affecting them and give them a sense of identity. Figure 1 shows Lloyd Kwast's model of culture.

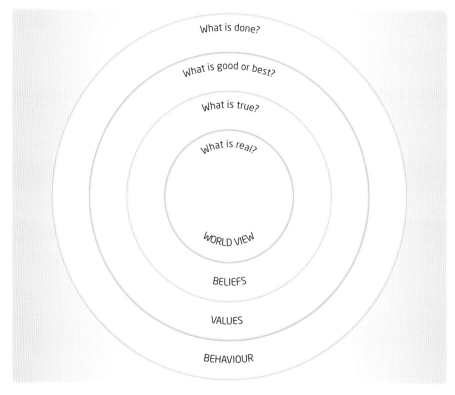

What is done?

What is good or best?

What is true?

What is real?

WORLD VIEW

BELIEFS

VALUES

BEHAVIOUR

Figure 1 *Kwast's model of culture.*

The natural environment can significantly affect the lifestyle of the people in a country or region, thus shaping their culture. Differences in culture in a region or country may create tensions, as numerous examples over time have shown.

Cultural traits or characteristics can be recognised in terms of:

- language
- customs
- beliefs
- dress
- images

- music
- food
- technology.

An area that has been a rich source of cultural traits is known as a **cultural hearth**. The Tigris and Euphrates valleys in modern-day Iraq where the world's first cities developed is a major example. Culture diffuses outwards from cultural hearths. Culture is a major aspect of people's lives. It affects how people relate to family members, to other people in their community and to people further afield. Cultural development is a process and it is therefore dynamic rather than static. Outside influences may have a very significant impact on traditions that have developed over many years. Figure 2 is an assessment of Mexican culture from a source that looks at a range of cultures around the world.

Mexico's history has led to a wondrous blending of cultures. Find out what makes Mexican culture unique.

You have to visit Mexico once to witness the colorful culture that makes the country such a vivacious place to live in. The Mexican spirit is exemplified by the culture of the charro, or Mexican cowboy. It is a rich legacy of tradition and valor, of war and peace.

Once in Mexico, you can glimpse an intriguing blend of Native American traditions and Spanish colonial influences in Mexican culture. Mexicans have for centuries been known for their distinguished ceramics, music, painting, sculpture, textiles and poetry, but after the Spaniards arrived in the 16th century, Mexican art and culture saw an amalgamation of Native American arts with the European way of life. This led to the evolution of a unique Mexican culture. Interestingly, the growth of Mexican culture is not limited to Spanish colonization; greatly developed cultures, including those of the Olmecs, Mayas, Toltecs, and Aztecs, existed long before the Spanish conquest.

The colonial rule of the Spaniards, which lasted for nearly 300 years, saw the construction of many churches, which are a blending of Spanish architectural designs with the handiwork of Native American workers who built and decorated the buildings. These Christian churches were supposed to replace the pagan structures. Not just churches, even the basic design of most of Mexico's towns, are influenced by the design of many of the older cities in Spain. The indigenous arts were regarded as an important part of the national revival after the revolution. Renowned artists like Diego Rivera, David Alfaro Siqueiros and José Clemente Orozco were commissioned to decorate important public buildings with large, vivid murals on social and historical themes. Many of these buildings exist to this day as thriving communities with magnificent cultural heritages. Mexico City is the country's cultural epicenter of fine arts, museums, and music, but spectacular cultural treasures can be found throughout the country. Present day Mexico is bursting with murals and littered with galleries of contemporary and historic art, which are a highlight of the country for many tourists. Mexico City and Oaxaca are particularly considered to be booming in contemporary arts scenes. The country's vibrant folk-art tradition has also contributed to Mexican culture in a big way.

There is diversity of customs, language, dress and food in culturally vibrant Mexico. Spanish is the national language of Mexico. But Mexican Spanish differs from Castilian Spanish, the literary and official language of Spain, in two aspects: in Mexico, the Castilian lisp has more or less disappeared, and numerous indigenous words have been adopted. Around 50 indigenous languages are spoken by about 7 million people in Mexico. A majority of the Mexican population have a Catholic faith. Christianity was introduced to the residents by the colonial masters. As far as dressing goes, the people of Mexico who live in small villages normally wear trousers, sombreros, cotton shirts and ponchos; in cities people generally wear fashion borrowed from Europe and the US. Clothing in Mexico changes according to the season. However, one of the hallmarks of Mexican clothing is woven fabrics. Woven clothing is worn by many people in Mexico.

The people of Mexico are generally very warm and gracious and believe strongly in their family and religion. Exchanging proper greetings is considered very important among the Mexican social milieu. Though Mexican people are hard-working, they are not very rich. They believe in enjoying a reasonable quiet life, taking pleasure in their siestas.

Real Mexican food is quite unlike the dishes found in most Mexican and Tex-Mex restaurants in other countries. Tortillas, beans and chili peppers are the staple foods is of Mexican people. Tortillas are thin round patties made of pressed corn or wheat-flour dough cooked on griddles. Beans of different varieties are most commonly boiled and fried. They can be a main ingredient in a meal or served almost as a garnish. Jugos, which is a kind of fruit juice, is a popular drink and is available everywhere. Mexico is also famous for its alcoholic beverages – mezcal and tequila in particular.

Today, Mexican society is slowly evolving from a socialistic government setup to a more democratic society. The government has taken steps toward improving literacy and education in the past few years – an indicator of progress.

Figure 2 *Mexican culture.*

The mixing of cultures is a major dimension of globalisation. This has occurred through:

- migration, which circulates ideas, values and beliefs around the world
- the rapid spread of news, ideas and fashions through the mass media, trade and travel
- the growth of global brands such as Coca-Cola and McDonald's, which serve as common reference points – the terms 'Americanisation' and 'McDonaldisation' are often used to describe global consumer culture
- the Internet which has allowed individual and mass communication on a scale never available before
- the transport revolution which has facilitated the mass movement of people and products around the world.

The term **cultural hybridity** is used to describe the extent to which cultures are intermixed. This process has been important to the success of many TNCs. The power of brands and their global marketing strategies cannot be underestimated. The increasing knowledge of Western consumer culture in the former Soviet Union and Eastern Europe in the Cold War was an important factor in the eventual disintegration of the Eastern Bloc.

However, in spite of the significant impact of globalisation on cultures around the world, it is important not to exaggerate the changes that have taken place. Considerable cultural differences remain, with some writers using terms such as 'culture wars' and 'clashes of civilisations'.

Discussion point

What is the evidence of the mixing of different cultures in the area in which you live?

Theory of Knowledge

One of the reasons why the IB Diploma insists on the study of a second language is that this gives an insight into the way other people live and see the world (there are, of course, many other reasons). Has this been your experience with your group 2 language study? Do you think that studying the culture of another country would be a better way of achieving this aim? Or should both be required?

Aspects of culture

Language

Language is an essential part of national identity and culture, although it is not always restricted by geographical borders. Culture is transmitted through a range of activities involving language, including speech, literature and song. Human interaction depends almost totally on language.

Poster for the musical Cats *in Beijing.*

	1st language	2nd language	Total
	(million speakers)		
Mandarin Chinese	873	178	1051
Hindi	370	120	490
Spanish	350	70	420
English	340	170	510
Arabic	260	24	284
Portuguese	203	10	213
Bengali	196	19	215
Russian	145	110	255
Japanese	126	1	127
German	101	128	229

Table 1 *Major first and second languages around the world.*

	Number of languages	Total population (million)
Papua New Guinea	820	5
Indonesia	742	242
Nigeria	516	129
India	427	1080
USA	311	296
Mexico	297	106
Cameroon	280	16
Australia	275	20
China	241	1300
Congo, Dem. Rep.	216	60

Table 2 *Countries with the greatest variety of languages.*

Some languages have over 100 million native speakers. The United Nations has six **official languages**: Arabic, Chinese, English, French, Russian and Spanish. The official language is the language of a country, region or institution that is embedded in law. Table 1 shows the major first and second languages around the world, while Table 2 lists the countries with the greatest language variety.

Language is of vital importance in service provision. Bilingual countries are obvious examples where both languages need to be used to communicate with the total population, but some countries like the UK have a large number of ethnic minorities and local government in particular must provide means of communication on important matters.

Canada is an example of a **bilingual country**, with the two official languages of English and French. The province of Quebec is the centre of the French language in Canada. About 80% of the population of Quebec are French speakers. The French-speaking population outside Quebec is particularly evident in adjacent parts of New Brunswick and Ontario. French Canada is distinct in North America by culture, language and politics. In the early years of settlement the French were numerically dominant in Canada, being about three-quarters of the total Canadian population in the mid 18th century, but a century later French representation was down to 30%. It now stands at 23%. Over time French Canada has pressed for stronger legislation to protect the French language and referendums have been held in Quebec to decide if the province should

remain part of Canada or become an independent country. Voting has been close when referendums have taken place, but Quebec remains part of Canada.

Figure 3 shows the official languages of Africa. For many African countries the official language is a remnant of colonial rule, with the old colonial powers often retaining strong links with their former colonies. These links are political, economic, social and cultural. The evidence of cultural association is most obvious through a shared language, but it can also involve many other facets of life.

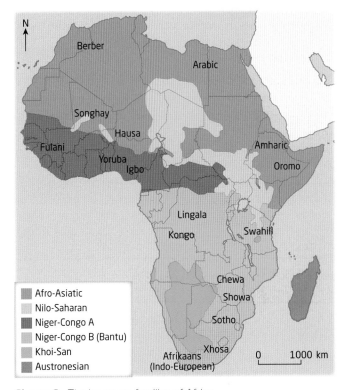

Figure 3 *The language families of Africa.*

Table 3 presents information about minority language groups in the European Union. All EU countries have minority language groups to an extent, but minority languages are much stronger in some countries than others. People from a minority language group sometimes feel very distinct from the majority population and language group in a country. Feelings of difference may be felt by both minority and majority groups which can lead to political tensions and spawn **separatist movements**.

Spain is an example of a country that has two significant minority language groups. As a minority and stateless language, Catalan is immediately associated with an actual region, a distinct community, and even with

Country	Main language spoken	Minority languages (examples)
Austria	German	Slovenian spoken by 20100 people in Carinthia and Styria regions
Belgium	French and Flemish	German spoken by 95000–100000 in German border area
UK	English	Welsh spoken by 500000 in Wales. Scottish Gaelic spoken by 67000, mostly in Highlands and Islands
Denmark	Danish	German spoken by 15000–20000 in Nord-Schleswig region
Netherlands	Dutch	West Frisian spoken by 450000 in Fryslan/Freisland region
Finland	Finnish	292000 Swedish speakers in southern and western Finland
France	French	Estimated 450000 Breton speakers in Brittany, 170000 Corsican speakers in Corsica
Germany	German	50000 Danish speakers in border regions
Greece	Greek	Other languages include Albanian and Bulgarian, but no recent figures available
Ireland	English	353000 (43.5%) have ability to speak Irish
Italy	Italian	German spoken in South Tyrol, French in parts of the Aosta Valley, but no official statistics available
Spain	Spanish	515000 Basque speakers in Basque country; 79% of the population of Catalonia can speak Catalan
Sweden	Swedish	Estimated 220000–300000 (4%) of population speak Finnish

Note: Some of these statistics are estimates. Countries like France and Greece do not collect details about language in their census but others do. For example, the UK Census asks people in Wales if they can speak Welsh. Respondents are generally asked to self-certify their ability to speak a language and their ability is not tested. Some ask about mother tongue, others about language ability. Therefore making comparisons is difficult.

Table 3 *Minority language groups in the European Union.*

Catalan nationalism. The global symbol of Catalan nationalism is the Barcelona football club. In the north of Spain over half a million people speak Basque. Some Basques feel so strongly about how different they are from the rest of Spain that they want their own separate country. A very small minority are members of the terrorist group ETA.

English has become the language of the 'global village' with a significant number of people around the world speaking English as a second language. This is often important to them in gaining access to the world of information and in providing greater employment opportunities. It also provides the greatest degree of access to global consumer culture.

Customs

Customs can be described as the established patterns of behaviour that are commonplace within a particular country, region or social setting. A custom is a long-standing practice handed down from one generation to the next. Some national customs are well known internationally, but most will not be until you conduct some research about them. It is useful to know something about the most important customs in a country before visiting. Such awareness is generally appreciated and it also avoids inadvertently causing offence. Japan has a number of particular customs:

- Bowing – an important form of respect. The duration and inclination of the bow is proportionate to the status of the person being addressed. It is very important for visiting politicians and business people to get this right and not cause offence.

- No tipping – to tip someone is seen as a little insulting. This is very different to many other countries where tipping is the expectation.

- Thresholds – people are expected to take off their shoes at the entrance of all homes, and most businesses and hotels. While this is common in a number of countries in terms of people's homes, it is very unusual in other

Beliefs

Arguably, the first true examples of global networks evolved in the form of world religions. Both Christianity and Islam can be viewed as global in their extent while the other four main religions of Hinduism, Buddhism, Judaism and Taoism are more regional in their scope (Figure 4).

Religious beliefs were a very strong aspect of culture in virtually all parts of the world in the past. However, **secularism** has gained a strong hold in many parts of the Western world in particular, so large sections of populations either have no religious beliefs at all or simply practise the traditional family religion but without real faith. Such societies can find other societies whose beliefs are very strong worrying and even threatening. Radical Islam is the most obvious case in point, but Christian fundamentalism is strong in places like the southern parts of the USA. In some Islamic countries religious leaders hold a great deal of power or may even control the country (a theocracy).

Iran's government is described as a 'theocratic republic'. Iran's head of state, or Supreme Leader, is an Islamic cleric appointed for life by an elected body called the Assembly of Experts. The Supreme Leader and other clerics determine if legislation is in line with Islamic law and customs (the Sharia) and can bar candidates from elections. Saudi Arabia's legal system is based entirely on Islamic law which puts prohibitions on many things including non-Muslim proselytism, alcohol, pork products and fornication. It also

Playing boules in the south of France.

countries for people to be expected to remove shoes in commercial establishments.

- Conformity – Japanese society is focused on the group rather than the individual. This is very different to societies in the West.

Celebrating St Patrick's Day on 17 March is perhaps Ireland's most well-known custom which communities in many other countries now also acknowledge. In Ireland St Patrick's Day is a public holiday. Virtually all countries have public holidays to celebrate particularly important aspects of their culture. Customs can also relate to leisure activities. In France, playing boules is a common custom, particularly among men at the weekend.

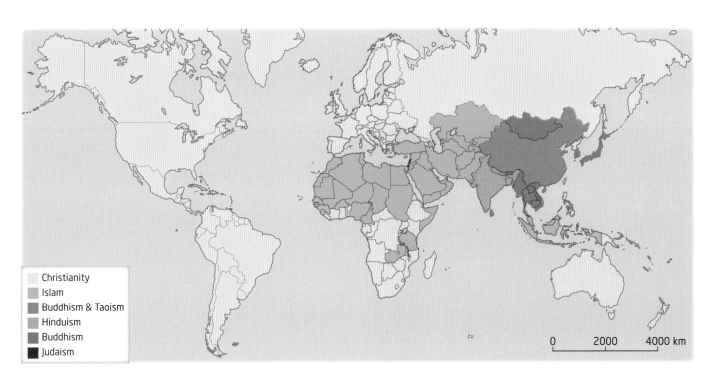

Christianity
Islam
Buddhism & Taoism
Hinduism
Buddhism
Judaism

0   2000   4000 km

Figure 4 *The world's major religions.*

Geographical skill

Describe the spatial distribution of religions illustrated in Figure 4. Make sure that you make reference to each continent, particularly where there is a mixture of religions.

Cultural dress – the burka.

dictates aspects of economic life, for example the rules for Islamic banking which differ significantly from those of capitalist commercial banks.

To complicate matters, Islam, like Christianity, is not one single unified religion. There are different branches or sects and the differences between them can lead to considerable tensions, such as with the Islamic Sunni and Shia sects in Iraq, and the Christian Protestants and Catholics in Northern Ireland.

Various secular ideologies have evolved alongside the development of national cultures. The conflict between capitalism and communism was the major global political divide in the second half of the 20th century.

Dress

Dress is an important part of daily life. Through clothing, individuals establish their individual sense of being as well as their place in society. Dress can mark out a person's job and their position in a community. In national terms dress may in part be a response to climate.

Cultural traits in terms of dress are far less distinctive in most countries than they used to be, as international casual and

business dress has become the global norm. It is usually the older age group in a country that clings to traditional dress when the younger generation has abandoned it. Traditional dress may be worn on certain special days. It can also be an important part of the tourist industry in many areas.

Dress not only marks economic and social change, but also important political watersheds. For example, the communist revolution in China in 1947 brought a strict uniformity in terms of dress. The opening up of the economy to the outside world from the late 1970s saw the norms on dress relaxed.

The dress code of a culture is often stricter for women than for men. In traditional Islam the burka is seen as essential for women to wear in public. This has resulted in fierce opposition in a number of countries, mainly in Europe. In January 2010 the head of President Nicolas Sarkozy's political party in France said that Muslim women wearing full-face veils should not be granted French nationality.

Images

Advances in telecommunications allow cultural images, of people and places, to flow around the world as never before. Cultural images may be:

- political
- economic
- social
- environmental
- historic.

Some images may be very recent while others have been perpetuated from earlier generations. For example, the

Buddhist monk in a UK temple.

The London Eye – a modern image of Britain.

Penny whistle musician, Africa.

popular images that many people have of the UK are of bowler hats, Buckingham Palace, London's red buses and the black London taxis. These are all traditional images. More modern images of the UK include Britpop and art, the English Premier League (football), David Beckham and the London Eye. The 32-capsule observation wheel overlooking the River Thames and the Houses of Parliament is the highest of its kind in the world and has become one of the most recognisable global images.

Imagery is important because it helps to portray a country in either positive or negative terms. Germany still suffers from images of the concentration camps of the Second World War and other aspects of the Nazi era. In contrast, images of modern Germany are frequently associated with the country's high standing in technology, particularly in relation to the car industry.

The images that people of a certain culture have of themselves are often quite different from the images that other people have of that particular culture. The latter are often **stereotypes** and as a result may bear little relation to reality. Stereotypes can cause offence and can become the cause of friction.

Music

Music is an essential part of most cultures, and because it does not depend on written or spoken communication explicitly for its major impact, it can diffuse easily from one culture to many others. However, because the global music industry is dominated by a small number of extremely large TNCs with their origins in the West, rock and pop music have transcended cultures more than any other genre.

The national anthem and possibly a few other particular pieces of music will be especially important in asserting national identity. This may also involve pride in the nationality of a particular composer or rock group. For example, Russia boasts a large number of internationally appreciated composers of classical music including Tchaikovsky, Shostakovich, Rachmaninoff, Stravinsky, Prokofiev and Rimsky-Korsakov. Classical music is an important part of Russian culture. In contrast, the US has a worldwide reputation for its pop and rock stars including Elvis Presley, Jimi Hendrix, The Eagles, Aerosmith, Madonna and Michael Jackson.

In some cultures, song is the dominant form of musical expression, while elsewhere instruments play a more important role. Sub-Saharan traditions emphasise singing, because song is used as an avenue of communication. Under global influences, traditional music and dance, although still practised, have decreased. New forms have emerged, however, that combine African and Western elements; they include West African highlife (showing certain Caribbean traits), Congolese popular music (reflecting Latin American influence), and in southern Africa sabasaba and kwela, both akin to American swing and jive music.

Food

Certain countries and cultures are internationally known for their food. The evidence is in restaurants with national identities. Italian, French, Mexican, Chinese, Indian and Thai restaurants are associated with particular countries and are also frequently found elsewhere. It is easy to think of the particular foods that are associated with such restaurants.

Why would it be a rarity to find restaurants associated with Russia, the UK, Germany and Bolivia in other countries?

Food is an important part of religious observance and spiritual ritual for many faiths. In Judaism 'kosher' means that a food is 'fit' or permitted. Foods must be prepared in the right way in order to be kosher; for example, animals that provide meat must be slaughtered correctly. Foods such as pork and shellfish are strictly forbidden. The Jewish 'food laws' originated more than 3000 years ago and contribute to a formal code of behaviour that reinforces the identity of a Jewish community. Food forms an integral part of religion in life for a practising Jew, but of course not all Jews follow this code.

In Islam, the concept of 'halal', meaning 'lawful or permitted', is applied to all areas of a person's life and includes regulations surrounding food. All foods are allowed (halal) except for those that are considered harmful. Prohibited foods (and other aspects of life) are called 'haram'. The list of haram foods includes pork, alcohol and any products that contain emulsifiers made from animal fats, particularly margarines.

Some Catholic and Orthodox Christians observe a number of feast and fast days during the year. For example, they may fast or avoid meat on Fridays and during Lent. Fish is a common alternative.

Research idea

Conduct a survey to list restaurants associated with countries in the area in which you live. What are the reasons for the location of these restaurants?

With growing Muslim populations more restaurants and food sellers now offer halal foods, New York, USA.

Technology

The development of new technology can result in cultural change. Gordon Childe used the term 'urban revolution' to describe the change in society marked by the emergence of the first cities some 5500 years ago. The catalyst for this period of rapid change was the Neolithic Revolution which occurred about 8000 BC. This was when sedentary farming, based on the domestication of animals and cereal farming, steadily replaced a nomadic way of life. The areas where these new techniques were introduced experienced much more rapid cultural change than the parts of the world excluded from such innovations. The Industrial Revolution began in the UK and many of its most important inventions are still associated with that country. In modern times Japan and Germany are particularly noted for their excellence in technology, a trait that a number of other countries are trying to emulate.

Cultures can differ significantly in their attitudes to different technologies. Here moral and ethical norms come into play. Examples include:

- nuclear electricity and power
- medical procedures such as abortion
- the use of contraception
- GM crops.

Some societies are more strongly against technologies that are perceived to have high environmental impact. Cultural norms with regard to human reproduction can also vary significantly.

Activities

1 Define (a) culture and (b) cultural traits.
2 Use an example to explain the meaning of a cultural hearth.
3 With reference to Figure 2 (page 143), write a 100-word summary of Mexican culture.
4 Explain cultural hybridity.
5 Why is language such an important part of culture?
6 Identify three well-known customs in the country in which you live. What is your opinion of these customs?
7 Why are differences in dress between cultures less prominent than they were 50 years ago?
8 Why is food a significant aspect of culture?
9 Give two examples of the way in which cultures can differ in their attitudes to technology.

The diffusion of cultural traits

Cultural diffusion is the process of the spreading of cultural traits from one place to another. Cultures change at different speeds across space and time. Cultures can move in both real space and cyberspace. Cultural traits can be diffused in a number of ways, in particular by the movement of workers, tourists and commodities. The influence of globalisation on cultural landscapes relates to the connectedness of that landscape to global networks and to the geographical and historical processes that have shaped a particular place or country. Places that have been largely bypassed by globalised cultural flows have been referred to as 'black holes'.

Historically, migration and the spread of empires were the most important sources of diffusion. Held *et al.* in *Global Transformation: Politics, Economics and Culture* argue that although cultural flows from the West to the rest of the world constitute the major global force, a partial reversal is taking place through complex patterns of migration, mass tourism and the growth of new sectors such as the world music industry.

The international movement of workers

In recent decades the international movement of workers has spanned a much wider range of countries than ever before. This refers to both countries of origin and destination. There are now about 100 million migrant workers around the world. Migration of labour is a key feature of globalisation and it makes a significant impact on the global economy. Worker migration has become increasingly feminised and is no longer as dominated as it once was by male migration. Migrant workers bring their own cultural traits from the countries they move from, but also pick up aspects of culture from their destination country. Such traits are transmitted back to their country of origin by (a) the short-term and permanent return of migrant workers to their home country and (b) by keeping in touch by phone, letter and ICT and sending goods back. All these modes of contact can communicate cultural aspects of the country the migrant is working in (Figure 5).

The great historic labour migrations including the Atlantic slave trade and the mass migrations from Europe to the 'New World' had a phenomenal impact on global cultural diffusion. In more recent times, with low rates of natural population increase in Western countries, migration has accounted for an increasing proportion of population growth. The result has been the establishment of significant diaspora populations in developed countries and growing cultural hybridity.

A recent example is the enlargement of the European Union in 2004 to include Eastern European countries such as Poland. A considerable number of Polish workers migrated to the UK. In areas such as London and Reading where the Polish community concentrated, shops providing goods and services to the expanding Polish community opened up and a number of Catholic churches began offering a weekend mass conducted in the Polish language. The building industry and hotels, pubs and catering attracted particularly large numbers of Polish workers. High immigration from Poland and a number of other countries increased the birth rate in the UK and widened the range of first languages spoken by children in schools. This placed considerable demands on many education authorities.

In the USA the large inflow of migrants from Latin America has resulted in a substantial increase in the proportion of Spanish speakers in the country. Many areas in the southern part of the USA, in states such as California, New Mexico, Texas and Florida, are effectively

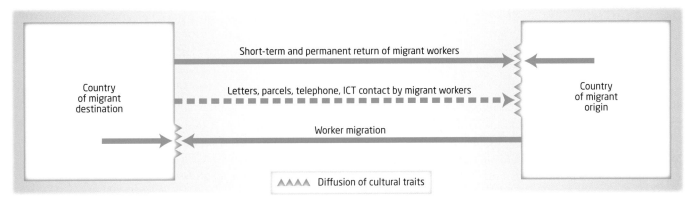

Figure 5 *Worker migration and cultural diffusion.*

bilingual. Many other traits of Latin American culture are also evident in the region. In turn, the contact that migrant workers have with their families and communities elicits a certain reverse flow of cultural traits as workers relate their experiences and send money home.

Mass tourism

International tourist arrivals reached a record of almost 900 million in 2007. Between 2000 and 2007 international tourist arrivals rose over 40%. This is an average of 4.5% a year, marking it out as a high growth industry. The growth in international tourism receipts was even stronger at almost 8% usually over the same period.

Recent decades have witnessed the globalisation of international tourism. Figure 6 shows international tourist arrivals by world region 2000–07. The highest rates of growth were in the developing world:

- The Middle East led the way with an average annual growth rate of 10%. Saudi Arabia and Egypt in particular showed strong growth as major resort destinations, while the United Arab Emirates is attracting a growing number of leisure and business travellers.

- The next highest rate of increase was in the Asia-Pacific region with an annual average growth of 8%. This was a result of (1) rapid economic expansion in the region, (2) increased marketing of tourism opportunities and (3) improved transportation infrastructure. Inbound tourism to China is rising rapidly, but outbound travel from China is a major factor in strong tourism growth across the entire Asia-Pacific region.

- Tourism in Africa rose by an average of 6%, led by the adventure tourism sector.

- In comparison with other parts of the developing world the tourism industry in Latin America and the Caribbean recorded much lower growth rates – 3% over the same time period. However, in this region the average growth figure hides a wide variation. Strong growth in many South and Central American countries contrasted with lower figures in the more mature destinations of the Caribbean and Mexico.

- Although the developed regions of the world remain the largest tourism destinations, their dominance is reducing and recent growth rates have been relatively low. For example, Europe and North America accounted for 69% of international arrivals in 2000, but

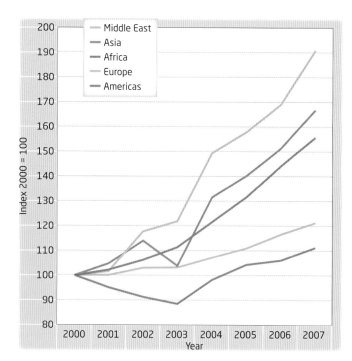

Figure 6 *Tourist arrivals by world region, 2000–07.*

by 2007 this had fallen to 62%. Europe still accounted for 54% of total international arrivals.

Large-scale international tourism results in varying degrees of cultural diffusion. In some countries it is only tourist enclaves that are significantly affected, whereas in others the impact is more widespread.

The core–periphery enclave model of tourism (Figure 7) proposed by S. Britton in 1981 stresses that in many developing countries the benefits/impact of tourism are very limited geographically. Most tourists come from the developed or core nations. In many developing countries (the periphery) tourists frequently stay in specially designated enclaves with all the required facilities immediately on hand. Outside of the resort enclaves there are a number of attractions (scenic, historic, cultural) at locations that can usually be reached and returned from within a day. At such locations the expected infrastructure is usually provided. Therefore the majority of the country is unaffected by tourism. As a result most tourists have little or no contact with local people and fail to experience the reality of life in the country they have chosen to visit.

The traditional cultures of many communities in the developing world have suffered because of the development of tourism. The adverse impact includes the following in varying degrees:

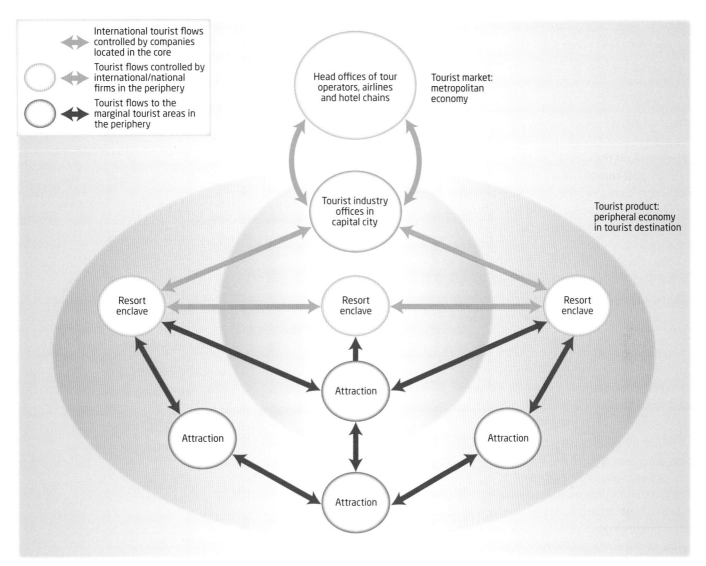

Figure 7 *Britton's enclave model of tourism.*

- There may be a loss of locally owned land as tourism companies buy up large tracts in the most scenic and accessible locations.

- Traditional values and practices may be abandoned by the local people.

- People may be displaced to make way for tourist developments.

- The structure of the local community can change.

- Large companies and governments can abuse the human rights of local people in the quest to maximise profits.

- Alcoholism and drug abuse increase as drink and drugs become more available to satisfy the demands of foreign tourists. It has also been suggested that the very obvious gap in wealth between local people and tourists can result in a certain 'despair' among some local people, particularly young adults, who find solace in alcohol and drugs.

- Tourism can increase levels of crime and prostitution, sometimes involving children. 'Sex tourism' is a big issue in certain locations such as Bangkok, but it is also prevalent in some degree in most locations visited by large numbers of international tourists. The issue of crime is more complex. Clearly the wealth that foreign visitors bring with them provides more opportunities for local criminals than existed previously but visitors may also commit various crimes themselves.

- Visitor congestion at key locations may hinder the movement of local people.

- Local people may be denied access to beaches in order to provide 'exclusivity' for visitors.
- Housing for local people can be lost as more visitors buy second homes in popular tourist areas.

The global movement of commodities

People around the world have a greater choice of international commodities than ever before, although in many developing countries the prices of such commodities are out of the reach of many people. However, even though people may not have the money to purchase a commodity, they become aware of the lifestyle it attempts to portray because of advertising.

As TNCs have sought to move beyond the often saturated markets of Western countries they have exported Western consumer culture to the developing world on a large scale. Walking around the central business district of virtually any large town or city in the developing world you will see large numbers of people wearing T-shirts and other clothes advertising major brand names for a range of different products. The global advertising industry is a major factor in the diffusion of cultural traits.

Western fast food chains such as McDonald's and KFC have played a considerable role in the increase in meat consumption in countries such as China. Diet is a cultural trait that is changing significantly in many newly industrialised countries. Along with such a change in diet often goes changes in eating habits, with fewer family meals as individual family members grab food on the go!

Some commodities spread cultural traits more directly than others. The **cultural or creative industries** are the most direct in spreading cultural traits. Such industries include

film, music, publishing, advertising, architecture, fashion, software, toys and games. Trade in cultural products has expanded rapidly in recent decades and is a major aspect of globalisation.

Culture shock

Cultural diffusion is not always a smooth process. Figure 9 shows two paths people can take during the four phases of long-term cross-cultural encounters. The term 'culture shock' was coined by Kalvero Oberg in 1954 to describe the difficulties that some people feel when confronted with a significantly different culture to their own.

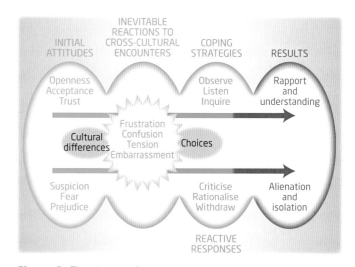

Figure 9 *The phases of long-term cross-cultural encounters.*

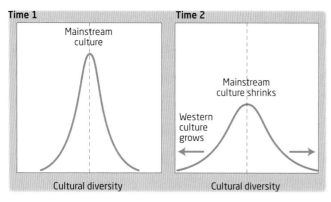

Figure 8 *The diffusion of Western culture into developing countries.*

Activities

1 Define 'cultural diffusion'.
2 Explain the difference between cultures diffusing in real space and cyberspace.
3 What is a 'black hole'?
4 With reference to Figure 5 (page 151) discuss the role of worker migration in the diffusion of cultural traits.
5 Describe the data presented in Figure 6 (page 152).
6 What roles have the international movement of tourists played in cultural diffusion?
7 How does the international movement of commodities affect the diffusion of cultural traits?

Review

Examination-style questions

1 a Describe cultural traits in terms of language, customs and beliefs.

 b Examine the importance of cultural traits in music, dress and food.

2 a Describe the general process of the diffusion of Western culture into developing countries.

 b Discuss the diffusion of cultural traits resulting from the international movement of workers, tourists and commodities.

Websites

www.ilo.org
International Labour Organization

Key terms

Culture the total of the inherited ideas, beliefs, values and knowledge which constitute the shared basis of social action.

Cultural traits individual components of a cultural complex which may be divided into three categories: sociological, ideological and technological.

Cultural hearth an area that is or has been a rich source of cultural traits.

Cultural hybridity the extent to which cultures are intermixed.

Official language the language of a country, region or institution that is embedded in law.

Bilingual country a country in which two languages are commonly spoken.

Separatist movements political parties or other organisations which believe that their region should separate from its current country to form a new country.

Customs the established patterns of behaviour that are commonplace within a particular country, region or social setting.

Secularism a view that rejects religion and religious considerations.

Stereotype a standardised mental picture that is held in common by members of a group and that represents an oversimplified opinion, prejudiced attitude or uncritical judgement.

Cultural diffusion the process of the spreading of cultural traits from one place to another.

Cultural or creative industries industries that involve the spreading or creating of culture.

13 Consumerism and culture

Domino's Pizza advertisement in Moscow.

Consumer culture, the mass media and brands

The spread of a global **consumer culture** has been important to the success of many TNCs. The **mass media** has been used very effectively to encourage consumers to 'want' more than they 'need'. Television and other media aim to create successful product images and to identify target consumer groups. The latter is a dynamic process as changes in income and attitudes can open up new markets. TNCs' market penetration and economic expansion depend upon the mass media for the dissemination of consumer culture. Without the mass media there would be no contemporary consumer society and no globalisation as we know it. Figure 1 illustrates the relationship between TNCs, the media and consumers.

The marketing industry uses all elements of the media to convey positive images and messages about the products and services of its clients (Figure 2). The Chartered Institute of Marketing defines marketing as 'the management process responsible for identifying, anticipating and satisfying customer requirements profitably'.

Advertising is the most high-profile aspect of marketing. Advertising seeks to turn predisposition into action. Grey Advertising International undertook a global analysis of television to determine its usefulness as an advertising medium and concluded:

> Television is undisputedly the key communications development of our era, shaping the values, attitudes and lifestyles of generations growing up with it. In countries where it operates as an unfettered commercial medium it has proven for many products the most potent of all consumer marketing weapons as well as a major influence in establishing corporate images.

However, while television is the most important element of the media in spreading consumer culture, the other avenues illustrated in Figure 2 are also powerful media. Internet advertising is increasing at a particularly rapid rate.

TNCs	MEDIA	CONSUMERS
Seeking to increase: • sales • market share • global spread	• Creating successful product images • Transforming 'wants' into 'needs' • Identifying 'target' consumer groups	• Accepting/rejecting product presentations • Having needs satisfied

Figure 1 *TNCs, the media and consumers.*

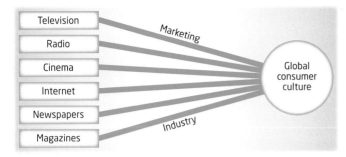

Figure 2 *The media spreading consumer culture.*

The global advertising industry generated revenues of $90.8 billion in 2008, according to BizResearch. This is forecast to rise to $107 billion by 2012. TV and cinema form the dominant channels in the global advertising market with 43.9% of the market value, but other media, particularly Internet advertising, are increasing rapidly. There is a strong link between the rate of investment in advertising and GDP growth in major markets. Overall, advertising contributes about 1% to global GDP.

Discussion point

Which elements of the media are most relevant to you in the choices you make about the purchase of goods and services?

In the modern age of sophisticated advertising, minute differences between products or small improvements in them can determine variations in demand. The power of **brands** and their global marketing strategies cannot be underestimated. This is particularly so in food, beverages and fashion. The increasing knowledge of Western

Billboard advertising Time *and other magazines.*

consumer culture in the former Soviet Union and Eastern Europe in the Cold War period was an important factor in the eventual disintegration of the Eastern bloc.

Consumption is now understood as more than just a material transaction process. Products have symbolic as well as material value so that their consumption is linked to the creation and expression of identities. Brands have increasingly become important symbols of identity. For example, in the USA wearing Adidas shoes and clothing became strongly linked to hip-hop culture. Other brands of clothing, shoes, jewellery, alcoholic drinks, cigarettes, perfume and other products all attempt to convey a certain message – one of enhanced status by consuming a product of high image value. Products that successfully signify status are rapidly diffused across the globe. According to W.E. Murray, 'When the objects, ideas and traits of a culture become part of the capitalist system of exchange and are bought and sold, a process of **cultural commodification** is said to be occurring.' Figure 3 looks at this process in greater detail.

Cultural commodification works both ways, with 'ethnic foods' becoming increasingly popular in Western supermarkets, alongside the marketing of ethnic districts in Western cities as noted locations for restaurants and other forms of entertainment, for local residents and tourists alike. Sampling of such alternatives to Western products is seen increasingly as a sign of sophistication.

Theory of Knowledge

Why do you think that global brands have been so successful in local markets all over the world? Is what they offer genuinely superior to established local products? Some analysts seem to think that marketing campaigns 'force' people to buy – but, unless we think purchasers have no preferences or will-power of their own, surely there have to be some positive reasons why they choose, say, Coke or McDonald's. What do you think?

Brand identity and brand image

Brands are among a company's most valuable assets. Strong brands have the power to create considerable competitive advantage. Powerful brands can:

- significantly increase revenue by ensuring higher demand and market share

How International Marketing Sells the Western Lifestyle

By Noreene Janus

No one can travel to Africa, Asia or Latin America and not be struck by the Western elements of urban life. The trappings of transnational culture – automobiles, advertising, supermarkets, shopping centers, hotels, fast food chains, credit cards, and Hollywood movies – give the feeling of being at home. Behind these tangible symbols is a corresponding set of values and attitudes about time, consumption, work relations, etc. Some believe global culture has resulted from gradual spontaneous processes that depended solely on technological innovations, increased international trade, global mass communications, jet travel. Recent studies show that the processes are anything but spontaneous; that they are the result of tremendous investments of time, energy and money by transnational corporations.

This 'transnational culture' is a direct outcome of the internationalization of production and accumulation promoted through standardized development models and cultural forms.

Creating Consumers

The common theme of transnational culture is consumption. Advertising expresses this ideology of consumption in its most synthetic and visual form.

Advertisers rely on a few repetitive themes: happiness, youth, success, status, luxury, fashion, and beauty. Social contradictions and class differences are masked and workplace conflicts are not shown. Campaigns suggest that solutions to human problems are to be found in individual consumption, presented as an ideal outlet for mass energies ... a socially acceptable form of action and participation which can be used to defuse potential political unrest. 'Consumer democracy' is held out to the poor around the world as a substitute for political democracy. After all, as the advertising executive who transformed the U.S. Pepsi ad campaign 'Join the Pepsi Generation' for use in Brazil as 'Join the Pepsi Revolution' explains, most people have no other means to express their need for social change other than by changing brands and increasing their consumption. Transnational advertising is one of the major reasons both for the spread of transnational culture and the breakdown of traditional cultures. Depicting the racy foreign lifestyles of a blond jetsetter in French or English, it associates Western products with modernity. That which is modern is good; that which is traditional is implicitly bad, impeding the march of progress. Transnational culture strives to eliminate local cultural variations.

Global marketing strategy is so effective that conscious subversion is hardly needed. The message 'we will sell you a culture' has resulted in the global advertising campaign, a single advertising message used in all countries where a product is made or distributed. Worldwide advertising is more economical and more efficient, although it may clash wildly with local conditions. Transnational corporations and international advertising agencies work hard at creating a consumer culture. Increasingly advertising campaigns are aimed at the vast numbers of poor in Third World countries. Even poor families, when living together and pooling their incomes, can add up to a household income of more than $10,000 per year, making them an important advertising target.

As one advertising professional commented, 'Once the TV set goes to work, the family is like a kid in a candy store. They're pounded by 450 commercials a week. They see all the beautiful things. And what they see, they want.'

Figure 3 *Cloning the consumer culture.*

- improve profitability by commanding premium prices and offering keen supplier terms
- reduce the costs of entry into new products due to a strong customer base.

Brand identity is everything the company wants the brand to be seen as. It may consist of features and attributes, benefits, performance, quality, service support, and the values that the brand possesses. **Brand image**, on the other hand, is the totality of consumer perceptions about the brand. Through advertising and other aspects of marketing, a company will try to achieve as close a correlation as possible between brand image and brand identity.

Table 1 shows the world's top 50 most valuable global brands according to BrandZ which uses the valuations calculated by analysts Millward Brown Optimor. The latter conclude that being recognisable in many markets is not by itself a passport to success. That requires adapting the brand and offer to be relevant in each particular market. Successful brands transcend their origins and create strong, enduring relationships with consumers across countries and cultures.

The power of the Internet is illustrated by the fact that Google and Microsoft occupy the first two positions. Coca-Cola, IBM and McDonald's complete the top five. Case studies of McDonald's and Coca-Cola follow on pages 161–166.

Rank	Brand	Brand value 2009 ($ million)
1	Google	100039
2	Microsoft	76249
3	Coca-Cola	67625
4	IBM	66622
5	McDonald's	66575
6	Apple	63113
7	China Mobile	61283
8	GE	59793
9	Vodafone	53727
10	Marlboro	49460
11	Wal-Mart	41083
12	ICBC (Asia)	38056
13	Nokia	35163
14	Toyota	29907
15	Ups	27842
16	Blackberry	27478
17	hp	26745
18	BMW	23948
19	SAP	23615
20	Disney	23110
21	Tesco	22938
22	Gillette	22919
23	Intel	22851
24	China Merchants Bank	22811
25	Oracle	21438
26	amazon.com	21294
27	Bank of China	21192
28	at&t	20059
29	Louis Vuitton	19395
30	HSBC	19079
31	Pampers	18945
32	Nintendo	18233
33	CISCO	17965
34	Verizon	17713
35	Porsche	17467

Rank	Brand	Brand value 2009 ($ million)
36	VISA	16353
37	Wells Fargo	16228
38	Santander	16035
39	docomo	15776
40	Mercedes-Benz	15499
41	Bank of America	15480
42	DELL	15422
43	Accenture	15076
44	Pepsi	14996
45	L'Oréal	14991
46	American Express	14963
47	Carrefour	14961
48	RBC	14894
49	Citi	14608
50	Honda	14571

Table 1 *The top 50 most valuable global brands.*

Manchester United – a famous sporting brand.

Generic brands

The influence of major brands is contained to a certain extent by the 'generic brands' produced by major supermarkets. Such generic brands generate larger profits for supermarkets and give them more control over production and price. When household incomes are squeezed during times of recession, the demand for generic brands usually increases. The marketing skills of companies like Wal-Mart and Tesco will ensure that presentation and pricing are such that generic brands do not appear to be cheaper alternatives of lower quality.

Consumer culture targets children

Advertising aimed at children is hardly new, but the scale and sophistication of today's marketing campaigns go far beyond traditional television ads, commercialising childhood to an unprecedented degree. Techniques of modern marketing include:

- invasive 'viral marketing' campaigns that turn children's friendships into word-of-mouth networks for spreading enthusiasm about new products
- covert sociological research into children's habits and preferences
- gimmicks such as hybridised 'advergames' that disguise brand-building and consumer product research as slick entertainment.

There has been growing concern about the way media-led consumerism is dominating children's lives. Susan Linn of the Campaign for Commercial-Free Childhood, writing in *State of the World 2010*, argues that commercialisation is undermining children's futures by eliminating playtime. Creative play of the unstructured child-directed variety is known to be extremely important for childhood development. This type of play has steadily declined because children are spending too much time watching TV, playing video games and surfing the Internet. It is no coincidence that investment in marketing to children has risen significantly. In 2009, American marketing companies spent $17 billion on marketing campaigns aimed at children. However, this is not just confined to the USA, it is a global trend.

The World Health Organization has identified marketing to children as a significant factor in the rise of childhood obesity. Other problems that have been associated with intense marketing to children include eating disorders, sexualisation, youth violence, family stress, and underage alcohol and tobacco use. A reaction to the association between such problems and marketing to children is beginning to gather pace. Quebec, for example, does not allow any television advertisements aimed at children under 13 years.

Research idea

Look at TV adverts on a mainstream channel for one hour in the early evening for three days. How many of the advertisements are aimed at least partially at children? Which companies and products are involved? How would you describe the techniques used in these advertisements?

Activities

1 Define (a) consumer culture and (b) the mass media.
2 Describe and explain the relationships between TNCs, the media and consumers.
3 What is cultural commodification?
4 Produce a 100-word précis of the text in Figure 3.
5 Explain the difference between brand identity and brand image.
6 Look at Table 1.
   a How many of these brands have you heard of?
   b Put as many of these brands as you can into industrial groups.
7 What are generic brands?
8 a Suggest why marketing campaigns have increasingly targeted children.
   b Discuss the problems associated with the growing commercialisation of childhood.

Case study

McDonald's: transnational franchising

With 31 000 restaurants in 118 countries and 1.4 million restaurant employees, the McDonald's hamburger chain has for long been the epitome of American multinational success, as well as a symbol of US imperialism for radical groups in many parts of the world. In spite of some recent well-publicised problems, McDonald's is still the king of fast food, serving nearly 58 million customers each day. The company logo, the set of Golden Arches, is one of the best-known business symbols in the world. Table 2 shows the brand values of the ten largest fast food chains according to the Millward Brown Optimor analysis. Some of these brands will be more familiar than others depending on where you live.

Rank	Brand	Brand value ($ million)
1	McDonald's	66 575
2	Subway	10 997
3	KFC	6 721
4	Starbucks	6 413
5	Tim Horton's	3 843
6	Pizza Hut	3 114
7	Wendy's	3 030
8	Burger King	2 429
9	Taco Bell	1 711
10	Arby's	661

Table 2 *The top ten fast food brands.*

McDonald's is an example of a brand **franchise** (Figure 4), a type of business organisation that has become extremely popular in recent decades because it can result in much more rapid expansion than following the traditional route where the core company owns everything. The more restaurants there are, the more McDonald's benefits from economies of scale. Today, over 70% of McDonald's restaurants worldwide are run on a franchise basis.

When the first McDonald's restaurant was opened in Britain in 1974, people queued for hours to get in. In 1994, the drive-through line on opening day in Kuwait City was seven miles long. The busiest McDonald's outlet is

McDonald's is an example of brand franchising. McDonald's, the franchisor, grants the right to sell McDonald's branded goods to someone wishing to set up their own business, the franchisee.

Under a McDonald's franchise, McDonald's owns and leases the site and the restaurant building. The franchisee buys the fittings, the equipment and the right to operate the franchise for 20 years.

To ensure uniformity throughout the world, all franchisees must use standardised McDonald's branding, menus, design layouts and administration systems. The licence agreement also insists the franchisee uses the same manufacturing or operating methods and maintains the quality of the menu items.

Figure 4 *A McDonald's franchise.*

in Moscow's Pushkin Square. When it opened in January 1990 it set the company record – which it still holds – for the largest number of servings in a single day. It has been estimated that:

- one in eight Americans has worked in a McDonald's at some point in their lives
- a third of all cows reared in the USA are needed to produce the company's burgers
- 8% of the US potato crop is used for the fries.

Initially the ingredients for the hamburgers were prepared in individual restaurants. However, from the late 1960s the meat, bread and fries have been mass produced and then delivered frozen to each franchise outlet.

The company has sought rapid growth since its inception in 1955, when Ray Kroc first franchised a company that had originated in 1937 as a California burger stand run by the McDonald brothers. Between 1965 and 1991 average annual revenue growth of 24% was based on innovative marketing and the enforcing of rigid standards of quality and cleanliness. Marketing was based on what one expert has described as the 'aspirational thing' – if you could eat hamburgers and drink Coke, you could taste part of the American dream.

However, as competition within the USA grew stiffer, McDonald's increasingly turned overseas to expand. In 1991, for the first time, McDonald's opened more outlets outside the USA than inside. In 1996, the peak year of expansion, the company opened 2000 restaurants globally. But the picture has not been so rosy in recent years. The

US market is virtually saturated and the company seems to have expanded too fast in countries where not enough people can afford a $1 hamburger. A Harvard business professor and author of an MBA thesis on the company says, 'McDonald's is suddenly reaching the boundaries of growth.'

Figure 5 shows the spatial extent of McDonald's global reach and also how the company has expanded over time. McDonald's is very poorly represented in Africa compared with other continents. Table 3 shows the countries with the most McDonald's restaurants. Almost 14 000 are in the USA, accounting for 43.5% of the global total. The rate of expansion has been particularly high in China where McDonald's opened 136 new outlets in 2008, the most of any country. McDonald's has established a new tradition in China by popularising American-style birthday parties. It has achieved this largely by its direct television marketing to children. What was at first the exception in Chinese middle-class communities is fast becoming the norm.

1	USA	13918
2	Japan	3755
3	Canada	1414
4	Germany	1333
5	UK	1190
6	France	1133
7	China	1012
8	Australia	782
9	Brazil	562
10	Spain	393
11	Italy	379
12	Mexico	379
13	Taiwan	349

Table 3 *Countries with the most McDonald's restaurants in 2008.*

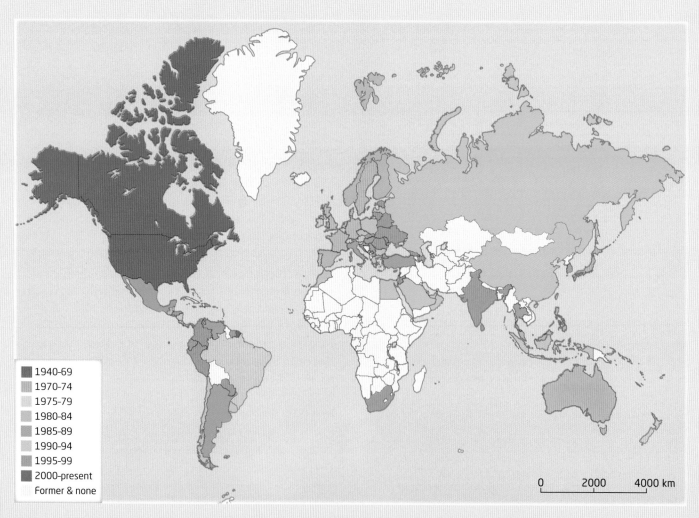

1940-69
1970-74
1975-79
1980-84
1985-89
1990-94
1995-99
2000-present
Former & none

0   2000   4000 km

Figure 5 *Global expansion of McDonald's since 1940.*

5 Sociocultural exchanges

Geographical skill

With reference to Figure 5 and Table 3, explain the global spread of McDonald's.

McDonald's McArabia meal.

Overall revenue for 2008 totalled $23.5 billion. McDonald's European operations generated the largest percentage amount at 42.2% with total sales of $9.9 billion. This was followed by McDonald's US restaurants with 34.3% of total global revenue. However, restaurants in Asia-Pacific, the Middle East and Africa achieved the highest sales percentage gains over the previous year. European revenue was led by strong sales in Russia, France and the UK.

Critics of the company put its recent change of fortunes down to the following:

- increasing competition, both in the USA and abroad – new, more health-conscious fast-food restaurants are rapidly raising their market share
- falling quality survey ratings against competitors
- a poor recent record of product innovation
- poor locational choices for some new outlets
- the increasing attraction of vegetarianism and scares over meat products (BSE, foot and mouth etc.)
- the impact of books such as *Fast Food Nation*.

Business analysts say that unless McDonald's can respond quickly to its perceived problems, its era of rapid expansion may well be over. However, the company is investing heavily to respond to recent challenges with measures which include:

- improving the quality of its present product range
- promoting higher-margin food such as the grilled-chicken flatbread sandwich
- getting in on the 'fast-casual' dining boom in the USA by buying chains such as Chipotle Mexican and Boston Market.

In recent years McDonald's has made serious efforts to adapt its menus to local tastes. For example, the company's Sichuan spicy menu product known as the China Mac became extremely popular at the Beijing Olympic Games. In China, McDonald's has a very middle-class image and this is true for other developing countries where it is located. As the number of people in the middle-income group rises in newly industrialised countries, it is not surprising that McDonald's is looking to expand in these countries in particular. The competitive advantages of McDonald's are such that it would be difficult for new domestic companies to offer stiff competition.

There is no guarantee that even the most powerful TNCs will maintain their market share. In fact Starbucks, not McDonald's, is now America's most expansionist food chain. In 2002 analysts became particularly nervous about litigation from obese Americans who blame McDonald's for their health problems. Some compared these lawsuits to the litigation that has cost tobacco companies billions of dollars. However, in January 2003 America's fast-food industry breathed a sigh of relief when a judge kicked out a lawsuit brought by a group of obese teenagers from the Bronx district of New York.

In the past McDonald's has been the target for environmental groups concerned about a variety of activities involving the company. Issues have included the destruction of rainforest to provide grazing land for 'McDonald's cattle' and the large amount of waste packaging that has to be disposed of.

McDonald's is not only an important global entity in its own right. It has also given its name to a process or set of principles (McDonaldisation) that is said to have spread around the world. According to Ritzer these principles are:

- efficiency – McDonaldisation compresses the timespan and the effort expended between a want and its satisfaction

- calculability – it encourages calculations of costs of money, time and effort as the key principles of value on the part of the consumer, displacing estimations of quality
- predictability – it standardises products so that consumers are encouraged not to seek alternatives
- control of human beings by the use of material technology – this involves not only maximal de-skilling of workers but control of consumers by means of queue control barriers, fixed menu displays, limited options, uncomfortable seats, inaccessible toilets and 'drive-through' processing

McDonald's continues to adapt its product range to consumer demand. It has recently introduced McCafé, a coffee house concept which the company brought into most of its US outlets in 2009.

Coca-Cola

Coca-Cola, with its headquarters in Atlanta, Georgia, is the world's largest soft drinks company. Coca-Cola is rated as the most recognised trade mark in the world. It has been claimed that the term 'Coca-Cola' itself is the second most widely understood in the world after 'OK'!

Besides the well-known Coca-Cola and Coke brands, it also produces Fanta, Sprite, Barq's, Minute Maid orange juice, POWERade and Dasani water. Coca-Cola originated as a soda fountain beverage in 1886 selling for 5 cents a glass. Early growth was encouraging, but it was only when a strong bottling system developed that Coca-Cola became the world-famous brand it is today. The company works with more than 300 bottlers to produce, deliver, market and sell products around the world. Table 4 lists the top ten soft drinks brands by brand value according to the Millward Brown Optimor analysis.

Coca-Cola advertisement.

Coca-Cola/Coke has not suffered in the recent global financial crisis in the way that many other global brands have. In the first half of 2009 its worldwide sales increased by 3%. The same thing happened in the year after the Wall Street Crash of 1929. It seems that when people do not have the money to spend on more expensive items they can still resort to cheaper pleasures such as the world's most famous soft drink.

In 1930 the company made a profit of $13 million, operating in over 25 countries. In 2008 its profits totalled $5.8 billion on sales of $31.9 billion from about 200 countries. Coke became a global brand much earlier than many of its modern-day competitors. Now, more than ever, it relies on its sales outside of its core region in North America. In recent times sales in North America and Europe have been stagnant, particularly for its main brand Coca-Cola. Figure 6 compares sales in North America with those in India and China since 2004. In the second quarter of 2009, Coke recorded sales growth of 33% in India and 14% in China while showing a decrease in North America. However, in terms of per capita consumption Coke is looking to make much greater headway into the markets

	Brand	Brand value ($ million)
1	Coca-Cola	53 315
2	Coke (Diet, Light and Zero)	14 310
3	Pepsi	12 761
4	Red Bull	8 154
5	Fanta	4 575
6	Sprite	3 511
7	Dr. Pepper	2 799
8	Gatorade	2 399
9	Diet Pepsi	2 234
10	Mountain Dew	2 221

Table 4 *The top ten global soft drinks brands.*

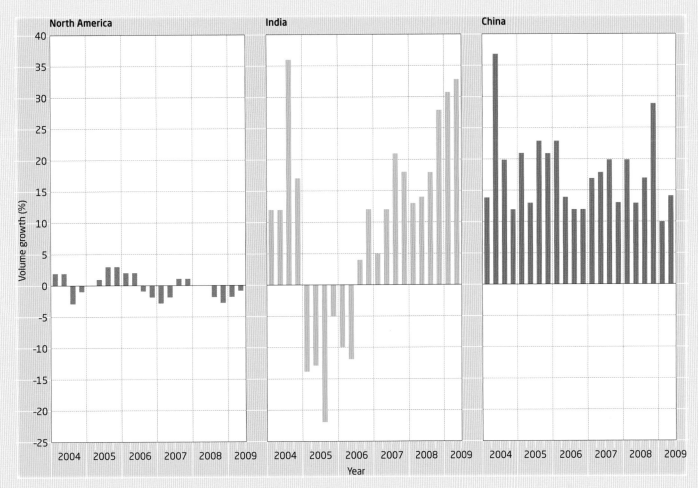

Figure 6 *Coca-Cola: volume growth by region (North America, India and China), 2004–09.*

of India and China, along with the markets of other newly industrialised countries where products such as Coca-Cola are becoming increasingly affordable. In the USA average per capita consumption of Coke products is 412 bottles a year, but only 28 in China and 7 in India.

Coke first entered the Chinese market in 1927 but halted operations in 1949, the year of the communist revolution. Coke returned to China in 1979 when the Chinese government announced important economic reforms to engage more openly with the global economy. By 2001, China had become the company's seventh largest market. In 2008 rising sales placed China as Coke's third largest market after the USA and Mexico.

Because soft drinks are a low-value/high-bulk product, companies in this industry aim to locate production as close to markets as possible. Thus the number of bottling plants in China has been increasing rapidly (Figure 7). Coke now has distribution in almost every province. The opening of the bottling plants in Jiangxi and Xinjiang required an investment of over $30 million by the company. Coca-Cola and its bottlers now operate 38 bottling plants in Greater

China, employing more than 30 000 people directly and indirectly and creating around 300 000 jobs. The company opened a new $90 million research and development centre in Shanghai in March 2009.

Coke has been involved with a number of social projects in China which include:

- building schools and libraries in rural China in partnership with Project Hope
- contributing to disaster relief efforts in the Sichuan region – Coke is donating $12 million to build schools in the earthquake-affected areas
- being a co-investor with UNDP and the Chinese government to enhance clean water access and sanitation in rural areas.

The company also sponsored the Olympic Torch Relay and had a major advertising presence at the Olympic Games. Coke is the official Beverage Global Partner of Expo 2010 Shanghai. Social and economic relationships with key customer countries are now seen as an important part of the 'acceptability' of major brands. A major part of Coke's

Olympic advertising was to try to persuade the Chinese population to drink its product cold. Both tradition and a shortage of refrigeration means that soft drinks have more often than not been drunk warm.

Coke has adapted its product range to maximise sales in China. For example, the company has been selling soda bottles of 355 ml, a little more than half the size of its traditional bottle. With the small bottle at a significantly lower price than the standard product it is accessible in terms of cost to a much larger market.

Urumqi, Xinjiang, June 24, 2009 – The Coca-Cola Company and its bottling partner, COFCO Coca-Cola Beverages Ltd, continued their expansion in China with the opening of two new bottling facilities this week in less developed central and western China. The new facilities are testimonies to Coca-Cola's long-term commitment to China as part of a recently announced USD $2 billion 3 year investment plan aimed at bolstering further growth in one of the world's largest and fastest growing beverage markets.

From today consumers in China's westernmost province, Xinjiang, will be able to consume locally-produced Coca-Cola products with the establishment of the new COFCO bottling plant, located along the historic Silk Road. The bottling facility will provide a strategically important platform for continuous growth of Coca-Cola in north-western China where Xinjiang, with over 20 million consumers, is the largest province.

Yesterday, The Coca-Cola Company and COFCO officially opened another new bottling plant in China. Located in Nanchang, Jiangxi Province, this plant will provide refreshing Coca-Cola products to the 44 million consumers in this central province of China.

The new investment has directly created 796 new jobs at the two bottling plants, and is more broadly expected to create an additional 8000 jobs with upstream suppliers and a wide variety of service providers.

Figure 7 *Coca-Cola accelerates expansion in China.*

In 2008, Coke's brands accounted for 52.5% of China's carbonated drinks market. This compares with Pepsi's 32.8%. Both companies invest heavily in marketing campaigns in an attempt to boost market share. Coke has recently used sport as its main marketing image while Pepsi has concentrated on pop music culture. However, the market leader in China is not a cola but lemon-lime Sprite which is a Coca-Cola brand.

Coke has invested $1.6 billion in China since 1979 and has plans to invest a further $2 billion between 2010 and

2013. Coke sees the continuing process of urbanisation in China as an important factor in increasing its potential market. The company was disappointed when the Chinese government recently blocked the proposed $2.4 billion takeover of Chinese juicemaker Huiyuan. China was concerned that the merger would give Coke too large a share of the soft drinks market.

In India, Coke was the number one soft drinks brand between 1958 and 1977. The company left India as the business environment turned nationalist. The Indian government had demanded that the company reveal its formula and become a minority owner to an Indian company. Coke returned to India in 1993, five years after Pepsi, as the country's business environment had become friendlier to foreign investment. It purchased an existing bottling network along with a number of local brands. In its first decade back in India, Coke invested in excess of $1 billion and recorded its first profits in 2001.

In 2003, both Coke and Pepsi came under intense pressure from an environmental group called the Centre for Science and Environment which alleged that samples of both companies' drinks tested high for pesticide residue. Problems were later found with the testing procedure but sales were affected sharply in the short term.

Reacting to consumer demand, Coca-Cola has made a significant move to healthier options such as Coke Zero. Of course its competitors have followed suit. Successful marketing continues to be essential for Coca-Cola to maintain its leading position.

 **Activities**

1 What is a franchise?
2 Explain how economies of scale are important to a large organisation like McDonald's.
3 Suggest reasons for the extremely high brand value of McDonald's (Table 2) compared with the other major fast food brands.
4 How has McDonald's reacted to changing consumer demand?
5 What is the origin of Coca-Cola?
6 List Coca-Cola's major brands.
7 Describe the data presented in Figure 6.
8 Why has Coca-Cola invested so much money in expanding in China and India?
9 Explain how Coca-Cola has adjusted its marketing to gain popularity in developing countries.

Review

Examination-style questions

1 a How have TNCs spread consumer culture around the world?

   b What has been the role of the media in this process?

2 a Describe the origin and characteristics of one branded commodity you have studied.

   b Examine the spatial and temporal pattern of adoption of this branded commodity on a global scale.

Websites

www.brandz.com
BrandZ

www.globalissues.org
Global Issues: social, political, economic and environmental issues

www.globalpolicy.org
Global Policy Forum

www.worldwatch.org
Worldwatch Institute

Key terms

Consumer culture the equation of personal happiness with consumption and the purchase of material possessions.

Mass media a section of the media specifically designed to reach a large audience. The term was coined in the 1920s with the advent of nationwide radio networks, and mass-circulation newspapers and magazines.

Brand a distinguishing name and/or symbol intended to identify a product or producer.

Cultural commodification when the objects, ideas and traits of a culture become part of the capitalist system of exchange and are bought and sold.

Brand identity image and values associated with a brand.

Brand image the totality of consumer perceptions about the brand.

Franchises businesses that are based upon the name, logos and trading methods of an existing organisation.

14 Sociocultural integration

KEY QUESTIONS

- What is the role of diasporas in preserving culture in the UK and in the adoption of minority traits by the host society?
- What has been the impact of cultural diffusion on the Xingu through the influence of international interactions?
- In what ways can international interactions result in the homogenisation and dilution of a culture?
- How can cultural imperialism be defined and identified?

East European food store in North London – East European migration to the UK rose significantly with the expansion of the EU in 2004.

A **diaspora** refers to the scattering of a culture from its homeland and was originally used with reference to the movements of the Jewish people. In more recent times the large-scale emigration of the Irish for more than a century after the Potato Famine of the 1840s has been generically referred to in Ireland as the 'Wild Geese', signifying movement over often long distances to many different destinations. The Irish diaspora is particularly strong in English-speaking countries such as the USA, UK and Australia. Until the communications revolution, diasporas maintained contact with the country of origin mainly by direct contact through travel and by letter and newspapers. In recent decades ICT has provided new-found space for diasporic cultural interactions.

Diasporas extend across traditional boundaries and in this process they create new cultural forms that challenge accepted hierarchies and cultures. For example, the concept of Britishness takes different forms in the disparate parts of the former British Empire with the blending of British and local cultures. Diasporas can profoundly transform nation-state cultures over a period of time.

Diasporas in London and the UK

London is arguably the most cosmopolitan city in Europe. Some commentators go further and view London as the most multiracial city in the world. The diverse **ethnicity** of the capital is exemplified by the fact that over 200 languages are spoken within its boundaries. The lobby group Migration Watch estimates that two-thirds of immigration into Britain since the mid 1990s has been into London. Within the UK the process of **racial assimilation** is much more advanced in London than anywhere else. Almost 30% of people in London were born outside the UK compared with 2.9% in the North East. In 2000 16% of all new solicitors in London were black or Asian, and a third of London's doctors are now non-white. London has the highest proportion of each ethnic minority group apart from Pakistanis, of whom there is a higher proportion in Yorkshire.

Just over 50% of London's people described themselves as white British in the 2001 census. A further 14% are either white Irish or 'white Other' (Europeans, Americans, Australians, New Zealanders etc.). There are now more ethnically African residents (8%) in London than black Caribbean. The largest Asian community is Bangladeshi (5%).

An Indian pub in Southall, London – Southall has the largest Indian community in the UK.

Ethnic groups are:

- distinct groups that are smaller than the dominant group in their society
- groups whose members share cultural traditions, values and a language
- groups whose members recognise themselves as a separate group and are recognised as such by others in society.

London's non-white population, 28.8% of the capital's total, is the largest of any European city. Demographers at the Greater London Authority predict that, due to continuing immigration, this will rise to a third of London's population within the next ten years. The biggest growth will be in London's Asian communities, which still have relatively large families, and also black Africans, due mainly to migration. It is also likely that the number of British-born children of Afro-Caribbean and mixed parentage will increase at a significant rate.

Spatial distribution

Figure 1 (page 170) shows the distribution of the non-white ethnic group population in London according to the 2001 census. A much more complicated picture still would be presented by examining figures at ward and enumeration district levels where the concept of the **urban mosaic** really becomes apparent. For example,

in Tower Hamlets the Bangladeshi population ranges from 58.1% in the ward of Spitalfields and Banglatown to 10% in the Bow East ward. Detailed analysis of census data shows that the ethnic Asian population lives in wards with higher levels of ethnic minority concentration than the black population.

The highest proportion of most ethnic groups in Britain can be found in one London borough or another (Figure 1). This is also true for religious groups. According to Ben Arogundade, author of *Black Beauty*, 'Geographically, future London will remain split into **integrationist communities**, such as Portobello or Shepherd's Bush, and separated enclaves such as Southall.'

Factors affecting concentration

A range of factors affect ethnic concentration:

- There is a tendency for more recent immigrants to live in wards with a high ethnic minority concentration.
- Those who are not fluent in English are more likely to live in areas with a high ethnic minority concentration.
- Those in the highest social classes live in areas with a lower concentration of ethnic minority communities.
- Higher levels of qualification are also associated with lower levels of ethnic minority concentration.
- The more paid workers there are in a household, the less likely they are to live in areas with a high concentration of ethnic minority population.

Civil demonstration in East London, June 2010.

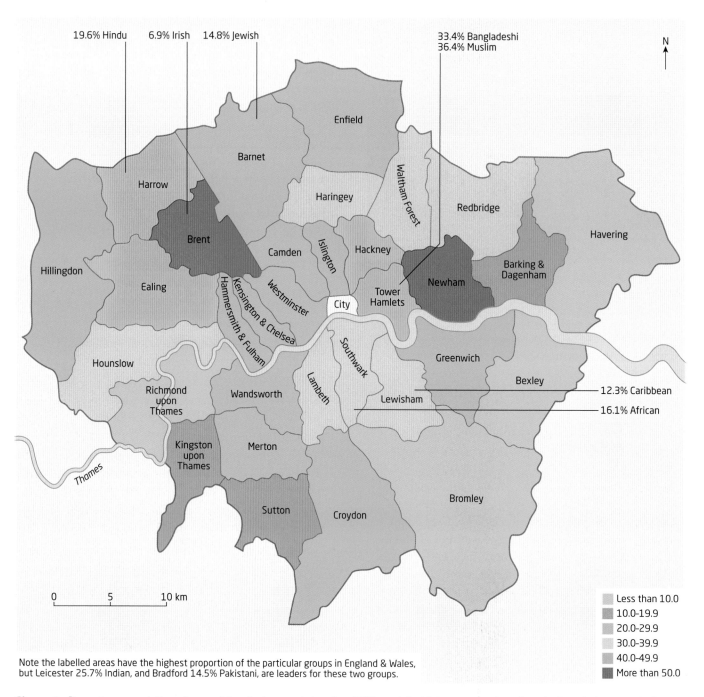

19.6% Hindu   6.9% Irish   14.8% Jewish

33.4% Bangladeshi
36.4% Muslim

N

Enfield

Barnet

Harrow

Haringey

Waltham Forest

Redbridge

Havering

Brent

Camden

Islington

Hackney

Hillingdon

Ealing

Westminster

Kensington & Chelsea

Hammersmith & Fulham

Tower
Hamlets

City

Newham

Barking &
Dagenham

Hounslow

Southwark

Greenwich

Bexley

Richmond
upon
Thames

Wandsworth

Lambeth

Lewisham

12.3% Caribbean

16.1% African

Kingston
upon
Thames

Merton

Thames

Sutton

Croydon

Bromley

0   5   10 km

Less than 10.0
10.0-19.9
20.0-29.9
30.0-39.9
40.0-49.9
More than 50.0

Note the labelled areas have the highest proportion of the particular groups in England & Wales,
but Leicester 25.7% Indian, and Bradford 14.5% Pakistani, are leaders for these two groups.

Figure 1 *Percentage population of non-white ethnic group in London, 2001, and the highest proportion of particular ethnic groups in England and Wales.*

Ethnic villages

The concept of ethnic villages often appears in newspapers, magazines and academic journals. Ethnic villages to a greater or lesser extent show clear evidence of the groups residing within their areas in terms of shops, places of worship, schools, cinemas, newspapers, social facilities, advertising and of course street presence. For example, the German school in Richmond and the nearby German bakery, the only one in London, have become key reference points for the capital's German community. The French Lycée (a school) in Kensington assumes a similar role. The UK is home to the second largest expatriate French population after the USA, with a very significant proportion of this group living in London. Evidence of the presence of larger and non-white ethnic groups is of course much more obvious.

The following list of ethnic villages in London comes from a variety of recent publications including *The Economist* and various articles in the *London Evening Standard*:

- Arabs in Bayswater
- West Indians in Brixton
- Punjabis in Southall
- Bangladeshis in Tower Hamlets
- Algerians and Moroccans in Finsbury Park
- Kosovans and Albanians in Enfield and Newham
- Iraqis in Barnet
- Congolese in Croydon
- Germans in Richmond
- Brazilians in Bayswater
- Turks in Hackney and Haringey
- Chinese in Soho
- Koreans in New Malden.

South Asians in London

The terms 'Asian' or 'South Asian' refer to peoples with ethnic origins from the Indian subcontinent (India, Bangladesh, Pakistan, Sri Lanka).

- 35% of all Asians in the UK live in the London area (Figure 2).
- 54% of all Bangladeshis living in the UK live in London, 41% of Indians, but only 19% of Pakistanis.
- There are approximately three Indians to every one Pakistani or Bangladeshi living in London.
- The Indian communities are concentrated in the boroughs of Ealing, Brent and Harrow; Pakistani communities in Walthamstow, Newham and Ealing; and Bangladeshis in Tower Hamlets, Newham and Camden.
- London has the largest concentration of Indians in the UK (437 000).
- The unemployment rate for Bangladeshis is considerably higher than for any other group in London.
- The London Pakistani community (142 000) is only the third largest in the UK, after the West Midlands (155 000) and Yorkshire and Humberside (146 000).
- Southall and surrounding districts contain the largest Sikh community in the world outside the Punjab in India. Three weekly Punjabi newspapers are published here.

From the 17th century, Indian domestics, servants and nannies (ayahs) began to be brought to London and elsewhere in the service of East India Company agents

There are many Korean businesses in New Malden, which has the largest concentration of Koreans in the UK.

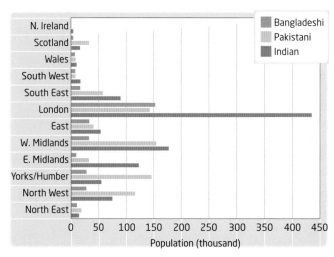

Figure 2 *The distribution of the Asian community in the UK.*

and British families returning from India. Some were returned to their home country when they were no longer required but others remained, residing mainly in Aldgate and later Hackney. Indian sailors (the lascars), first recruited to fill the manpower gap caused by the death or desertion of British sailors in India, crewed the Company's East Indiamen (ships) and later, as an all-lascar labour force, the steam-powered liners such as P&O and Clan Line. Although transients, a number jumped ship in British ports. By the mid 19th century small communities of Indian seamen had settled near the London docks in Stepney, and later in Poplar and Canning Town. As the opportunities for work at sea decreased, many became traders in the nearby market areas of Wentworth Street and Petticoat Lane.

The 1920s witnessed the arrival of Indian professionals and students in London, along with a number of single Sikh males from the Punjab. It was at this time that Indian restaurants began to appear, the first one opening in Leicester Square. Asian shops and places of worship also began to be established during the inter-war period.

The turmoil that surrounded Indian Independence and the partition that led to the state of Pakistan in 1947 resulted in considerable migration to London. The newcomers included doctors, teachers, ex-Army officers and farmers. Some found employment in their specialist areas but most had to settle for jobs in London where labour shortages existed. Thus many settled in Southall and other industrial areas where factories were short of labour. There is therefore a strong correlation between initial ethnic communities and large industrial areas with a high demand for unskilled, semi-skilled and skilled labour.

During the 1960s, 1970s and early 1980s, Indian people arrived in London not just from India but from other countries such as Uganda, Kenya, the Caribbean and Fiji, frequently responding to very strong push factors, for example the expulsion of Asians from Uganda under the regime of Idi Amin. Migration from the Indian subcontinent continued in the following decades with a considerable emphasis on the extended families of those already resident in Britain. The strong emphasis on education in many Asian families has resulted in significant upward mobility for subsequent generations, with geographical dispersal into higher-income areas. There are now significant Asian communities in wards of relative affluence in London and Asian children represent a considerable group in London's independent schools.

Other ethnic groups

The following are some examples of smaller ethnic groups in London.

- *Chinese* There have been Chinese people in London since the late 18th century, with the community concentrated near the docks in Limehouse until the Second World War. Since the 1950s Soho has become the main focus of Chinese presence in the capital. London's Chinese population now numbers more than 60,000 due to immigration not only from China itself but also from Hong Kong, Singapore, Malaysia and Vietnam. Secondary concentrations of Chinese can be found in Lewisham, Camden, Hackney and Lambeth.

- *South Africans* There were over 18 000 South African-born Londoners according to the 1991 census. Today the figure is much higher. Areas with above average numbers of South Africans are Wimbledon, Earl's Court, Fulham, St John's Wood, Wood Green, Acton and Willesden. These are primarily young white South Africans with British passports who find economic opportunities better in London than in their homeland.

- *The Orthodox Jewish Community of Stamford Hill* This traditional Jewish group, numbering 16 000 people, speak Yiddish as well as English, with the men wearing beards, black hats and long black coats. They shelter their children from the influence of the media, educating them in around 25 private schools in the Stamford Hill area. Families are generally large, sometimes with ten or twelve children.

- *South Koreans* Of the 24 000 or so South Koreans living in Britain, about 20 000 live in London and the adjoining county of Surrey. The South London suburb of New Malden is the firm focus of this community with many businesses, including a Korean college, owned by and catering for the local Korean population. The size of the Korean community has grown dramatically since 1989 when emigration restrictions were eased in South Korea.

Preserving culture

Figure 3 illustrates the way in which diasporas to a greater or lesser extent preserve the culture of their country of origin in the UK. The degree of concentration of diasporas is a significant factor affecting the strength of cultural retention. In general, the greater the degree of concentration, the more likely that the language of the country of origin will be used in social contact. However, this is secondary to using the language of origin in the home. The degree of ethnic concentration also affects the wider range of cultural norms of ethnic groups. Frequency of usage, as opposed to making a token gesture, is an important factor in preserving culture in a meaningful form. Cultural institutions, particularly places of worship, play a major role in maintaining tradition by bringing people together on a regular basis, often encouraging traditional language and dress and other cultural norms.

Continuing migration from the country of origin is a strong factor in preserving culture in its true form as opposed to hybridised forms which can evolve with weaker links with the country of origin. Frequency of return to the country of origin can also play an important role as family and friends will expect to see a continuation of cultural traits.

Roger Ballard in his analysis of British South Asians noted how efficiently these groups can participate in mainstream society in terms of the conventional expectations of Britain's dominant ethnic majority, while at the same time maintaining a strong attachment to their cultural roots. They have done this by organising their domestic lives on their own terms. UK society is generally perceived as being more tolerant towards ethnic minorities than many other countries that have experienced a high rate of immigration. This has helped minority groups to perhaps practise their culture more openly than might otherwise be the case.

The adoption of minority traits

The host society in the UK has been susceptible to the adoption of minority traits over time. Figure 4 (page 174) illustrates the main factors responsible. Intermarriage is more likely between the host society and some ethnic groups than others. When it occurs it opens up minority culture in a much more direct way than any other factor.

The rapid expansion of international tourism in recent decades has made it more likely for the majority population in the UK to have travelled to some of the countries of origin of minority groups in the UK. This aids greater understanding of cultural differences and makes the adoption of minority traits more likely. The greater the range of influences the host society is exposed to, the more likely that minority traits will be adopted.

Multiculturalism has been a significant element in education in the UK in recent decades. Children learn about other cultures in a number of subjects and thus have a better understanding of different cultures than previous generations. Higher levels of understanding reduce the barriers to the adoption of minority traits due to greater appreciation of the positive elements of alternative cultures.

Food traditions and habits are comparatively portable and the diet of the UK, like most countries with a history of immigration, bears the imprint of many past migrations. As an ethnic group builds up numerical strength in a country

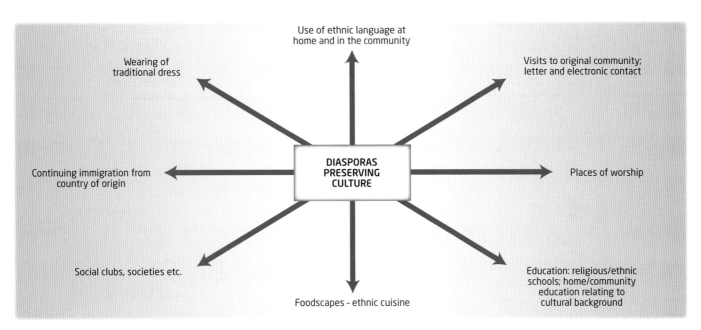

Figure 3 *The role of diasporas in preserving culture.*

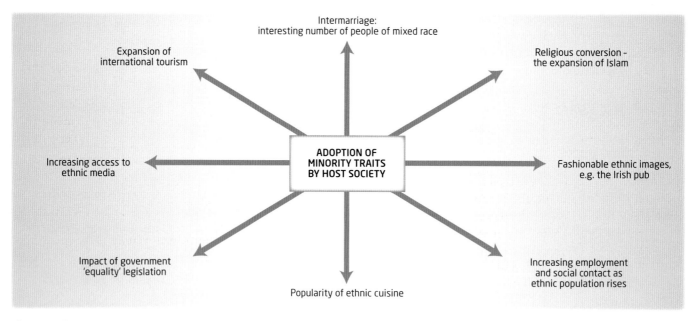

Figure 4 *The adoption of minority traits by host societies.*

like the UK, businesses will be more likely to respond to their product demands. Such 'diasporic foodways' can have a significant impact on the host society.

Activities

1 What is a diaspora?
2 Describe the data presented in Figure 1 (page 170).
3 What are the main factors affecting ethnic concentration in the UK?
4 With reference to Figure 2 (page 171), describe the distribution of the Asian community in the UK.
5 Use Figure 3 (page 173) to examine the role of diasporas in preserving culture.
6 With the aid of Figure 4, discuss how minority traits are adopted by host societies.

The impact of cultural diffusion on an indigenous and remote society

The second international decade of the world's **indigenous peoples** began on 1 January 2005. This initiative by the United Nations has five main objectives:

- promoting non-discrimination and inclusion of indigenous peoples in the design, implementation and evaluation of international, regional and national processes regarding laws, policies, resources, programmes and projects
- promoting full and effective participation of indigenous peoples in decisions that directly or indirectly affect their lifestyles, traditional lands and territories, their cultural integrity as indigenous peoples with collective rights or any other aspect of their lives, considering the principle of free, prior and informed consent
- redefining development policies that depart from a vision of equity and that are culturally appropriate, including respect for the cultural and linguistic diversity of indigenous peoples
- adopting targeted policies, programmes, projects and budgets for the development of indigenous peoples, including concrete benchmarks, and particular emphasis on indigenous women, children and young people
- developing strong monitoring mechanisms and enhancing accountability at the international, regional and particularly the national level, regarding the implementation of legal, policy and operational frameworks for the protection of indigenous peoples and the improvement of their lives.

The adoption of the second decade reflects increasing concern about the precarious condition of many

indigenous peoples around the world. UNESCO aims to strengthen collaboration between indigenous organisations, governments, NGOs and UN agencies. A major step forward was the adoption in September 2007 of the UN Declaration on the Rights of Indigenous Peoples by the UN General Assembly. The Director General of UNESCO described the 2007 declaration as a 'milestone for indigenous peoples and all those who are committed to the protection and promotion of cultural diversity and intercultural dialogue'.

A case study of the Xingu people in Brazil's Amazon Basin can be found on pages 176–177.

Discussion point

Why do you think there is so much international concern about the well-being of indigenous peoples?

International interactions and the homogenisation and dilution of culture

Cultural interaction has been conceptualised in three general ways, which can overlap:

- Assimilation – when a culture loses its original traits because it is overwhelmed by a more dominant culture. Such a process if extended globally would result in spatial **homogeneity**. This school of thought is put forward by the 'hyperglobalists' who see the spread of Western culture resulting in the homogenisation of global culture.

- Acculturation – this occurs when one group assumes the traits of others but also retains some of its own characteristics. The spatial outcome of this process is cultural hybridity or glocalisation. Proponents of this viewpoint have been called 'transformationalists' who

see globalisation leading to an intermingling of cultures, creating new hybrids and networks.

- Autarkism – this is when a culture reasserts its traits in the face of a perceived or actual threat from another culture. On a large scale this process would result in localisation and 'mosaicked heterogeneity'. Critics of the hyperglobalist view argue that their claims are greatly exaggerated and that national cultures still remain strong.

Cultural imperialism

The term **cultural imperialism** seems to have emerged in the 1960s along with other terms of radical criticism. It can be defined as the practice of promoting the culture or language of one nation in another. It is often the case that the former is a large, powerful nation and the latter is a smaller, less affluent one. Cultural imperialism can take the form of an active, formal policy, or a general attitude. Although the process has gained general acceptance, some social scientists see it as an artificial concept.

Cultural imperialism can be traced back to the Greek and Roman Empires and arguably to civilisations in even earlier times. A major period of cultural imperialism began in the colonial period. A number of European countries

Figure 6 *Cultural imperialism?*

Case study

The Xingu people of the Amazon Basin

The 26 000 km² Xingu National Park and Indigenous Peoples Reserve in Brazil's Amazon Basin was established in 1961 as South America's first indigenous National Park. It is the second largest Park in Brazil behind Jau, marking the first Indian territory recognised by the Brazilian government. The Park surrounds the Xingu river which flows north through north-eastern Mato Grosso and central Para state to join the Amazon river near its mouth (Figure 5). This is a protected tribal territory administered by the communities living within its boundaries. The indigenous people of the Park have become increasingly affected by the economic and cultural activities prevalent outside of its borders. These activities are generated not just from within Brazil, but on an international scale.

Figure 5 *Location of the Xingu river.*

The Xingu people represent 15 tribes and all four of Brazil's indigenous language groups, but share similar belief systems, rituals and ceremonies. In the centuries since the penetration of the Europeans into South America, they fled deeper into the Amazon Basin to escape from outside influences. At the end of the 19th century the population numbered 3000, but by the mid 20th century this number

had been reduced by foreign epidemic diseases such as flu, measles, smallpox and malaria to less than 1000. Many indigenous populations around the world have been affected in this way by diseases brought in by outsiders.

The protected status of the region, alongside efforts by the government to improve the health of the peoples living in the National Park, has contributed to the number of Xingu living in the 32 settlements increasing again to over 3000 inhabitants at present, half of them younger than 15 years. Their demographic characteristics reflect an earlier stage of demographic transition than Brazil as a whole. Experts believe that at least one of the tribes would have become extinct if the Park had not existed.

Xingu villages are set out on a large scale that is readily apparent from the air:

- The Xingu live in traditional longhouses which are large communal dwellings housing up to 40 people. A longhouse would be large enough to accommodate a passenger jet aircraft. The longhouses take at least six months to build, with the foundations made from as many as 30 tree trunks and the roof made from hundreds of narrower trunks. The whole building is covered with a thatch made from grass reeds that stretches down to the ground. There are no windows, with light only entering through doorways. Small fires help to keep mosquitoes at bay.

- An area of sacred ground is set aside to bury the dead.

- Paths lead out to communal vegetable gardens growing manioc and other crops.

- Daily bathing is part of traditional life. This takes place in nearby lagoons and begins with a bath at dawn. Xingu people will also bathe at times throughout the day in an attempt to escape the heat.

- Traditional wooden canoes are still used to navigate the local small creeks. Fish are an important part of the diet. Fishing methods range from hooks and lines to spear-fishing.

- The playing of sacred flutes is an important part of Xingu custom.

The expansion of commercial agriculture into the rainforest has had a major impact on the Xingu. Much of the National Park is surrounded by soya farmland as the cultivation of this crop has pushed further and further into the rainforest. This has had an impact on both the culture and the environment of the Xingu. Effluent from adjacent farming activities is polluting the Xingu river and its

A Xingu longhouse with Xingu people engaged in traditional Huka-Huka wrestling.

tributaries and new hydro-electric dams are encroaching on the Xingu people's ability to continue a sustainable lifestyle.

The diffusion of mainstream Brazilian and global culture into the lives of this indigenous population has prompted considerable debate both inside and outside the Park. It is now usual for a longhouse to have a television, which has transformed part of the daily routine of the Xingu. It has been largely through television that they have become more aware of the products available to modern consumer society. Some products, such as solar panels, which power water pumps and radio transmitters as well as televisions, are seen as beneficial by almost all Xingu people, but general consumer goods have caused more controversy. There are concerns that cash-bought goods have created friction and jealousy and that Xingu society is gradually changing from one where the emphasis was on the community to one that has become more individualistic. There are plans to use solar panels to power satellite Internet stations which will extend the influence of consumer culture into the lives of Xingu communities even further.

Modern dress is now part of daily life, with traditional costumes limited to ceremonial occasions. Traditional canoes are gradually being replaced by motorised aluminium launches. Football has spread rapidly in popularity in the Park. Most Xingu communities now compete in weekly football leagues and football has become a popular viewing activity in the longhouses. The advertising that goes with commercial football has become an increasingly familiar sight in terms of local dress.

Tourism is beginning to have an impact on the region in a more significant way. Although relatively small scale at present, it is likely to increase as international tourists seek out more remote environments and communities. Some communities in the Park provide accommodation for tourist groups and this is proving to be a significant source of income. The inevitable result is the purchase of more goods from the outside world.

The major current threat to the way of life of the Xingu is the resurrected plan to construct the Belo Monte dam and its accompanying reservoir. The Belo Monte dam is just one of nearly 100 dams planned for Brazil's Amazon to deal with the nation's soaring energy demands. The dam will divert the flow of the tributary Xingu river. Critics say the dam will destroy vast areas of pristine rainforest, disrupt sensitive ecosystems, and force the relocation of 12 000 people. Numerous small dams have been built on tributaries in the upper Xingu region which have affected fishing opportunities for the Xingu. Dams are a major factor in fish stocks worldwide because they restrict the movement of fish up and down waterways, and often prevent them from reaching spawning areas.

A television documentary was made in 2010 by the Brazilian NGO FASE, entitled *Xingu: Why We Don't Want Belo Monte*. This provided an opportunity for the Xingu to show their intense opposition to the project. Marijane Lisboa, a reporter on human rights for the environment, points out that indigenous groups lose not just the means to assure their basic needs but also their history. Without their territory, their history loses its meaning; they are intimately connected to the land. The tension between the well-meaning desire of many Brazilians to preserve and protect the Indian way of life and the drive to open up remote areas to economic development and settlement remains unresolved.

Thus the traditional lifestyle of the Xingu is being influenced by (a) large-scale agriculture which is mainly satisfying the growing global demand for soybeans, (b) Brazil's increasing energy requirements and (c) global consumer culture brought in by both television (and soon the Internet) and increasing direct contact with the outside world.

Activities

1 Describe the location of the Xingu National Park and Indigenous Peoples Reserve.
2 Discuss the threats to the traditional life and culture of the Xingu.

were involved in the acquisition of colonies epitomised by the so-called 'Scramble for Africa'. The British Empire was the largest in territorial extent and reached its maximum just before the First World War. In the colonial period Western culture was diffused around the world. The widespread independence of colonies during the 1940s, 1950s and 1960s ended the first stage of cultural imperialism, one of direct political domination.

After independence most colonial powers still exerted a strong influence on their former colonies. This influence was now largely economic, but also cultural and indirectly political. An example of the last is providing aid to a former colony, which can create a certain dependency. In this neo-colonial period the influence of TNCs has become very powerful indeed. Those on the political left also see major transnational institutions, particularly the World Bank, the IMF and the WTO, as facilitating this process. As the world's greatest economic power, the USA has led the spread of Western culture to other parts of the world. A number of writers have singled out McDonald's as playing a major role in this process. The term 'McDonaldisation' has become part of the literature on globalisation. In 1993, G. Ritzer in *The McDonaldisation of Society* defined McDonaldisation as the process through which the organisational, productive and representational principles of McDonald's were redefining globalisation. McDonald's itself would argue that it has made considerable efforts to ensure that its menus reflect the local market.

Cultural imperialism is said to be responsible for the decline and sometimes extinction of local cultures in many parts of the world where much traditional wisdom has been lost in the process. This has been likened to the decline in biodiversity leaving a depleted ecosystem.

W.E. Warwick looks at evidence in five areas to examine the arguments that support cultural imperialism. These are:

- Language – there are concerns that half of the world's 6000 languages will be extinct by 2100. About 60% of current languages have fewer than 10 000 speakers. Although Mandarin is more widely spoken as a first language, English dominates international communication.

- Tourism – on a number of counts tourism can claim to be the world's largest industry. The landscapes of mass tourism are similar in most parts of the world, as are the cultural traits of so many Western tourists when they visit developing countries.

- Global brands – major brands and the images they project are of Western consumer culture. American brands in particular, such as Coca-Cola, Nike and McDonald's, have had a phenomenal impact around the world.

- Media – national media systems have lost considerable ground to global media networks. Around 20–30 large TNCs dominate the global entertainment and media industry. The great majority have their headquarters in Western countries, with the USA most heavily represented. Some writers use the term 'electronic colonialism' to refer to the power of media giants such as Google, Microsoft, Disney and Time Warner.

Theory of Knowledge

The MEDIA programme of the European Union seeks to strengthen the European audio-visual industry, for example through promoting the production and circulation of European films. Its past and future spending will total more than 1 billion euros. Why should money be spent in this way, if most people's first choice is to watch Hollywood films? Is it important, as some have said, for people to see themselves and their own way of life on screen?

- Democracy – the liberal democracy of the West has spread rapidly in recent decades at the expense of communism and other forms of non-democratic rule. Most people would see this as a good thing, but some will argue that it has reduced the diversity of governance methods that other cultures exhibit, which in some cases have strong historical roots.

A variation on the cultural imperialism scenario is the notion of a universalised hybrid culture which is homogenous but not entirely Western in character. This is illustrated for example by the number of words in the English language such as 'pyjamas' and 'shampoo' that come from the Indian subcontinent as a consequence of British colonisation of that region. Modern globalisation has taken these words, along with the rest of the English language, around the world. Another example is Chilean Spanish which includes the influence of Mapudungun, the language of the indigenous Mapuche.

Both of the above views are not without their critics. Some writers argue that such views are Eurocentric and overlook the power of locality and local culture. There are certainly examples of reassertion of ethnic and cultural differences such as the revival of a number of small European languages in recent decades.

The Independent

UK | **World** | Business | People | Science | Media | Education

Home > News > World > Africa

It was all polite smiles and meticulous protocol as Jacob Zuma met the Queen yesterday afternoon. But just hours before he left for his state visit to Britain, South Africa's flamboyant President revealed what he really thought of his hosts.

In an astonishing interview given shortly before he boarded his flight to London, Mr Zuma launched a scathing attack on the British, accusing them of being cultural imperialists with colonial attitudes who still viewed Africans as 'barbaric'.

'When the British came to our country they said everything we did was barbaric, was wrong, inferior in whatever way,' he told The Independent's sister group of newspapers in South Africa. 'Bear in mind that I'm a freedom fighter and I fought to free myself, and also for my culture to be respected. And I don't know why they are continuing thinking that their culture is more superior than others.'

The catalyst for Mr Zuma's remarkable outburst was criticism from a number of British columnists who questioned the President's polygamy, a common and accepted practice among South Africa's Zulus.

Many visiting heads of state might have chosen to ignore the stinging barbs of tabloid journalism, but Mr Zuma – who has married five times and currently has three wives – is a political bruiser who enjoys taking on his detractors in public.

Rather than stick to the protocols of a state visit (pomp, splendour and no criticism of either the host or visiting nation) the South African President clearly felt compelled to speak out against what he perceived to be British cultural snobbery.

Figure 7 *Zuma visit*, The Independent, *March 2010.*

Activities

1   Explain the term 'the homogenisation of global culture'.
2   Discuss the three ways in which cultural interaction has been conceptualised.
3   Define 'cultural imperialism'.
4   What is the evidence to support the concept of cultural imperialism?

At the end of a recent state visit to the UK, President Jacob Zuma accused the British of being cultural imperialists (Figure 7). He made reference to British views when South Africa was a colony and he argued that the UK still viewed itself as superior to South Africa and other developing countries.

Research idea

Find another recent example where a developing country has accused a developed country of cultural imperialism. Examine the reasons for this accusation.

Review

Examination-style questions

1 a What has been the role of diasporas in preserving culture in one country?

b To what extent has the host society adopted minority traits?

2 a Describe the location and characteristics of one remote indigenous society.

b What has been the impact of cultural diffusion on this society?

Websites

www.thisislondon.co.uk/standard/
London Evening Standard newspaper

www.statistics.gov.uk/census2001
UK Office for National Statistics

http://rainforests.mongabay.com
Mongabay.com: information on rainforests

www.diaspora.org.uk
Diaspora: supporting refugees and asylum seekers

www.independent.co.uk
The Independent newspaper

http://wiki.media-culture.org.au
Wiki Media: search 'Cultural imperialism'

Key terms

Diaspora the scattering of a culture from its homeland.

Ethnicity the identification of individuals within particular ethnic groups.

Racial assimilation the gradual process of integration into the mainstream community. This process has three main strands which are broadly in chronological order: economic, social and political.

Urban mosaic the complex pattern of different residential areas within a city reflecting variations in socio-economic status which are mainly attributable to income and ethnicity.

Integrationist communities communities where a variety of ethnic groups intermix spatially and socially.

Indigenous people any ethnic group that inhabits a geographical region with which they have the earliest known historical connection.

Homogeneity a situation in which there is a lack of variation.

Cultural imperialism the practice of promoting the culture or language of one nation in another. It is usually the case that the former is a large, powerful nation and the latter is a smaller, less affluent one.

15 Loss of sovereignty

Political borders and the flow of goods, capital, labour and ideas

Loss of sovereignty

The Brazilian Embassy in Vienna.

Two narratives bound our era and, by degrees but unmistakably, our predicament: the story of consumerism and the story of globalization. In recent years, the two have combined to produce a single and singularly corrosive narrative. Consumerism has meant the transformation of citizens into shoppers, eroding America's sovereignty from within; globalization has meant the transformation of nation-states into secondary players on the world stage, eroding America's sovereignty from without. In collaboration, the trends are dealing a ruinous blow to democracy – to our capacity for common judgment, citizenship, and liberty itself.

Benjamin R. Barber, *Shrunken Sovereign: Consumerism, Globalization, and American Emptiness*

Hyperglobalists have predicted the end of the nation-state. Geographers have, on the whole, responded to such arguments in a balanced way; while acknowledging the transformed nature of political governance, arguments predicting the death of the state are seen as exaggerated.

Warwick E. Murray, *Geographies of Globalization*

The **nation-state** is a relatively new concept in global society. It is around 300 years old and before this time there existed a range of organisational forms governing territory. The emergence of the modern nation-state and a system of international relations is generally seen to have been established by the Treaty of Westphalia in 1713. The Treaty enshrined territorial **sovereignty**, borders and citizenship.

Until the last 50 years or so the world was largely organised by its nation-states. They were the regulating agents of change at virtually all scales. Today the global political situation is more like a 'web of interdependence' as some of the traditional powers of nation-states have evolved to other types of organisation (Figure 1). Some writers see it as paradoxical that the world now has more nation-states than ever before.

Many writers have voiced concern about the apparent loss of sovereignty of nation-states. The loss of sovereignty results from the voluntary or involuntary ceding of national autonomy to other organisations. The American sociologist Benjamin Barber, quoted above, views the changes taking place as anti-democratic and threatening the very foundations upon which the USA was built.

The Pentagon houses the United States Department of Defense – nations organise their own security, but most are also in alliance with other countries.

In the USA, conservatives see the creation of the first global criminal court, the International Criminal Court (ICC), as another step towards 'world government' that threatens US sovereignty. Thus the USA was not among the 120 nations that initially endorsed the creation of the court at a 1998 conference in Rome. Although President Clinton eventually signed so that the USA could remain engaged in negotiations, once it became clear that the court would come into existence without the changes sought by Washington, President Bush withdrew the USA from the Rome Treaty. Subsequently, Congress passed legislation that would authorise military action to free any American taken into custody on the direction of the ICC.

Globalisation not only pulls upwards in terms of nation-states losing some of the power they once had as international linkages become more and more important, it also pushes downwards, creating new pressures for local autonomy. For example, in Spain Basque separatists want their own state, as do many Kurds in the Middle East. According to the American sociologist Daniel Bell, nations are too small to solve the big problems but also too large to solve the small ones.

Theory of Knowledge

National identity is one component of people's sense of themselves (along with kinship, social position, sexuality, and political and social allegiances, for example). If loss of sovereignty leads to an erosion of national identity (which may or may not be the case), would this be a good or bad thing?

Figure 2 is an extract from the UK newspaper *The Guardian* commenting on the loss of sovereignty in the UK which has affected so many aspects of life in the country. Within the UK, the major concern of many people has been the gradual transfer of powers from the UK government to the European Union (EU). A new political party, the UK Independence Party (UKIP), was founded in 1993 to oppose such a transfer of power. Its principal aim is withdrawal from the EU. However, UKIP has only gained modest support to date. The growth of regional organisations such as the EU and other changes are usefully summed up in Ohmae's transition from the industrial age to the information age (Figure 3).

The borders between many EU countries have no controls at all. For example, if you drive between France and Spain, road signs will tell you that the border is being crossed and you will see the now derelict old border control buildings where once you would have had to show your passport. However, today people are free to drive across without stopping. France and Spain are part of the Schengen Agreement which allows movement from one country to another without border controls. Figure 4 (page 184) shows the 25 European countries which have signed the agreement. The Schengen Agreement may well act as a model for other parts of the

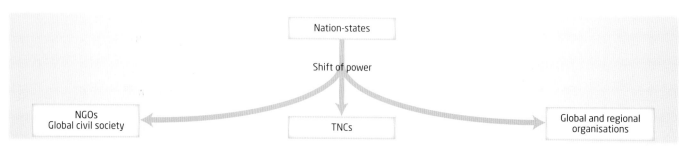

Figure 1 *Shift of power.*

By Will Hutton

Why are opponents to Europe's reform treaty so silent on the avalanche of foreign takeovers?

Over the past few years there has been an extraordinary loss of British sovereignty. One in five of our leading companies has become foreign-owned in a buying spree unprecedented in our or any comparable western country.

Nearly all our investment banks are foreign-owned, as are many of our utilities and strategic sectors, including steel production. Centrica, owner of British Gas, is widely expected soon to receive a bid from the Russian GazProm; and the Chinese government has just set up a $200bn fund to buy foreign companies, with Britain among its top targets.

About this Britain's newly minted nationalists – nearly all the right-of-centre press, the Conservative party and the UK Independence party – are mute. Manchester United supporters had a short-lived protest against the American takeover of their club, but apart from that the British seem remarkably relaxed about so much foreign ownership. No political party seems to think it matters.

But every editorial in every rightwing newspaper is fulminating against the EU reform treaty as a disastrous sellout. The establishment of an EU president who will hold office for two and a half years, the creation of a high representative for foreign policy, and a reduction in the number of commissioners are all deemed to constitute a mortal threat to our sovereignty. There may be explicit opt-outs from the charter of fundamental rights and matters to do with the justice system – the only areas where the reform treaty enlarges EU competence – but that won't stop the foaming-at-the-mouth brigade from making wild charges about the continental dagger at the heart of all things British.

Figure 2 *'A real loss of sovereignty' in the UK,* The Guardian, *2007.*

world in the future. This is a world where regional identity becomes increasingly important; a sort of midway position between the nation-state and a fully globalised world.

Within the EU the recent economic crisis has had a particularly adverse effect on the southern European countries. Greece has been the worst affected and has required considerable financial help from the EU to keep its economy afloat. In February 2010, Herman Van Rompuy, the EU's president, called for the creation of an 'economic government that shifts responsibility for economic planning from national authorities to the EU level'. It seems that nation-states are most vulnerable in times of crisis! In terms of foreign policy, more than 50 EU embassies have opened across the world since the

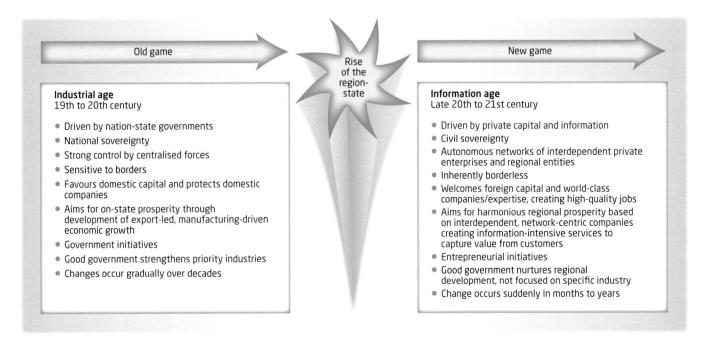

Figure 3 *Ohmae's industrial and information ages.*

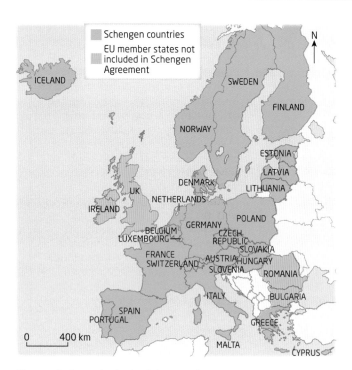

Figure 4 *Countries in the Schengen Agreement.*

Lisbon Treaty came into force at the beginning of 2010. Undoubtedly more will follow. At the moment there are no plans to close national embassies in the foreign countries concerned, but this cannot be ruled out in the future.

Most political borders are not the obstacles they once were and as a result goods, capital, labour and ideas flow more freely across them than ever before. However, a relatively small number of countries maintain extremely strict border controls. Such nations are regarded as authoritarian regimes by the rest of the world. Examples include Iran, North Korea, Burma, Cuba and, to a lesser extent in recent years, China.

Discussion point

Do you feel that the country in which you live has lost some of its sovereignty? Explain the reasons for your opinion.

The flow of ideas

The political barriers to movement vary considerably according to the type of transfer under consideration. As Figure 5 shows, ideas can move across political boundaries much more easily than capital, goods and

labour. The development of the Internet and other forms of communication and transport have resulted in a phenomenal increase in the flow of ideas and images around the world. This has created enormous benefits, but also considerable tensions in some countries. For example, it has created a great deal of unease between Islamic countries and an increasingly secular rest of the world.

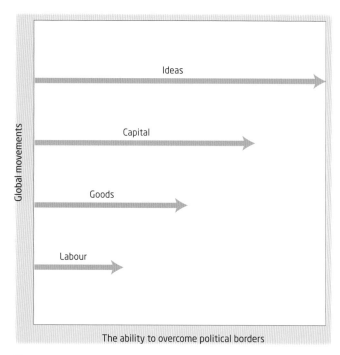

Figure 5 *Ideas, capital, goods and labour – the ability to overcome political borders.*

The increasing pace of globalisation in recent decades has been paralleled by the rise of **religious fundamentalism**. Many writers see the latter as a direct and indirect reaction to the former. In the West the term 'fundamentalism' invariably means Islamic fundamentalism. The fundamentalist revival in Islam that began in the 1970s is, rightly or wrongly, a major concern to many people and governments in the West. This is because this 'aggressive' faction of Islam largely rejects Western modernisation and secularism. The call is for 'Islamisation' whereby:

- Sharia law replaces secular law
- education centres on the Koran
- the economic system is oriented to redistribution rather than the accumulation of wealth by individuals
- cultural products (TV, music etc.) are tightly controlled.

The irony for many people in the West is that globalisation has made a pan-Islamic movement possible. For many outside the West, globalisation and secularism go hand in hand whereby increasing wealth spawns moral decadence. However, the influence of fundamentalism on other religions should not be underestimated. The development of the New Christian Right in the USA has had a significant influence on attitudes and policy-making in that country.

The development of global civil society has been an important aspect of the diffusion of ideas around the world. It has spawned new networks of communication which are not government- and company-based. These networks monitor the actions of governments and companies, spreading their criticisms rapidly to all those who want to take an interest. Political protests now occur almost simultaneously in countries far apart because of the power and effectiveness of instant global communication. In 1999 NGOs worldwide used the Internet to coordinate a massive protest against the WTO meeting in Seattle. This proved to be a blueprint for global civil society organisation thereafter.

The flow of ideas has allowed many more individual connections to be made as more people see similarities between themselves and people in other countries. National governments set the agenda for their populations less today than at any time in the past. If a government is perceived to be pursuing poor policies, the criticisms of other governments, organisations and individuals are available to the citizens of that country via the Internet and other forms of media. Even when countries try to block such connections they cannot do so entirely.

The erosion of a national language can also be associated with loss of sovereignty. For example, in many European countries a significant proportion of the population speak English and as this trend has increased it has raised questions about national identity. Many writers see English as the language of the 'global village'.

Capital

On a more tangible level the dimension of the world economy that is most globalised is the market for raising loans and capital. Prior to the deregulation of the global financial markets the activities of banks, insurance companies and investment dealers had been confined largely within national boundaries. Over the last 20 years most countries have significantly reduced the restrictions on capital flows, permitting more foreign investment in their financial markets and economies and allowing their own citizens and companies to invest abroad. With the removal of regulations the financial sector scanned the globe for the best returns on investments. Recent decades have witnessed a considerable increase in the growth of large, sophisticated institutional investors that have the power to shift huge sums of money around the globe.

Technological innovations and faster information flows, helped by a sharp rise in total savings being channelled into financial instruments across borders, have fostered the dramatic globalisation of capital flows. The cost of such cross-border flows has fallen significantly. The IMF, the World Bank and the OECD have exercised considerable influence over capital flows by legitimising financial opening as sound and desirable.

In 2006, the annual value of cross-border capital flows reached $8.2 trillion (Figure 6), nearly three times the level in 2002 and an eightfold increase since 1990. Since 1990, global capital flows have grown faster than the value of world trade, world GDP and the world's financial assets.

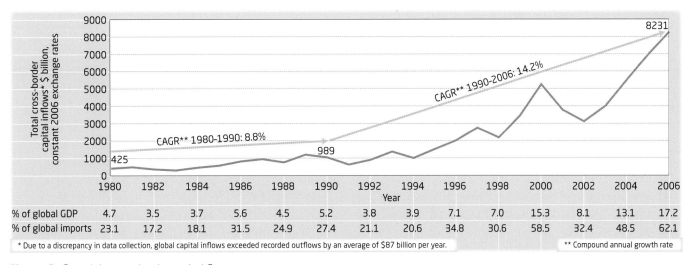

	1980	1982	1984	1986	1988	1990	1992	1994	1996	1998	2000	2002	2004	2006
% of global GDP	4.7	3.5	3.7	5.6	4.5	5.2	3.8	3.9	7.1	7.0	15.3	8.1	13.1	17.2
% of global imports	23.1	17.2	18.1	31.5	24.9	27.4	21.1	20.6	34.8	30.6	58.5	32.4	48.5	62.1

* Due to a discrepancy in data collection, global capital inflows exceeded recorded outflows by an average of $87 billion per year.   ** Compound annual growth rate

Figure 6 *Growth in cross-border capital flows.*

Examples of such capital flows are:

- US companies building factories in China
- European citizens buying Latin American stocks
- Middle East investors buying equity stakes in UK banks
- Chinese companies taking stakes in African commodity producers.

Although most countries see this as beneficial, there are concerns. The main worry is that 'hot money' can surge into a country suddenly and move out just as fast, causing considerable financial difficulty in countries where this happens. Critics of globalisation see this lack of national control over financial flows as another aspect of the way democracy is being undermined by the operation of the global financial system.

The recent global financial crisis has shown how little control national governments have over the large transnational banks and other major financial institutions. If a major TNC decides to pull out of a country there is little that the government of that country can do to stop it. Rising unemployment and loss of taxes are concerns for all governments. Sometimes financial inducements are offered under the guise of the government sharing the burden of a difficult trading situation.

Goods

The origin and continuing basis of global interdependence is trade. The World Trade Organisation and its predecessor the GATT have overseen a dramatic decrease in the barriers to trade. The role of the WTO has already been considered in Chapter 5. However, a range of other agreements between groups of countries have also significantly changed the nature of international trade. Figure 7 shows the extent to which trade expanded in the first decade of the new millennium.

Regional trade agreements

Regional trade agreements have proliferated in the last two decades. In 1990 there were fewer than 25; by 1998 there were more than 90. The most notable of these are the EU, NAFTA in North America, ASEAN in Asia, and Mercosur in Latin America. The United Nations refer to such organisations as 'geographically discriminatory trading arrangements'. Nearly all of the WTO's members belong to at least one regional pact. All such arrangements have one unifying characteristic: the preferential terms that trade participants enjoy over non-participating countries. Although no regional group has as yet adopted rules contrary to those of the WTO, there are some concerns:

- Regional agreements can divert trade, inducing a country to import from a member of its **trade bloc** rather than from a cheaper supplier elsewhere.
- Regional groups might raise barriers against each other, creating protectionist blocs.
- Regional trade rules may complicate the establishment of new global regulations.

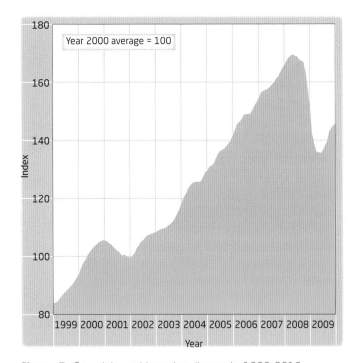

Figure 7 *Growth in world merchandise trade, 1999–2010.*

There is a growing consensus that international regionalism is on the ascendency. The EU, NAFTA and ASEAN+ (associated agreements with other countries) triad of regional trading arrangements dominate the world economy, accounting for about two-thirds of all world trade. Whether the regional trade agreement trend causes the process of world trade liberalisation to falter in the future remains to be seen.

Apart from trade blocs there are a number of looser trade groupings aiming to foster the mutual interests of member countries. These include:

- the Asia Pacific Economic Cooperation forum (APEC): its 21 members border the Pacific Ocean and include Canada, the USA, Peru, Chile, Japan, China and Australia – the member countries have pledged to facilitate free trade
- the Cairns Group of agricultural exporting nations: formed in 1986 to lobby for freer trade in agricultural products, its members include Argentina, Brazil, Canada, New Zealand, Australia, the Philippines and South Africa.

Bilateral free trade agreements

Bilateral trade agreements have been popular with a significant number of countries, but many economists argue that bilateral deals are a less effective route to trade liberalisation. Because trade within bilateral agreements is conducted on preferential terms, these pacts discriminate against third countries. The concern of many is that as more and more bilateral agreements are signed, the aim of a more seamless global economy will be hindered by a patchwork quilt of agreements. Because of this the EU, which is party to a number of bilateral agreements, plans to launch no new negotiations until after the Doha round of WTO talks ends.

Trade blocs

A trade bloc is a group of countries that share trade agreements among themselves. Since the Second World War there have been many examples of such groups joining together to stimulate trade and to obtain other benefits from economic cooperation. The following forms of increasing economic integration between countries can be recognised:

- Free trade areas – members abolish tariffs and quotas on trade between themselves but maintain independent restrictions on imports from non-member countries. NAFTA is an example of a free trade area.

- Customs unions – this is a closer form of economic integration. Besides free trade between member nations, all members are obliged to operate a common external tariff on imports from non-member countries. Mercosur, established on 1 January 1995, is a customs union joining Brazil, Paraguay, Uruguay and Argentina in a single market of over 200 million people.

- Common markets – these are customs unions which, in addition to free trade in goods and services, also allow the free movement of labour and capital.

- Economic unions – these organisations have all the characteristics of a common market but also require members to adopt common economic policies on such matters as agriculture, transport, industry and regional policy. The EU is an example of an economic union, although it must be remembered that its present high level of economic integration was achieved in a number of stages. When Britain joined in 1973 the organisation could best be described as a common market. The increasing level of integration has been marked by changes in the name of the organisation. Initially known as the European Economic Community, it later became the European Community and finally, from November 1993, the European Union.

Discussion point

To what extent will the EU become a model for other continents to follow?

Labour

In contrast to financial markets and the flow of goods and services, labour markets are far behind in the process of globalisation, largely because of the restrictions governments impose on immigration. However, the natural attachment that people feel for their 'home' region is also a significant factor in the **immobility of labour**.

In a genuinely globalised market there would be no restrictions on the movement of labour. However, at present no country in the world allows free international movement of labour. Labour is arguably the most controversial of the flows illustrated in Figure 5 (page 184). People may become insecure about their jobs if significant numbers of people with similar skills are coming into a country. International labour migration has become a significant political issue in a number of countries.

When countries are short of labour and this factor threatens economic growth, immigration rules are generally relaxed to allow more workers to come into a country. However, when the supply of labour in a country exceeds the demand, immigration rules are often tightened. This has certainly been the story in the past and it still applies to much of the world. The main exceptions

El Camino de Santiago – an example of EU funding in Spain.

are where international agreements have been signed to allow the free movement of labour between countries. The largest-scale example is the EU.

Free movement of people is one of the fundamental freedoms guaranteed by EU law (Article 39 of the European Community Treaty) and is also an essential element of European citizenship. EU rules on the free movement of workers also apply to member states of the European Economic Area (i.e. to Iceland, Liechtenstein and Norway). The relevant rights are complemented by a system for the coordination of social security schemes and by a system to ensure the mutual recognition of qualifications.

As more countries have joined the EU, popular destination countries have been allowed to introduce 'transitional measures' to ensure that too many foreign workers do not arrive in a very short period of time. However, all such restrictions on current member countries will end either in 2011 or 2014. This will mean that there will be no restrictions on the movement of labour between the 27 member countries. It will be interesting to see to what extent this provides a model for other regional groupings.

Activities

1 Define (a) nation-state (b) sovereignty.
2 Read the text in Figure 2 (page 183). In what ways does Will Hutton feel that the UK has lost sovereignty?
3 Discuss the changes from the 'industrial age' to the 'information age' shown in Figure 3 (page 183).
4 a What is the Schengen Agreement?
  b Suggest why so many European countries have joined the Agreement.
  c Suggest why some countries like the UK decided not to join and instead to retain control over their borders.
5 Describe and explain the differences illustrated by Figure 5 (page 184).
6 Look at Figure 6 (page 185). How did cross-border capital flows change between 1980 and 2006?

The North American Free Trade Agreement

The North American Free Trade Agreement (NAFTA) came into effect on 1 January 1994 with the objective of eliminating most tariffs and other restrictions on free trade

and investment between the USA, Canada and Mexico by the year 2003. All remaining tariffs were removed as scheduled on 1 January 2008.

Although the idea of a North American trade bloc had been around for some time, the formation of NAFTA in the 1990s was hastened by three factors:

- the ever-increasing economic challenge from Western Europe and Asia
- the completion of the internal market of the EU and the establishment of the European Economic Area (EEA) in 1993
- growing concern that nations left outside trade blocs would be commercially disadvantaged.

The first significant move towards a North American trade bloc was the signing of the Canada–United States Automotive Products Trade Agreement (Auto Pact) in 1965. In 1988 the two countries extended their relationship with the establishment of the comprehensive Canada–United States Free Trade Agreement (FTA or CUSTA). In 1990 Mexico formally requested a free trade relationship with its northern neighbours and after four years of intense negotiation NAFTA was approved by the governments of all three countries. In effect, the terms of the 1988 FTA were extended to include Mexico, whose economy was then less than 5% the size of those of the USA and Canada combined. This established a unique relationship between a relatively poor developing nation and two of the world's richest countries. Never before had a trade bloc included members of both the developed and developing worlds. When NAFTA was established in 1994 its 390 million consumers, with a combined GDP of over $7.6 trillion, vied with the EEA (the EU and Iceland, Norway and Liechtenstein) to become the world's largest

Dockside, Seattle, one of the USA's major ports.

trade bloc. Today the NAFTA region has a population of 444 million people of whom 304 million live in the USA, 107 million in Mexico and 33 million in Canada.

The 1994 agreement planned for all tariffs on goods qualifying as North American to be phased out within ten years, although special rules applied to key sectors such as energy, agriculture, textiles and clothing. Trade in services would also be facilitated while other provisions would give relief or protection to 'sensitive industries' (e.g. some agricultural products like US sugar were given protection for 15 years) and technical and environmental standards. To lessen American concerns about Mexico, special 'supplemental agreements' or 'side deals' were added to NAFTA. These provide for annual reviews of 'import surges' or dumping of products and, if necessary, a penalty: a resumption of pre-NAFTA tariffs, usually for three years. In addition, three-country commissions monitor the enforcement of NAFTA-related national laws. Here any two nations can instigate an investigation of suspected breaches of regulations concerning environmental standards, health and safety in the workplace, minimum wages and child labour. Fines of up to $20 million can be imposed.

The objectives of NAFTA differ from the EU's Maastricht Treaty (1993) in a number of significant ways. The NAFTA agreement is limited to trade only and thus does not:

- permit free movement of labour
- attempt to redistribute wealth to poorer regions within its boundaries
- seek to establish a common currency
- seek political union
- aim to establish a customs union with common external tariffs
- affect existing border controls.

However, like the EU, NAFTA may allow other countries to join providing all current members agree. The objective of NAFTA's supporters is that the whole of Latin America will follow Mexico's example and eventually join. The establishment of Mercosur on 1 January 1995 was a major stage in this process. The members of this customs union are Brazil, Argentina, Paraguay and Uruguay. Mercosur has talked with the Andean Pact countries (Bolivia, Peru, Ecuador, Colombia and Venezuela) and Chile for the creation of a South American Free Trade Area as an important building block towards the establishment of a Free Trade Area of the Americas (FTAA) incorporating all the countries of North, Central and South America, as agreed during the 'Americas Summit' in Miami in December 1994. This idea of a trade bloc covering all of the Americas was reaffirmed by the Quebec Declaration in April 2001.

Not everyone is positive about the proposed FTAA. President da Silva of Brazil, when still in opposition, called the FTAA an 'attempt at annexing Latin America' by the USA. In September 2002 Brazil's Catholic bishops organised a plebiscite, inviting the public to express opposition to the proposed accord. Some Brazilians argue that the WTO is a better forum than the FTAA in which to achieve free trade.

NAFTA links 444 million people producing $17 trillion worth of goods and services. The USA recorded $967 billion in total (two ways) goods trade with Canada and Mexico in 2008, resulting in a goods trade deficit of $143 billion with its NAFTA partners. In contrast the USA posted a surplus in the trading of services of $26.5 billion (2007). Canada and Mexico were the top two purchasers of US exports in 2008. In turn, Canada and Mexico were the largest and third largest suppliers of goods imports to the USA in 2008. Figure 8 shows the growth of overall trade in goods among the USA, Canada and Mexico between 1993 and 2008. Regional business investment in the USA rose 117% between 1993 and 2007, as compared to a 45% rise in the 14 years previously. Trade with NAFTA partners now accounts for more than 80% of Canadian and Mexican trade, and more than a third of US trade.

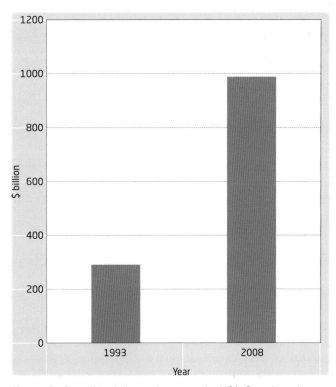

Figure 8 *Overall trade in goods among the USA, Canada and Mexico 1993 and 2008.*

The impact on the USA

The arguments for and against NAFTA have been debated most fiercely in the USA, where the strongest proponents of NAFTA have been multinational corporations, economists and key political figures such as ex-President Clinton. The classical economic argument, following Ricardo's *Theory of Comparative Advantage*, is that all three countries would be better off with free trade as they would specialise increasingly in what they are best at.

Trade unions and environmental groups have led the argument against NAFTA. The major debate in the USA focuses on the issue of trade with Mexico. Trade unions have long feared that free trade with Mexico will result in wage and benefit reductions if US firms are to remain competitive against cheap Mexican labour. They also foresee US companies moving to Mexico to take direct advantage of lower wage rates as well as being attracted south of the border by less demanding environmental legislation.

Ship passing through locks on the Great Lakes waterway system between the USA and Canada.

Many environmental groups such as the powerful Sierra Club have been strong critics of NAFTA. They envisaged more severe environmental degradation in Mexico where environmental laws are lax and often unenforced. The Sierra Club also predicted that US environmental legislation would be watered down in the name of staying competitive with Mexico.

Transnational corporations that have moved operations to Mexico have, as expected, reaped higher profits. However, the trade deficit with Mexico has increased with no signs of the situation being reversed. But the predictions of an almost immediate adverse impact on the US economy as a whole did not materialise as growth remained strong in the USA throughout the 1990s. Nevertheless a significant number of American workers are less well off now than before the advent of NAFTA. Critics of NAFTA within the USA frequently cite the growth of the merchandise trade deficit as

evidence for their point of view. However, NAFTA trade only accounts for 16% of the overall merchandise trade deficit. Public Citizen, a pressure group opposed to NAFTA, has attacked the organisation over a wide range of issues, calling it a 'trade agreement from hell'.

The impact on Canada

Although there are significant exceptions, most organisations and individuals in Canada hold favourable views about NAFTA because the benefits of the agreement seem very clear-cut. Since the formation of NAFTA, the Canadian economy has grown at the fastest rate of all three countries. Mexico's growth rate has been the slowest. Table 1 shows Canada's considerable surplus in merchandise trade with its NAFTA partners and the importance of two-way flows of foreign direct investment. One in five jobs in Canada is linked to international trade.

Merchandise trade

	2008 (Canadian $ billion)	% change from previous year
Canadian exports to NAFTA	381.3	+5.7
Canadian imports from NAFTA	245.1	+3.1

Foreign direct investment stock

	2008 (end of year, Canadian $ billion)	% change from previous year
Canadian FDI in NAFTA	314.6	+33.8
FDI in Canada from NAFTA	293.9	+0.3

Table 1 *Canada's 2008 merchandise trade and FDI with its NAFTA partners.*

Canada's trade with its NAFTA partners has been growing much faster than its trade with other countries. Canada has always been conscious of the limited size of its domestic market and saw huge benefits of having open access to the USA and Mexico. As Canada is distant from Mexico it has not experienced some of the difficulties that have arisen between the USA and Mexico because of their common border. However, environmental groups in Canada have voiced similar concerns to those raised in the USA.

CBD of Vancouver, Canada's third largest city and a major port.

Canadian critics of NAFTA are concerned that Canada is now too tightly bound economically with the USA and as a result is already beginning to lose some of its sovereignty because of the huge difference in economic and political power of the two countries.

Timber – a big export product from Canada to the USA.

The impact on Mexico

Supporters of NAFTA in Mexico say the new market has forced Mexican companies to adopt higher foreign standards and business practices, gradually improving the competitiveness of Mexican business. As the Mexican economy is locked into the economies of the USA and Canada it makes it impossible for the country to revert to the disastrous protectionist policies of the past. Mexican supporters of NAFTA also stress the degree to which manufacturing industry has diversified since the formation of NAFTA.

However, not all Mexicans are so convinced about the merits of NAFTA. They argue that Mexico has swapped one kind of trade dependence for another. In the early 1980s oil dominated the country's economy, accounting for two-thirds of exports. Although the economy is more diversified now, the great majority of its exports go to the USA, making Mexico highly dependent on the US economy. A common expression in Mexican business circles is 'When the USA catches a cold, Mexico gets pneumonia'.

Mexican exports have increased not only because of US demand but also because of Mexican penetration of the US market. This reflects (a) the decline in barriers to trade and (b) the improved quality of Mexican goods. Mexico has achieved significant market penetration in food and live animals, beverages and tobacco, machinery and transport equipment, and miscellaneous manufactured articles.

Another criticism is that the Mexican government did too little to prepare the country for such a significant change. Mexican farmers have been particularly hard hit. The vast majority of farm plots are less than 10 hectares and operate with very modest equipment. Before NAFTA they were protected by import tariffs and government-guaranteed prices. Now they have to compete with large-scale high-technology American and Canadian agribusiness. The impact on the landscape of the north-western state of Sonora has been startling. The state used to be known as Mexico's breadbasket because wheat dominated agricultural production here. Now, due to the import of cheaper wheat from the USA and Canada, farmers have turned to nuts, peaches, asparagus, chickpeas, olives, cucumbers, watermelons and jalapeno chillis. Most of the production of the new crops is for export. Although change was already underway before 1994, the advent of NAFTA speeded up the process considerably.

Industry too has had its problems. Critics of the government claim that Mexico does not have an industrial policy apart from promoting *maquiladoras*. These are factories that import materials or parts to make goods for re-export. Maquiladoras existed long before 1994 but they have increased greatly in number since NAFTA came into effect. Although the jobs they provide are important to the economy, less than 3% of the maquiladoras' input is produced locally. Thus while rising exports have been helpful in reducing the trade deficit, they have not done much for the rest of the economy.

An ever-increasing number of Asian and European companies have established plants in Mexico in order to gain access to Mexico's NAFTA trade partners. Mexico is being used as a springboard to the USA and Canada in the same way that many foreign companies base operations in the UK to gain open access to the whole of the EU. At the same time, many US companies manufacture products in Mexico that are destined for the latter's trade partners throughout Latin America.

A clear-cut assessment of Mexico's NAFTA membership is difficult because many of Mexico's trade liberalisation policies were in effect before NAFTA began, prompted by Mexico's membership of GATT and its ongoing domestic reforms.

The future of NAFTA

Opinion about NAFTA remains divided, particularly in the USA. A reasonable statement about NAFTA would be that neither the critics' worst fears nor the supporters' rosiest forecasts have materialised.

Potential strains in relations between the USA and Canada were exposed in February 2009 when Barack Obama, on his first foreign trip as President, hinted at renegotiation of the North American Free Trade Agreement. The President made the promise to renegotiate NAFTA on the campaign trail in 2008 in response to protests in the Midwest that it was partly responsible for a drain on jobs from the USA. The Canadian government has also been concerned by other protectionist moves by Obama such as the 'buy America' provisions in his $787 billion economic stimulus package, which originally proposed that only US steel should be used for infrastructure projects. The 'buy America' provisions have since been watered down, with the USA saying it would not do anything that ran counter to existing trade agreements.

Research idea

Find out if the US government has followed up its desire to renegotiate aspects of the NAFTA agreement.

Activities

1 Briefly list the reasons for the formation of NAFTA.
2 What are the main differences between NAFTA and the EU?
3 Discuss the impact of NAFTA on the USA.
4 **a** Why are most Canadians in favour of NAFTA?
  b What are the concerns that some Canadians have about NAFTA?
5 To what extent have the benefits of NAFTA for Mexico outweighed the costs?

The shift of power from nation-states to TNCs

The increasing size and influence of TNCs in recent decades and their apparent challenge to the power of nation-states has been the subject of much debate, drawing a wide variety of opinion. There are those who say the power of nation-states has been radically diminished. Others argue that this is to overstate the situation, but they do acknowledge that there has been a shift of power from nation-states to TNCs.

The modern nation-state remains the principal form of political rule around the world. All TNCs have to operate within national and international regulatory systems. According to Peter Dicken, the 'new geo-economy' is being structured and restructured by the complex, dynamic interactions between companies and governments. However, many writers see a growing imbalance between national governments and TNCs in favour of the latter: W. Ellwood in *The No-Nonsense Guide to Globalisation* states: 'As corporations gain the upper hand, the fear of job losses and the resulting social devastation has created a downward pressure on environmental standards and social programs – what critics of unregulated corporate power call "a race to the bottom".'

Daniel Litvin argues that despite the global appearance of power and competence, transnationals usually end up out of their depth. Using examples from the 16th century to the present day he shows that these large corporate entities were much less in control of events than either they or their critics would wish us to believe.

Although nation-states have become less powerful in some ways, they remain of fundamental importance politically. They also exercise a range of constraints over companies through competition law and other regulations. Taxation is an important part of the picture. Corporate taxes make up a bigger share of government revenue than 20 years ago.

Figure 9 summarises the possible positive and negative effects of TNCs locating in developing countries. Although TNCs are frequently criticised for exploiting labour across the globe, workers in foreign firms in poor countries earn twice the national average.

A major criticism of TNCs is that they may undermine the push for democracy in dictatorial nations in their desire for political stability. As Benjamin Barber says in *McWorld and Jihad*, 'Capitalists may be democrats but capitalism does not need or entail democracy.'

TNCs exert power because of their size in terms of the number of people they employ directly and indirectly, the resources they use and the capital flows that they direct. They may also exert power in terms of the business sector in which they operate. In times of high energy prices and energy shortages, the large energy companies are in a very strong position when it comes to negotiating with national governments. Large media companies can influence public opinion and thus hold influence in the internal politics of countries and over international issues. In terms of the latter, lobbying by TNCs in the United Nations and other organisations has become an increasingly controversial issue.

If a major newspaper decides to switch allegiance from one political party to another it could influence the course of a general election. In the UK, the popular *The Sun* newspaper decided to back the Labour Party prior to the 1997 election after previously supporting the Conservative Party. Most political analysts saw this as an important factor in the Labour victory. *The Sun* is part of News Corporation, a huge media company founded by Rupert Murdoch, with interests in film, television, cable, magazines, newspapers and general publishing.

More and more major politicians have become aware of the importance of relations with the leaders of global industry. When President Hu Jintao of China visited the USA in 2006, his first meeting was not with US President George Bush in Washington, but with Bill Gates, the chairman of Microsoft. This was seen by many people as an example of the shift in power from nation-states to TNCs.

Deregulation and the freeing-up of markets has undoubtedly reduced the power of the nation-state as a mechanism for national economic management, with more and more important decisions being made by TNCs and global governance bodies such as the WTO, the IMF and the World Bank. The combination of deregulation and the Internet allows huge amounts of capital to flow across international boundaries without state monitoring or controls. The anti-globalisation movement in particular argues that this allows TNCs to play off one country against another, seeking lower wages from workers and lower taxes from governments. The consequences of this are poorer working conditions and inadequate social services.

Given their dominant position in politics, economics and technology, it is not surprising to find the big TNCs deeply involved in most of the world's serious environmental issues. And it is therefore not surprising that environmental groups are among those most concerned about the shift in power from nation-states to TNCs.

TNC influence on UN organisations

There is growing concern in many quarters that UN agencies, which have to listen to opinion from all sides, are wide open to manipulation and infiltration (Figure 10). A report by the World Health Organization (WHO) stated that junk food and fizzy drinks are making children obese, and that governments should clamp down on them. The rising tide of obesity is having a severe impact on the quality of life of millions of people in the rich world, and even killing some of them, and is now edging into poor

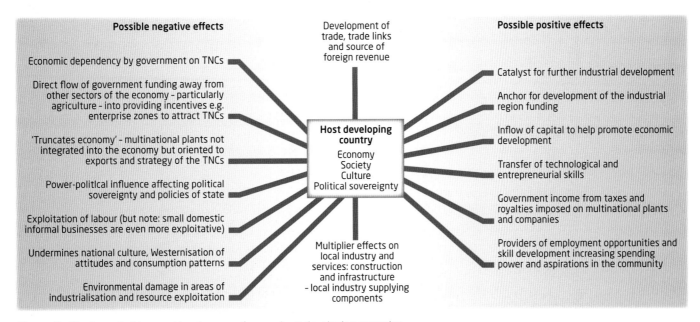

Figure 9 *The impact of transnational corporations on host developing countries.*

WHO 'infiltrated by food industry'

The food industry has infiltrated the World Health Organization, just as the tobacco industry did, and succeeded in exerting 'an undue influence' over policies intended to safeguard public health by limiting the amount of fat, sugar and salt we consume, according to a confidential report obtained by the Guardian.

The report, by an independent consultant to the WHO, finds that:
• food companies attempted to place scientists favourable to their views on WHO and Food and Agricultural Organisation (FAO) committees
• they financially supported non-governmental organisations which were invited to formal discussions on key issues with the UN agencies
• they financed research and policy groups that supported their views
• they financed individuals who would promote 'anti-regulation ideology' to the public, for instance in newspaper articles.

'The easy movement of experts – toxicologists in particular – between private firms, universities, tobacco and food industries and international agencies creates the conditions for conflict of interest,' says the report by Norbert Hirschhorn, a Connecticut-based public health academic who searched archives set up during litigation in the US for references to food companies owned or linked to the tobacco industry.

He finds that there is reasonable suspicion that undue influence was exerted 'on specific WHO/FAO food policies dealing with dietary guidelines, pesticide use, additives, trans-fatty acids and sugar.'

'The food industry is considerably engaged in genetically modified foods and the tobacco industry has studied the matter closely with respect to its product; there is evidence the tobacco industry planned also to influence the debate over biotechnology.' The WHO and FAO need the scientific input of the food industry, says the report, but that input must be transparent and subject to open debate.

'One industry-led organisation, International Life Sciences Institute (ILSI), has positioned its experts and expertise across the whole spectrum of food and tobacco policies: at conferences, on FAO/WHO food policy committees and within WHO, and with monographs, journals and technical briefs.'

Some of the strongest criticism in the report is levelled against the ILSI, founded in Washington in 1978 by the Heinz Foundation, Coca-Cola, Pepsi Cola, General Foods, Kraft (owned by Philip Morris) and Procter & Gamble. Until 1991 it was led by Alex Malaspina, vice-president of Coca-Cola.

Dr Malaspina established ILSI as a non-governmental organisation 'in official relations' with the WHO and secured it 'specialised consultative status' with the FAO.

Eileen Kennedy, global executive director of ILSI, said that the funding of its regional groups came exclusively from industry, while the central body received money from the branches, from government and from an endowment set up by Dr Malaspina. Nonetheless, she said, ILSI regarded itself as an independent body.

Figure 10 *Influence on United Nations organisations.* The Guardian, *January 2003.*

countries to co-exist with malnutrition. The large TNCs in the food and drinks industry do not accept this claim and are using all the influence they can muster to challenge the conclusions of the WHO.

The WHO report recommended that:

- governments should clamp down on TV ads pushing sugar-rich items to impressionable children

- governments should consider heavier taxes on such products

- schools should scrap vending machines.

The British Soft Drinks Association denies the link between its products and obesity, attributing the latter to sedentary lifestyles.

Previously the WHO has accused the tobacco TNCs of sabotaging efforts to control tobacco consumption through pressure tactics against the agency and other international organisations. A WHO report accused the tobacco industry of:

- using numerous third-party organisations such as trade unions to try to influence the WHO

- secretly funding 'independent' experts to conduct research and publish papers that would challenge WHO findings

- setting up press conferences to draw attention away from events organised by the WHO related to anti-smoking efforts.

Comparing the wealth of TNCs with that of nation-states

On globalization's parallel track, demarcated by markets rather than territorial boundaries, corporations and firms have displaced nation-states as the key players on the international scene. They more often use the political institutions created by nation-states to work their will than they are used by those states to enact sovereign political objectives. Even philanthropies such as the Clinton Foundation, the Gates Foundation, and the Ford Foundation have become weighty actors in the international marketplace, boasting an economic clout that many nation-states cannot begin to exercise.

Benjamin Barber, *Shrunken Sovereign: Consumerism, Globalization, and American Emptiness*, 2008

Although **wealth** is a fundamental concept in economics, the definition of the concept has varied. This has been one reason for the debate about how to compare the wealth of TNCs with that of nation-states. The wealth of a nation can be defined as 'the total amount of economically relevant private and public assets including physical (natural), financial, human, and "social" capital'. So the traditional way of using Gross Domestic Product (GDP) to indicate a country's wealth provides only a partial picture. The GDP of two countries could be the same, but the wider aspects of wealth might vary so much that the quality of life of the citizens of the two countries is very different indeed.

For TNCs, the traditional measure of wealth is the revenue generated from sales in a year. The figures for the largest TNCs are colossal, dwarfing the GDPs of many of the world's nations. Table 2 shows the revenues and profits (or losses) of the world's ten largest corporations in 2009. The data comes from the US business magazine *Fortune* which produces an analysis and ranking of the world's 500 largest corporations every year.

Royal Dutch Shell led the ranking with a revenue of $458 billion. The top three corporations were all in excess of $400 billion. All of the top ten recorded revenues of over $200 billion. By way of comparison, Table 3 shows data from the International Monetary Fund for estimated GDP in 2009. The top six countries in the world are shown, along with a selection of 18 other countries. The total revenue of Royal Dutch Shell is virtually the same as the total GDP of Belgium, which ranks 20th in the world. Only 41 countries had a GDP more than the revenue of

Toyota Motor which is in 10th place in terms of the world's major TNCs. Bolivia ranks 100th in the world with a GDP of only $17 billion. This is less than the profits made by Royal Dutch Shell, Exxon Mobil, BP and Chevron. This is an indication of the power that large TNCs can exert, particularly in relatively small economies.

However, companies that record large revenues do not always make a profit and some large TNCs have made spectacular losses. In some cases, consistent losses over a number of years have caused the complete collapse of some leading TNCs so that they disappear entirely from the ranking lists. This does not happen to nation-states – so far, at least!

Rank	Company	Revenue ($ billion)	Profits ($ billion)
1	Royal Dutch Shell	458	20
2	Exxon Mobil	442	45
3	Wal-Mart Stores	405	13
4	BP	367	21
5	Chevron	263	24
6	Total	235	16
7	Conoco-Phillips	231	-17
8	ING Group	227	-1
9	Sinopec	208	2
10	Toyota Motor	204	-4

Table 2 *Revenue and profits of the world's top ten TNCs, 2009.*

The method of comparing the revenue of major TNCs with the GDP of countries has been criticised by a number of observers. Martin Wolf, writing in the *Financial Times*, stated that these calculations 'rest on an elementary howler', with the might of corporations being judged by sales but that of countries by value-added (GDP). According to Wolf the incompatibility of these two measures, grossly overestimating the power of corporations, has led to a 'paranoid delusion'.

In a similar vein, Philippe Legrain in *Open World: the Truth about Globalisation* says the method of comparison is like comparing apples and pears. He argues that a proper comparison would look at the value-added for both entities (TNCs and countries). To do this for TNCs it is necessary to deduct the costs of production from the revenue generated. Under this method a much smaller number of TNCs would make it into the combined (TNCs and countries) wealth ranking. Figure 11 compares the views of Naomi Klein, who is happy to compare the revenues of TNCs with the GDP of countries, with the position of Philippe Legrain. This is an academic debate that shows no sign of compromise.

Rank	Country	$ billion
1	USA	14 266
2	Japan	5 048
3	China	4 757
4	Germany	3 235
5	France	2 634
6	UK	2 198
15	South Korea	800
20	Belgium	461
25	Norway	368
30	Denmark	308
35	Colombia	228
40	Hong Kong	208
45	Nigeria	168
50	Algeria	134
55	New Zealand	109
60	Morocco	90
65	Libya	60
70	Slovenia	49
75	Azerbaijan	42
80	Lithuania	36
85	Kenya	30
90	Latvia	24
95	El Salvador	22
100	Bolivia	17

Table 3 *Selected countries: GDP by world ranking, 2009.*

'Corporations are much more than purveyors of the products we all want; they are also the most powerful political forces of our time…Shell and Wal-Mart bask in budgets bigger than the gross domestic product of most nations…of the top hundred economies, fifty-one are multinationals and only forty-nine are countries.'

Naomi Klein, *No Logo*

'It is simply not true. The statement [opposite] is arrived at by comparing companies' sales and countries' gross domestic product (GDP). But this is like comparing apples and pears. A less misleading comparison – between companies' value-added and countries' value-added, their GDP – reveals that only two companies make it into the top fifty creators of value-added, and thirty-seven into the top hundred.'

Philippe Legrain, *Open World: the Truth about Globalisation*

Figure 11 *Countries and corporations: alternative views*

Geographical skill

a Explain the two methods of comparing the power of TNCs with that of countries.
b Which method do you favour and why?

Activities

1 Discuss the evidence that TNCs have become more powerful in recent decades.
2 With reference to Figure 9 (page 193), examine the advantages and disadvantages of TNCs to their host developing countries.
3 Suggest how TNCs can influence the United Nations and other international organisations.

Theory of Knowledge

What implications does the increasing power of TNCs have for citizenship and democracy?

Review

Examination-style questions

1 a Describe the formation of a trade bloc you have studied.

   b What has been the impact on its member countries?

2 a Why are so many countries keen to attract TNC investment?

   b What are the disadvantages that TNCs can bring to host developing countries?

Key terms

Nation-state an independent state inhabited by all the people of one nation and one nation only.

Sovereignty the exclusive right to exercise, within a specific territory, the functions of a nation-state and be answerable to no higher authority.

Religious fundamentalism movements favouring strict observance of religious teaching (Islam, Christianity, Hinduism etc.).

Websites

www.guardian.co.uk
The Guardian newspaper, UK

www.worldaffairsjournal.org
World Affairs journal

www.globalissues.org
Global Issues: social, political, economic and environmental issues

www.globalpolicy.org
Global Policy Forum

Trade bloc a group of countries that share trade agreements between each other.

Immobility of labour the effect of barriers to the movement of workers between jobs and geographical regions.

Wealth the total amount of economically relevant private and public assets including physical (natural), financial, human and 'social' capital.

16 Responses

KEY QUESTIONS

- How and why has there been a resurgence of nationalism in Bolivia as it attempts to retain control of its resources and culture?
- What are the characteristics and functions of anti-globalisation movements?
- How has the USA attempted to control immigration?

Communist Party office in a French town – the Communist Party in France and elsewhere has highlighted many of the problems associated with globalisation.

Responding to globalisation and loss of sovereignty

The progress of globalisation and the associated loss of sovereignty felt in many countries has led to various responses at different levels. In some countries such as Bolivia, Venezuela and Russia, governments have reasserted control over key economic sectors which were under the control of foreign transnational companies. Some development economists argue that the colonialism of the past has been replaced by neo-colonialism where control is economic rather than political.

In the past such views were aimed at Western TNCs, but now the targets have become wider. An article published in *Time* magazine in December 2009 entitled 'The World of China Inc' stated that the spreading reach of Chinese companies in poor nations is sparking a backlash against the way they do business. At first many countries welcomed Chinese investment, but now there are concerns about the balance of benefits and the influence that China has on national governments because of China's huge economic power.

The first era of significant Chinese interest in Africa was in the 1950–60s when China was trying to gain influence in various parts of the world as a counter to both Western capitalism and to the then Soviet Union, its ideological rival in communism. China supported African liberation movements and later helped a number of African countries in such fields as building railways, education and health.

The second era of Chinese interest in Africa, which dates broadly from the mid 1990s, has been based on international trade and on securing considerable quantities of a wide array of raw materials to feed its phenomenal industrial development (Figure 1). Africa has also been identified as a growing market for Chinese goods.

China's total investment in Africa in 2006 is estimated at $6.3 billion. It has become Africa's third biggest trade partner after the USA and France, 30% of China's oil imports come from Africa and it has signed trade initiatives with more than 40 African states.

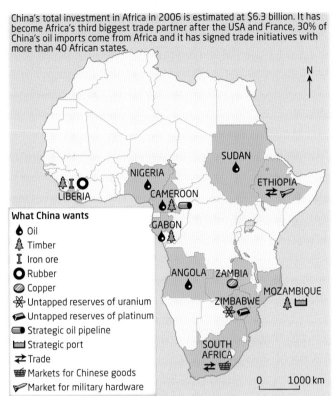

What China wants

- 💧 Oil
- 🌲 Timber
- Ⅰ Iron ore
- ⬤ Rubber
- ⬭ Copper
- ☢ Untapped reserves of uranium
- ◗ Untapped reserves of platinum
- ⬭ Strategic oil pipeline
- ⊟ Strategic port
- ⇄ Trade
- 🛒 Markets for Chinese goods
- ➤ Market for military hardware

0   1000 km

	What China gives
Cameroon	China cancelled $100 million debt owed to it by Cameroon.
Gabon	Agricultural experts to help small scale farmers.
South Africa	Deal to supply South African citrus fruits to China.
Sudan	Huge sales of military hardware. China buys two-thirds of Sudan's oil and has been criticised for not using its economic leverage to pressurise the Sudanese government into resolving civil war in Darfur.
Ethiopia	The China–Ethiopia Friendship Road which rings the capital, Addis Ababa, and a road-building programme around the country.
Angola	$5.8 billion no-strings-attached loans package to repair war-torn national infrastructure.
Zambia	Investment in copper mines and smelts, loan of $39 million to improve roads.
Zimbabwe	Economic aid and investment, allowing Robert Mugabe's regime to avoid Western pressure for political reform.
Mozambique	Aid and debt relief, road-building programme. Purchases prawns and cashew nuts.
Nigeria	$2.3 billion for a 45% share of an offshore oil block. Grants for anti-malarial medicine.
Liberia	$5 million in aid, building 100 secondary schools and 30 hospitals destroyed during civil war. 275 scholarships for Liberians to study in China.

Figure 1 *China's investment in Africa.*

In some countries **immigration** has become a key issue as people have felt threatened in various ways by the sociocultural changes that significant levels of immigration may bring. Various groups of people and organisations have reacted against globalisation and become part

Religious procession in a Spanish village – traditional values are still strong in communities like this.

of national and international **anti-globalisation movements.** Anti-globalisation movements have gained increasing media attention and are undoubtedly having an impact on policy-makers at the national and international levels. Religious leaders have also become increasingly concerned the obsession with consumerism brought about by globalisation.

Activities

Read the case study on pages 200–202 then answer these questions.

1 **a** What is resource nationalisation?
   b Why has Bolivia pursued this policy?
   c How in the long term could this policy prove to be
       (i) of benefit to Bolivia (ii) a disadvantage to Bolivia?
2 Why have Bolivia's recent policies to cope with globalisation created tension with the USA?
3 Comment on the data illustrated in Figure 3.

Case study

Bolivia: managing the impact of globalisation

Bolivia (Figure 2) has recently introduced a **resource nationalisation** policy to regain an important aspect of its sovereignty and to use the expected increase in national income to combat inequality and poverty. Along with Cuba and Venezuela it forms the so-called 'radical block' of nations in Latin America which are concerned about US economic power in the region and the exploitative action of TNCs in general.

Total population 2007	9.5 million
Crude birth rate 2007	28/1000
Crude death rate 2007	8/1000
Life expectancy 2007	65 years
Infant mortality rate 2007	48/1000
Adult literacy rate 2000–07	90%
GNI per capita 2007	$1260
% of population using improved drinking water sources, 2006	86%
Debt service as a % of exports of goods and services, 2006	8%
ODA inflow, 2006	$581 million

Table 1 *Bolivia factfile.*

Figure 2 *Location of Bolivia.*

Bolivia is South America's poorest country with a gross national income (GNI) per capita of only $1260 in 2007 (Table 1). In the 1980s and 1990s the Bolivian government introduced free market reforms. Such reforms were required by the World Bank if Bolivia was to continue to receive aid. **Privatisation** was at the heart of this agenda. Investors, usually foreign, were allowed to acquire 50%

ownership and management control of public sectors such as electricity, telecommunications and the state oil corporation, in return for an agreed level of capital investment. Although the Bolivian government had little choice, it also wanted to link economic growth with equity so that poorer people would gain more benefit from Bolivia's participation in the global economy. The measures to achieve this included:

- a type of decentralisation called Popular Participation
- education reform to improve access to opportunities for the poor.

These two strategies were mainly targeted at improving the lives of the indigenous and mestizo (mixed race) populations. These population groups scored significantly below the national average on virtually every indicator of the quality of life. However, very limited progress with these objectives led to frequent changes in government due to public disquiet. A significant change occurred in December 2005 when Evo Morales of the Movement Toward Socialism (MAS) was elected as the country's first indigenous president. He was elected on a pledge to challenge the free market reforms that most people felt the country had been pressurised into adopting. There was widespread concern that these policies benefited large TNCs and the rich in Bolivia to the detriment of the poor and the environment. There were concerns voiced in a number of other countries which were in a similar situation. Bolivia has the highest income inequality in Latin America and the sixth most unequal in the world (Figure 3). This is a situation that will take time to change.

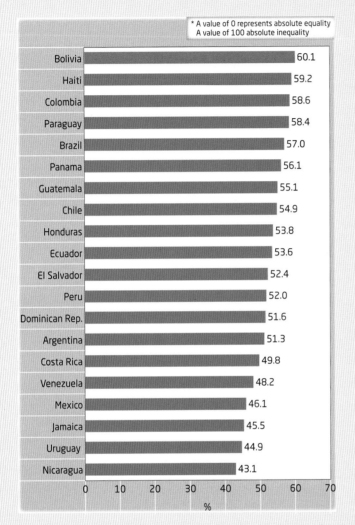

* A value of 0 represents absolute equality
A value of 100 absolute inequality

Bolivia	60.1
Haiti	59.2
Colombia	58.6
Paraguay	58.4
Brazil	57.0
Panama	56.1
Guatemala	55.1
Chile	54.9
Honduras	53.8
Ecuador	53.6
El Salvador	52.4
Peru	52.0
Dominican Rep.	51.6
Argentina	51.3
Costa Rica	49.8
Venezuela	48.2
Mexico	46.1
Jamaica	45.5
Uruguay	44.9
Nicaragua	43.1

%

Figure 3 *Income inequality in Latin America.*

In May 2006 President Morales nationalised the country's gas and oil industry. Bolivia has the second largest natural gas reserves (48.7 trillion cubic feet) in Latin America, but produces only a small amount of oil for domestic use. The foreign energy companies were told they had six months to sign new operating contracts or leave the country. All agreed to sign new contracts which will result in higher revenues for the government. Now, all foreign energy companies have to deliver all their production to the state-run YPFB for distribution and processing.

Overall, Bolivia has taken control of 82% of the oil and gas in the country, leaving the remainder to foreign

companies. Although Bolivia suffered much international criticism for its action, many aspects of Bolivia's resource nationalisation actually replicate Norway's oil management policies. Norway is very much a 'respected' member of the international community. The new government in Bolivia saw regaining control of the country's natural resources as a vital first step towards generating the revenue to achieve much needed development.

The process of resource nationalisation has not only affected TNCs from the developed world, but also its South American neighbour Brazil. Brazil's state-controlled oil company Petroleo Brasileiro SA produces 70% of Bolivia's natural gas. Bolivia argues that Brazil gets the gas at a very low rate which is about half of what gas costs in the USA. Brazil feels that the price is fair, given the fact that it built the gas pipeline between the two countries at a cost of $2.5 billion.

In 2006 President Morales said, 'Nationalisation will not stop at oil and gas resources, we'll extend it to land.' Brazilians grow more than a third of the soybeans in Bolivia and the concerns of these farmers about losing their land has led to discussions between the two governments. Bolivia has stated that its main concern is illegal or undocumented occupation of Bolivian land, especially land within 50 km of the Brazilian border, territory that Bolivia's constitution prohibits foreigners from owning.

Bolivians hold a certain resentment against some of their South American neighbours. Since the middle of the 19th century, Bolivia has lost about half its territory in natural resource disputes, the largest amount going to Brazil. Bolivia lost its Pacific coastline as a result of the 1879–84 War of the Pacific against Chile. This war was largely fought over guano (bird dung) which is used as a fertiliser.

Bolivia is adopting a socialist model of regional commerce and cooperation as opposed to what it sees as 'US-backed free trade'. Bolivia views the concept of the Free Trade Area of the Americas as an attempt by the USA to 'annex' Latin America. The government is trying to attract foreign investment while at the same time giving the state a larger role in managing the economy.

The privatisation of water has been a major issue. The resulting large increases in water bills provoked huge demonstrations such as in Cochabamba, Bolivia's third largest city. The Bolivian government withdrew its water contract with Bechtel and its operating partner Abengoa. As a result the companies sued the Bolivian government for $50 million. However, in 2006 the companies agreed to abandon their legal action in return for a token payment.

A protest against water privatisation in Bolivia.

country. The US ambassador was accused of 'conspiring against democracy' and encouraging rebel groups who were protesting in eastern Bolivia. In November 2008, the USA suspended duty-free access for Bolivian exports and President Morales suspended US Drug Enforcement Administration operations, accusing its agents of espionage.

Bolivia has a problem with the USA's drug war in South America. The USA wants to end the production of coca and thus reduce cocaine production to zero. Although Bolivia is against the trade in illegal drugs it wants to preserve the legal market for coca leaves and promote the export of legal coca products. The reduction in the coca crop has hit the incomes of many people on low incomes.

The Bolivian government is concerned by the number of people moving abroad to find work to earn money for their families. Limited employment in Bolivia is a major problem. In many cases children are left behind with no-one to care for them. In 2007 the Bolivian government announced it was to create 360 000 jobs by 2010, but it has fallen well short of this due at least partly to the global financial crisis.

The actions of the USA in 'pressurising' Colombia and Peru into free trade agreements have damaged Bolivian exports to these countries. Sixty per cent of Bolivia's main farm export, soybeans, goes to Colombia. Now Bolivia is concerned that cheap, subsidised US food will undercut much of Bolivia's market in Colombia.

In April 2006 Bolivia signed the people's trade agreement with Venezuela and Cuba. The latter has agreed to take all of Bolivia's soybean production as well as other farm products at market prices or better. Venezuela will also send oil to Bolivia to meet domestic shortages in production. Cuba has agreed to supply doctors.

In September 2008, President Morales ordered the US ambassador to Bolivia, Philip Goldberg, to leave the

Like many countries that rely heavily on the export of raw materials to earn foreign currency, Bolivia has a sizeable foreign debt. At the end of 2006, Bolivia owed $3.2 billion to foreign creditors.

In December 2009 Evo Morales was re-elected as President of Bolivia, winning more than 60% of the vote. His left-of-centre Movement Toward Socialism party gained majorities in both the 36-seat Senate and the 130-member Lower House. Supported strongly again by the largely poor indigenous population, Morales promises to push through further social and economic reforms. Before Morales came to power in 2005, Bolivia had had five presidents in five years. There seems to be a perception amongst a majority of Bolivians that the country is moving towards a fairer society with a government determined to ensure a better balance of benefits from foreign investment than was the case in the past.

A UN human rights report on Bolivia published in 2008 welcomed the positive advances made by the government in the areas of economic, social and cultural rights. The report highlighted programmes like the 'dignity pension' for the elderly and the 'Juancito Pinto' voucher for schoolchildren in poor rural areas, as well as the 'yes I can' literacy campaign.

Anti-globalisation movements

As the global economy and society have changed in recent decades, an increasing number of organisations have become vociferous in their opposition to the way in which globalisation has been operating. Such anti-globalisation movements are particularly critical about the actions of TNCs and the international organisations that set the rules for global finance and trade. Critics of the way that globalisation is operating highlight the following:

- the widening gap between rich and poor at the global level and in many individual countries
- decision-making power being concentrated in fewer and fewer hands
- the erosion and loss of local cultures
- loss of sovereignty of nation-states
- the destruction of biological diversity
- the increase in environmental problems as the scale of economic activity increases
- the increase in regional tensions in some parts of the world.

A large number of organisations are critical of the way the global economy and society operates. The following organisations are often quoted as being substantial anti-globalisation organisations:

- Focus on the Global South
- People's Global Action
- Landless People's Movement in South Africa
- Revolutionary International Organisation
- The Homeless Workers Movement in Brazil
- Grassroots Global Justice in the USA.

Those that have major concerns about globalisation, the so-called anti-globalisation 'movement', come from a wide variety of backgrounds:

- popular fears about the power of big business
- trade unionists worried about jobs filtering down to lower wage economies
- environmentalists who say that TNCs are disregarding the environment in the rush for profits and market share
- those fearful of the erosion of national sovereignty and culture
- small businesses afraid that they will become the victims of global economies of scale
- poverty campaigners who say that the West's gain has been at the expense of developing countries.

All these groups and others came together to demonstrate against the WTO in Seattle in December 1999 and at subsequent international conferences. Approximately 60 000 people took to the streets of Seattle and used peaceful protest and civil disobedience to disrupt the WTO negotiations. Mark Ritchie, President of the Institute of Agriculture and Trade Policy, described the demonstrations at the Seattle Conference as 'the first post-modern global gathering…the nations of the South combined with representatives of civil society to write a new chapter in global governance'.

Trade union groups of various backgrounds are heavily involved in the anti-globalisation movement. One of the main concerns of many labour groups is that the losers to international trade are not being properly compensated. They argue that too often the short-term negative effects of international trade on labour are being ignored. In addition, trade union groups worry about the rights and freedoms of their members. According to the International Forum on Globalization, globalisation has been characterised by a sharp increase in unemployment in both the developed and developing worlds. The privatisation of public utilities has been a significant factor in this process. Labour groups point to the high social costs associated with unemployment which private companies do not seem to care about.

Anti-globalisation groups often refer to 'market failures'. This is often in reference to TNCs, primarily because the size of many of these corporations has allowed them to circumvent or subvert rules made in an earlier era. Prominent writers in the anti-globalisation movement point out that there is a place where competition ends and market power begins. They argue that at that point government has to take over to curb the excesses of companies that become too powerful.

'Market creep' is another term that is often used by anti-globalisers. This refers to the idea that democracy is being replaced by something more market driven. Issues such as democracy and human rights are moral issues, and TNCs, it is argued, are frequently 'morally ambivalent'.

In her book *The Silent Takeover*, Noreena Hertz states: 'Corporations have become behemoths, huge global giants that wield immense political power' and in the process of their evolution 'justice, equity, rights, the environment, and even issues of national security fall by the wayside'. Hertz quotes a *Business Week* survey which found that three-quarters of Americans thought that business had gained too much power over many aspects of their lives.

Focus on the Global South

Focus on the Global South (Focus) is a non-governmental organisation established in Bangkok in 1995 and is affiliated with the Chulalongkorn University Social Research Institute. Focus combines policy research, advocacy, activism and grassroots capacity building in order to generate critical analysis and encourages debates on national and international policies related to corporate-led globalisation, neo-liberalism and militarisation. Focus's main objectives are to:

- dismantle oppressive economic and political structures and institutions
- create liberating structures and institutions
- promote demilitarisation and peace-building, instead of conflict.

Focus states that these three goals are brought together in the 'paradigm of deglobalisation'. This term describes the transformation of the global economy from one centred around the needs of TNCs to one that focuses on the needs of people, communities and nations and in which the capacities of local and national economies are strengthened. The deglobalisation paradigm forms the basis of Focus's work which spans five thematic areas: Defending and Reclaiming the Commons; Trade; Peace and People's Security; Alternatives; and China.

Research idea

Produce a factfile on an anti-globalisation movement operating in the country in which you live.

Control of major international organisations

A serious issue for the anti-globalisers is the apparent control that a relatively small number of countries have over the major international organisations (Figure 4). There are now significant moves to make changes to the way decisions are made in these organisations. In March 2009, British Prime Minister Gordon Brown stated he would support ending a six-decade-long gentlemen's agreement under which leadership of the World Bank and IMF has been divided up between Americans and Europeans. During a visit to Brazil, Gordon Brown, said, 'The International Monetary Fund, the World Bank and all the international institutions must

change now to meet the new realities.' The UK has also indicated its support for enlarging the UN's Security Council from its present membership of only five countries.

> **The United Nations** The five permanent members of the UN Security Council (the USA, UK, France, Russia and China) each have the power of veto not only over decisions concerning war and peace, but also over all attempts to amend or review the UN charter.
>
> **The International Monetary Fund and the World Bank** Altering the constitution of either body requires an 85% vote. The USA alone possesses 17% of the votes in each organisation.
>
> **The World Trade Organisation** In principle, every nation has an equal vote within the WTO. In practice, the rich world shuts out the poor world from key negotiations.

Figure 4 *Control of major international organisations.*

Climate change protestors, London, December 2009.

Globalisation and the environment

Environmentalists argue that the economics of globalisation is concerned primarily with internal costs, largely ignoring external costs such as environmental impact. While companies make profits, society has to pay the bill. There is a great deal of evidence that the planet's ecological health is in trouble. Between 1950 and 2000 humankind consumed more of the world's natural capital than during its entire previous history. According to the ecologist Robert Ayres, 'We may well be on the way to our own extinction.' Cuts enforced by the IMF have reduced spending on the environment in a number of countries. There is detailed consideration of the environmental aspects of globalisation in the core theme book *Patterns and Change*.

Redesigning the global economy

Critics of the way globalisation is proceeding at present argue for a number of significant changes to the global system including the following:

- the establishment of a global central bank
- a revamping of the IMF to make it more democratic
- a 'Tobin tax' on international financial transactions to reduce speculation
- the establishment of a global environmental organisation to monitor and reduce the impact of economic activity
- the control of capital for the public good.

The major overall objective is that the two prime movers of the global economy, the economically powerful nation-states and TNCs, become more accountable to the people of the planet and that all the impacts of economic activity are taken into account in the decision-making process. The goal must be to spread the benefits of globalisation more widely so that all peoples feel included in the global improvement in the quality of life.

Discussion point

What do you think of the suggestions for redesigning the global economy?

Activities

1. What do you understand by the term 'anti-globalisation movement'?
2. Briefly discuss the main concerns of anti-globalisation movements.
3. **a** Why has there been so much criticism about the way major international organisations have been run in the past?
   b How do you think these organisations should change in the future?

The USA: Controlling immigration

Immigration has had a phenomenal influence on the demographic history of the USA. Since 1820 almost 60 million people have entered the country (Figure 5). During this time both the rate of entry and the origin of immigrants have changed considerably. The highest recorded rate for any decade was 10.4 per 1000 between 1901 and 1910, when 8.75 million newcomers arrived, although some decades in the 19th century were not far behind in proportional terms. The high rate of immigration continued until the outbreak of hostilities in Europe in 1914, whereupon it sharply abated from 12.3 per 1000 in 1914 to 3.2 per 1000 in 1915. It has rarely risen above the latter figure since, apart from a few exceptional years in the early 1920s and in recent years. The main reason for this was a growing concern among the American public about the numbers and origin of migrants.

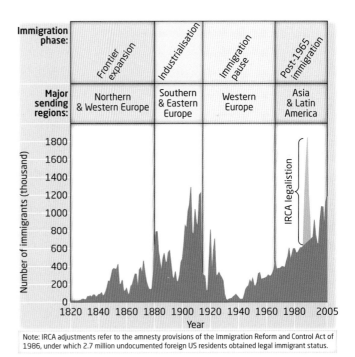

Note: IRCA adjustments refer to the amnesty provisions of the Immigration Reform and Control Act of 1986, under which 2.7 million undocumented foreign US residents obtained legal immigrant status.

Figure 5 *Legal immigration to the USA, 1820–2005.*

In 1924 a system of 'national origins quotas' was introduced which operated with only slight modification until 1965. This legislation was designed to reduce migration significantly and, in particular, to stem the influx of Eastern and Southern Europeans who entered the USA

Customs and Border Protection officer, Mexico/USA border.

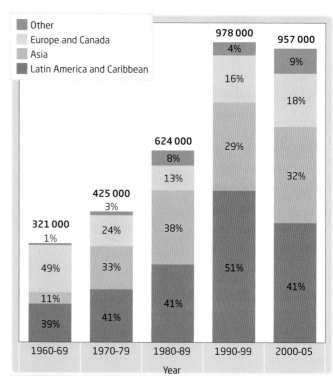

Note: Percentages may not add up to 100 because of rounding. The annual numbers are averages for each period.

Figure 6 *Annual number of legal US immigrants by decade and region of origin, 1960–2005.*

in extremely large numbers at the turn of the 20th century. Anti-Chinese restrictions had already been in force for many years to fence off Chinese contract labourers. In fact Asian-Americans had to wait until the middle of the 20th century before they were entitled to vote. The new system aimed to preserve the ethnic balance which existed in the country at the time of the 1920 census, offering the largest quotas of entry permits to British, Irish and German immigrants (70% in total).

The racist overtones of this system, resulting in considerable internal and international opposition, led to its abolition in 1965. The 1965 Act, which became fully effective in July 1968, set an annual limit of 120 000 immigrants from the Western Hemisphere (the Americas) and 170 000 from the Eastern Hemisphere. People from every country within each hemisphere now had an equal chance of acceptance. However, immigration has exceeded this level considerably because relatives of US citizens are admitted without numerical limitation. The Immigration Act of 1990 raised immigration quotas by 40%.

As the **intervening obstacles** were lowered for potential migrants from a number of world regions, so the ethnic composition of new arrivals changed significantly. Europe, the previous major source region, has been overtaken since 1970 by the rest of the Americas and by Asia (Figure 6), a trend that is likely to continue in the future. The considerable increase in immigration in the 1990s, coinciding in the early part of the decade with a period of intense economic recession, reopened the immigration debate in the USA in a big way. By the late 1990s about one million immigrants were entering the USA each year. This number comprised 730 000 legal immigrants, 200 000 illegal aliens, and 100 000 refugees. About 70% of legal

immigrants are allowed in for the purposes of family reunification. Between 1990 and 2000, the number of foreign-born American residents increased by 6 million to just over 25 million. As Figure 6 shows, this high level of immigration has continued into the new millennium. Half of the 50 million new inhabitants expected in America in the next 25 years will be immigrants or the children of immigrants.

Figure 7 shows the status of foreign-born US residents in 2005. Of this total, 31% were naturalised US citizens, but almost as many were unauthorised migrants. Figure 8 analyses the legal status of foreigners living in the USA.

The inflow of migrants into the USA during the 1980s and 1990s has been termed 'the second great migration of the 20th century'. This trend is still in progress. One of its main consequences is the gradual change in ethnic balance. According to the 1950 census America was 89% white and 10% black with other races making a very minor contribution indeed. In 1970 the main minority populations were blacks (12%), Latinos (5%) and Asians (1%). Now Latinos account for around 14% of the population, and if current trends continue, in 20 years' time they will dominate Texas and California.

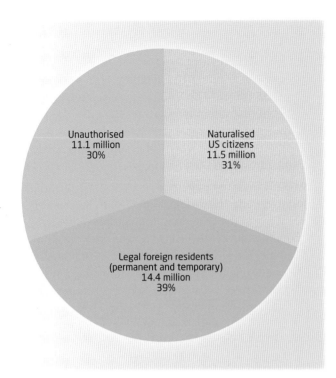

Unauthorised
11.1 million
30%

Naturalised
US citizens
11.5 million
31%

Legal foreign residents
(permanent and temporary)
14.4 million
39%

Figure 7 *Status of foreign-born US residents, 2005.*

Chinatown in San Francisco.

Geographical skill

Produce a 100-word summary of the information presented in Figure 8. Make sure that you refer to all the sub-sections in the article.

All persons in the United States are either US citizens or aliens, persons who are citizens of another country. There are four major types of aliens: immigrants, refugees, temporary legal migrants, and unauthorized foreigners.

Legal immigrants are citizens of other countries who have been granted a visa that allows them to live and work permanently in the United States and, generally after five years, to become naturalized US citizens. Immigrant visas are now credit-card type documents, but they used to be printed on green paper and legal immigrants are still referred to as 'green card holders.' Over 1.1 million immigrants (including refugees) were admitted in FY05, up from 950 000 in FY04.

Refugees and asylees are persons allowed to stay in the United States because of fear of persecution at home because of race, religion, nationality, membership in a particular social group, or political opinion. Refugees are resettled in the United States from abroad, often after leaving their countries and waiting in a third country until they are admitted to the United States to begin life anew. The numbers fluctuate according to events abroad and changes in US laws.

Asylees or asylum applicants are foreigners who arrive in the United States and request refugee status. Refugees and asylees may become legal permanent residents after a year in the United States.

Temporary legal migrants are foreigners in the United States for a specific purpose, such as visiting, working, or studying. Some 32 million temporary legal migrants were admitted in FY05. Almost 90 percent were temporary visitors for pleasure (tourists) or business visitors. These counts of arrivals do not include Mexicans with border crossing cards that allow shopping visits or Canadian visitors. Temporary migrants who enter and leave the United States several times are counted each time they enter.

The United States has 25 types of non-immigrant visas, such as A1 visas for foreign government officials, B-visas for business visitors and tourists, F-visas for foreign students, H-visas for foreign workers, O- and P-visas for foreign athletes and entertainers, and TN visas for Canadians and Mexicans entering the United States to work under NAFTA's migration provisions. Visitors who are nationals of specific countries such as Canada and the UK are not required to have entry visas; however, most are included in the counts of arrivals. In 2006 there were 27 such visa-waiver countries.

Unauthorized, undocumented, or illegal migrants are foreigners in the United States without a valid visa. An estimated 11 million unauthorized foreigners were living in the United States in March 2005, including 6 million unauthorized Mexicans. The number of unauthorized foreigners has been rising by about 525 000 a year.

Figure 8 *Legal status of foreigners living in the USA.* Source: Population Bulletin, Volume 61, No. 4, 2006.

Among other things, immigrants are helping to move the country's demographic centre of gravity south-westward as immigration into the USA is very spatially selective (Figure 9). The big 'immigrant states' are California, New York, Florida, Texas and Illinois. In 1990 these states were home to 75% of US immigrants. By 2005 this total had fallen to 59% as immigrants move into new parts of the country.

There are three main reasons for the concentration of immigration:

- first, the location of existing immigrant communities which are well established in these states

- second, the availability of employment in the most populous states in the country

- finally, the land border with Mexico for California and Texas, and Florida's proximity to Caribbean countries.

The benefits and costs of immigration to the USA

The general attitude to immigration in the USA has always been much more positive than in Europe, although that is not to say that significant opposition has not existed. There has also been a great deal of debate about the degree of economic advantage.

Various attempts have been made to quantify the economics of immigration:

- A study carried out for Congress by the National Academy of Sciences (NAS) in 1997 concluded that immigration provided a net benefit to the American economy of around $10 billion a year in an economy worth $8 trillion. The NAS study calculated that competition from immigrants resulted in a 3% cut in wages of local people who had only a high-school certificate, with the worst-hit group usually being immigrants from the previous wave.

- An OECD survey published in 1997 concluded that immigration is financially beneficial to the American economy in the long term. Immigrants themselves take more out of the economy than they put in. For example, foreign-born residents are 35% more likely to receive public assistance than native-born residents, and the former, on average, pay 32% less in tax during their lifetime than the latter. The payback comes with the children of immigrants who, on average, pay far more to the state in taxes than they take from it. However, it takes 40 years after an immigrant enters the country, the OECD calculates, before the financial gain to the state outweighs the cost. For the public purse, the most lucrative immigrant is a 21-year-old with a higher-level education.

- Harvard economist George Borjas in his book *Heaven's Door* argues that the economic benefits brought by the latest 20-year wave of immigrants are less than for the immigration period 1950–70 due to a fall-off in levels

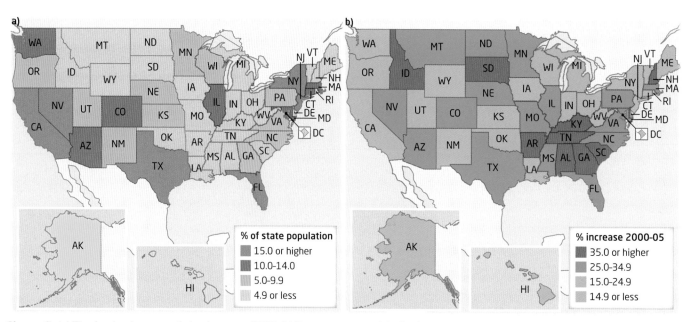

Figure 9 *(a) The foreign-born population by state, 2005. (b) Percentage growth in foreign-born population by state, 2000–05.*

of skill. He proposes that the USA should admit only 500 000 immigrants each year and select the most highly skilled. Borjas argues that rich Americans gain most from immigration. At home they gain from cheap nannies, cleaners and gardeners, while if they own businesses many benefit from relatively cheap immigrant labour. However, for the native-born poor the arrival of unskilled workers has made it harder to find jobs in an economy that demands even more education.

- The New Immigrant Survey Pilot published by the Rand Corporation in 1999 reached a different conclusion with regard to the skill level of immigrants. This study of legal immigrants only found that the newcomers' median length of schooling was 13 years, one year more than for the native population, and that new immigrants were more highly educated than their predecessors. However, it should be noted that the Borjas study included both legal and illegal immigrants. The Rand Corporation survey also concluded that for any male newcomer the immediate effect of getting to America is equivalent to winning $10 000. Over a lifetime, the gain totals $300 000.

The overall conclusion from the various recent studies is that in the long term the USA gains from immigration but that the immigrants gain even more.

Business in America generally favours immigration because:

- it has a general deflationary impact on wage rates by increasing the pool of labour, particularly in the semi-skilled and unskilled areas
- without immigration some industries, such as those in the field of high technology, would face severe skill shortages – one in four new businesses in Silicon Valley is started by someone of Indian or Chinese origin
- some industries, such as agriculture in California, rely on the blatant large-scale employment of illegal immigrants.

As the number of immigrants has increased in recent years so has their political clout. Of the two main political parties, the Republicans have wanted more control on immigration over the years but, as the number of immigrant voters has risen, the rhetoric has been toned down.

Still a 'melting-pot'?

The term 'melting-pot' originates from a play of that name, written by Israel Zangwill, which opened in Washington in 1908. The speaker is David, a young composer: 'America is God's Crucible, the great Melting-Pot where all the races of Europe are melting and reforming... Germans and Frenchmen, Irishmen and Englishmen, Jews and Russians –

into the Crucible with you all! God is making the American!' The imagery comes from steelmaking which was the high-technology industry then. The analogy was that the USA would fuse together a diversity of cultures and create a typically American way of life.

Many observers are, however, cynical about the validity of the melting-pot theory of majority–minority relations. This has sometimes been expressed by the formula $A + B + C = A$, where A, B and C represent different ethnic groups and A is the dominant one. Over time the other groups gradually conform to the attitudes, values and lifestyle of the dominant group while A will change only marginally.

In a major challenge to the melting-pot theory Charles Truxillo, a professor of Chicano (Latino) studies at the University of New Mexico, recently predicted that before the end of the 21st century California, southern Colorado, Texas, Arizona and New Mexico would secede from the USA to form a new sovereign Hispanic nation.

Assimilation into the host community is of major importance both to immigrants themselves and to native-born Americans. A 1999 study by the National Immigration Forum analysed four measures of assimilation – home ownership, citizenship, learning English, and intermarriage – and concluded that recent immigrants are following much the same pattern as previous generations. As other studies have found, attitudes become more Americanised with each succeeding generation. A recent poll by the *Washington Post* of 2500 Latinos showed that nine out of ten recent arrivals think it is important to change to fit in but a similar proportion think it is also important to retain part of their culture. These attitudes are similar to those of previous ethnic groups who have entered the USA in large numbers.

Activities

1. With reference to Figure 5 (page 205), describe the pattern of legal immigration to the USA between 1820 and 2005.
2. Describe and explain the trends and changes shown in Figure 6 (page 206).
3. Comment on the status of foreign-born US residents illustrated in Figure 7 (page 207).
4. Describe and explain the spatial distributions shown in the two maps in Figure 9 (page 208).
5. Assess the perceived advantages and disadvantages of a sustained high level of immigration into the USA.

Review

Examination-style questions

1 a For a country you have studied, examine the growing concerns it has had about the impact of globalisation.

   b How has this country acted to reassert its sovereignty?

2 a Why is there concern in some countries about high levels of immigration?

   b For a country you have studied, discuss its attempts to control migration.

Websites

www.focusweb.org
Focus on the Global South

www.prb.org
Population Reference Bureau

www.census.gov
US Census Bureau

www.boliviaweb.com
Bolivia Web interactive

Key terms

Immigration the migration of people into a country from other countries.

Anti-globalisation movements organisations and other groupings of people calling for reform of the global economic system to make it more equitable and democratic.

Resource nationalisation when a country decides to take part, or all, of one or a number of natural resources under state ownership.

Privatisation the transfer of businesses from the state to the private sector.

Intervening obstacles the difficulties encountered by a migrant or potential migrant in the movement from origin to destination.

17 Glocalisation and the adoption of globalisation

Defining glocalisation

Globalisation was defined in Chapter 1 as 'The growing interdependence of countries worldwide through the increasing volume and variety of cross-border transactions in goods and services and of international capital flows, and through the more rapid and widespread diffusion of technology'. The impact of globalisation is that people in both developed and developing countries can be significantly affected by decisions taken long distances away by transnational corporations and major international organisations. Globalisation has led to the homogenisation of landscapes and cultures to varying degrees. John Meyer has used the term 'isomorphism' to describe the way in which common features can be found in many different parts of the world. **Isomorphism** is a scientific term which means replication of the same form yet separated from the main source.

There can be little doubt that there has been a trend towards global uniformity, but the process of globalisation does not and will not erase all differences. Many of the various groups of people concerned by the process of globalisation see **glocalisation** as combating the worst aspects of globalisation, at least to a partial extent. However, there are those who reject globalisation in its entirety and want to see a completely new global economic system based on the principles of **equity** and **sustainability**.

Glocalisation is a combination of the words 'globalisation' and '**localisation**'. The latter means confined or restricted to a particular location. Figure 1 shows how Colin Hines, the author of *Localisation. Global Manifesto*, views

Arsenal's Emirates Stadium – the English Premier League club is sponsored by one of the world's fastest-growing airlines.

Corporate Globalization - the ever-increasing integration of national economies into the global economy through trade and investment rules and privatization, aided by technological advances. These reduce barriers to trade and investment and in the process reduce democratic controls by nation states and their communities over their economic affairs. The process is driven by the widespread lobbying of large corporations who use the theory of comparative advantage, the goal of international competitiveness and the growth model to achieve the maximization of their profits. It is occurring increasingly at the expense of social, environmental and labour improvements and rising inequality for most of the world.

Localization - a process which reverses the trend of globalization by discriminating in favour of the local. It ensures that all goods and services that can reasonably be provided locally should be. Depending on the context, the 'local' is predominantly defined as part of the nation state, although it can be the nation state itself or occasionally a regional grouping of nation states.

The policies bringing about localization are ones which increase control of the economy by communities and nation states. The result should be an increase in community cohesion, a reduction in poverty and inequality and an improvement in livelihoods, social infrastructure and environmental protection, and hence an increase in the all important sense of security.

Localization is not about restricting the flow of information, technology, trade and investment, management and legal structures which further localization, indeed these are encouraged by the new localist emphasis in global aid and trade rules. Such transfers also play a crucial role in the successful transition from globalization to localization. It is not a return to overpowering state control, merely governments' provision of a policy and economic framework which allows people, community groups and businesses to rediversify their own local economies.

The route to localization consists of seven interrelated and self-reinforcing policy areas. The basic steps are:

- reintroduction of protective safeguards for domestic economies;
- a site-here-to-sell-here policy for manufacturing and services domestically or regionally;
- localizing money such that the majority stays within its place of origin;
- local competition policy to eliminate monopolies from the more protected economies;
- introduction of resource taxes to increase environmental improvements and help fund the transition to the Protect the Local, Globally approach;
- increased democratic involvement both politically and economically to ensure the effectiveness and equity of the movement to more diverse local economies;
- reorientation of the end goals of aid and trade rules such that they contribute to the rebuilding of local economies and local control.

Under these circumstances, beggar-your-neighbour globalization gives way to the potentially more co-operative better-your-neighbour localization.

Figure 1 *Explaining globalisation and localisation.*

localisation. Here 'local' is viewed as being part of a country, a country as a whole or occasionally as a grouping of countries.

Glocalisation has roots in geography, sociology, anthropology, economics and other disciplines. Its meaning can differ slightly according to its subject context. In business, glocalisation is seen very much as the tailoring of products and **marketing** to meet spatial variations in consumer demand. For example, language localisation is an important aspect of marketing products to different countries so that the labelling of a product is in the language of the country it is being sold in. 'Dub localisation' is a term used in the media to refer, for example, to films and television programmes initially produced in English being presented in other languages so

that such programmes become accessible to a much wider audience. Maynard (2003) states:

> In the marketing sense, glocalisation means that companies have to deal not only with worldwide considerations, but also, very expressly, with the specific rules and conditions of each country in which they operate. Glocalisation represents the need for multinationals to be global and local at the same time. Put simply, whereas globalisation is a move toward centralisation, glocalisation is a move toward decentralisation.

Some business leaders believe that centralisation is necessary to maintain control, pointing to companies that have undergone disastrous consequences when problems at the local level have not been picked up early enough by headquarters. An example often quoted in recent years is how the once highly regarded Arthur Anderson consulting firm collapsed in the Enron scandal when its global nucleus lost track of what the local was doing. The local at the time was in the USA. Other companies see the objective of total global control as being impossible to achieve and recognise the importance of delegation to local hubs.

Sainsbury's 'Local' shop: in the UK the large supermarket chain markets its smaller food stores as 'Local'.

Glocalisation is where the global and the local interact (Figure 2) to produce hybridised outcomes. Here local populations are no longer viewed as the victims of global cultural change but as interpreters of such processes. The word 'glocal' refers to individuals and communities that 'think globally and act locally'. This signifies the capacity to bridge scales. Since the mid 1990s, glocalisation has gradually come to occupy an increasingly central place in studies of globalisation. The fact that virtually all major global companies now recognise that they have to think locally to be competitive shows how far the concept has come in less than two decades. Glocalisation stresses the need for cultural accommodation.

The influence of **Westernisation** is the dominant process of globalisation, but its impact varies around the world, blending and mixing in different ways. For example, in former British colonies the influence of long association with the UK varies considerably because of the individual

ways in which the cultures of the UK and different developing countries have blended (Figure 3). The 'modification' that occurs varies not only over space but also over time.

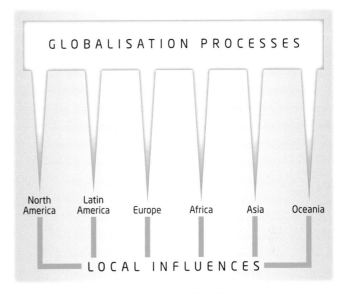

Figure 2 *Globalisation processes and local influences.*

Glocalisation recognises that all human activities are localised in that they are grounded in specific places, even though they may be heavily influenced by processes

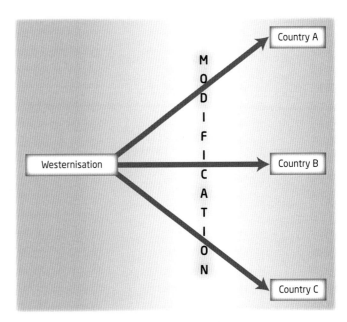

Figure 3 *The modification of Westernisation.*

operating at the regional and global scales. Even if the products and services have been brought in from abroad, the people delivering these products and services are invariably local people who will have at least some influence on the local business environment. Local consumers will also exert a varying degree of influence on globalised products and services in terms of how they respond to what is on offer.

The term 'glocalisation' has been applied to a variety of circumstances:

- The process of linking local, regional and global scales (also referred to as the micro, meso and macro scales).

- Using ICT to provide local services on a global or transregional basis. Although the Internet has been a key element in the process of globalisation, its role as a localising agent cannot be ignored. More and more web applications have been glocalising their approach to meet consumer demand. Many minority languages have developed their own websites as an important part of maintaining and extending such languages in their home regions. Websites can play an important role in maintaining other aspects of culture as well.

- Individuals, households and organisations maintaining interpersonal social networks combining local and global interactions. With the considerable expansion of global migration over the last 30 years, diasporas have become significant in many countries.

- Transnational corporations establishing local organisation structures to work more effectively with local cultures. TNCs have come to recognise that a 'one size fits all' approach has limited appeal in many markets around the world.

- The customisation of global products and services to suit local laws or culture. This can have a major impact on sales due to the importance of 'product acceptability' in local communities.

- The declaration of a city or other locality as world territory with responsibilities and rights on a global scale. More and more people at a local level now recognise that their actions can have a global impact (Figure 4).

An increasing number of local businesses are joining national, regional or global networks to help them compete with much larger enterprises. For example, a single-location flower shop may become a member of Interflora so that a customer can go into a flower shop in Ireland and arrange for a bunch of flowers to be delivered to someone in another country.

It is generally accepted that glocalisation supports the diversity of local cultures, markets and identities.

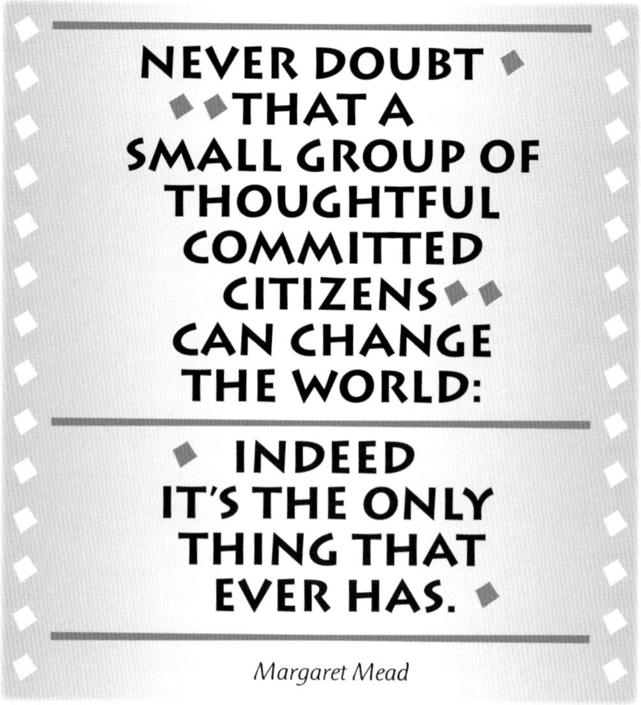

NEVER DOUBT THAT A SMALL GROUP OF THOUGHTFUL COMMITTED CITIZENS CAN CHANGE THE WORLD:

INDEED IT'S THE ONLY THING THAT EVER HAS.

Margaret Mead

Figure 4 *Margaret Mead quote.*

People the world over recognise the power of globalisation and many see its benefits, but they are keen to maintain their local culture at a certain level. The degree of tolerance between the two processes varies from place to place.

Thomas Friedman in his book *The Lexus and the Olive Tree* argues that technology is making globalisation inevitable, but people also long to have cultural roots, the latter being represented by their olive trees.

Figure 5 shows how the Co-operative Bank sees itself in terms of local and international relationships. The bank only invests in what it considers to be ethical activities in terms of both human rights and the environment. It stresses its obligation to its employees and their families and also its transgenerational role. Another bank, HSBC, styles itself as 'the world's local bank', trying to show a 'human touch' and create brand affinity with a worldwide audience.

In 2005, the Disney Corporation opened its new theme park in Hong Kong, a joint venture between Disney and the Hong Kong government. The familiar Disney format was adapted to ensure its Asian visitors felt comfortable. A key part of this process was following the advice of a 'feng shui' master in terms of the aspect and layout of the park. An important element was to ensure that the restaurants were distinctly local in flavour. Nevertheless,

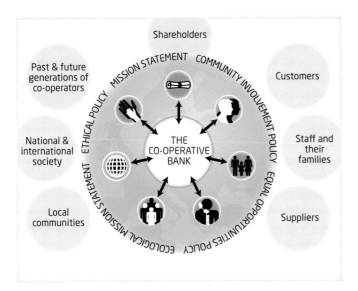

Figure 5 *The Co-operative Bank.*

A branch of Co-operative Bank, London.

Disney did encounter opposition. The interesting point is that most of it came from outside Hong Kong. Although Disney did much to glocalise its efforts it still could not satisfy some global activist groups. Very often global civil society, in terms of groups outside a particular country, provide invaluable support to local civil society, but at times their views can differ. Figure 6 shows the interactions occurring in the Disney example but it applies to many other issues of a controversial nature.

Friedman has referred to such opposition from outside a country as 'globalution' or 'revolution from beyond'. The number of issues that have attracted global attention from civil society groups has grown significantly over the past decade. Experience gained in the opposition to one development or action may be quickly applied to another situation in a different country. Before the Internet age, TNCs had a good chance of containing opposition within a particular host country. Now this is virtually impossible due to Internet blogging and other forms of cyberaction.

Geographical skill

Look at Figure 5. Comment on the way in which the Co-operative Bank tries to present itself.

Support for local shops and commerce is increasingly important in a global market.

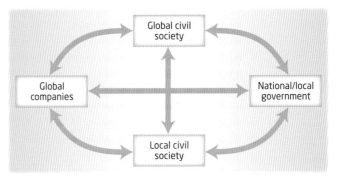

Figure 6 *Global companies, governments and civil societies.*

Japanese origin

The origin of the term 'glocalisation' comes from Japanese business practices where the Japanese word *dochakuka* means 'global localisation'. Originally it referred to methods of adapting farming techniques to local conditions, but later it became a marketing strategy for Japanese business in the 1980s. The term was popularised in the English-speaking world in the 1990s by the British sociologist Roland Robertson and the Canadian sociologists Keith Hampton and Barry Wellman. Early use of the term has also been ascribed to Manfred Lange in 1990 when he described the interplay of local, regional and global interactions as 'glocal'. Robertson maintains that the widespread fear that local cultures are being overwhelmed by global, allegedly homogenising, processes is unwarranted in so far as the diffusion between and across sociocultural formations of any set of ideas or values must of necessity adapt to particular, local circumstances if they are to 'stick' (unless imposed by military force and surveillance). He states:

> Globalization is without meaning unless it takes with the utmost seriousness that this concept involves the complex linking of socially constructed 'localities'. Moreover, the present concern with the local being overwhelmed by the global is but another way of saying that (reified) localities are becoming too interconnected. There is, then, no small irony in the fact that the emphasis on the protection of the local has been produced in global terms (Robertson, 1997). The local has been globalized; just as the global has been localized.

Theory of Knowledge

There is a pervasive notion that people only make choices or take actions that are in their own best interests (this lies behind the idea that globalisation must adapt to local circumstances if it is to be accepted). What kinds of processes, other than military force, might lead to other kinds of choices or actions?

NGOs: the Glocal Forum

A number of NGOs are actively working to promote glocalisation, including the Glocal Forum (Figure 7). This is a non-profit organisation 'dedicated to the promotion of international inter-city relations in pursuance of a new balance between global and local forces'. The Glocal Forum was founded in 2001 with the First Annual Glocalisation Conference held in May 2002. The conference brought together mayors and city representatives from all over the world. The Glocal Forum emphasises the central role of cities in international relations. The city-to-city approach works to bring together local leaders from both developing and developed countries. Since its inception, over 140 cities have joined the Glocal Forum Network. Figure 8 shows the cities involved in the Glocal Forum Network, with more likely to join in the future. Nearly 100 international agencies and companies have also worked with the Glocal Forum in forwarding the glocal development vision.

The Glocal Forum argues that glocalisation empowers local communities, linking them to global resources, facilitating development and providing opportunities for local communities to direct positive social change in the areas that most directly affect them. An example of the glocal approach is the 'We Are the Future' programme which aims to secure a better future for children and young people in post-conflict areas. This programme was initiated with Child Centres in six developing, post-conflict cities – Addis Ababa, Asmara, Freetown, Kabul, Kigali and Nablus.

Research idea

Select one city from Figure 8 (check the names of the cities on www.glocalforum.org) and find out the extent of its involvement with the Glocal Forum network.

Activities

1 Define 'globalisation'.
2 With reference to Figure 1 (page 212), discuss the meaning of 'localisation'.
3 Discuss the origin of the term 'glocalisation'.
4 Summarise the objectives of the Glocal Forum.
5 Look at Figure 8. Describe and suggest reasons for the distribution of cities that are members of the Glocal Forum Network.

Glocalization – What does it mean?

In today's globalized and primarily urban world, the dream of universal stability and prosperity has, unfortunately, not come true. Children on one side of the world have the most innovative sources of knowledge and technology at their fingertips, while children on the other side of the world die from a lack of nutrition and even the most basic of health services.

The Glocal Forum believes in the urgent need to recognize the interests and cultural identities of those who were left out of global economic expansion and has therefore developed a new strategy for international relations called 'Glocalization.'

Glocalization is a new paradigm for international relations and an innovative practice of development cooperation. The Glocalization strategy empowers local communities, linking them to global resources and knowledge while facilitating initiatives for peace and development. It provides opportunities for the local communities to direct positive social change in the areas that most directly affect them, and to shape an innovative and more equitable international system.

In particular, Glocalization attributes a special role to cities as international actors, and to city-to-city cooperation as a tool to counter global challenges and promote economic development and peacebuilding activities. Through enhanced connectivity, city-to-city networks can have access to the resources of the private and public sector and utilize these resources to address local needs, thus increasing the impact and cost-effectiveness of development projects for sustainable peace. Cities and local authorities represent the focal point of Glocalization. However, Glocalization is carried out by a number of key players – from the public sector, to international institutions and private sector companies – small and large, local and global.

Glocalization entails a shift in the international system, from a framework based on a balance of power between nation states, to a balance of cultural interests and local needs with global opportunities, always taking into account the importance of local actors as agents of change. By creating a new socio-economic balance, Glocalization has far-reaching benefits for both developed and developing countries, emphasizing social equity as a basis for international stability and ensuring a more secure and stable global environment to bring about development and peace. Glocalization brings together civil societies, local administrations and the private sector, on the one hand, and international organizations and national governments on the other, while fostering dialogue between parties through city-to-city partnerships, youth empowerment and information and communications technology.

For more insight on Glocalization strategy, please see the *Glocalization Manifesto* published by the Glocal Forum, December 2004.

Figure 7 *The Glocal Forum.*

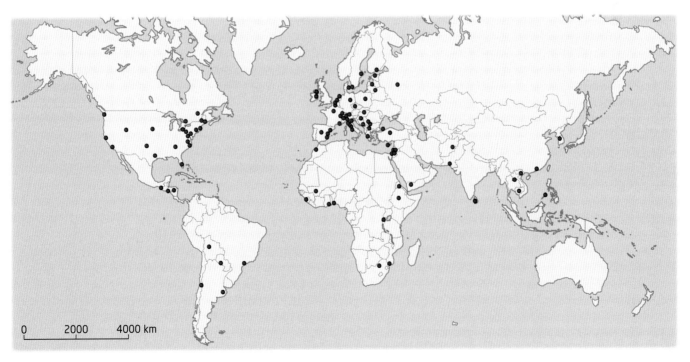

Figure 8 *Cities in the Glocal Forum Network.*

The adoption of globalisation

Commercial activities at the local level have become globalised to varying degrees. The level and rate of adoption have varied from place to place for a number of reasons.

The level of economic development of countries and regions

Globalisation has reached its greatest extent in the developed world (Figure 9) and has had the lowest level of impact in the world's least developed countries (LDCs). The latter group of countries is recognised by the United Nations as the poorest countries of all. These countries often argue that they have been bypassed by the benefits of globalisation, but have not been immune from its disadvantages. In some locations the impact of major mining operations or tourist enclaves may be very significant indeed.

The most rapid rate of change is invariably taking place in the newly industrialised nations such as China, India and Brazil. A high level of foreign direct investment invariably influences host countries in a number of ways that can be classified as economic, social, environmental and political. Within countries there can be substantial regional variations in the adoption of globalisation, with most evidence of the process in the economic core region

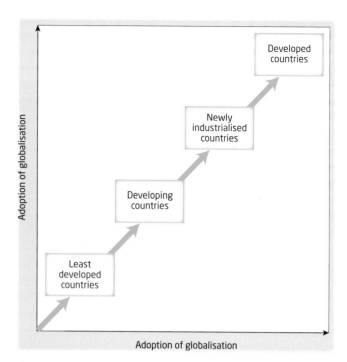

Figure 9 *Adoption of globalisation by economic development of countries.*

or regions. Global influences are usually evident at a much lower level in peripheral areas. J.R. Friedman noted that there were different types of peripheral areas in countries by dividing the periphery into upward transition areas, downward transition areas and resource frontiers. Figure 10 applied Friedmann's structure to Brazil. The

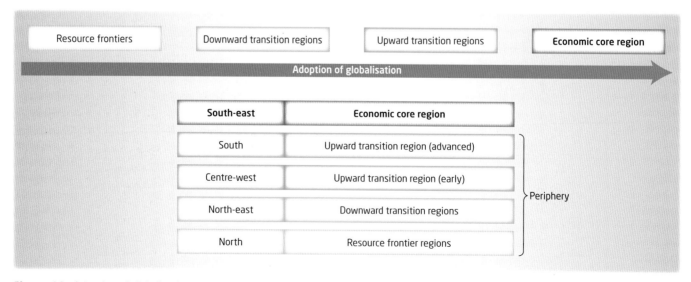

Figure 10 *Adoption of globalisation by regions within Brazil.*

Amazon region can be viewed as the country's resource frontier with very significant foreign direct investment involved in the development of natural resources, but with other elements of globalisation still only evident at a relatively low level. In the early stages of industrialisation the gap between core and periphery invariably widens, but after a certain level of development is reached the gap generally narrows. As it does so, the difference in the adoption of globalisation also decreases (Figure 11).

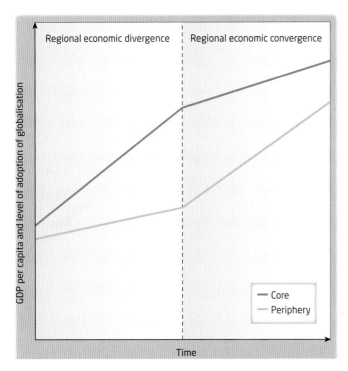

Figure 11 *Regional economic divergence and convergence.*

The size of markets in terms of population

There is also the important factor of the total purchasing power of a country when TNCs are examining potential markets for their products. Many retail companies work on the principle of threshold populations when assessing the profitability of alternative locations. This is standard business practice in both developed and developing countries. Where production is the main concern, the labour force in terms of size and quality is a major location factor. Quality is of course the main factor as a large potential labour force in itself has no attraction unless it possesses the skills required by major companies or it can be trained to acquire such skills.

Starbucks: an expanding global presence.

One of the most obvious ways in which many communities are affected by globalisation is when a major retailer such as Wal-Mart decides to open a new outlet in the locality. This will bring advantages in the form of greater consumer choice, probable lower prices and the creation of new jobs. However, such large retail outlets can have a huge adverse effect on existing businesses and alter the structure of the local business community considerably. Because large retail organisations can achieve significant economies of scale such as negotiating the lowest possible prices from suppliers as they order in such large quantities, they can squeeze out smaller-scale local retailers. As this process has happened time and time again, communities yet to be directly affected have been forewarned. Local groups in many parts of North America have actively opposed the opening of new Wal-Mart stores.

Contrasts between urban and rural areas

Capital cities, particularly if they are the largest urban areas in a country, generally exhibit the highest levels of globalisation. Economic, political and sociocultural factors combine to attract high levels of foreign interest, investment and presence. Foreign embassies will be located in capital cities and they will often have strong links with the companies of the country they represent. Embassy staff will also have certain expectations with regard to the availability of goods and services which businesses, either global or local, will be eager to exploit. Thus capital cities are the logical places for more ambitious indigenous businesses to develop which may gradually take on globalised traits in order to compete with foreign-owned companies. Examples are local versions of KFC and McDonald's.

The contrast with rural areas may be very stark indeed. The marketing of global products may well be in evidence in rural areas, but the availability of such products outside of the main urban centres may be very limited indeed.

The level of infrastructure

The success of commercial activities in any locality depends to a considerable degree upon the level of infrastructure and the quality of infrastructure services available to businesses. Improvements in transport and communications such as motorway construction, the opening of a new airport and the spread of utilities can pave the way for the gradual influx of globalised commercial activities. Major ports in developing countries often exhibit higher levels of globalisation than urban areas of a comparable size inland. Improvements in accessibility often set off an upward spiral of development which gradually illustrates more global influence.

In some parts of the developed world rural settlements are connected by no more than dirt tracks.

Cultural acceptance of global business

Some countries are more open to outside influences than others. This is apparent for various levels of economic development. For example, in the developed world commercial activities and attitudes in the UK are more

globalised than in France. The latter has managed to retain considerably more by way of tradition and culture. This is particularly evident when comparing smaller urban areas in both countries, with more limited intrusion of obvious globalisation evident in France. France has always been uneasy with the mass-market American culture that companies like McDonald's have come to epitomise.

In 2007, in the period before the French presidential election, Nicholas Baverez, a political commentator, stated: 'The main issue facing France today is how we deal with globalisation. Will we embrace globalisation or will we keep pretending it doesn't exist for another five years?' The election debates highlighted the uneasy relationship France has with the notion of globalisation. The socialist leader Ségolène Royal wanted to punish companies that moved production sites abroad and called for a Europe that protected its citizens from the adverse effects of globalisation. She said she would re-nationalise the electricity and gas industries and argued for a higher minimum wage.

Many French people associate globalisation primarily with outsourcing abroad which inevitably means the loss of jobs in France. The former President Jacques Chirac said that free-market economics was just as dangerous an ideology as communism because it failed to allow countries to protect themselves when they needed to most.

Union leaders in France have vowed to protect France's welfare state from globalisation. All parties have promised to fight speculative capitalism and the filter-down of jobs from the country to lower wage economies. In few other EU countries is the anti-globalisation movement so powerful. This explains, at least to some extent, the diplomatic tensions that sometimes occur between France on the one hand and the USA and the UK on the other.

Government reaction to foreign direct investment and the presence of foreign businesses

Some governments are much more open to global influences than others. North Korea is the most closed society in the world with the government doing everything it can to keep its population unaware of what is happening in the outside world (Figure 12). The impact of globalised commercial activities is virtually zero and, because of the intense poverty of the country, localised commercial activities are also very limited. In late 2009 North Korea took steps to curb unofficial economic activity and suppress inflation, issuing a revalued currency and sharply limiting

Case study

Glocalisation in Singapore

Such has been the pace of economic growth in Singapore since the 1960s that it is now classed as a High Income Economy according to the World Bank classification. The country's export-oriented growth in the 1980s was dominated by ICT and computer peripherals. From the 1990s the emphasis has been on biotechnology with the government aiming to create a knowledge-based economy. Singaporeans have a very positive attitude towards technology which has been important to the country's success. Such an attitude has made the country open to foreign technology and investment.

Economic development and social change in Singapore have not followed a pure free-market model. The country's government has played a major role in guiding market forces. The government of Singapore has been much more interventionist than most Western governments in overseeing both economic and social change. The country relied to a large extent on foreign TNCs to launch economic growth, but it also built up a high rate of savings through its Central Provident Fund as a major source of independent investment.

A high standard of education has been fundamental to economic development in Singapore. Higher education in Singapore is a hybrid version comprising the original British model and the American model, along with a number of local characteristics. It has enough of the global to give it worldwide credibility, but also enough of the local to provide a certain uniqueness.

Glocalisation is also evident in the style of housing. Ninety per cent of the population lives in housing blocks built by the government and then sold to citizens. The country borrowed the so-called international style of very basic and practical designs, but incorporated a new concept of public space called void-decks. These are places for weddings, funerals or other communal gatherings. In other design features as well, the merging of the Western and local is evident.

In many aspects of television and other forms of entertainment there is evidence of glocalisation, although some examples amount to no more than imitation.

Cultural fusion has been clearly evident in the economic and social changes that have occurred in the country since the 1960s. This process has also been observed in a number of other Asian countries, such as Malaysia. The populations of these countries have generally embraced the benefits of economic growth, but have been keen to put their own cultural mark on it. At the same time governments have seen the need to play a significant role in navigating the way forward.

---

the amount of old money people can exchange for new bills. These measures appeared to be a crude attempt to severely punish people involved in black market trading, which had begun to take root in North Korea in recent years as the country's central planning system broke down. Since a famine that killed many North Koreans and shook the rationing system in the mid 1990s, the North's centrally planned economy, with state-run stores that sell goods at government-set prices, has co-existed with an unofficial economy where people sell home-grown food or goods smuggled in from China. North Korea's government had become worried that the unofficial economy had grown too large, undermining the dominance of government control. North Korea uses its large armed forces to control dissent within the country and its nuclear weapons to create tension with what it sees as hostile countries on the international front.

A North Korean factory worker was publicly executed by firing squad this week after conveying news out of the secretive communist state via his illicit cell phone.

The man, surnamed Chong, made calls to the defector using an illegal Chinese mobile phone, the broadcaster said, citing a North Korean security agency official it did not identify. The report didn't say when the phone calls were made. The execution took place by firing squad in late January in the eastern coastal city of Hamhung, according to Open Radio for North Korea, a broadcaster specializing in the isolated country.

The arms factory worker was accused of revealing the price of rice and details of deplorable living conditions to a friend who defected to South Korea, Open Radio for North Korea revealed. The station, a grantee of the National Endowment for Democracy, broadcasts into the reclusive state.

The radio broadcasts and underground reporting are the product of a working partnership of North Korean defectors and South Korean human rights activists.

Figure 12 *North Korea – Open radio exposes closed society.*

Economic activity at the local level

Over 70% of the world's GDP is produced domestically within national boundaries, nearly 90% of what Americans consume is produced within the 50 states of the USA.

Much of what we consume cannot be traded internationally since many services such as hairdressing, retailing and restaurants, have to be provided locally. These services are the fastest-growing sector of most developed economies. Three-quarters of what Britons buy in the shops is made domestically and 90% in the UK within the EU. Even if all the remaining trade barriers were abolished, more subtle barriers would remain, such as differences in accounting, tax and regulatory standards.

Where people have a choice between a local or global good or service, a number of factors influence their decision. Clearly price and quality are major factors, but accountability is also important and consumers may favour a local option because of this factor.

A local shopping centre in Dubai with locally provided services.

over-exaggerated in the boom years of the 1990s and that the much more difficult economic and political climate of the first decade of the 21st century requires a more considered assessment of the interconnectedness of nations around the world. It seems that the term 'globalony' was coined in 1943 by US Congresswoman Clare Boothe Luce to trash what Vice President Henry Wallace liked to call his 'global thinking', particularly a plan to promote world peace by building airports all over the world.

The current decade will be crucial in setting the path for the medium term. The global financial crisis of 2008–10 may well turn out to have been a blessing in disguise, when the worst aspects of globalisation became very apparent while there was still time to address the significant flaws in the global system.

Discussion point

To what extent is the production of goods and services in the region in which you live local rather than global? Come to a decision on each economic activity in turn.

Is continued globalisation inevitable?

Most people feel it is inevitable that globalisation will continue to develop, but this cannot be taken for granted. As *The Economist* pointed out in a special report on the subject:

> The lesson of the early 20th century, easily forgotten during the boom years of the 1990s, is that globalisation is reversible. It was derailed by war (in 1914) and by economic policy during recession (in the early 1930s). This time global integration might stall if the risk and cost of doing business abroad rises (perhaps as a consequence of heightened fears about security), or if governments once more turn their backs on open trade and capital flows. Either of these threats could prove decisive. The question is, will they?

An article in *Newsweek* entitled 'The New Buzzword: Globalony' argues that the extent of globalisation was

Activities

1 With reference to Figure 9 (page 218), how does the level of economic development of countries and regions influence the adoption of globalisation?
2 Explain how the adoption of globalisation can vary between urban and rural areas.
3 With the help of Figures 10 and 11, discuss the factors that influence differences in the rate of adoption of globalisation within countries.
4 Suggest why some countries are more resistant to the incursion of globalisation than others.
5 Why does a significant degree of economic activity remain at the local level?

Review

Examination-style questions

1 Distinguish between the terms 'globalisation' and 'glocalisation'.

2 To what extent have commercial activities at a local scale become globalised?

Websites

www.glocalforum.org
The Glocal Forum

www.citymajors.com
Citymajors.com: about the world's cities

Key terms

Isomorphism a scientific term which means replication of the same form yet separated from the main source.

Glocalisation where the global and the local interact to produce hybridised outcomes.

Equity the state, quality or ideal of being just, impartial and fair.

Sustainability meeting the needs of the present without compromising the ability of future generations to meet their own needs.

Localisation confined or restricted to a particular location.

Marketing the commercial processes involved in promoting and selling and distributing a product or service.

Westernisation a particular form of modernisation in which the methods and values of Western industrial capitalism are the basis of the changes that are occurring.

18 Local responses to globalisation

KEY QUESTIONS

- What have been the responses of civil society to globalisation in terms of the adoption, adaptation (glocalisation) or rejection of globalised goods, services and cultural traits?

- What are the relative costs and benefits of local commercial production to the producer, the consumer and the local economy, compared with the costs and benefits of globalised production?

Civil society protest, London, March 2009.

The responses of civil society to globalisation: adoption, adaptation and rejection

Global civil society positions

Global civil society covers a considerable spectrum of views. Figure 1 is a useful classification of the positions of the major groups within global civil society. Clearly some people will support the current model of globalisation. These may be people who feel they have done well under the process and those who see no realistic alternative. They will point to rising living standards in developed countries and the development of successive generations of newly industrialised countries. On the issue of lower-income developing countries they may argue that it is only a matter of time before these countries see significant development. If not, then they may point to internal issues such as poor and corrupt government which are difficult for the outside world to tackle.

Others completely reject globalisation in virtually all its forms. This camp ranges from anti-capitalist movements to forms of religious fundamentalism and authoritarian and socialist states. Authoritarian regimes such as North Korea and Iran see globalisation as a vehicle for the USA and its allies to extend neo-colonialism. Their concerns are not only the economic and cultural threats of globalisation, but also a military fear (unjustified to most Western eyes). In Latin America, Cuba, Venezuela and Bolivia in particular are extremely critical of what they see as American and other Western imperialist influences operating through the mechanism of TNCs.

The 'reformists' aim to civilise globalisation so that the economic benefits are much more widely shared both between and within countries. The pursuit of human rights and social justice are key aspects of this strategy. This camp is represented by a considerable number of international NGOs. **Trade unions** also come into this grouping.

The 'alternatives' want to opt out of globalisation and pursue lifestyles that reject current trends. Establishing local alternative economies is a significant way of following this path.

Civil anti-capitalist protest, London, March 2009.

The overall influence of civil society is the subject of much debate. It has undoubtedly expanded considerably over the past decade or so. Some writers see it as a major force in global politics already, while others argue that civil society still remains embryonic. The latter see civil society becoming an increasing force in the coming decades. Political parties in democratic countries are already beginning to adapt to this changing environment. Its impact at present is greatest in the developed world, but people's expectations are rising in the developing world as they come to expect more from their political leaders. They recognise the power that instant global publicity can have.

Sustainability is an important objective for many if not most people who are unhappy with globalisation as it stands. Figure 2 illustrates how both individuals and companies can adjust current practices to gradually move to a more sustainable society. General consumer behaviour

	Types of actors	Position on globalisation	Position on plant biotechnology	Position on global finance	Position on humanitarian intervention
Supporters	Transnational business and their allies	Favour global capitalism and the spread of a global rule of law	Favour plant biotechnology developed by corporations, no restrictions necessary	Favour deregulation, free trade and free capital flows	Favour just wars for human rights
Rejectionists	Anti-capitalist social movements; authoritarian states; nationalist and fundamentalist movements	Left oppose global capitalism; right and left want to preserve national sovereignty	Believe plant biotechnology is 'wrong' and dangerous and should be abolished	Favour national protection of markets and control of capital flows; radical rejectionists want overthrow of capitalism	Oppose all forms of armed intervention in other states, intervention is imperialism or 'not our business'
Reformists	Most NGOs; many in international institutions; many social movements and networks	Aim to civilise globalisation	Do not oppose technology as such but call for labelling information and public participation in risk assessment; sharing of benefits	Want more social justice and stability; favour reform of international economic institutions as well as specific proposals like debt relief or Tobin tax	Favour civil society intervention and international policing to enforce human rights
Alternatives	Grass roots groups, social movements and submerged networks	Want to opt out of globalisation	Want to live own lifestyle, rejecting conventional agriculture and seeking isolation from GM food crops	Pursue an anti-corporate lifestyle, facilitate colourful protest, try to establish local alternative economies	Favour civil society intervention in conflicts but oppose use of military force

Figure 1 *Global civil society positions on globalisation.*

in many countries has made some progress in shifting towards the 'global citizen' approach, but there is a long way to go until true sustainability can be achieved, and progress varies considerably from one country to another.

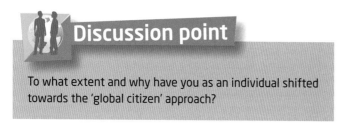

Figure 2 *Shifting from traditional to sustainable business.*

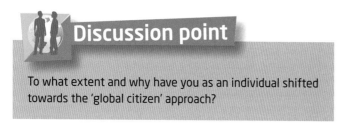

Discussion point

To what extent and why have you as an individual shifted towards the 'global citizen' approach?

Corporate social responsibility is a vital element in the path towards sustainability. Here the financial bottom line of the traditional company needs to be replaced by **triple bottom line accounting**. The latter involves not just economic accounting but also social and environmental accounting. Socially responsible companies look at all the costs and benefits of the actions they take.

Present levels of consumption are creating an unsustainable demand for many resources. As the world globalises, the effects of excess demand cross borders and have an impact on societies economically, socially and environmentally. There are two aspects to the problem:

- the impact of developed-world consumption on the environment of developing countries
- the impact of developing countries acquiring developed-world consumption habits.

Getting the global community to agree on a common course of action will become even more important in the future with the scale of 'spillovers' generated by a more interconnected world and global economy.

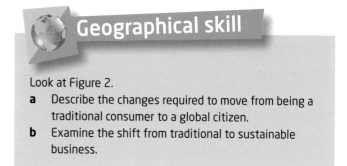

Geographical skill

Look at Figure 2.
a Describe the changes required to move from being a traditional consumer to a global citizen.
b Examine the shift from traditional to sustainable business.

Much probably depends on the availability and price of key natural resources such as oil. Figure 3 shows four extreme scenarios presented in a report by the business consultants PricewaterhouseCoopers. Scenario 2 provides maximum sustainability while Scenario 3 is the worst situation with regard to impact on the environment.

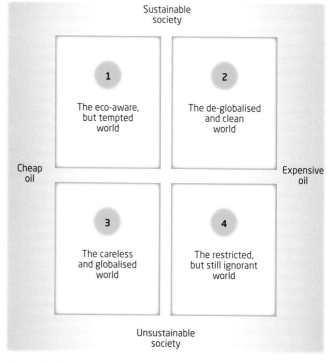

Figure 3 *Extreme scenarios.*

Adaptation

In spite of the dominant position of global brands, products are often adapted to local conditions. For example, mutton is used instead of beef in McDonald's outlets in India and vegetable oil is used for frying. Another example is the Barbie Doll which comes in 30 different national varieties.

In terms of the media, local television, radio and newspapers often strike a different note over important issues compared with the international media giants. During the Iraq and Afghanistan wars the Arab news network Al Jazeera frequently took a different stance to the Western media concerning what was happening in both countries. At times it was highly critical of Coalition actions in a way that many Western news agencies might have found difficult.

In China, while the country has embraced capitalism in terms of managing the economy of the country, it has maintained authoritarian politics, arguing that this is the system best suited to China. Socialism persists in other countries too, such as Cuba, Vietnam and North Korea. The change from communism to democratic rule in Russia seems to have taken a few steps backward in recent years, with critics of the Russian government arguing that its democracy is more cosmetic than real.

Street directions in Beijing in both Mandarin and English.

At the extreme, the response to globalisation, if it is perceived to be the reason for unfair treatment, may be violent. One explanation can be found in public choice theory. This states that even if the benefits are greater than the costs, if the costs are concentrated among the few while the benefits are enjoyed by the majority, the opponents of the process of globalisation will be more motivated than its supporters. This is partly why so much effort has gone into trying to solve conflicts such as the Middle East. Peace is much more likely when all groups feel they have a stake in prosperity. Glocalisation can play an important part in this process.

Trilateral meeting: Obama, Netanyahu and Abbas, London, 2009.

Trade union responses to globalisation

It has often been stated that while capital is global, labour remains local. However, national trade unions are increasingly forging alliances with their foreign counterparts in order to protect their members' interests.

The Global Union Research Network (GURN) was established in 2004 to encourage trade unions and other interested parties to study labour movement responses to developments in the global economy. The International Labour Organization (ILO) plays a significant role in safeguarding workers' rights.

Historically, collective bargaining has been organised within national boundaries, but recently there have been signs of change. Such change has been driven by the family of Global Union institutions: the International Trade Union Confederation (ITUC), the OECD's Trade Union Advisory Committee (TUAC) and particularly the ten sectoral Global Union Federations (GUFs). The last have led the way in negotiating the growing number of International Framework Agreements with TNCs. This is a way of moving beyond companies' voluntary codes of practice which can simply be a marketing ploy.

International Framework Agreements constitute a formal recognition of social partnership at the global level. Companies signing such agreements commit themselves to respect workers' rights on the basis of the core ILO Conventions. An example is the framework agreement signed between Building and Wood Workers' International (BWI) and the Swedish furniture company IKEA which has helped raise labour standards in countries as diverse as China, Malaysia and Poland.

However, there are practical problems in extending the reach of framework agreements so that they adequately cover the networks of suppliers and subcontractors to TNCs. This is a significant issue, as large companies increasingly outsource aspects of work that were once core functions. The increasing scale of labour migration has also presented a challenge. One response has been the increase in advice given to workers migrating to other countries. Initiatives include the seconding of a worker from the Polish union federation Solidarity to the British Trades Union Congress, to help to organise Polish migrants into British unions.

Activities

1 Define 'global civil society'.
2 Discuss the different responses of civil society to globalisation presented in Figure 1.
3 Explain the different scenarios shown in Figure 3.
4 Outline the responses of trade unions to globalisation.

Local commercial production compared with globalised production

The costs and benefits of globalised production

There are many advantages for economic activity in working at the global scale. These are after all the reasons why so many companies have attempted to make the transition from national to international entities. Such advantages include:

- Sourcing of raw materials and components on a global basis reduces costs.
- TNCs can seek out the lowest-cost locations for labour and other factors.
- High-volume production at low cost in countries such as China helps to reduce the rate of inflation in other countries and has helped living standards to rise.
- Collaborative arrangements with international partners can increase the efficiency of operations considerably.
- Selling goods and services to a global market allows TNCs to achieve very significant economies of scale.
- Global marketing helps to establish brands with huge appeal all around the world.

Country	Possible advantages	Possible disadvantages
USA: headquarters	Positive employment impact and stimulus to the development of high-level skills in design, marketing and development in Beaverton, Oregon; direct and indirect contribution to local and national tax base	Another US firm that does not manufacture in its own country – indirect loss of jobs and the negative impact on balance of payments as footwear is imported; trade unions complain of an uneven playing field because of the big contrast in working conditions between developing and developed countries
Vietnam: outsourcing	Creates substantial employment in Vietnam; pays higher wages than local companies; improves the skills base of the local population; the success of a global brand may attract other TNCs to Vietnam, setting off the process of cumulative causation; exports are a positive contribution to the balance of payments; sets new standards for indigenous companies; contribution to local tax base helps pay for improvements to infrastructure	Concerns over the exploitation of cheap labour and poor working conditions; allegations of the use of child labour; company image and advertising may help to undermine national culture; concerns about the political influence of large TNCs; the knowledge that investment could be transferred quickly to lower-cost locations

Figure 4 *The potential advantages and disadvantages of TNCs: Nike to the USA and Vietnam.*

However, the critics of globalisation have continually pointed out the costs of global production. The operations of Nike and other companies that operate in, or outsource to, cheap labour economies have come under considerable criticism. Such criticism has not just been about the impact on poorer economies but also about the effect of such TNC organisations on the headquarters nation. However, there can be little doubt that the operations of TNCs also bring considerable benefits to both types of country. If this were not so then governments would place greater restrictions on the actions of TNCs. This would be possible despite the considerable influence they have. It is also important to note that the operation of TNCs is at times very controversial and opinions may vary widely. What one expert may construe as on balance an advantage, another expert may view the other way. Figure 4 attempts to summarise the potential advantages and disadvantages of Nike to the USA, its headquarters location, and to Vietnam, where 34 subcontracted Nike factories operate.

In response to years of 'sweatshop allegations', Nike produced a 108-page report in 2005 which gave the most comprehensive picture to date of the 700 factories producing its footwear and clothing. The report published the addresses of all contract factories. The report detailed admissions of abuses including:

- restricting access to toilets and drinking water
- denying workers at least one day off in seven
- forced overtime
- wages below the legal minimum
- verbal harassment.

The pressure group Human Rights First described the report as an important step forward in improving conditions for workers in poor countries. Phil Knight, the Chairman of the company, said he hoped Nike could become a global leader in corporate responsibility.

Figure 5 looks at the impact of globalised production on the UK. The costs and benefits can be classified into economic, social, political and environmental perspectives.

Perspective	Benefits	Problems
Economic	As one of the world's most 'open' economies, the UK attracts a very high level of foreign direct investment, creating significant employment and contributing to GDP; a high level of investment abroad by UK companies also increases national income. Financial deregulation has enhanced the position of the City as one of the world's top three financial centres. Low-cost manufactured products from China and elsewhere have helped keep inflation low.	High job losses in traditional industries due to global shift and deindustrialisation. TNCs can move investment away from the UK as quickly as they can bring it in, causing loss of jobs and corporation tax. Speculative investment, causing economic uncertainty, has increased with financial deregulation. There is a widening gap between the highest- and lowest-paid workers.
Social	Economic growth has facilitated high levels of spending on education and health in particular. Globalisation is a large factor in the increasingly cosmopolitan nature of UK society. The transport and communications revolution has transformed lifestyles.	A strong economy has attracted a very high level of immigration in recent years with increasing concerns that this is unsustainable.
Political	Strong trading relationships with a large number of other countries brings political influence; as a member of the EU, Britain can extend its influence to areas where it was not previously well represented.	Voter apathy as many people see loss of political power to EU and major TNCs. International terrorism is a growing threat with increasing ethnic diversity, rapid transportation and more open borders.
Environmental	Deindustrialisation has improved environmental conditions in many areas; increasing international cooperation to solve cross-border environmental issues gives a better chance of such problems being addressed.	Population growth has an impact on the environment with the increasing demand for land, water and other resources. Rapid industrial growth in China and elsewhere has an impact on the global environment, including the UK.

Figure 5 *The UK: examples of the benefits and problems of globalisation.*

The costs and benefits of local commercial production

Local commercial production can result in significant benefits to producer, consumer and local economy.

Producer

Local companies should have greater knowledge of the local market compared with markets further afield. Direct and regular contact with their customers should make them aware of exactly what local customers want and give them the ability to react quickly to changes in local consumer demand. Personal relationships based on face-to-face contact can be built up with customers, resulting in strong customer loyalty. However, the purchasing power of the local market may be limited and larger companies may need to market well beyond their local customer base to achieve the volume of sales they desire. Many large national and international companies are where they are now because of initial success in their local market areas.

Consumer

There is a strong tendency among consumers to associate local production with quality. This is particularly so with agricultural products when consumers can see, at least to a certain extent, the methods of production used. Local producers and consumers may be linked in an economic sense in terms of the employment of family and friends and also perhaps in terms of social networks. Such bonds

are a strong incentive to do business. Consumers who make a point of seeking out local producers are sometimes referred to as active consumers as opposed to passive consumers who are more likely to be influenced by the advertising of large companies. However, many products may not be produced locally and those that are may not fit the needs of many local consumers in terms of price, fashion and quality.

Thatching a roof in Dorset, UK – an ancient skill possessed by a relatively small number of tradespeople today.

Local economy

Strong local commercial production can set off a significant multiplier effect in the local economy. Strong local businesses can initiate upward spirals of development. The starting point is the creation of jobs. The higher the proportion of the population in employment, the greater the purchasing power of the community. A healthy local economy needs as diverse an employment base as possible. Local government finance relies to a considerable extent on the business rates levied on local companies. The more money that is available from this source, the more local authorities have available to spend on services within their jurisdiction. The local economy benefits in particular when strong linkages are forged between local businesses. The result is invariably a stronger multiplier effect than if this is not the case.

The success of local production depends to a certain extent on the actions of local and national politicians. The level of business rates and other forms of taxation can prove a significant factor. Investment in industrial estates, business parks and shopping centres is also crucial, along with ensuring a good level of accessibility. Local businesses frequently organise themselves into chambers of commerce or similar establishments to ensure that their views are made known to local politicians, and where appropriate at the national scale.

Case study

The rapid rise of halal business

Muslims have found many of the goods and services offered by standard globalisation processes to be, in various ways, inappropriate to their religion and culture. As a result businesses at different scales have reacted to this substantial latent demand. At first this involved businesses at the smaller scale, but now many of the world's major TNCs recognise the economic power of the Islamic market.

The Islamic market offers goods and services that comply with Islamic law and the teachings of the Koran. Overall this economic sector accounts for demand considerably over $1 trillion a year. The purchasing power of the world's 1.6 billion Muslims has increased significantly. Table 1 shows the global distribution of the Muslim population.

Continent	Population 2008 (million)	Muslim population 2008 (million)	% Muslim
Africa	967.0	462.4	47.8
Asia	4050.6	1103.7	27.2
Europe	735.2	51.5	7.0
North America	331.7	7.1	2.2
South America	576.8	2.4	0.4
Oceania	33.5	0.5	1.5
Total	**6694.8**	**1627.6**	**24.3**
Muslim population is increasing at 1.84% per year Muslim population 2009 = 1 657.6 million			

Table 1 *The global distribution of the Muslim population.*

The **halal** food market has expanded rapidly over the last decade and is valued at an estimated $632 billion a year in 2008. This equates to about 16% of the global food industry (see Figure 6).

A growing number of hotels such as the Jawhara Hotel chain cater for Muslim travellers. Such hotels do not stock alcohol, expect a conservative dress code and are generally perceived as quiet environments compared with the average 'global' hotel. Hotels like this are becoming increasingly popular with non-Muslim travellers who appreciate quiet and calm.

Major TNCs have become increasingly aware of Islamic purchasing power. Companies such as Nestlé, McDonald's and Tesco have been quick to expand their Muslim-friendly products in countries where demand is perceived to be strong. KFC is testing halal-only outlets in Muslim areas of the UK.

Halal shop, Malaysia.

Governments and regions in the Middle East and Asia have been keen to invest in this rapidly growing market. Regional 'halal hubs' have emerged, providing manufacturing centres and logistical systems that maintain product purity during manufacturing, shipping and storage. Elsewhere in the world the halal market has brought about some interesting changes:

- Halal slaughtering facilities have been constructed in Brazil because this country exports large quantities of chicken to Saudi Arabia. Similar facilities have been built in New Zealand which exports lamb to Muslim countries.

- Halal warehouses have been built in Rotterdam to ensure that the storage of halal goods conforms to Islamic law. Rotterdam is Europe's largest port and is a major transshipment point. Europe's Muslim population has been rising steadily and is now around 51.5 million.

- Cosmetics companies produce products that do no contain alcohol or animal fats.

- The Burooj company, operating in the Persian Gulf, designs spas and swimming pools that segregate the sexes.

- Nokia has free downloadable recitations from the Koran and maps showing the locations of major mosques in the Middle East.

- The expansion of Islamic banking: Islamic law forbids banks from charging interest. Customers pay fees instead. Islamic banking only accounts for about 1% of the global market at present, but it is growing at a rate of around 15% a year.

In the West, the USA, Brazil, Canada, Australia, New Zealand and France are the biggest halal suppliers. In the East, Thailand is the biggest exporter of halal certified products, after which the Philippines, Malaysia, Indonesia, Singapore and India are the leading halal products suppliers to the world.

The large expansion in the range of goods and services produced for the Muslim market partly reflects the considerable social changes under way in the Muslim world. Many more Muslim women have full-time jobs now than even ten years ago. This not only affects the level of purchasing power, but also the type of goods and services in demand.

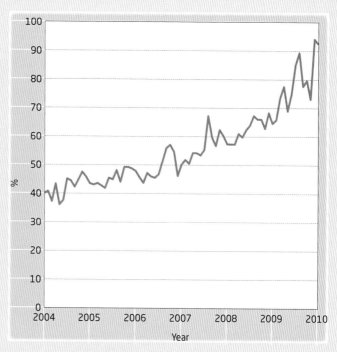

Figure 6 *Google searches for 'halal'.*

Use the Internet and other sources to assess the strength of halal business in the country in which you live.

The issue of generic pharmaceuticals

No set of globalised products has come under greater challenge than pharmaceuticals. The problem has been the relatively high prices set for drugs for which there is a desperate need in large quantities in developing countries. The local response against the global pharmaceutical giants started in Africa but quickly spread to other parts of the world. The prices and accessibility of drugs to combat AIDS has been a particular issue. Stephen Lewis, a former Canadian ambassador to the United Nations, called this issue 'the greatest human tragedy of our age'.

Countries like India and Brazil, along with a range of civil society groups, have led the protests against the policies of the pharmaceutical TNCs. Gradually the pharmaceutical industry has agreed to lower prices and even allowed the manufacturing of **generic drugs**.

Pharmaceutical companies are now all too aware of the large audiences that major civil society groups can reach. For example, the Switzerland-based company Novaris established relationships with African countries and the global activist organisations that supported these countries at an early stage in its marketing drive in order to promote itself as a socially responsible company.

Local civil society in Southall, London.

Community-supported agricultural programmes

Community-supported agriculture (CSA) is increasing in popularity in the USA and similar schemes are expanding in other countries. This is a way for consumers to buy local, seasonal food directly from farmers. A farmer offers a certain number of 'shares' to the public. Typically the share consists of a box of vegetables, but other farm products may be included such as eggs, homemade bread, cheese and meat. Interested consumers purchase a share (a membership) and in return receive a box of seasonal produce each week throughout the farming season. The advantages for farmers are:

- marketing produce early in the year, before the longer farming days begin
- receiving payment early in the season, which helps with cash flow
- getting to know the people who eat the food they grow.

The advantages for consumers are:

- buying and eating fresh food with all its nutritional benefits
- being exposed to new vegetables and new ways of cooking
- visiting the farm at least once a season, providing an educational opportunity for both adults and children
- developing a relationship with the farmer who grows their food.

Tens of thousands of families have joined CSAs, and in some areas of the USA there is more demand than there are CSA farms to fill it. The government does not track CSAs, so there is no official count of how many CSAs there are. LocalHarvest has the most comprehensive directory of CSA farms in the USA, with over 2 500 listed on its grassroots database.

Community garden, New Orleans, USA.

 **Activities**

1 Discuss the costs and benefits of TNC operations in host developing countries.
2 Examine the reasons for the rapid increase in halal businesses.
3 Why have pharmaceutical companies come under such pressure from civil society?
4 What are the reasons for the popularity of community-supported agricultural programmes?

Review

Examination-style questions

1 a Discuss civil society responses to globalisation in general.

 b Evaluate the response of civil society to one particular issue.

2 a Evaluate the relative costs and benefits of local commercial production to the producer.

 b Consider the costs and benefits to the consumer and the local economy.

Websites

www.islamicpopulation.com
Muslim Population Worldwide

www.oxfam.org.uk
Oxfam

www.opendemocracy.net
Open Democracy

www.ilo.org
International Labour Organization

www.localharvest.org
LocalHarvest

www.greenpeople.org
Green People

Key terms

Trade union an organisation of workers who have banded together to achieve common goals such as pay and better working conditions.

Corporate social responsibility a concept whereby organisations take responsibility for their impact on society and the environment.

Triple bottom line accounting involves not just economic accounting but also social and environmental accounting.

Halal an Arabic term designating any object or action that is permissible to use or engage in.

Generic drug a drug that is exactly the same as a brand-name drug and which may be manufactured and marketed after the brand-name drug's patent expires.

19 Alternatives

KEY QUESTIONS

- What is the role of civil societies in raising awareness of local and global environmental, social and cultural issues?
- How do civil societies support local economic activity and the strengthening of local cultural values?
- What are the positions held by anti-globalisation groups?
- What is the quality of life of a contemporary non-globalised society?

Local civil society protest about fair pay for teachers, London, 2008.

Advanced globalisation

There can be little doubt that the process of globalisation has some way to go. When it will be complete, if ever, is a source of much debate, as are the likely outcomes. Some see the process as offering enormous opportunities, while others are fearful of its extension. The literature on the subject frequently cites the following as the consequences of advanced globalisation:

- the elimination of geography as a controlling variable in the global economy
- the disappearance of the nation-state
- economic synchronisation across the globe
- companies with no specific territorial location or national identity
- the disappearance of distinctions between developing and developed countries as structures of wealth and poverty become detached from territory
- English as the common public language of the globalised system.

According to Waters, 'The rise in global consciousness, along with higher levels of material interdependence, increases the probability that the world will be reproduced as a single system.' Although there has been a strong movement towards a single system in recent decades, the degree of conflict around the world emphasises that there is a lack of agreement on what shape the single system should take in the future. Robertson argues that globalisation is neither necessarily a good thing nor a bad thing but that its moral character will be determined by the people of the planet. Since the Seattle demonstration in 1999 the level of concerned debate about the best way forward has increased. Fewer people are now prepared to leave it just to governments and international economic organisations to decide.

Professor Benjamin Barber, director of the Walt Whitman Center at Rutgers University and a critic of the way economic globalisation is currently working, has stated, 'We are living in a McWorld. We need to globalise democratic institutions in order to keep economic globalisation in check.' Barber has highlighted drugs, pornography and the 'war on children' as the major negative impacts of globalisation. Many see the growing influence of global civil society as a major factor in countering the negative aspects of globalisation. The general message coming from this disparate array of individuals and organisations is that the starting point is to fundamentally change the way in which the global economy is organised.

Critics of the way globalisation is proceeding at present argue for a number of significant changes to the global system including:

- the establishment of a global central bank
- a revamping of the IMF to make it more democratic
- a 'Tobin tax' on international financial transactions to reduce speculation
- the establishment of a global environmental organisation to monitor and reduce the impact of economic activity
- the control of capital for the public good.

The major overall objective is that the two prime movers of the global economy, the economically powerful nation-states and transnational corporations, become more accountable to the people of the planet and that all the impacts of economic activity are taken into account in the decision-making process. The goal must be to spread the benefits of globalisation more widely so that all peoples feel included in the global improvement in the quality of life.

Local radio can do much to raise and debate local issues.

Alternative paths

In terms of global interactions there are broadly three alternative paths to follow:

- business-as-usual with the current model of capitalism
- a restructured capitalism with much stronger objectives in terms of both equity and the environment
- abandoning capitalism and introducing a new world order.

Under the business-as-usual scenario only very limited efforts are made in terms of environmental sustainability and human equity, with the likelihood of both problems getting worse. There has been so much opposition to this stance that the global community is already moving away from it, albeit at a relatively slow pace according to critics. It is the flaws in the current model that many people hold responsible for the global financial crisis of 2008/09 and previous periods of global financial instability, and for most of our concerns about the environment. The overriding motive for most economic activity has been profit, with other concerns frequently given no more than lip-service.

Although there are many radicals who say that the world's major problems cannot be solved unless we abandon the current economic and political structures and start afresh, most people would see this as unrealistic and unachievable. However, the supporters of such change argue that a number of countries have in the past changed from capitalist to communist systems, and some have changed back again to capitalism. In an era of enhanced political cooperation (compared with the Cold War era), international agreement on a new world order might be possible.

The most likely new path is a restructured capitalism with broader quality-of-life objectives. Ironically this has probably become more likely as a result of the recent global financial crisis which made many of the problems of the current system all too transparent. Civil society has already played a crucial role in moving towards the objective of a restructured capitalism and it will undoubtedly move more and more centre stage in the future.

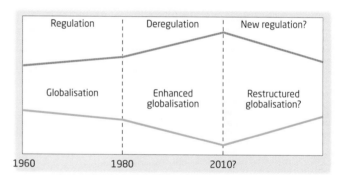

Figure 1 *Model of recent and future stages of capitalism.*

Figure 1 shows in diagrammatic form how the situation might change in the coming decades. The globalisation of the 1960s and 1970s occurred under much heavier regulation of finance and trade by both individual countries and international organisations compared with that of the last three decades. The deregulation of financial markets has presented expanding opportunities for many large companies and has resulted in much larger and more complex capital flows around the world. This has resulted in massive profits for some and rising living standards for the world's middle- and higher-income groups.

However, many of the world's poor have seemingly been left behind and environmental problems have reached such a scale that no one in the future will be unaffected. David Harvey in his book *A Brief History of Neoliberalism* argues that the greater freedoms given to TNCs in recent decades as state control receded was not an inevitable shift of power but one that reflected the interests and desires of the capitalist class. Such was the power of this movement that people with alternative ideas were portrayed as being out of touch with reality.

An important recent change has been the enlargement in the number of countries meeting regularly to discuss the global economy (Figure 2). The meeting of the finance ministers of the Group of Seven (G7) was formed in 1976 when Canada joined the Group of Six (USA, Japan, UK, Germany, France and Italy). The G8 is the annual meeting of the heads of government of these seven countries with the addition of Russia in 1997. The EU is also represented within the G8. The addition of Russia acknowledged that country's importance both economically and politically. The G20 was established in 1999, in the wake of the 1997 Asian financial Crisis, to bring together major advanced and emerging economies to stabilise the global financial market.

Every continent is represented by the G20 group of nations. However, smaller countries and in particular the poorest nations of the world still feel they have little say in policy formation. Global civil society is playing a key role in promoting the agenda of the poorest nations.

G7 →	G8 →	G20
USA	USA	USA
Canada	Canada	Canada
Japan	Japan	Japan
UK	UK	UK
Germany	Germany	Germany
France	France	France
Italy	Italy	Italy
	Russia	Russia
		South Africa
		Argentina
		Brazil
		Mexico
		China
		South Korea
		India
		Indonesia
		Saudi Arabia
		Turkey
		Australia
		European Union

Figure 2 *G7 to G20.*

An alternative view of capital

Jonathon Porritt in his book *Capitalism as if the World Matters* (2005) argues that more and more people in senior posts in both government and business around the world have grasped the importance of sustainable development. Such change is incremental rather than transformational, but it is beginning to make a difference. Porritt became a leading figure in the Green movement in the early 1980s and in the 1990s he was co-founder of Forum for the Future which set out an agenda for global sustainability.

Porritt states: 'there need be no fundamental contradiction between sustainable development and capitalism'. This is so, providing less attention is paid to economic growth in itself and more attention to human well-being and the environment. Porritt is an optimist about making progress towards a green society. Developing this discussion, Porritt argues for an expansion of the traditional view of capital. The latter is viewed in terms of 'stocks' of capital (land, machines, money). Porritt's five-capital framework broadens this view considerably to include:

- natural capital which is required to maintain a functioning biosphere, supply resources and dispose of wastes
- human capital which provides the knowledge and skills to create manufactured capital
- social capital which establishes the institutions that provide the stable human environment within which economic activity can occur
- manufactured capital which is the products and infrastructure that provide people with economic wealth
- financial capital which provides the lubricant to keep the whole system operating.

Developing more sustainable approaches in all of these areas can bring important improvements in well-being and the environment. This involves a change in thinking from preoccupation with short-term economic gain to a longer-term approach that re-engages with the natural world. This can be achieved through a reform agenda rather than revolution. Porritt's views are in contrast to the prevailing views of many radical academics and NGOs which see the only way forward as a completely different world order.

Fish landed at a small port in France – destined for local consumption.

Discussion point

What do you think of Jonathan Porritt's 'alternative view of capital'?

Theory of Knowledge

The recent global financial crisis has galvanised thought about the way the global economy works. The flaws of the current system have become all too apparent and people are anxious that similar problems should not reoccur in the future. Human knowledge frequently advances more rapidly during problem periods. You may have come across the notion of paradigm shift, relating to revolutionary changes in scientific thinking (Newtonian mechanics giving way to relativity is one oft-quoted example). Is such change happening in politics and economics now, in your view? Where might we end up?

Civil society supporting local economic activity

A recent discussion on the subject entitled *Alternatives to Economic Globalisation* edited by J. Cavanagh and J. Mander encouraged people to act in a number of different ways to support local economic and other activities and be more conscious of the global environment. As individual consumers, people were urged to:

- be an informed consumer by knowing how a good is produced, who produced it and how it is disposed of

- buy local to reduce food miles and stimulate the local economy
- join a community-supported agricultural programme or support local farmers' markets and urban gardens
- support **fair trade** to ensure that producers in developing countries are getting a reasonable price for their products.

The publication also focused on what people can do as workers. The advice included:

- joining a trade union to help support workers' rights in the community
- being aware of the power of worker pension funds to ensure that funds are invested ethically
- forming and supporting worker-owned cooperatives which are a good alternative to hierarchical business structures.

Under such organisations workers own and operate the enterprise themselves. Individuals also have a role to play as depositors and investors by:

- holding accounts with socially responsible banks or credit unions to ensure that their money is not used in unethical ways
- investigating how their bank or other financial organisation invests in local community development
- using credit cards that donate to important causes
- supporting 'local currency' movements where they exist.

The 'alternative money' schemes referred to in the last point, located in some cities, particularly in the USA, represent a partial alternative to engaging in the dominant economy. Under such schemes communities agree to use a local 'scrip' currency, rather than formal currency, for some of their needs, and to exchange services at agreed rates. The objective is to recycle funds within a community, keeping resources local.

As a local citizen the individual can become involved in a number of practical ways such as:

- discussing alternatives to economic globalisation in the community
- participating in local community organisations and encouraging links between different organisations
- organising local eco-initiatives drawing on the experience of successful schemes in other locations around the world
- supporting voter education and registration efforts in the community – voter apathy only encourages the 'status quo'.

An aspect of civil society: volunteer educating local villagers, Dhaka, Bangladesh.

Civil society in Burkina Faso, helping women start up their own small businesses.

Figure 3 shows the influence that pension funds can have on major companies. The controversial issue of Canada's oil (tar) sands is covered in the companion textbook for the core module, *Patterns and Change*. More and more people are now aware of the economic power of pension funds and are keen to voice their opinion on how and where such funds should be invested. Pension funds have never been under such pressure to behave in an ethical manner. This is a significant way in which civil society can have an important influence on global finance.

Microcredit and social business: the Grameen Bank

The development of the Grameen Bank in Bangladesh has illustrated the power of **microcredit** in the battle against poverty. The Grameen foundation uses microfinance and innovative technology to fight global poverty and bring opportunities to the poorest people. The bank provides tiny loans and other financial services to poor people to start their own businesses. Women are the beneficiaries of most of these loans. A typical loan might be used to buy a cow and sell milk to fellow villagers or to purchase a piece of machinery which can be hired out to other people in the community. The concept has spread beyond Bangladesh to reach 3.6 million families in 25 countries. Muhammad Yunus highlights **social business** as the next phase in the battle against poverty in his book *Creating a World Without Poverty*. He presents a vision of a new business model that

• US and Australian pension funds join rebellion on BP oil sands

A collection of influential international investors have added their support to a shareholder rebellion over BP's plans to invest in the controversial Canadian oil sands.

Pension funds from the US and Australia say they will back a resolution at BP's annual general meeting next week that calls for the oil group to publish a report on the financial and environmental risks involved in developing oil sands.

The California Public Employees' Retirement System (CalPers), the

• $10bn: The cost of BP's Canadian oils sands venture, which covers an area in Alberta the size of England

California State Teachers' Retirement System (CalStrs) and the Vermont Pension Investment Committee said yesterday they will vote in favour of the resolution – which BP management is opposing – as will AMP Capital Investors and Christian Super in Australia.

Jack Ehnes, chief executive of CalStrs, said: 'The environmental risks associated with oil sands development come with long-term financial risk for CalStrs profolio.'

The investors that have

committed to the resolution hold stakes of less than 0.5pc in BP, but CalStrs and CalPers are among the top 10 largest pension funds in the world and their support is a blow to the oil giant.

Oil sands, also known as tar sands, are controversial because extracting the oil requires significant amounts of energy – giving off more carbon dioxide and costing more than conventional methods, as well as potentially scarring the landscape.

Figure 3 The power of pension funds.

combines the operation of the free market with the quest for a more humane world. Yunus argues that poverty is created by economic, social and political systems and not by the laziness, ignorance or moral failings of the poor. He sees the role of women as 'drivers' of the 'coming revolution' and technology as a crucial enabler.

Research idea

Look at the Grameen Bank's website (www.grameen-info. org) to find out more about microcredit.

Activities

1 Debate the stages illustrated in Figure 1 (page 236).
2 To what extent is the enlargement of the main groupings of countries discussing the global economy, from 7 or 8 to 20 (Figure 2), a move in the right direction?
3 Present a brief summary of Figure 3.
4 Discuss the role of the Grameen Bank.

The quality of life of a contemporary non-globalised society: rural Mongolia

There are very few parts of the world that remain completely untouched by interactions with the outside world, but there are a number where such interaction has been very limited. The people living in these areas can be considered to be non-globalised societies. An example of such a non-globalised society is the majority of rural Mongolia (apart from areas close to Ulaanbaatar and a few other urban areas), which is characterised by:

- traditional family structures with a strong emphasis on the extended family
- the importance of local customs and hospitality
- populations living at extremely low densities, equalling the lowest in the world

Children outside their ger in southern Mongolia.

- a heavy reliance on agricultural activities, particularly herding
- difficult environmental conditions in both summer and winter
- traditional housing in the form of gers, often involving changes of location as herds are moved in search of fodder
- relative inaccessibility, with most parts of the country lacking paved roads – movement by horseback is common and only 4×4 vehicles can make progress in many areas
- low incomes and limited material possessions – repair and reuse have long been important strategies to make possessions last
- very limited service provision reflected in lower health and education standards in many provinces compared with the capital city
- low levels of personal contact with other countries.

Although Mongolia is three times the size of France in land area, the country has a population of only 2.7 million. About 40% of the total population lives in the capital city, Ulaanbaatar. A major reason for this high level of population centralisation is the harsh conditions in much of rural Mongolia. About a third of the population live as nomadic herders on sparsely populated grasslands, most in very isolated locations. This is a major factor in their non-globalised status. In recent years, droughts and unusually cold and snowy winters have decimated livestock, destroying the livelihoods of hundreds of thousands of households. Many have moved to Ulaanbaatar where they live in impoverished conditions, mainly on the periphery of the city. This exemplifies the concept of the **urbanisation of poverty**.

	Total population (thousand)	Urban population (%)	Rural population (%)
1990	2 149.2	54.6	45.4
2000	2 407.5	57.2	42.8
2003	2 504.0	58.5	41.5
2004	2 533.1	59.1	40.9
2005	2 562.3	60.2	39.8
2006	2 594.8	60.9	39.1
2007	2 626.6	61.0	39.0

Table 1 *Urban and rural populations of Mongolia, 1990–2007.*

Figure 4 shows the provinces (*aimags*) of Mongolia and the location of the capital city. The most difficult conditions are experienced in the Gobi Desert regions of the south. Bayan-Ölgii is the highest Mongolian *aimag*, reaching a height of 4374 metres.

Table 1 shows the continuing urbanisation of Mongolia in recent decades. Table 2 shows how the **maternal mortality rate** varies between Ulaanbaatar and the *aimags*. Although there has been significant improvement in both, the gap between the capital city and the surrounding regions is still significant. In 2007 the **infant mortality rate** for Ulaanbaatar was 14.7/1000, while the *aimag* average was 20.3/1000. The respective figures for the child mortality rate were 18.8/1000 and 24.6/1000.

Significant environmental issues that affect the quality of life in rural Mongolia are:

- overgrazing
- deforestation
- soil erosion
- desertification.

According to 2006 census data, there are 1 707 000 herding households in Mongolia, of which 40% live

Figure 4 *Mongolian aimags (provinces).*

	1990	2000	2003	2004	2005	2006	2007	2015
Country average	199.0	158.5	109.5	98.6	93.0	69.7	89.6	50.0
Ulaanbaatar average	126.0	171.1	138.0	79.8	73.3	71.8	73.7	–
Aimag average	230.0	153.4	93.7	109.6	105.7	68.2	102.0	–

Table 2 *Maternal mortality rates.*

Geographical skill

Describe and suggest reasons for the variations in Mongolia's maternal mortality between 1990 and 2007.

Urban poverty in Ulaanbaatar, Mongolia.

below the poverty line. Since 1996 the poverty of herding households has not decreased. A more detailed survey examined the livelihood conditions of rural herding households and found over 60% in the lowest of four income categories (Table 3).

% poor	% low-middle income	% middle income	% upper-middle income
60.7	33.7	5.4	0

Table 3 *Livelihood conditions of rural herding households.*

The survey also examined the social position of rural herding households and found that 73.3% were classed as poor in terms of social position. Herders are living under direct risk of adverse environmental conditions. Over 97% of the herders interviewed considered climate change and environmental change a reality in their area. The environmental conditions they referred to were:

- heavy snowfall
- reduction of drinking water
- frequent drought and *dzud* (severe winter) events
- drying up of rivers and springs
- reduction in haymaking yield
- reduction of feeding value of pasture land
- sand movement and intensification of desertification.

Herders also commented on a fall in the number of forage plant species, animal fatness and bodyweight, and consequently a decrease in the production of meat and milk as well as wool, cashmere and moult hair.

Because of the migrant nature of herding, education is a problem for herding families. A partial solution is to bring travelling schools to rural Mongolia (Figure 5). Only about half of Mongolian children receive any form of early childhood education.

Thus, in terms of harsh environments and material assets, rural Mongolians would appear to have a very poor quality of life, but most appear to gain very significant pleasure from the positive attributes of their environment and from their communities. This is difficult to quantify, but it is the conclusion of various studies and the first-hand experience of the author and his son. The latter has lived in Mongolia for the past two years and visited a range of rural communities. Although Ulaanbaatar suffers from high levels of urban pollution, air quality in rural areas away from the capital is generally very high. Although winters are very cold, precipitation and cloud cover are extremely limited and thus clear skies are the norm.

Various international agencies have been working to improve the quality of life in rural Mongolia. The Strengthening Livelihoods in Rural Mongolia is a 12-year programme to enhance livelihood security and

Zavkhan, Mongolia, 22 September 2007 – A father reins his camel to a halt and coaxes the animal to bend its legs until its belly rests on the dry earth. His son slides off and with a quick wave goodbye turns and runs to a white felt tent known as a 'ger' – the traditional home in this region.

However, this particular ger is not a home; it is a specially adapted kindergarten for children of herder families who rarely have a fixed residence. Inside, the teacher is showing the young students how to sing a popular folk song.

This travelling preschool is working with the nomadic nature of the people here: if the children can't come to the school, take the school to the students. This ger travels seven to eight times each year, bringing education within the reach of families far from town.

Preschool is a rare luxury in rural western Mongolia, where nomadic families migrate with their herds several times each year, often settling far from any town. Only about 54% of Mongolian children receive any form of early childhood education.

Mobile schooling for mobile families

'Compared to the fixed kindergartens, this form is more convenient. It provides much needed early childhood education for very young children because it suits the lifestyle of the herder families in the area,' said a teacher named Badamragchaa.

UNICEF supports an effort to improve access to education in rural western Mongolia, where enrolment is lower than in most of the country, and drop-out rates are sharply higher, particularly among boys.

'What we have noticed is that those boys who are not finishing school are from herding families and from families who did not have the opportunity to put the children in the preschools,' said UNICEF representative Bertrand Desmoulins.

Figure 5 *Travelling schools bring education to migrant herder children.*

sustainability by increasing the capacity of communities and local institutions to reduce vulnerability throughout rural Mongolia. The project is funded by the World Bank, the European Commission, the Japanese PHRD Grant and the Government of Mongolia. Examples of the programme's work include:

- rehabilitating wells under the pastoral risk management component to provide watering points for livestock and allow herders to move their livestock away from overgrazed pastures close to settlements
- rehabilitating hay and fodder storage facilities to store hay reserves
- providing loans to herders to increase hay production
- providing ambulances for rural health care centres and improving the medical equipment in such centres
- repairing bridges to improve accessibility in isolated areas
- rehabilitating potable water supplies where such facilities have seriously deteriorated.

Activities

1. Why can much of rural Mongolia be considered to be a non-globalised society?
2. Describe the scenes shown in the two photographs of rural Mongolia (pages 240 and 242).
3. What are the environmental issues that have affected the quality of life?
4. Describe the data in Tables 2 and 3.
5. Prepare a brief summary of the information presented in Figure 5.

Review

Examination-style questions

1 **a** Describe the role of civil societies in raising awareness of global issues.

 b Discuss the role of civil societies in supporting local issues.

2 **a** Describe the location and other geographical characteristics of a contemporary non-globalised society you have studied.

 b Evaluate the quality of life of this society.

Websites

www.globaloceans.org
Global Forum on Oceans, Coasts and Islands

www.unctad.org
United Nations Conference on Trade and Development

www.developmentgateway.org
Development Gateway

www.worldbank.org.mn
Mongolian Quarterly, World Bank

www.mongolianmatters.com
Mongolian Matters

www.unicef.org
Unicef

www.globaltolocal.com
Global To Local: climate change and sustainability consultants

www.grameen-info.org
Grameen Bank

Key terms

Fair trade a movement that aims to create direct long-term trading links with producers in developing countries and ensure they receive a guaranteed price for their product on favourable financial terms.

Microcredit tiny loans and financial services to help the poor – mostly women – start businesses and escape poverty.

Social business forms of business that seek to profit from investments that generate social improvements and serve a broader human development purpose.

Urbanisation of poverty the increase in the proportion of people in poverty in a country who live in urban areas.

Maternal mortality rate annual number of deaths of women from pregnancy-related causes per 100 000 live births.

Infant mortality rate the number of deaths of children under one year of age per 1000 live births.

Index

Acknowledgements

The author and publishers are grateful for the permissions granted to reproduce materials in either the original or adapted form. While every effort has been made, it has not always been possible to identify the sources of all the materials used, or to trace all copyright holders. If any omissions are brought to our notice, we will be happy to include the appropriate acknowledgements on reprinting.

Texts

p. 3 Model of the global economy, Fig. 1.1 (p.2) from *Global Shift* by Peter Dicken, Fourth edition 2003, SAGE and Guilford Press; pp. 8–12 figures and data from KOF Index of Globalization, Dreher, Axel, 2006: *Does Globalization Affect Growth?*; p. 19 Alpha global cities map used by permission of the Department of Geography, University of Loughborough; pp. 23, 24, 170, 171, 199 figures from *Geo Factsheet* no.s 247, 157 and 219, used by permission of Curriculum Press; p. 37 airline route networks diagram used by permission of Gergana Bounova, MIT; pp. 16, 62, 193 figures from *Access to Geography: Globalisation* © 2003 Paul Guinness and pp.108, 109, 153 from *Advanced Geography: Concepts and Cases* © 1999 Paul Guinness and Garrett Nagle – reproduced by permission of Hodder Education; p. 44 'The exploding internet' from the *New Scientist*, including data on internet traffic from TeleGeography; p. 45 'East Africa gets broadband' © The Economist Newspaper Limited, London, 2010; p. 49 E-democracy concept by Steven Clift www. publicus.net; pp. 60–61 figures from the World Investment Report 2009 © United Nations Publications Board, used with permission; p. 64 poster used by permission of Christian Aid; p. 70 'Lamy's lament on trade liberalism' by Larry Elliot, © Guardian News & Media 2010; p. 70 figure from *Edexcel A2 Geography*, P. Byrne, Pearson Education Ltd; p. 76 map used by permission of J.T. Kilpinen, Valparaiso University; p. 77 map from *Changing Faces, Changing Places: Mapping Southern Californians*, J.P. Allen & E. Turner, Centre for Geographical Studies, California State University, Northridge, 2002; pp. 84–90 figures and text by permission of A.T. Kearney; p. 89 interview by Diksha Dutta from www.globalservicesmedia.com; p. 96 'Meat consumption' and 'Vertical integration' from *Geographical*, April 2009; p. 97 'Meat firms sued over illegal deforestation' by David Adam, © Guardian News &

Media 2009; pp. 113–114 Blacksmith Institute, www. blacksmithinstitute.com; p. 116 article from Antara; p. 117 'From toxic waste to toxic assets, the same people always get dumped on' by George Monbiot, © Guardian News & Media Ltd 2009; p. 123 map by Philippe Rekacewicz, UNEP/GRID-Arendal; p. 124 'The Chernobyl accident' from the UNSCEAR website, http://www.unscear.org/ unscear/es/chernobyl.html; p. 127 'Greenpeace plans to build fortress on Heathrow runway site' by Matthew Taylor, © Guardian News & Media Ltd 2010; pp. 128–130 tables and figures © Crown copyright: 'Public attitudes and behaviours towards the environment', DEFRA, September 2009; p. 143 © Monirupa Shete/Buzzle.com; p. 147 map from www.mapsofworld.com; p. 154 Cultural differences figure taken from *Cross-Cultural Connections: Stepping Out and Fitting in Around the World* by Duane Elmer, © 2002 by Duane H. Elmer, used by permission of InterVarsity Press, PO Box 1400 Downers Grove, IL 60515 www.ivpress.com; p. 158 'Cloning the consumer culture' by Noreene Janus from the Centre for Media Literacy website, first published in 1986 in *Cultural Survival Quarterly*; p. 161 McDonald's franchise text used with permission from McDonald's Restaurants Ltd; p. 166 'Coca-Cola accelerates expansion in China' – reprint courtesy of the Coca-Cola Company, © 2010 The Coca-Cola Company; p. 179 'Zuma visit', © the *Independent*, March 2010; p. 183 'A real loss of sovereignty' by Will Hutton, © Guardian News & Media Ltd 2007; p. 194 'WHO "infiltrated by food industry"' by Sarah Bosely, © Guardian News & Media Ltd 2003; pp. 205, 206, 207, 208 Population Bulletin data from *Yearbook of Immigration Statistics*, DHS, 2005 – J.S. Passel, *The Size and Characteristics of the Unauthorized Migrant Population in the U.S.* – data from the Pew Hispanic Centre; p. 212 explaining globalisation text by Colin Hines, author of *Localization – A Global Manifesto* (Earthscan); p. 221 'Open radio exposes closed society', Michael Allen, *Democracy Digest*, 2010; p. 225 'Global civil society positions on globalisation' from *Introducing Global Civil Society* by H. Anheier, M. Glasius, M. Kaldor, (2001) by permission of Oxford University Press; p. 239 'US and Australian pension funds join rebellion on BP oil sands', Graham Ruddick © Telegraph Media Group Limited, 2010; p. 243 'Travelling schools bring education to "herder children"' by Steve Nettleton, 2007, UNICEF

...graphs

p. 11 Lou Linwei/Alamy; pp. 12r, 87, 142 age fotostock/ Robert Harding; pp. 14, 23, 240, 242 Chris Guinness; p. 18 James Morgan/Shutterstock; p.25 image broker/ Alamy; p. 34 Mike Harrison/Getty Images; p. 43 Jean Pierre Amet/BelOmbra/Corbis; p. 43r Fredrik Renander/ Alamy; p. 49 Duncan Hale-Sutton/Alamy; pp. 50, 77 Peter Horree/Alamy; p. 59 Dennis MacDonald/Alamy; pp. 61, 202 Getty Images; p. 64 Ian/Volger/Mirrorpix; p. 65 KPA/Zuma/Rex Features; p. 73 Christine Osborne Pictures/Alamy; p. 75 Keith Dannemiller/Alamy; p. 79 Ted Soqui/Corbis; p. 82 irishphoto/Alamy; p. 89 Robert Conant/Photolibrary; p. 93 J.P. Laffont/Sygma/Corbis; p. 93r Richard Wareham Fotographie/Alamy; p. 100 Directphoto.org/Alamy; p. 107 Steve Vidler/SuperStock; p. 110b blickwinkel/Alamy; p. 111 Chad Ehlers/Alamy; p. 115 Ulrich Doering/Alamy; p. 122 Ria Navosti/Science Photo Library; p. 128 Visions of America LLC/Alamy; p. 128r Jose Fuste Raga/Corbis; p. 135br JTB Photo/ SuperStock; p. 137r Ron Bedland/Alamy; p. 139 Lionel Derimais/Alamy; p. 148r Picture Contact/Alamy; p. 149r Gallo Images/Alamy; p. 150 David Grossman/Alamy; p. 159 Robert Wilkinson/Alamy; p. 169r David Hoffman/ Alamy; pp. 171t, Andrew Dunsmore/Rex Fatures; p. 171b van Hilversum/Alamy; p. 177 Reuters/Corbis; p. 182 Morton Beebe/Corbis; p. 204 Steve Bell/Rex Features; p. 206 Fred Graves/Reuters/Corbis; p. 215 Michael Prince/ Corbis; p. 222 Megapress/Alamy; pp. 224, 225 Matthew Chattle/Alamy; p. 227r Rex Features; p. 231 Rob Walls/ Alamy; p. 233 Jim West/Alamy; p. 235 Janine Wiedel Photolibrary/Alamy; p. 236 China Tourism Press/Getty Images; p. 239t Karen Kasmauski/Science Faction/Corbis; p. 239b Andy Aitchison/In Pictures/Corbis

All other photographs reproduced with the kind permission of Paul Guinness.

(**Key:** l = left, r = right, t = top of page, b = bottom of page)